Forms of Life

D1205875

signale
modern german letters, cultures, and thought

Series editor: Peter Uwe Hohendahl, Cornell University

Signale: Modern German Letters, Cultures, and Thought publishes new English language books in literary studies, criticism, cultural studies, and intellectual history pertaining to the German-speaking world, as well as translations of important German-language works. *Signale* construes "modern" in the broadest terms: the series covers topics ranging from the early modern period to the present. *Signale* books are published under a joint imprint of Cornell University Press and Cornell University Library in electronic and print formats. Please see http://signale.cornell.edu/.

Forms of Life

Aesthetics and Biopolitics
in German Culture

Andreas Gailus

A Signale Book

Cornell University Press and Cornell University Library
Ithaca and London

Cornell University Press and Cornell University Library gratefully
acknowledge the College of Arts & Sciences, Cornell University, for
support of the Signale series.

Copyright © 2020 by Cornell University

All rights reserved. Except for brief quotations in a review, this book, or
parts thereof, must not be reproduced in any form without permission in
writing from the publisher. For information, address Cornell University
Press, Sage House, 512 East State Street, Ithaca, New York 14850.

First published 2020 by Cornell University Press
and Cornell University Library

Library of Congress Cataloging-in-Publication Data

Names: Gailus, Andreas, author.
Title: Forms of life : aesthetics and biopolitics in German culture /
    Andreas Gailus.
Description: Ithaca [New York] : Cornell University Press, 2020. |
    Series: Signale: modern German letters, culture, and thought |
    Includes bibliographical references and index.
Identifiers: LCCN 2019050397 (print) | LCCN 2019050398 (ebook) |
    ISBN 9781501749803 (hardcover) | ISBN 9781501749810 (paper-
    back) | ISBN 9781501749964 (epub) | ISBN 9781501749971 (pdf)
Subjects: LCSH: Vitalism in literature. | German literature—History
    and criticism. | Biopolitics—Germany. | Aesthetics, German.
Classification: LCC PT49 .G35 2020 (print) | LCC PT49 (ebook) |
    DDC 830.9—dc23
LC record available at https://lccn.loc.gov/2019050397
LC ebook record available at https://lccn.loc.gov/2019050398

CONTENTS

Part III Deformation

PREFACE

> The greatness . . . of true art . . . was to regain, to recover, to
> make us recognize that reality at a distance from which we
> live, from which we separate ourselves more and more as the
> conventional knowledge which we substitute for it grows
> thicker and more impermeable, that reality which we would
> run the risk of dying without having known, and which is
> quite simply our life. True life, life finally discovered and
> illuminated, the only life therefore really lived, is literature;
> that life which, in a sense, at every moment inhabits all men
> as well as the artist.
>
> —MARCEL PROUST, *IN SEARCH OF LOST TIME*

In one interpretation, Proust's reflections, taken from the last volume of his *In Search of Lost Time*,[1] participate in a deeply romantic

---

1. Marcel Proust, *À La Recherche Du Temps Perdu* (Paris: Editions Galli-
mard, 1999), 2284. I was reminded of this passage by Didier Fassin, who also uses
it as the starting point for a critique of contemporary academic analyses of life. See

conception of art and aesthetic life. Since our ordinary life is enveloped in clichés and repetitions, "true life, life finally discovered and illuminated" can only be found in its aesthetic elaboration, which is therefore universal and transcendent. Art redeems life, creating beauty out of the inane chatter of daily existence. But the passage may also be read in a more expansive and less elitist way. On this second reading, literature shows us the infinite particularity and richness of the life that we already live and that inhabits all men at every moment. The task of literature, so understood, is not to move away from ordinary life but deeper into it, and in doing so, help us see that our seemingly banal lives contain all the splendor and richness of the simultaneously immanent and transcendent in art. In short, "life . . . really lived, is literature," just as literature, properly written, is life.

Proust's novel corroborates the more expansive reading. On the one hand, given its autobiographical frame, Proust's *Recherche* is still linked to the older conception of life as individually bounded and narratively ordered, as bio-graphy. On the other hand, the novel's infinitesimal detail systematically overruns the autobiographical frame and the limits it imposes on narrative and subjective revelation. Literature thus discloses a life that is simultaneously singular and universal, a life that, while inhabiting all men at every moment, nonetheless does so uniquely in each. Thus, even where it challenges traditional conceptions of auto-bio-graphy, Proust's *Recherche* is still committed to what we may call "subjective" life: a life that is, at least in part, irreducibly perspectival and singular, bound up with and experienced through a particular body and mind.

This is precisely *not* the kind of life that we encounter in contemporary discussions of political life. When Michel Foucault introduced his concepts of biopower and biopolitics in the late 1970s, he explicitly set aside notions of lived experience, subjectivity, and existence in order to bring into focus a new conception of "life" that

---

his "True Life, Real Lives: Revisiting the Boundaries between Ethnography and Fiction," *American Ethnologist* 41, no. 1 (2014): 7. While my reading of this quote initially echoes Fassin's, I ultimately take it in a different direction. As should become clear in what follows, Fassin's work as a whole has similarly influenced my approach to several aspects of the modern discourse of life.

cuts across individual bodies and biographies. The subject of biopolitical life is a "new body, a multiple body, a body with so many heads that, while they might not be infinite in number, cannot necessarily be counted. Biopolitics deals with the population,"[2] and it focuses "on the species body, the body imbued with the mechanics of life and serving as the basis of biological processes: propagation, births and mortality, the level of health, life expectancy and longevity."[3] To produce this "species body," biopolitics draws on forms of knowledge that systematically bracket the experiential dimension of life: biology, which conceives of life as organic matter, and statistics, which subordinates individuals to the numerically distributed classes they comprise. This impersonal conception of life also informs post-Foucaultian work on biopolitics. Whether it examines nineteenth- or early twentieth-century notions of race and eugenics or analyzes recent developments in biotechnology and genetic engineering, biopolitical research moves in a direction that is diametrically opposed to the approach to life that we find in Proust's novel, for whom the singularity of sensory, mnemonic, and intellectual reception grounds the infinite totality of the world we all share.

Foucault's style, which may be said to turn Proust's exquisite attentiveness to detail against itself, adds a unique twist to this more general turn away from experience. In certain particularly beautiful and arresting passages of his work, Foucault gives us a kind of Proustian microanalysis—an analysis, however, not of human life and experience as such, but of its biopolitical organization. Foucault, too, writes a kind of literature, but one whose subject matter is the life of the disciplinary technologies and biopolitical mechanisms that permeate our bodies and shape our presumed subjectivity from the inside out. Thus, despite his denial that power issues from above, "life," for Foucault, is just the amorphous, passive material upon which the implements of power impose their form. Put

---

2. Michel Foucault, *"Society Must Be Defended." Lectures at the College de France, 1975–1976*, trans. David Macey (New York: Picador, 2003), 245.

3. Michel Foucault, *The History of Sexuality. Volume I: An Introduction*, trans. Robert Hurley (New York: Vintage Books, 1980), 139.

differently, biopolitics examines the imposition—from without—of discursive and disciplinary regimes of life and subjectivity upon the subject. In doing so, it leaves the subject itself unthought and ignores much modern writing on the structure of subjective experience, or the "lived experience" that a broadly conceived vitalist tradition from Herder to Bergson and beyond has theorized philosophically and explored aesthetically. This reductivist animus is present in virtually all biopolitical writings on "life," whether conceived of in terms of populations, "bare life," or "life itself."

The following pages aim to show that something essential is lost in this elimination of the aesthetic and experiential dimension of life. To be clear, my goal is not to oppose art to politics or existence to power but to examine their dialectical entanglement in order to develop a richer model of the relationship between life and its biopolitical manipulation. For the reductionism of biopolitical research cuts both ways: in marginalizing subjective life, biopolitics fails to capture the profound violence of biopolitical determination; and in focusing on the external technologies of power that shape life, biopolitics denies life its intrinsic value and force, undertheorizing it in ways that carry serious political and ethical implications. My claim is that in order to address these shortcomings we need a more comprehensive and complex understanding of life, one that I try to capture under the roughly Wittgensteinian rubric of *forms of life*. Such an understanding, moreover, requires foregrounding the role of aesthetics in general, and literature in particular. As I will argue throughout the book, it is the literary archive, mostly ignored in biopolitical research, that gives us the richest account of "lived experience" and its interaction with changing technologies of power and knowledge. In this sense, my book makes an explicit case for the importance of the arts and humanities in coming to terms with our biopolitical modernity.

A few words about the governing rubric and title of my book. While Wittgenstein uses the phrase "form of life" (singular) primarily to highlight the tacit background of practices that supports and limits meaning-making and rational justification, I employ the phrase (in its plural form) to emphasize the variegated and multitudinous morphology of human life. Human life is *essentially* heterogeneous. Rather than cohering in a unifying, determinate form, it unfolds in the active and open-ended interweaving of a multiplicity of modalities and forms: biological and ethical, political and psychical, aesthetic and biographical, sensory and legal, etc. In this sense, a form of life is always a composite, made up of many forms, each of which is shaped by its own logic and dynamic, imposing itself upon its adjacent forms which in turn impose themselves upon it. What we experience as inner restlessness is always in part the result of these competing forms of life or vitalities within us.

It should be clear then that the following pages are not, and indeed cannot be, directed towards establishing a definition of "life." This is not because life is irrational but because stipulating definitions is itself part of a narrow region of rationality—a particular language game—characteristic of scientific practice. As Wittgenstein and Nietzsche have shown, the call for definitions is bound up with the presumed sovereignty of abstract, invariable rules and laws—a presumption at odds with the fluidity and complexity of living forms.[4] Instead of seeking to define the timeless essence of "life," each of my chapters analyzes, through the close reading of a text or body of texts, a specific historical alignment of forms of life that in their multiplicity defy the demands of definition. To give just one example, Goethe's writings in the 1790s are shaped by the effort to combine a metamorphic theory of biological form, an understanding of liberal governmentality, a theory of novelistic form, and a new conception of socialization and individual biography. While Goethe's model of vitalism comes under attack by later authors, all the texts I consider foreground the dynamic heterogeneity of human life, whose extravagant morphology they seek to capture in conceptual or aesthetic form. It is for this reason that I treat these texts not merely as historical objects but as expressions of theoretical moments of reflection on "this complicated form of life" (Wittgenstein

---

4. For example, see Nietzsche, "Only that which has no history can be defined" (GM II, §13; KSA 5:317); Wittgenstein, "For in the flux of life, where all our concepts are elastic, we couldn't reconcile ourselves to a rigid concept" (LWPP I, §246).

PPF §1) that we *are*. The main concern of my book is not historiographic but philosophical and systematic, even existential.

Talk of "existential" here will strike some readers as ahistorical, but this may be the result of too narrow a conception of both existence and history. If the concept of "life" cannot be defined, this is ultimately because it designates that which we are already entangled in. To speak about life is to speak from within it. Rather than constituting a limitation of knowledge about life, however, this self-referentiality is the condition of its possibility. As Kant was the first to emphasize, we can understand life around us only because we are ourselves living creatures. While Kant frames his inquiry in quasi-transcendental terms, his literary and philosophical successors increasingly draw attention both to the cultural and political determinants of life, including their own, and to the necessary historicity and perspectivism of their own discourse and lived experience. Each of the authors I examine interprets "life" from within a specific historical constellation—a specific configuration of life—that conditions what can, at that moment, be lived and thought. There is no exclusive, preeminently "objective" perspective to occupy in this regard, no "view from nowhere."[5]

This is of course true of my own discourse as well. Although I provide no definition of life, my use of the term is nonetheless circumscribed by what, informed by my historical and contemporary sources, I take as "characteristic" features of both life and its concept. First, living things are both subject and object of processes of formation, formed and formative. Neither exclusively imposed from without nor determined from within, the form of living things is shaped by the interplay of intrinsic and extrinsic forces. Second, vital forms are not static entities but dynamic processes; life is mobile and plastic, or as Goethe says, *metamorphic*. Third, following Thomas Khurana, I will suggest that we conceive of the protean character of the living in terms of the dialectic of force and form. From this perspective, a form is a precarious structural balance that is subject to constant pressures exerted on it from internal and ex-

---

5. Thomas Nagel, *The View from Nowhere* (Oxford: Oxford University Press, 1986).

ternal forms and forces. Fourth, forms of life are essentially composite, that is, they are made up of other forms of life. As Nietzsche argues, this is already true of biological organisms, which are composed of countless smaller organisms, each of which asserts its own existence and will to power. This heterogeneity becomes particularly complex and unstable in *human* life, which, due to its embeddedness in symbolic life, unfolds through the representation and internalization of myriad cultural forms of subjectivity, sociality, and civility. Trees may be subject to political and economic processes, but not because they represent or recognize themselves in them. Only human life is traversed by the symbolic.

The following pages will seek to flesh out these rather abstract claims. The introduction situates my book within the context of contemporary debates about life, spells out the relevance of Wittgenstein's later thought to my argument, and explains how literature provides access to the political interiority of human life unavailable to contemporary theories of biopolitics. It also motivates the geographical and temporal specificity of my book, arguing that German culture from the late eighteenth to the mid-twentieth century developed an expanded conception of life as the dynamic drive toward form. I suggest that this dynamic process of formation was seen by many in the German tradition as fundamental not merely to metabolic and bodily life, but equally to the vital processes of aesthetic, psychic, and sociopolitical phenomena.

The three sections of my book outline three structural moments in the German discourse on form and its relation to life. Part I—"Life as Formation"—examines the conceptualization of life as formative form around 1800. Kant's *Critique of the Power of Judgment* is the first book in the German tradition to articulate the new dynamic notion of life as a convergence of mind and nature (chapter 1). For Kant, aesthetic experience is important because it (a) involves an intensification of the life of the mind (including the social dimension of mind as *sensus communis*) and (b) enables us to develop a regulative notion of organic life. Kant's claim is that to understand the peculiar organization of natural beings, we must view them as products of an intrinsic formative activity, and hence as in some way analogous to the mind's power of cognitive and perceptual synthesis, which we experience most vividly in our encounter with beauty. Aesthetic experience allows us to grasp the nature of human, or symbolic, life and its place within the natural world. Goethe's biological and literary writings of the 1790s radicalize Kant's insights (chapter 2). On the one hand, he emphasizes the "metamorphic" fluidity of both natural forms and human cognition; on the other, he stresses the erotic and social dimension of subjectivity. For Goethe, human life is singularly precarious because it is subject to libidinal investments and the unruliness of the imagination. To develop properly, human life must therefore be regularized by social forms that (re)direct its innate vitality—it must assume a second-order, socialized naturalness. Goethe's novel *Wilhelm Meister's Apprenticeship* associates the creation of this second nature with liberal forms of governing, depicting liberalism's normative force as a necessary, if at times violent, supplement to human life. With Goethe, vitalism opens itself to biopower.

Part II—"The Conflict of Forms"—examines the radicalization of this violent dimension in Kleist and Nietzsche. While Kant and Goethe model life as a self-organizing form, Kleist and Nietzsche highlight its divided and conflictual nature, depicting it as driving beyond form into the territory of deformation and disarticulation. In Kleist, this anti-organicism manifests in a poetic practice that emphasizes both the self-interrupting power of language and the prosthetic character of human life (chapter 3). Whereas Kant's and Goethe's autopoetic models seek to reconcile art and life, Kleist's heteropoietics frames art as an artificially intensified mode of life: art exceeds ordinary life, not by providing it with a beautiful form, but by extracting and magnifying its capacity to exceed itself, to break its own form, to become hybrid. In contrast to the Idealist notion of the human imposition of value upon life, Nietzsche makes life not only the highest value but understands it as a process of valuation (chapter 4). Moreover, since valuation is conceived as the assertion of self against the assertion of countless other selves, Nietzsche's vitalism is intrinsically antagonistic and heterogeneous. For Nietzsche, life is a struggle down to the smallest cell, and formation (*Bildung*) is always also deformation and overcoming, including the overcoming of previous forms of self. Under the rubric of the will-to-power, Nietzsche thus thinks of life as a force that both produces and exceeds all conceptual distinctions and oppositions; life becomes a problem and task that is at once biological and political, aesthetic and ethical, theoretical and practical.

Part III—"Deformation"—explores modernist figurations of life in Gottfried Benn and Robert Musil, both of whom develop their poetics through an engagement with and rejection of earlier models of vitalism. Benn's avant-garde Rönne novellas, written during World War I, deconstruct the Kantian belief in the mind's capacity to unify sensory data, replacing the latter's emphasis on formal unity with an emphasis on linguistic and bodily disarticulation (chapter 5). Himself a medical doctor, Benn writes literature in part as a pathology report, finding in the focus on disintegrating bodies and subjectivities an opening toward a new prose and therefore a new way of conceptualizing the human *bios*. Robert Musil's unfinished magnum opus, *The Man Without Qualities*, analyzes the petrification of the classical model of *Bildung* under conditions of a heightened biopolitical modernity (chapter 6). Where Goethe presented social forms as stabilizing human life, Musil depicts a world in which calculative reason has absorbed all singularity into statistical patterns of norm and deviation, splitting language and culture into impersonal scientific knowledge on the one hand and vacuous, dilettante chatter on the other. Musil's unfinished novel examines the violent fallout of the resulting inexpressibility of life (nationalism, madness, hypermasculinity) and explores, in its second part, new forms of speaking, thinking, and desiring capable of restoring life to experience and existence. The epilogue articulates in compressed and axiomatic form my major theoretical positions and claims.

A book that claims to outline the discourse of life in German culture from the late eighteenth to the mid-twentieth century is by necessity highly selective. While omissions are therefore inevitable, the lack of a sustained discussion of two thinkers—Hegel and Freud—requires some explanation. Hegel's attempt to overcome the Kantian opposition between (natural) necessity and (human) freedom builds on the understanding of life developed in Kant's third *Critique* and Goethe's biological writings. Insofar as Hegel's philosophy may be said to conceive "of a freedom that realizes it-self in and through life: a freedom of life,"[6] his work systematizes conceptual impulses discussed in the first two chapters of my book. But this systematization also smooths over tensions within the new discourse of life that are more clearly visible in the earlier writings. Rather than considering these tensions as theoretical failures, I read them as marks of the essential heterogeneity of life itself. From this perspective, Kant's and Goethe's reflections are more revealing than Hegel's more encompassing philosophical discourse. The situation concerning Freud is different. While influenced by Nietzsche's philosophy and certain trends within nineteenth-century biology, Freud's thinking about the interweaving of psyche and soma is not only highly original but historically complex, undergoing constant revisions, from the early neurological model of the mind in the "Project for a Scientific Psychology" (1895) to his protean work on sexuality and his later more speculative reflections on the role of the destructive forces in human life. Engaging with this enormous body of work in anything but a superficial manner would have exceeded the limits of a manageable chapter and transformed the architecture of the book. In the end, the number of chapters is only the pragmatic aspect of a more fundamental limit that has inevitably shaped this book—the limitations of my own life and thought.

Like all forms of life, my book has taken shape through the constant interaction and exchange with other people and institutions. A significant portion of it was written during a fellowship year at the University of Michigan's Institute for the Humanities. I wish to thank the director of the institute, Sid Smith, and my fellow fellows—especially Christiane Gruber, Jean Hébrard, Yanay Israel, Farina Mir, Mireille Roddier, Marjorie Rubright, Megan Sweeney, and Shana Melnysyn—for their encouragement and feedback, and the

6. Thomas Khurana, abstract for *The Freedom of Life: Hegelian Perspectives*, ed. Thomas Khurana (Berlin: August Verlag, 2013); and more recently and comprehensively, Khurana's outstanding *Das Leben der Freiheit. Form und Wirklichkeit der Autonomie* (Frankfurt am Main: Suhrkamp, 2017). As will become obvious, I am much indebted to Khurana's work on the concept of life in German Idealism.

institute and its staff for creating a marvelous working environment. The gift of time during my fellowship is but one of the many ways in which the University of Michigan has supported my work. I count myself lucky to be part of an institution that values research, and to be surrounded by so many incredibly smart and generous colleagues and friends. I could not have written this book without the unflagging support and kindness of Kerstin Barndt, Julia Hell, Marjorie Levinson, Johannes von Moltke, Yopie Prins, Helmut Puff, Scott Spector, and Silke-Maria Weineck. Silke, Marjorie, and Scott read the entire manuscript at a later stage and offered me a perceptive account of what I had been trying to argue; Danielle Lavaque-Manty, Christopher Skeaff, and Johannes gave much-needed feedback early on. Didier Fassin generously shared unpublished material with me. Elizabeth McNeill's outstanding work as a research assistant saved me from many goofs. I also benefited greatly from comments I received in the course of presenting parts of this project at various universities. My biggest thanks go to: Leslie Adelson, Michel Chaouli, Paul Fleming, Peter Gilgen, Arne Hoecker, Niklaus Largier, Christine Lehleiter, Helmut Müller-Sievers, John Noyes, Annette Schwarz, Erica Weitzman, and John Zilkosky. It is through the words of others that I found my own.

Monthly culinary feasts with Danielle Lavaque-Manty, Mika Lavaque-Manty, and Sue Juster offered welcome breaks from the asceticism of writing. David Halperin, Gayle Rubin, and Rostom Mesli convinced me that champagne is an essential feature of human life. And when I was in danger of getting lost in my head, Giangi, Sadie, and Arya reminded me of the other side of things, the life of instincts and the pleasures of unthinking movement.

Working with Cornell University Press was a true delight. I am grateful to Peter Uwe Hohendahl for his early interest in my project; to the members of the *Signale* board for their speedy (and favorable!) evaluation of the manuscript; to Kizer Walker, Mahinder Kingra, and Bethany Wasik for shepherding the book through the various stages of publication; and to Erin Davis for her attentive copyediting of my manuscript. The two reviewers for the press, Michel Chaouli and Jeffrey Librett, gave me valuable feedback on the manuscript; I trust they recognize their suggestions in the final product.

Finally, there are two people whose importance to this project goes well beyond what I can adequately thank them for here—my friend Russell Newstadt, and my partner and wife Lisa Disch. I cannot imagine what this book would have looked like without Russell's friendship and support; all I know is that it would have been infinitely poorer. Whenever I felt stuck and tempted to take shortcuts or gloss over inconsistencies and inaccuracies, Russell's insistence on conceptual precision and argumentative clarity forced me to dig deeper and find better formulations. There is no idea in this book that has not been shaped by our conversations. As for Lisa, I still cannot believe my luck in being able to share my life with her. Her boundless enthusiasm for the world has been a constant source of optimism and strength for me, and while I will never be able to fully match it, I am profoundly grateful for being able to live in its forcefield. Without her faith in me, my doubts would have gotten the better of me. This book is for her.

Earlier versions of chapters 2 and 5 appeared in *Germanic Review* (2012) and *New German Critique* (2018). I am grateful to publishers Taylor & Francis and Duke University Press for permission to reuse the material.

Abbreviations

Benn

GW   *Gesammelte Werke in der Fassung der Erstdrucke.* 4 vols. Edited by Bruno Hillebrand (Frankfurt am Main: Fischer, 1982–1989).

KP   *Künstlerische Prosa.* Edited by Holger Hof (Stuttgart: Klett-Cotta, 2006).

SW   *Sämtliche Werke.* Edited by Gerhard Schuster (Stuttgart: Klett-Cotta, 1986).

Goethe

FA   *Sämtliche Werke: Briefe, Tagebücher und Gespräche.* 40 vols. Edited by Friedmar Apel et al. (Frankfurt am Main: Deutscher Klassiker Verlag, 1989–).

HA   Goethes *Werke*. Hamburger Ausgabe in 14 Bänden.
      Edited by Erich Trunz (Hamburg: C. H. Beck, 1981).
MA   *Sämtliche Werke nach Epochen seines Schaffens.*
      Münchner Ausgabe. 21 vols. Edited by Karl Richter et al.
      (Munich: Carl Hanser Verlag, 1985–).
WMA   *Wilhelm Meister's Apprenticeship*. In *The Collected
      Works*, vol. 9. Edited and translated by Eric A. Blackall
      in cooperation with Victor Lange (New York: Suhrkamp
      Publishers, 1989).
WML   *Wilhelm Meisters Lehrjahre. Ein Roman*. Edited by Hans
      Jürgen Schings (Munich: Carl Hanser Verlag, 1988).

Kant

AA   *Kant's Gesammelte Schriften*. Edited by Königlich
      Preußischen Akademie der Wissenschaften. 28 vols.
      (Berlin: G. Reimer, 1902–).
CPJ   *Critique of the Power of Judgment*. Translated by Paul
      Guyer and Eric Matthews (Cambridge: Cambridge
      University Press, 2000).
CPR   *Critique of Pure Reason*. Translated by Paul Guyer and
      Allen W. Wood (Cambridge: Cambridge University Press,
      1999).
KrV   *Kritik der reinen Vernunft* (Hamburg: Felix Meiner,
      1956).
KU   *Kritik der Urteilskraft*. In *Kant's Gesammelte Schriften*.
      Edited by Königlich Preußischen Akademie der Wissen-
      schaften, vol. 5 (Berlin: G. Reimer, 1908), 165–486.

Kleist

EF   "Empfindungen vor Friedrichs Seelandschaft." In *Sämtliche
      Werke und Briefe: Münchner Ausgabe*, vol. 2. Edited by
      Roland Reuss and Peter Staengle (Munich: Carl Hanser
      Verlag, 2010), 362–63.

FF   "Feelings before Friedrich's Seascape." Translated by Silke-Maria Weineck. *Germanic Review* 85, no. 1 (2010): 65.

MT   "Über das Marionettentheater." In *Sämtliche Werke und Briefe: Münchner Ausgabe*, vol. 2, 425–33.

MvO   "Die Marquise von O . . ." In *Sämtliche Werke und Briefe: Münchner Ausgabe*, vol. 2, 107–47.

SW   *Sämtliche Werke und Briefe: Münchner Ausgabe*. Edited by Roland Reuss and Peter Staengle (Munich: Carl Hanser Verlag, 2010).

Musil

D   *Diaries, 1899–1941*. Translated by Philip Payne (New York: Basic Books, 1998).

MoE   *Der Mann ohne Eigenschaften*. Edited by Adolf Frisé (Reinbek bei Hamburg: Rowohlt, 1981).

MwQ   *The Man Without Qualities*. Translated by Sophie Wilkins (New York: Alfred A. Knopf, 1995).

PS   *Precision and Soul: Essays and Addresses*. Translated by Burton Pike and David S. Luft (Chicago: Chicago University Press, 1995).

PSE   *Prosa und Stücke. Kleine Prosa. Aphorismen. Autobiographische Essays und Reden. Kritik*. Edited by Adolf Frisé (Reinbek bei Hamburg: Rowohlt, 1978).

T   *Tagebücher*. Edited by Adolf Frisé (Reinbek bei Hamburg: Rowohlt, 1976).

Nietzsche

A   *Der Antichrist*. In *Sämtliche Werke*, vol. 5, 165–254.

BGE   *Beyond Good and Evil*. Translated by Judith Norman (Cambridge: Cambridge University Press, 2002).

BT   *The Birth of Tragedy and Other Writings*. Translated by Ronald Speirs (Cambridge: Cambridge University Press, 1999).

CW   *The Case of Wagner*. In *The Anti-Christ, Ecce Homo, Twilight of the Idols and Other Writings*. Translated by Judith Norman (Cambridge: Cambridge University Press, 2005), 231–63.

FW   *Die fröhliche Wissenschaft*. In *Sämtliche Werke*, vol. 3, 343–652.

GD   *Götzen-Dämmerung*. In *Sämtliche Werke*, vol. 6, 55–162.

GEM   *Zur Genealogie der Moral*. In *Sämtliche Werke*, vol. 5, 245–412.

GM   *On the Genealogy of Morals*. Translated by Carol Diethe (Cambridge: Cambridge University Press, 1997).

GT   *Die Geburt der Tragödie*. In *Sämtliche Werke*, vol. 1, 9–156.

JGB   *Jenseits von Gut und Böse*. In *Sämtliche Werke*, vol. 5, 9–244.

KSA   *Sämtliche Werke. Kritische Studienausgabe in 15 Bänden*. Edited by Giorgio Colli and Mazzino Montinari (Berlin: Walter de Gruyter, 1967–1977).

MR   *Morgenröthe*. In *Sämtliche Werke*, vol. 3, 9–332.

WP   *The Will to Power*. Translated by Walter Kaufmann and R. J. Hollingdale (New York: Vintage Books, 1967).

Wittgenstein

LWPP *Last Writings on the Philosophy of Psychology*. Translated by C. G. Luckhardt and Maximian A. E. Aue (Oxford: Blackwell, 1982).

PI   *Philosophical Investigations*. Translated by G. E. M. Anscombe, P. M. S. Hacker, and Joachim Schulte (Hoboken, NJ: Wiley-Blackwell, 2009).

PPF   *Philosophy of Psychology: A Fragment*. In *Philosophical Investigations*, 182–243.

R   *Remarks on the Philosophy of Psychology*. Translated by
        G. E. M. Anscombe (Chicago: University of Chicago
        Press, 1980).
ÜG   *Über Gewißheit* (Frankfurt am Main: Suhrkamp, 1970).
Z   *Zettel*. Translated by G. E. M. Anscombe (Oxford:
        Blackwell, 1967).

INTRODUCTION

"There is much that is formidable (*polla ta deina*)," the chorus in Sophocles's *Antigone* intones, "but nothing more formidable than man (*ouden anthrōpou deinoteron*)."[1] And nowhere is this terrible supremacy more visible, the ode continues, than in man's violent subduing of nature. No matter how marvelous and intricate the natural world may be, man's "wind-swift thought (*anemoen phronēma*)," his ingenuity and cunning, finds a way to impose itself and bend nature's forces to his design. He bears himself across the "furious chasms of the sea" in ships, and wears away the "imperishable earth (*Gān aphthiton*)" with yoked horses. Pondering and plotting, he draws down to earth the "race (*phylon*) of airborne

---

1. Sophocles, *Sophoclis: Fabulae*, ed. Hugh Lloyd-Jones and N. G. Wilson (Oxford: Oxford University Press, 1992), lines 332–75 (passage translated by Russell Newstadt). See also Martin Heidegger's famous reading of the ode in his *Introduction to Metaphysics*, trans. Gregory Fried and Richard Polt (New Haven, CT: Yale University Press, 2004), 163–84.

birds" with slings and pulls to the surface the "tribes (*ethnē*) of those native to the sea" with "woven nets." And when he is not busy killing, man tames and trains, captures and cultivates, the beasts that roam in the mountains, the "rough-maned stallion," the "unvanquished bull." He, the "all too clever (*periphradēs*)" human being.

Sophocles's "Ode to Man" reads as an eerie premonition of our contemporary environmental catastrophe. Though written more than two thousand years ago, Sophocles's language already suggests the global transformation of entire species and classes ("tribes" and "races") of animals, as well as the inversion and denaturing of the seemingly imperishable natural elements of heaven and earth. There is even, perhaps, a sense of more invasive and disruptive technologies to come, even if their precise shape and reach remains unimaginable to Sophocles.[2] What Sophocles does not envision, however, is that man's interventions might not simply transform nature but render human life within it impossible to sustain. And with this possibility, which has become not only imaginable but increasingly probable, the very opposition between nature and human nature that still structures Sophocles's text begins to crumble. At a time when the fallout of our carbon-driven civilization has raised sea levels and heated the atmosphere, what used to be called "nature" has become almost indistinguishable from human manipulation. We are at once near to and a great distance from Greek tragedy.

In view of these developments, it is not surprising that we are witnessing a profusion of interest in questions of life. If the rather amorphous notion of "life" has become a keyword inside and outside academia, this is both because life itself is everywhere under threat, and because the traditional categories for distinguishing its various regions—categories such as nature and culture, politics and biology, humans and nonhumans—are dissolving in front of our

---

2. The invasiveness of modern technology goes hand in hand with a transformation of what counts as living matter. This is perhaps most obvious in the realm of medical intervention, which is no longer limited to cutting or curing individual bodies but has learned to manipulate genes or transfer cells. For a discussion of the biopolitical implications of these changes, see Petra Gehring, *Was ist Biomacht? Vom zweifelhaften Mehrwert des Lebens* (Frankfurt: Campus Verlag, 2004), esp. 17–35.

eyes. Hence the political and conceptual orientation of most contemporary academic work engaged with questions of life: environmental history and science and technology studies attend to the nexus of waste, toxicity, and power while challenging the nature-culture binary;[3] animal studies highlight the brutal practices of the food industry while questioning the humanistic bias of our ethical categories;[4] and under the rubric of biopolitics, scholars study biomedicine[5] or the treatment of refugees[6] in view of a politics that reduces political subjects to mere living beings.

However, vital as these issues are, I want to step back from the present moment and look to the historical period when the basic questions and terms at play in today's contemporary discussions of life enter the stage. To be sure, as Sophocles's tragedy shows, reflections on the status of human life within nature are perennial. But these reflections cross a significant and, for us, still relevant conceptual threshold at a specific point in time. Before the issue of human beings' reorganization of natural life assumed *material* urgency in the twentieth century, it became a matter of *intellectual* urgency in the last decades of the eighteenth century, especially in Germany. As Foucault already indicated many years ago, it is during this period that our modern notion of "life"—of life understood as a productive force or vital principle that organizes living beings from

---

3. See, for instance, Brett Walker, *Toxic Archipelago: A History of Industrial Disease in Japan* (Seattle: University of Washington Press, 2011), and the articles in the journal *Environmental Humanities*, among many others. For a particularly imaginative way of rethinking life in the context of environmental crisis, see Timothy Morton, *Ecological Thought* (Cambridge, MA: Harvard University Press, 2012).

4. Cary Wolfe, *Before the Law: Humans and Animals in a Biopolitical Frame* (Chicago: University of Chicago Press, 2012).

5. Gehring, *Was ist Biomacht?*; Nicholas Rose, *The Politics of Life Itself: Biomedicine, Power, and Subjectivity in the Twenty First Century* (Princeton, NJ: Princeton University Press, 2006).

6. Didier Fassin, "Humanitarianism as a Politics of Life," *Public Culture* 19, no. 3 (2007): 499–520. Fassin is careful to distinguish between Foucaultian biopolitics and his own notion of a "politics of life." See his "Another Politics of Life is Possible," *Theory, Culture and Society* 26, no. 5 (2009): 44–60, and my discussion below.

within—emerged.[7] Enlightenment vitalists no longer conceived of living beings as complex machines, as had been the case within the broadly Cartesian framework that dominated natural history until the mid-eighteenth century, but as manifestations of an intrinsic activity—an inner force—that shapes and moves them. Although some of these debates also took place in France,[8] they gathered steam in Germany after 1775, giving rise to a powerful discourse of life that was distinct in two ways: first, because it placed an unusually strong emphasis on "development," insisting on the dynamic context of life;[9] and second, because in Germany this new dynamic notion of "life" was extended beyond the biological realm to reconceptualize the logic of social and cognitive processes. To adopt a formulation from Thomas Khurana and Christoph Menke, in intellectual debates in Germany life appears as "a peculiar type of form and formation. Life figures as the subject and object of processes of formation,"[10] whether political, practical, aesthetic, or

---

7. Michel Foucault, *The Order of Things: An Archeology of the Human Sciences* (New York: Vintage Books, 1970), esp. 226 ff. On the emergence of a synthetic notion of life during this period, see also François Jacob, *The Logic of Life: A History of Heredity* (New York: Pantheon Books, 1974); Timothy Lenoir, *The Strategy of Life: Teleology and Mechanics in Nineteenth-Century German Biology* (Chicago: University of Chicago Press, 1989); Stephen Asma, *Following Form and Function: A Philosophical Archeology of Life Sciences* (Evanston, IL: Northwestern University Press, 1996); and, more recently, Peter Reill, *Vitalizing Nature in the Enlightenment* (Berkeley: University of California Press, 2005), who dates the rise of vitalism to the 1750s.

8. Reill, *Vitalizing Nature in the Enlightenment.*

9. Asma, *Following Form and Function,* 48, stresses the singularity of the German case most forcefully: "One of the strongest themes that should be impressed upon us concerning German nature philosophy and its morphology is the singular focus on 'development.' The Germans, wrestling with questions of form and function, always placed their inquiry firmly in the dynamic context of life . . . a point which was not appreciated by French and British naturalists until well after von Baer's work had been appropriated [after 1850]."

10. Thomas Khurana and Christoph Menke, "Form and Formation of Life," *Constellations* 18, no. 1 (March 2011): 6–7. See also Christoph Menke, *Kraft. Ein Grundbegriff ästhetischer Anthropologie* (Frankfurt am Main: Suhrkamp, 2008). For a detailed understanding of the concept of life in German Idealism, see Khurana's *Das Leben der Freiheit* and "Die Kunst der zweiten Natur. Zu einem modernen Kulturbegriff nach Kant, Schiller und Hegel," *WestEnd—Neue Zeitschrift für Sozialforschung* 1 (2016): 35–55. Particularly important for my work is

biological. The point of this extended notion of life was not to biologize culture but to overcome the Cartesian dualism of body and mind in favor of a more nuanced differentiation between natural and symbolic processes. After all, if mind *and* body are self-active and formative, then biological life may still be different from symbolic life but no longer its absolute Other.

It was Kant's *Critique of Judgment* (1790)—the subject of chapter 1—that brought out the larger philosophical implications of Enlightenment vitalism. In articulating a conceptual framework that drew art, nature, and cognition into close proximity, Kant inaugurated a discourse of life centered on the complex interaction between natural and symbolic processes. My claim is that this expanded conception of life and its attention to force and form is of historical and critical importance. As I will argue in more detail, most contemporary discussions, including the discourse on biopolitics, tend to reduce life to the effect of the technologies and instruments of power and knowledge brought to bear on it. Put schematically, contemporary theories place the implements of structuring, symbolizing, and forming life on the side of resources *external* to life, conceiving of the latter as the minimal potential for, or the infinitely malleable matter of, living common to all specific forms of life. The problem with this approach is that it strips life of its vitality—its *intrinsic* force and form—thus failing to capture both its buoyancy and the full reach, indeed the violence, of its biopolitical manipulation. To gain a better sense of our biopolitical modernity, I argue, we need a richer and more plastic notion of life, one attuned to the interplay and conflict between its different modalities, what, in part following Wittgenstein, I will call *forms of life*. I want to suggest that the German discourse of life with its emphasis on the dialectic of force and form and its attention to the interconnection of natural, aesthetic, and political processes of formation provides us with an essential resource for articulating such a model.

Khurana's earlier essay on the dialectic of force and form: "Force and Form: An Essay on the Dialectics of the Living," *Constellations* 18, no. 1 (March 2011): 21–34.

My book, then, engages with contemporary debates on life from the perspective of a tradition that is rarely explicitly discussed. In the first place, this tradition arises in Germany and Austria, rather than France and England, and more specifically in what we may call a vitalist strand of thinking in German-speaking culture. Second, it emerges in the period between 1780 and 1940, which significantly precedes contemporary biopolitical and environmental debates. In fact, the bulk of my book concerns two historical moments—one around 1800, the other in the early decades of the twentieth century—during which conceptions of human and nonhuman life undergo important transformations. Finally, I suggest that in order to grasp the forms of life and existence in modernity, we need to draw on the literary and aesthetic archive, which is often ignored within contemporary debates on life.[11] To be clear, I do not wish to deny that our current predicament is largely the product of political and scientific technologies. My claim is just that the conceptual underpinnings and existential implications of these technologies are

---

11.   There are important exceptions to this neglect in the literature on biopolitics, the most powerful being the work of Eric Santner. See his *On Creaturely Life: Rilke, Benjamin, Sebald* (Chicago: University of Chicago Press, 2006), *The Royal Remains: The People's Two Bodies and the Endgames of Sovereignty* (Chicago: University of Chicago Press, 2011), and *The Weight of all Flesh: On the Subject-Matter of Political Economy* (Chicago: University of Chicago Press, 2015). I discuss Santner's work in more detail in the "Seeing-As" section of this chapter. Another important book that defends the place of art and the humanities within the context of a broader theory of life is Carsten Strathausen's excellent *Bioaesthetics: Making Sense of Life in Science and the Arts* (Minneapolis: University of Minnesota Press, 2017). Strathausen draws on aesthetic theory, especially Kant's *Critique of the Power of Judgment*, to draw out parallels between aesthetic and biological processes while at the same time pushing back against recent appeals to use biology and neuroscience in order to articulate the dynamics of cultural artifacts. Building on Francesco Varela's and Humberto Maturana's account of the nonlinear causality of living matter, Strathausen argues that recursivity and autopoiesis are essential both to living organisms and art and aesthetics. From this perspective, "bioaesthetics" is defined as an "interdisciplinary approach to the study of culture that moves beyond the speculative theory of art that has dominated the humanities since the nineteenth century, without, however, succumbing to the broad universalist claims that characterize today's biologism and new Darwinism" (24). Whereas the bulk of Strathausen's work is devoted to a critique of these contemporary theories, my book focuses on the engagement with, and transformation of, Kant's insights within German literature and philosophy.

most clearly articulated in literature and philosophy, owing to the privileged place of form and formalization in both enterprises. Hence the title of this book, *Forms of Life*, which is meant to signal the importance of form, and thus aesthetics, for understanding our biopolitical modernity.

Why literature? What is it that literature and aesthetics can add to contemporary discussions of life? To begin to answer these questions, it will be helpful to recall a comment on the semantics of "life" by Georges Canguilhem, one of Foucault's most influential teachers: "By life, one can hear the present or the past participle of the verb to live—the living (*le vivant*) and the lived (*le vécu*)," which correspond respectively to "the universal organization of matter" and to "the experience of individual human beings." And he adds: "The second meaning is, according to me, commanded by the first one, which is more fundamental. It is in the sense that life is the form and power of the living that I would like to treat relations between concept and life."[12] Canguilhem's bracketing of lived experience, as Didier Fassin has remarked, shapes much of today's discourse on life. This is true of the path taken by scholars such as Paul Rabinow, Sarah Franklin, and Nikolas Rose[13] "with their simultaneous and convergent definition and use of the idea of the 'life itself' . . . the side of life sciences and biomedical interventions on living matter."[14] But it is also true for major conceptions of biopolitics, be it Agamben's notion of "bare life" extracted from its psychological and social milieu or Foucault's emphasis on population control and institutional operations. In fact, in his 1978 introduction to the new edition of Canguilhem's *The Normal and the Pathological*, Foucault explicitly invoked Canguilhem's distinction between living matter and lived experience to situate his own work in opposition to

---

12. Georges Canguilhem, *Études d'histoire et de philosophie des sciences* (Paris: Vrin, 1983), 335 (my translation).

13. Paul Rabinow, *Making PCR: A Story of Biotechnology* (Chicago: University of Chicago Press, 1996); Sarah Franklin, *Life itself: Global Nature and the Global Imaginary* (London: Sage, 2000), esp. 188–227; Nicholas Rose, *The Politics of Life Itself: Biomedicine, Power, and Subjectivity in the Twenty-First Century* (Princeton, NJ: Princeton University Press, 2006).

14. Fassin, "Another Politics of Life Is Possible."

inquiries centered on the notion of experience, which he associated with the works of Merleau-Ponty and Sartre.[15] I will not analyze Foucault's critique of phenomenology or the philosophy of the subject;[16] suffice it to note that the notion of experience is virtually absent from Foucault's larger works of the late 1960s and the 1970s. Whether he analyzes discourses, as in *The Order of Things*, or technologies of power and knowledge, as in *Discipline and Punish* and *The History of Sexuality*, Foucault's main focus is on the broader epistemic and institutional structures that determine what counts for the subject *as* experience. Put somewhat differently, Foucault's approach to human life in the late 1960s and the 1970s is predominantly vertical—it is a third person, top-to-bottom approach that analyzes experience, if at all, in terms of processes of individualization that are regulated by impersonal mechanisms imposed on the subject from above.[17] But this approach highlights only one, albeit highly important, perspective on human life—the institutional perspective, whether mediated through scientific epistemes, disciplinary or surveillance mechanisms, statistics, or regimes of truth; hence Fassin's call to bring other media and perspectives into the conversation. While situating himself in the tradition of work inspired by Canguilhem and Foucault, Fassin, an anthropologist who has written extensively on refugees, humanitarianism, and the politics of AIDS, directs his social science colleagues to the resources of the aesthetic: "In their approach to life, social scientists have most recently been inspired by philosophers who theorize the living rather than the lived, biology more than the ethics of life, biopolitics more than the experience of life, but it might be time for them to reengage in a conversation with novelists, poets, playwrights and

---

15. Michel Foucault, introduction to *The Normal and the Pathological*, ed. Georges Canguilhem (New York: Zone Books, 1997), 8.

16. On Foucault's critique of phenomenology, see Leonard Lawlor, *The Implications of Immanence: Towards a New Concept of Life* (New York: Fordham University Press, 2006), 57–69, and Todd May, "Foucault's Relation to Phenomenology," in *The Cambridge Companion to Foucault*, ed. Gary Gutting (Cambridge: Cambridge University Press, 2006), 284–311.

17. See the "Foucault" section of this chapter.

filmmakers—that is, creators who use, as they do themselves, life as the matter of their creation."[18]

This is the conversation that I hope to engage with in this work. Like Fassin, my turn to aesthetics is not meant to deny the importance of more abstract takes on human life, nor do I wish to recover some kind of inner experience that exists prior to broader social and symbolic processes. By lived experience—*Erlebnis*—I mean not a private datum or event shielded from the world but a network of dissonant forces and vectors that crisscross self and other, body and mind, drive and law. Experience, in other words, is the registering of a multiplicity of perspectives, grammatically parsed in the configuration of first-, second-, and third-person indices. Inextricably bound up with a first-person perspective, while simultaneously unfolding in the second-person realm of social interaction—the to-and-fro of conversational and bodily engagement in which human beings project a sense of self and respond to the sense of self projected by others[19]—experience, so understood, is equally shaped by countless third-person narratives, impersonal scripts, practices, and technologies that regulate social life and structure the self's relation to itself and others. As I will show in more detail, aesthetic media in general, and literature in particular, are singularly equipped to simulate and explore this heterogeneous structure of experience and subjectivity. Literature's attention to the interplay of multiple perspectives and discourses, its polylogical structure, enables it to model both the texture of embodied experience and its interweaving with broader social processes.

In the view I propose, then, literature's sensitivity to changes in the political, social, and scientific organization of life is not a matter of accident; questions of life and questions of aesthetics are *intrinsically* connected. Aesthetic media record psychic and sociopolitical life in the most intimate regions of inner and outer space, registering in moods, bodily sensations, perception, modes of speaking, and seemingly trivial details the ideas, anxieties, and obsessions of

---

18. Fassin, "True Life, Real Lives," 7.
19. See Webb Keane, *Ethical Life: Its Social and Natural Histories* (Princeton, NJ: Princeton University Press, 2016), 110–22.

a particular era. This attention to detail has become particularly relevant in our biopolitical modernity. As Eric Santner elegantly puts it, the notion of biopolitics names a constellation "where life becomes a matter of politics and politics comes to inform the very matter and materiality of life."[20] I would add that if the theory of biopolitics is to have any explanatory relevance at all, it must account for the emergence of an historically specific form of power, one characterized by two interrelated features: by the "reduced importance of fixed social roles and the egalitarian reduction of politics to the life shared by all, irrespective of status, gender, or even species,"[21] and by the development of new technologies of power aimed at colonizing and shaping the ordinary lives of citizens. It is modern literature that registers these changes most clearly. Put very schematically, until the eighteenth century, individuality had been a matter of fame, and literature depicted the representative individual through heroic narratives that commemorated the extraordinary deeds associated with his name. With the beginning of the eighteenth century, and, in particular, with the rise of the novel, this heroic conception of life receded into the background. The modern novel, with its distinctly antiheroic bias, shifted the focus of narrative amplification from the great individual to the chatter and minutiae that structure the lives of ordinary people. In doing so, it opened up for inspection both the operations of psychic or cognitive life and the new social and political forces that shaped it. Put differently, the novel explored experience not as the passive registering of external reality but as what molds and is molded by the social and natural life of which it is a part. And what came to be known in the last decades of the eighteenth century as "aesthetics" was precisely an attempt to articulate, in philosophical and conceptual language, this dynamic intertwinement of mind, body, and (natural and sociopolitical) environment.

---

20. Santner, *On Creaturely Life*, 12.

21. Malcolm Bull, "States Don't Really Mind Their Citizens Dying (Provided They Don't All Do It at Once): They Just Don't Like Anyone Else to Kill Them," *London Review of Books* 26, no. 4 (2004): 5.

To anticipate arguments more fully developed in the first two chapters, the relevance of the new discipline of aesthetics to questions of life was fourfold. First, aesthetics, especially as developed in Kant, drew attention to the formative and dynamic character of cognitive processes—to the fact that the forms the mind generates are restricted neither by rational, categorical, or practical purposes nor by existing natural forms. In this sense, aesthetics highlighted the freedom of the mind, its creative and imaginative capacity to *give form to life*. Second, insofar as this freedom is felt in aesthetic experience as a pleasurable enlivening (*Belebung*) of the mind's various faculties, aesthetics showed that the mind possesses its own peculiar kind of vitality, a mode of life that is both similar to and different from natural life. Third, whereas Cartesian and other intellectualist accounts of thinking divorced cognition from the body, aesthetics emphasized the interplay between affect and judgment, thus highlighting both the embodied character of cognition and the conceptual dimension of experience. Fourth, art came to be charged with the task of giving representative form to this new episteme of living interrelationships among different modalities of life. Art was conceived as the reflective medium in which nature and mind, self and language, social organization and imagination, sense and sensibility intersect and collide. Itself the source of a peculiar aesthetic vitality not reducible to its manifest content, art also came to represent and embody the multifariousness of forms of life, thereby making the new, extended notion of life intuitively, affectively, and symbolically accessible.

I am not saying, then, that literature is the only aesthetic medium attentive to the dynamics of social and psychic life. All aesthetic media are perceptually and conceptually self-reflective; that is, all art foregrounds the ways our senses, nerves, moods, and words disclose the world that in turn shapes them. But literature, at least until the arrival of technological media at the end of the nineteenth century and arguably beyond it, is singularly equipped to portray the intertwining of life and experience. Think of its ability to expand and compress time and space, to quickly shift scale and perspective, or to crystallize language into metaphors that compress otherwise distinct semantic fields. To these traditional resources we must add the specific devices modern literature developed to penetrate and represent the interplay of psychic and social life: a newly pliable and common hero;[22] the fashioning of narrative episodes as open opportunities rather than rigid conflicts;[23] elaborate techniques for representing consciousness and its intertwinement with communication, such as free indirect discourse;[24] and an increasing emphasis on citation, polyphony, and heteroglossia, enabling fictional texts to absorb multiple idioms, including the faceless languages of both science and cliché.[25] In thus embracing and magnifying the complex texture of modern everyday life, literature performed two distinct yet potentially connected feats: it explored, in hitherto unknown depth and detail, the forms and processes of subjective life; and it thereby made visible—in fact, opened to observation and reflection—the spaces in which the new capillary forms of power sought to install themselves.

Against this admittedly schematic sketch, we can distinguish three approaches of examining the connection between modern literature and modern biopolitics. First, literature can be seen to extend the projections and calculations of power into dimensions of human life otherwise inaccessible to more official forms of biopolitics such as health policy and population control. On this reading, literature's articulation of subjectivity and experience is a ploy enabling it to drive the mechanisms of normalization deep into the subject, molding not just the bodies of citizens but also their minds and souls, their "individuality." This is the line of thought Foucault himself

---

22. See Franco Moretti, *The Way of the World: The Bildungsroman in European Culture* (London: Verso, 1987), 21, for whom Goethe's *Wilhelm Meister* is the prototypical modern "pliant" protagonist. For an illuminating discussion of the issue of averageness in German literature, see Paul Fleming, *Exemplarity and Mediocrity: The Art of the Average from the Bourgeois Tragedy to Realism* (Redwood Hills, CA: Stanford University Press, 2009).

23. Moretti, *The Way of the World*, 45–46.

24. Dorrit Cohn, *Transparent Minds: Narrative Modes for Presenting Consciousness in Fiction* (Princeton, NJ: Princeton University Press, 1984).

25. On polyphony and heteroglossia in the modern novel, see M. M. Bakhtin, *Problems of Dostoevsky's Poetics*, Theory and History of Literature 8, ed. and trans. Caryl Emerson (Minneapolis: University of Minnesota Press, 1984) and M. M. Bakhtin, *The Dialogic Imagination: Four Essays* (Austin: University of Texas Press, 1983).

gestured at and which, following him, D. A. Miller has pursued most brilliantly.[26] But literature's affective reach also opens up a second, less negative connection to politics. Literature's capacity to articulate experience in its most intimate details makes it highly sensitive to biopolitical transformations. If biopower truly runs *through* our lives, as the discourse on biopolitics claims, then aesthetic media—and literature in particular—are uniquely equipped to register, and give symbolic and imaginative expression to, this imbrication of bodies, mind, and power. Aesthetics, so understood, is neither a sophisticated arm of the biopolitical regime nor its radical other; it is a mode of thinking that grasps the manipulation of life in modernity from *within* this very life.

And there is a third connection between literature and life, one that ultimately points beyond the paradigms of biopolitics. Imagine or recall standing in front of a painting. As you approach the canvas, the visual field undergoes a radical transformation, as the figures and forms seen from afar dissolve into a bewildering mix of pigments, brushstrokes, dots, and layers of paint. Something of that sort happens to the realist impulse of modern art. As the parameters of description become more fine-grained, the organizing frames of realist narrative—characters, plots, objects, recognizable situations, generic story lines—begin to disintegrate. Move the narrative gaze closer to the minutiae of thinking and the unity of character dissolves into a stream of consciousness; reduce the scale of description and the codes of fashion give way to a world of tactile and visual sensation. What I am depicting here is not just the historical transformation from realism to modernism (think late Henry James)

---

26. See Michel Foucault's remarks on modern literature in "Lives of Infamous Men," in *Power: The Essential Works of Michel Foucault*, ed. James D. Faubion, vol. 3, *Power*, ed. James D. Faubion (New York: The New Press, 1997), 157–75, according to which "literature belongs to the great system of constraint by which the West obliged the quotidian to enter into discourse" (174). The most compelling and formally interesting interpretation of modern literature along these lines is by D. A. Miller, *The Novel and the Police* (Berkeley: University of California Press, 1988). Miller locates the primary normalizing function of the novel in its use of free indirect discourse. A kind of rhetorical panopticon, free indirect discourse, under the cover of neutrality, operates by "qualifying, canceling, endorsing, subsuming all the other voices it lets speak" (25).

but a dialectic movement internal to *all* art, a dialectic that becomes particularly evident in the context of modern literature's realist orientation. For while realist literature is called upon to give representative shape to ordinary life, its own plenitude of expression constantly exceeds the forms of life it depicts. To be sure, this dialectic between form and expression is not restricted to German literature. It is perhaps a defining feature of all forceful art, and is in clear evidence in authors as diverse as Melville, Flaubert, George Eliot, Proust, Joyce, and Beckett. But the German tradition is unusual because (a) it places the dialectic of form and expression at the core of a new field of philosophical inquiry and (b) frames this inquiry explicitly as a reflection on *life*. When Kant, in the opening pages of the *Critique of the Power of Judgment*, defines the specificity of aesthetic experience in terms of the intensified "feeling of life" (*Lebensgefühl*)[27] beauty generates in the beholder, he simultaneously connects art to, and distinguishes it from, the then emerging biological conception of "life." With Kant, aesthetic experience comes to be understood as a particular kind of animation (*Belebung*), as an emphatic mode of aliveness that exceeds all natural and ordinary forms of life (in fact, transports the subject beyond self, opening up another experience). German writings on art up to Adorno hold on to this emphatic idea of *aesthetic life*, reflecting in various ways on its entanglement with the scientific and political organization of natural and social life. These post-Kantian reflections take a variety of forms, including an insistence on the disaggregation of art and social life (as in Nietzsche's claim that "only as an *aesthetic phenomenon* is existence and the world eternally *justified*"[28]) and the increasing problematization of the very possibility of experience in modernity (see chapters 5 and 6). But even the most extreme critics of experience hold on to an emphatic insistence on the vital resources of art. Driving such critiques is an ultimately ethical and political stance: the belief that aesthetic life, while hypersensitive to the mechanisms of social manipulation, is not reduc-

---

27.   KU § 1; AA 5:204; CPJ 90.
28.   Friedrich Nietzsche, *The Birth of Tragedy and Other Writings* (Cambridge: Cambridge University Press, 1999), 33 (Nietzsche's emphasis).

ible to it, and that art opens up a critical and experimental space in which alternative modes of being in the world—alternative forms of aliveness—can be tried out and imagined. In short, it is precisely the formal plasticity of aesthetic media—their formative power—that enables them to serve as a laboratory for the projection of as yet unrealized possibilities of being, and thus, of new forms of life that point beyond the biopolitical paradigm.

The detailed discussion of these aesthetic experiments will have to await the individual chapters of the book. I will now (1) make the case for my focus on German-speaking culture, (2) outline salient features of the rise of vitalism in the second half of the eighteenth century, (3) situate my work in relation to Foucault's, and (4) sketch my appropriation and expansion of the Wittgensteinian conception of *Lebensform*.

Why Germany?

German-speaking culture has been obsessed with figures and tropes of life since the second half of the eighteenth century. From Kant's *Critique of Judgment* (1790) to Freud's distinction between life and death drives (published in 1920)[29]; from the Romantic philosophy of life (*Lebensphilosophie*)[30] to Nazi projects of geographic expansion (*Lebensraum*)[31] and biological purification (*lebenswert*, *lebensunwert*);[32] and from the life reform (*Lebensreform*)

29. Sigmund Freud, "Beyond the Pleasure Principle," in *The Standard Edition of the Complete Psychological Works of Sigmund Freud*, vol. 18, ed. James Strachey (London: Hogarth Press and the Institute of Psychoanalysis, 1955), 1–64.

30. Friedrich Schlegel, *Philosophie des Lebens* (1827), in *Kritische Friedrich-Schlegel Ausgabe*, ed. Ernst Behler (Munich: Ferdinand Schöningh, 1969), 101–308.

31. The term *Lebensraum* was coined by the German geographer Friedrich Rautzel at the end of the nineteenth century and employed by the Nazis to legitimate their imperialist policy. See Woodruff D. Smith, *The Ideological Origins of Nazi Imperialism* (Oxford: Oxford University Press, 1989), esp. 83–111 and 231–58.

32. Peter Weingart, Jürgen Kroll, and Kurt Bayertz, *Rasse, Blut und Gene. Geschichte der Eugenik und Rassenhygiene in Deutschland* (Frankfurt am Main: Suhrkamp, 1992), esp. 523–32.

movement of the early 1900s[33] to Husserl's theory of "life-world" (*Lebenswelt*, 1936)[34] and Wittgenstein's notion of forms of life (*Lebensformen*, 1945)[35]—to name only a few of the relevant mileposts—the term "life" has been central to philosophical, political, cultural, and aesthetic movements in Germany. In fact, talk of life pervades and defies political, disciplinary, and religious boundaries. The word *Lebensform*, for instance, was coined in the context of Romantic philosophy in the 1820s,[36] entered biological terminology a few decades later,[37] became a popular term of conservative cultural-political criticism after World War I,[38] and migrated in the 1930s into Wittgenstein's philosophy of language on the one hand and the Nazi discourse on eugenics on the other.

This fluidity of the term "life"—its movement across vastly different semantic fields—has allowed it to inform almost every period of German culture and politics. Vitalist thought emerged in the second half of the eighteenth century as a cultural, political, and epistemological battle cry in literature and natural history (see the next section). To a generation increasingly suspicious of the social and political determinism of aristocratic society, the supposition of a "vital force" operating at the heart of nature and culture provided a powerful model for an emergent society based on expres-

---

33. John Alexander Williams, *Turning to Nature in Germany: Hiking, Nudism, and Conservation, 1900–1940* (Redwood Hills, CA: Stanford University Press, 2007).

34. Edmund Husserl, *The Crisis of European Sciences and Transcendental Phenomenology* (Evanston, IL: Northwestern University Press, 1970).

35. Ludwig Wittgenstein, *Philosophical Investigations* (Hoboken, NJ: Wiley-Blackwell, 2009).

36. Stefan Helmreich and Sophia Roosth, "Life Forms: A Keyword Entry," *Representations* 112 (2010): 31–33.

37. Helmreich and Roosth, "Life-Forms," 34.

38. See Oswald Spengler, *Der Untergang des Abendlands: Umrisse einer Morphologie der Weltgeschichte* (Munich: C. H. Beck, 1918), and the work of Ludwig Klages, especially his *Der Geist als Widersacher der Seele (1929–32)* (Leipzig: J. A. Barth, 1929–32). On Klages's philosophy of life, its influence on Benjamin, and its connection to Nazi politics, see Nitzan Lebovic, *The Philosophy of Life and Death: Ludwig Klages and the Rise of a Nazi Biopolitics* (New York: Palgrave, 2013), esp. chapters 5 and 6, and Richard Wolin, "Introduction to the Revised Edition," in *Benjamin: Aesthetics of Redemption* (New York: Columbia University Press, 1982), esp. xxix–xi.

siveness and individual freedom. In the 1780s, Friedrich Heinrich Jacobi (1743–1819) inserted another thread into this discourse of life. Drawing on Spinoza's monism—the idea that matter and thought are modes of a single infinite substance—Jacobi argued that rational thought inevitably led to "nihilism" (a term he invented) and that faith and feeling alone were able to sense the unity of life.[39] An initial expression of what later came to be called *Lebensphilosophie*, Jacobi's existentialist critique of philosophy and his contention that all of our knowledge claims—indeed, our entire life—rested on ungrounded beliefs, on feeling rather than reason, deeply influenced post-Kantian thinkers. Meanwhile Kant's own reflections on the self-organizing structure of cognitive and natural processes in the *Critique of Judgment* seemed to provide further confirmation of the continuity of mind and nature. Thus, Enlightenment vitalism gave way to Romantic *Naturphilosophie*, and a new metaphysical notion of "life" came to underwrite organic conceptions of state and society,[40] work in biology and medicine,[41] and new theories of art and the novel.[42]

---

39. See Friedrich Heinrich Jacobi, *Über die Lehre des Spinoza in Briefen an den Herrn Moses Mendelssohn* (Hamburg: Felix Meiner, 1785), his 1815 *Vorrede* to his complete works, and his novel *Eduard Allwill* (1792). For an excellent English selection of Jacobi's work, see *The Main Philosophical Writings and the Novel Allwill*, ed. and trans. George di Giovanni (Montreal: McGill-Queen's University Press, 1994). On holistic monism and Jacobi's influence on post-Kantian philosophy, see Paul Franks, *All or Nothing: Systematicity, Transcendental Arguments, and Skepticism in German Idealism* (Cambridge, MA: Harvard University Press, 2005), esp. 162–76.

40. Ethel Matala De Mazza, *Der verfaßte Körper. Zum Projekt einer organischen Gemeinschaft in der Politischen Romantik* (Freiburg: Rombach, 1999); Gerhard Dilcher, "The Germanists and the Historical School of Law: German Legal Science between Romanticism, Realism, and Rationalization," *Rechtsgeschichte* 24 (2016): 20–72; and Ernst-Wolfgang Böckenförde, "Organ, Organismus, Organisation, politischer Körper," in *Geschichtliche Grundbegriffe. Historisches Lexikon zur politisch-sozialen Sprache in Deutschland*, vol. 4, ed. Otto Brunner, Werner Conze, and Reinhart Koselleck (Stuttgart: Klett-Cotta, 1978), esp. 579–613.

41. Robert J. Richards, *The Romantic Conception of Life: Science and Philosophy in the Age of Goethe* (Chicago: University of Chicago Press, 2004).

42. Rüdiger Campe, "Form und Leben in der Theorie des Romans," in *Vita aesthetica. Szenen ästhetischer Lebendigkeit*, ed. Armen Avanessian, Winfried Menninghaus, and Jan Völker (Zurich, Berlin: diaphanes, 2009), 193–212.

Although the positivist orientation of mid-century biology often tended to reduce "life" to a physicochemical process, a rich understanding of the intertwinement of biological and social life continued to inform both post- and anti-Hegelian strands of German thought throughout the nineteenth century. Thus Marx and Nietzsche, albeit very differently, closed the gap between organic processes on the one hand and the domain of value and evaluation that Idealist conceptions of "life" had continued to uphold on the other. Radicalizing Hegel, Marx argued that all human value derived from embodied human labor, and described the labor process itself in evocative organic terms as mediating the "metabolism between human and nature [*Stoffwechsel zwischen Mensch und Natur*]."[43] Nietzsche went even further, conceiving of organic life *itself* in terms of valuation: "Valuations [*Werthschätzungen*] lie in all functions of the organic being." (KSA 11:26 [72]; see chapter 4 of the current volume). By the end of the nineteenth century, and under the influence of both Nietzsche's philosophy and a persistent anti-Darwinism within German science,[44] the term "life" became a rallying point inside and outside academia. "The epoch between roughly 1895 to 1914," Petra Gehring observes, "marks a caesura in the history of 'life' because the concept begins to separate itself from the notion of nature—and more precisely from the nature/culture difference. A new, ontologically extended concept of life undercuts that difference and absorbs, as a *concept without counterconcept*, nature as well as culture and 'the social.'"[45] "Life" thus came to stand for the dynamics of values and the vitality of con-

---

43. Karl Marx, *Das Kapital. Kritik der politischen Ökonomie*, vol.1 (Berlin: Dietz Verlag, 1951), 192.

44. Nicholas Saul, "Darwin in German Literary Culture, 1890–1914," in *The Literary and Cultural Reception of Charles Darwin in Europe*, ed. Thomas F. Glick and Elinor Schaffer, vol. 3 (London: Bloomsbury, 2014), 46–77.

45. See Petra Gehring, "Wert, Wirklichkeit, Macht: Lebenswissenschaften um 1900," *Allgemeine Zeitschrift für Philosophie* 34, no. 1 (2009): 118, and "Biologische Politik um 1900: Reform? Therapie? Experiment?," in *Kulturgeschichte des Menschenversuchs im 20. Jahrhundert*, ed. Birgit Griesicke, Marcus Krause, Nicolas Pethes, and Katja Sabisch (Frankfurt am Main: Suhrkamp, 2009), 48–77. Gehring's title, *Biologische Politik*, is taken from a book by Wilhelm Schallmayer, who coined the formulation in 1905. See Gehring, "Biologische Politik," 53.

flict, action, and decision. It became a rallying point for social movements critical of industrialization (*Lebensreformbewegung*) and a catalyst for developments in philosophy, sociology, law, aesthetic theories of form, and psychology.[46] At the same time, the period saw the emergence of a whole set of biomedical and biopolitical discourses aimed at creating a more powerful and prosperous society.[47] This rhetorical explosion across different disciplines and political camps continued after 1914, heightened by the experience of war: literature and art increasingly evoked images of bodily deformation, rotten flesh, and biological decay;[48] a group of mostly conservative thinkers published books on what came to be called *Staatsbiologie*;[49] Benjamin opposed "bare" to "just" life in his defense of revolutionary violence;[50] and conservative critics of the Weimar Republic such as Carl Schmitt dreamt of a state of exceptions when "the power of real life breaks through the crust of a mechanism that has become torpid by repetition."[51] Thus when National Socialism used biological tropes for political purposes, it

---

46. To name some important figures in these areas: *Lebensphilosophie*: Wilhelm Dilthey and Georg Simmel; literary form: György Lukács's *Die Seele und die Formen*; politics and law: Wilhelm Schallmayer, *Vererbung und Auslese im Lebenslauf der Völker* and Heinrich Matzat, *Philosophie der Anpassung*. For the broader turn toward holism and organicism in early twentieth-century German science, see Anne Harrington, *Reenchanted Science: Holism in German Culture from Wilhelm II to Hitler* (Princeton, NJ: Princeton University Press, 1996).

47. For a survey of primary sources and an excellent discussion of critical approaches to early twentieth-century biopolitics, see, in addition to Gehring's "Wert, Wirklichkeit, Macht," Edward Ross Dickinson, "Biopolitics, Fascism, Democracy: Some Reflections on Our Discourse about 'Modernity,'" *Central European History* 37, no. 1 (2004): 1–48.

48. See chapter 5.

49. Jakob von Uexküll, *Staatsbiologie* (Berlin: Gebrüder Paetel, 1920); Karl Binding, *Zum Werden und Leben der Staaten* (Munich: Duncker Humblot, 1920); Oscar Hertwig, *Der Staat als Organismus. Gedanken zur Entwicklung der Menschheit* (Jena: Gustav Fischer, 1922).

50. Walter Benjamin, "Critique of Violence," in *Reflections: Essays, Aphorisms, Autobiographical Writings*, ed. Peter Demetz (New York: Schocken Books, 1978), 277–300.

51. Carl Schmitt, *Political Theology: Four Chapters on the Concept of Sovereignty*, ed. and trans. George Schwab (Chicago: University of Chicago Press, 1985), 15. As the opening of the paragraph from which this quote is taken states unambiguously, Schmitt understands his thinking as a "philosophy of concrete life."

could draw on a long-standing tradition, including eugenic and bio-medical discourses dating back to the Wilhelminian empire,[52] as well as organicist theories of the state that, from Romanticism on-ward, had pitted the "natural" communitarianism of German cul-ture against the "mechanical" rationalism (France) or "atomistic" individualism (England) of Western civilization.[53]

There is a theoretical lesson to be drawn from this brief histori-cal survey. The fluidity and plasticity of the notion of life makes the term both intellectually stimulating and politically dangerous: stim-ulating because the language of life opens up a conceptual and an-alogical space to explore connections between regions of reality that are indeed intertwined—nature and cognition, biology and politics, humans and animals, etc.; and dangerous because this very malle-ability makes possible, in fact invites, potentially catastrophic acts of reductionism, as evidenced most clearly in National Socialism's systematic biologization of politics, art, and ethics. Hence the two imperatives that will guide the inquiry that follows: first, a full en-gagement with the discourse of life in modernity must theorize the promises *and* dangers this discourse holds; and second, any suitably robust notion of life must articulate the multifariousness of differ-ent yet interconnected forms of life—political and psychical, bio-

---

52. In the last decades, historiographic attention to the biopolitical discourse in Germany has served to emphasize continuities between the imperial, Weimar, and Nazi periods. Thus in the introduction to an important volume on the conti-nuities of early twentieth-century German history, Geoff Eley argued in 1996 for a "reperiodization of the late nineteenth and early twentieth centuries to stress the coherence of the years between the 1890s and 1930s as a unitary context in which definite themes of national efficiency, social hygiene, and racialized nationalism coalesced." Geoff Eley, ed., "Introduction 1: Is There a History of the Kaiser-reich?," in *Society, Culture, and the State in Germany, 1870–1930* (Ann Arbor: University of Michigan Press, 1996), 31. In the meantime, the literature corrobo-rating this claim has grown. For a rich bibliography, see Dickinson, "Biopolitics, Fascism, Democracy," who, however, warns against overemphasizing the drift toward totalitarianism in German biopolitical discourses, arguing that dreams of social and biological perfectibility are central to modernity and shaped not only totalitarian visions but also democratic policies, both in Germany and other West-ern countries. Dickinson's claim resonates with Gehring's discussion about dis-courses of life around 1900 and with my own understanding of the politically flexible nature of concepts of life in German culture.

53. See Böckenförde, "Organ, Organismus."

logical and ethical, aesthetic and biographical. An archive that includes Kant as well as Hitler reminds us that the notion of life defies conceptual and political reduction.

There is yet another reason why this archive deserves special scrutiny: earlier German thinking about life continues to influence scholarly paradigms in English-speaking academia. In contemporary practical philosophy, the recourse to collective forms of life as normative grounds repeatedly draws on Kant's third *Critique* and the works of Hegel and Wittgenstein;[54] cultural ecology and ecocriticism rediscover German *Naturphilosophie*;[55] scholars in animal studies draw on texts by Rilke, Uexküll, and Heidegger;[56] political theorists seeking to recover vitalism for democratic purposes return to early twentieth-century German biology;[57] and all while Nietzsche's philosophy of force, Marx's theory of value, and Hegel's ideas on plasticity, powerfully reinterpreted by French and Italian thinkers, shape debates across the humanities and social sciences.[58]

54. Michael Thompson, *Life and Action: Elementary Structures of Practice and Practical Thought* (Cambridge, MA: Harvard University Press, 2008).

55. Hubert Zapf, *Literature as Cultural Ecology: Sustainable Texts* (London: Bloomsbury, 2016), 62–63; Kate Rigby, "Romanticism and Ecocriticism," in *The Oxford Handbook of Ecocriticism*, ed. Greg Garrard (Oxford: Oxford University Press, 2014), 60–79. For a good survey of the environmental imagination in German literature and philosophy, see Sabine Wilke, *German Culture and the Modern Environmental Imagination: Narrating and Depicting Nature* (Amsterdam: Brill Rodopi, 2015).

56. Giorgio Agamben, *The Open: Man and Animal* (Redwood Hills, CA: Stanford University Press, 2003); Wolfe, *Before the Law*.

57. See Jane Bennett, *Vibrant Matter: A Political Ecology of Things* (Durham, NC: Duke University Press, 2010). Bennett's recovery of the work of the German biologist Hans Driesch highlights the tendency of much of this "new vitalism" to disambiguate the modern discourse of life and undertheorize its political complexity. Thus while Bennett devotes twenty pages to Driesch's work, even calling him "the star of this chapter" (64), she fails to mention that in 1935 Driesch used his theory of vitalism to justify Hitler and his *Führerprinzip*. This omission is all the more glaring because Bennett, in the same chapter, cites an article by Canguilhem that discusses Driesch's connection to Nazism.

58. Nietzsche: Gilles Deleuze, *Nietzsche and Philosophy* (New York: Columbia University Press, 1983); Roberto Esposito, *Bíos* (Minneapolis: University of Minnesota Press, 2008); Marx: Michael Negri and Antonio Hardt, *Empire* (Cambridge, MA: Harvard University Press, 2001) and Melinda E. Cooper, *Life as Surplus: Biotechnology and Capitalism in the Neoliberal Era* (Seattle: University of

Nowhere is this influence more tangible than in the field of biopolitical theory. There is, first of all, the sheer weight of German history. Even scholars critical of Agamben's hyperbolic claim that the "camp is the nomos of the modern"[59] are unlikely to deny that postwar thinking about the politics of life unfolded in the wake of Auschwitz, the most extreme and paradigmatic site of biopolitical violence. Moreover, the very term "biopolitics" dates back to early twentieth-century German debates. It emerged in the early 1900s simultaneous in the racial hygiene theories of Wilhelm Schallmayer, who spoke in 1905 of "*biologische Politik*,"[60] and in the writings of the Swedish political thinker Rudolf Kjellen, who drew on the work of Friedrich Ratzel, a German geographer credited with coining the notion of *Lebensraum* in its geopolitical meaning.[61] Kjellen's most developed theory of the state, published in Swedish as *Staten som lifsform* (*The State as a Life-Form*; 1916), was almost immediately translated into German, where it triggered a wave of biologically inflected political theories, such as Jakob von Uexküll's *Staatsbiologie* (1920), Karl Binding's *Zum Werden und Leben der Staaten* (1920), and Oskar Hertwig's *Staat als Organismus* (1922).[62]

Washington Press, 2015); Hegel: Catherine Malabou, *The Future of Hegel: Plasticity, Temporality and Dialectic* (New York: Routledge, 2004).

59. Giorgio Agamben, *Homo Sacer: Sovereign Power and Bare Life* (Redwood Hills, CA: Stanford University Press, 1998), §7.

60. Wilhelm Schallmayer, *Beiträge zu einer Nationalbiologie* (Jena, Germany: Hermann Costenoble, 1905), 63–150.

61. Kjellen assimilated Ratzel's concept of *Lebensraum* into an organic theory of the state that rested on two main analogies with the natural world. On the one hand, like natural organisms, the state is "attached to its own soil and will die if it loses this connection. . . . Here we focus on a trait that the state shares in common with the plant world, like a forest." On the other hand, the state-as-nation is treated as a single ethnic individual, or a "potenziertes Individuum." Rudolf Kjellen, *Staten som lifsform*, cited in C. Abrahamsson, "On the genealogy of Lebensraum," *Geographica Helvetica* 68 (2013): 37–44, 41.

62. The impact of this new "biological conception of the state [*biologische Staatsauffassung*]" was strong enough that Carl Schmitt, on the occasion of a new translation of Kjellen's book, felt compelled to defend the latter against its German interpreters and to emphasize the "many functions" of the term *Leben*. Kjellen's vitalism, Schmitt claims, builds on "older organic theories of the state" and is at its core directed against the "liberal restriction and reduction of the state [*liberale Einschränkung und Herabminderung des Staates*]." The state needs the language of

Thomas Lemke and Roberto Esposito have recently drawn attention to Kjellen's work, situating it in the context of German political thought of the 1920s.[63] According to Esposito, Kjellen and his immediate German successors mark a new phase in the "immunitarian" paradigm that had underpinned Western conceptions of political and communal life since Hobbes. Especially in Jacob von Uexküll's intensification of Kjellen's vitalism, Esposito sees the theoretical harbinger of a totalitarian thanatopolitics that protects the unity of the community by pathologizing, and killing off, the unruly manifestations of life threatening to de-form that unity. Against this deadly model of "negative biopolitics," Esposito opposes the idea of an "affirmative biopolitics" that, in embracing the vulnerability of bodies and the plasticity of life, allows for more democratic and open forms of community and governance.[64] What is important for my argument is that Esposito develops his concepts of "affirmative" and "negative" biopolitics in dialogue with an historically and locally specific archive. While negative biopolitics culminates in a line ranging from Kjellen and Uexküll to Hitler and Nazi eugenics, the theory of affirmative biopolitics draws on, besides Merleau-Ponty and Canguilhem, the philosophical thought of Nietzsche, Husserl, Heidegger, and Arendt.[65] Contemporary biopolitical

---

life not because it is at its core biological but because it is a *mythical* entity. "The treatise that lies before us is in a highly characteristic and interesting way an antiliberal book. Although this might not be the intention of its author, and thus without any conscious tendency, the book works toward infusing the great myth of the 'state' with new life. This is where the ultimate meaning of the notion of life and its application to the state lies." Carl Schmitt, "Politik und Friedensvertrag" in *Wirtschaftsdienst* 10 (1925): 1010.

63. Thomas Lemke, *Biopolitics: An Advanced Introduction*, trans. Eric Frederick Trump (New York: New York University Press, 2011), 9–10; Esposito, *Bíos*, 16–18.

64. Esposito, *Bíos*, 146–94.

65. In Arendt's case, Esposito draws on her reflection on "natality" and her idea of life as a constant renewal (*Bíos*, 177–79). Husserl is important for Esposito because of his influence on Merleau-Ponty. Esposito devotes a rich chapter to Nietzsche, depicting him as the philosopher that exposes and attacks the modern immunitary paradigm while ultimately failing to fully overcome it (*Bíos*, 78–110). Heidegger features prominently in Esposito's book, prior to *Bíos*, entitled *Communitas: The Origin and Destiny of Community* (Redwood Hills, CA: Stanford University Press, 2009), and represents, with Nietzsche, the furthest point thought

theory thus takes shape through an engagement with twentieth-century German discourses of life.

An even stronger dependence on this material can be found in Giorgio Agamben's work. Roughly 145 of the 190 pages of *Homo Sacer* are devoted to the interpretation of German history or thinkers, and the percentage is only moderately lower in *The Open*, whose crucial concept, the idea of a modern "anthropological machine," rests entirely on Agamben's reading of German sources from the late nineteenth and early twentieth century.[66] It is not just that Agamben's pages are littered with better- and lesser-known German names;[67] with the exception of Aristotle and Foucault, all of his major theoretical and historical reference points are to an archive that is spatially and temporally circumscribed: his "state of exception" is derived from Schmitt, the concept of "bare life" (and much more) from Benjamin,[68] and its utopian counter-notion—what Agamben calls "form-of-life"—from Heidegger.[69] And then, of course, there is "the camp," the "biopolitical paradigm of the modern." In fact, since for Agamben the camp is not just the "nomos of the modern" but also the culmination of a fateful metaphysical tradition that begins with Aristotle, German history around 1941

---

had come in 1945 to understanding the deadly dialect of modern politics and life. On the importance of Heidegger, see for instance Esposito's comment "that Heidegger's thought emerges in the first half of the twentieth century as the only one able to support the philosophical confrontation with biopolitics" (*Bíos*, 152).

66. Agamben, *The Open*, 33–85, where Agamben discusses the works of: Ernst Haeckel (33–35), Heymann Steinthal (35–37), Jacob von Uexküll (39–47), Rainer Maria Rilke (57–59), Martin Heidegger (49–77), and Walter Benjamin (81–84).

67. Some examples of better-known names: Arendt, Benjamin, Eichmann, Freud, Haeckel, Hegel, Heidegger, Himmler, Hitler, Hölderlin, Husserl, Kafka, Kantorowicz, Kelsen, Nietzsche, Rilke, Rosenzweig, Schelling, Schmitt, Scholem, von Uexküll. Some lesser-known names: Fischer, Reiter, Roscher, Steinthal.

68. Khurana also highlights Agamben's indebtedness to Benjamin's messianism. See Khurana's "Desaster und Versprechen. Eine irritierende Nähe im Werk Giorgio Agambens," in *Die gouvernementale Maschine. Zur politischen Philosophie Giorgio Agambens*, ed. Janine Böckelmann and Frank Meier (Münster: Unrast, 2008), 29–44.

69. As Khurana points out, Agamben's definition of "form-of-life" in *Means without End* "is almost a word-to-word citation of a passage from §9 in Heidegger's *Being and Time*." Khurana, "Desaster und Versprechen."

comes to be conceived as the fatal telos of Western civilization. To readers familiar with Hegel and Heidegger, even the *structure* of Agamben's argument looks German.

German sources also loom large in Foucault's writings on biopolitics. While Foucault rarely cites German philosophy, most of the empirical evidence he uses to corroborate his larger conceptual claims come from German history. What Foucault calls biopower— "the set of mechanisms through which the basic biological features of the human species became the object of a political strategy"[70]— is said to emerge in eighteenth-century Germany, where small principalities created health agencies focused on regulating and improving the biological welfare of the population;[71] and when Foucault introduces the concept of biopolitics in his *History of Sexuality*, he does so in the context of a sustained critique of modern discourses on sexuality whose main representatives hail from German-speaking cultures.[72] Finally, Foucault's 1978 lectures on modern governmentality, in which he studies "liberalism as the general framework of biopolitics,"[73] draw heavily on a specific tradition: Foucault analyzes in detail German postwar liberalism, discusses its theoretical roots in the Weimar Republic, emphasizes the importance of the experience and analysis of Nazism for the founding members of neoliberalism, and even goes so far as to draw parallels between the neoliberalism of the Freiburg-school and the neo-Marxism of the

---

70. Michel Foucault, *Security, Territory, Population: Lectures at the College de France, 1977–1978*, ed. Michel Senellart, trans. Graham Burchell (New York: Palgrave Macmillan, 2007), 1.

71. Michel Foucault, "The Birth of Social Medicine," in Faubion, *Power*, 134–57. Foucault devotes several pages to explaining "why and how state medicine was able to appear first in Germany" (139), arguing that it was precisely the lack of unified political power and advanced economic development in Germany that allowed it, rather than France or England, to develop both a science of the state and a medical practice "devoted to the improvement of public health" (140).

72. Joachim Heinrich Campe and Christian Gotthilf Salzmann feature as examples for the dissemination of "procedures of confession" in the eighteenth century (63), Heinrich Kaan, Albert Moll, Richard von Krafft-Ebing, and of course Freud are the major representatives of nineteenth-century sexology that is the main target of Foucault's book.

73. Michel Foucault, *The Birth of Biopolitics: Lectures at the College de France, 1978–1979*, ed. Arnold Davidson (New York: Palgrave Macmillan, 2008), 22.

Frankfurt School.[74] In sum, from 1976 to 1979—the period during which Foucault uses the concepts of biopower and biopolitics—each significant articulation of his theory unfolds by way of a sustained engagement with German material.

What are we to do with this persistent tension between a general theory of political modernity and its reliance on a locally specific archive? How to evaluate this asymmetry between claim and evidence, a lopsidedness that is particularly pronounced in the case of Agamben, who derives from a rather narrow archive—German thought and history from 1920 to 1945—nothing less than the political logic of Western civilization? Although I am suspicious of Agamben's political ontology, my overall goal in highlighting this asymmetry is not to impugn the notion of biopolitics but to give it more texture. First, I want to emphasize that the texts Esposito, Foucault, and Agamben regularly invoke to articulate their theories belong to a rich and involved discourse that dates back to the late eighteenth century, and that paying attention to this larger context will enable a better understanding of both the early twentieth-century debates and the contemporary theories derived from them. Second, we will see that contemporary theories of biopolitics consistently disregard the aesthetic strand within the German discourse of life. I will show that this disregard results in an overly schematic notion of both life and (bio)politics, and that attention to the aesthetic and literary dimension provides a more fine-grained picture of the transformation of human life in modernity. In my proposed reading, aesthetics ultimately points to a more heterogeneous and dynamic model of life than is available in contemporary theory, a model that suggests not only that "life" articulates itself in countless systemic forms of life (aesthetic, political, psychic, organic, etc.) that are both intertwined and in tension with one another, but also that each of these systemic forms is *intrinsically* divided, split be-

---

74. Foucault, *The Birth of Biopolitics*, esp. 105–17. See also Thomas Lemke's insightful discussion of Foucault's engagement with German neoliberalism, "'The Birth of Biopolitics': Michel Foucault's Lecture at the Collège de France on Neo-Liberal Governmentality," *Economy and Society* 30, no. 2 (2001): esp. 192–97.

tween processes of formation and deformation, and between form and force.

Enlightenment Vitalism

Concepts and systems of thoughts are subject not only to the instability of their internal logic but also to pressures exerted on them by transformations in the natural and social environment in which they operate. When the world changes, so ultimately do the categories meant to organize and structure it. Something of this sort happened to seventeenth- and eighteenth-century models of natural history, whose principal aim was the classification of species not according to patterns of change and development but on the basis of visible, static structures. Natural history was descriptive; it sought to provide, in the form of a tableau, grid, or catalogue, a systematic survey of the whole of animate nature constructed according to genus and species. This spatial arrangement of knowledge reflected the belief in an "inner bond between logic and biology";[75] catalogue and tableau acted as representational mirrors of a nature whose inner organization followed Aristotelian class concepts. In the second half of the eighteenth century, this bio-logic came under external political and internal systematic pressures: political, because the insistence on fixed natural classes came in conflict with an increasing demand for greater social mobility; and systematically, because natural history's descriptivism gave rise to an accumulation of data that defied systematization. As the "rapidly increasing number of newly discovered species led to the proliferation of classificatory systems and nomenclatures,"[76] the catalogues of natural history, and thus nature itself, came to look less like an organized whole than a

---

75. Ernst Cassirer, *Problem of Knowledge: Philosophy, Science, and History since Hegel* (New Haven, CT: Yale University Press, 1966), 124.

76. Dorothea von Mücke, "Goethe's Metamorphosis: Changing Forms in Nature, the Life Sciences, and Authorship," *Representations* 95 (Summer 2006): 27; see also Wolf Lepenies, *Ende der Naturgeschichte: Wandel kultureller Selbstverständlichkeiten in den Wissenschaften des 18. und 19. Jahrhunderts* (Frankfurt am Main: Suhrkamp, 1986).

bewildering hodgepodge of empirically derived, and hence contingent, similarities. As Kant put it in the first introduction to his *Critique of Judgment*, natural history leaves us with "such an *infinite multiplicity* of empirical laws and such a *great heterogeneity of forms* of nature" as to make any systematic inquiry into nature impossible.[77]

What was necessary, therefore, was to place natural inquiry on new conceptual footings, to ground it in a principle that could unify empirical research from within. It is in this context that we must place the emergence of the modern conception of "life," of life understood as a productive force or vital principle that organizes living beings from within. In *The Order of Things*, Foucault famously conceived of this emergence in terms of an abrupt break between discontinuous orders of knowledge. According to Foucault, the spatial and classificatory models of seventeenth- and eighteenth-century natural history suddenly gave way to a new type of knowledge—a new episteme—that framed empirical phenomena as the expression of an underlying and continuous dynamic process. Foucault shows how, around 1800, the idea of an invisible dynamic continuum appeared in seemingly diverse fields of inquiry, resulting in the formulation of a number of metaobjects—"life," "labor," "history"—around which the new nineteenth-century sciences of biology, economics, and philological linguistics formed. While Foucault's claim that the modern order of knowledge is internally related to a new concept of life remains crucial, his emphasis on epistemic breaks and his restriction of knowledge to disciplinary knowledge is problematic. Recent studies have shown that natural history's inability to account for the dynamic character of living things came under criticism as early as 1750, and from a variety of angles. An early focal point for this critique was the question of animal generation.[78] Should generation be thought of in terms of

---

77. Immanuel Kant, *Critique of the Power of Judgment* (Cambridge: Cambridge University Press, 2000), 203.

78. For these debates, see Helmut Müller-Sievers, *Self-Generation: Biology, Philosophy, and Literature around 1800* (Stanford, CA: Stanford University Press, 1997), 26–48; Peter H. Reill, *Vitalizing Nature in the Enlightenment* (Berkeley: University of California Press, 2005), 56–70.

divine preformation, according to which "God had created all living things at the beginning of time and then encased these minutely fully formed entities in seeds or *germes*,"[79] as the mechanistic framework of natural history held? Or should the birth of new life be understood in more dynamic terms, as the effect of an "always active organic matter, always tending to mold itself" as Buffon argued in 1749?[80] Buffon's antimechanical stance gained traction over the following decades, giving rise to an Enlightenment vitalism that sought to overcome the sharp separation between mind and nature underlying the classical episteme. For reasons both intellectual and political,[81] this new vitalism was particularly forceful in Germany, where from the 1770s onward a number of thinkers began to dissolve the mind-body dichotomy "by positing the existence in living matter of active or self-activating forces, which had a teleological character."[82] Moreover, some of these thinkers did not restrict the new idea of vital forces to the narrowly understood natural realm but extended it to explain human history, cultural development, and aesthetic creation. Foucault's account thus needs to be amended: the modern notion of "life" did not originate with nineteenth-century biology, as Foucault claimed, but emerged several decades earlier from within Enlightenment thought, and in the context of a broader—aesthetic and scientific—reflection on the plasticity of natural and cultural forms.

---

79. Peter H. Reill, *Vitalizing Nature*, 56 (Reill's emphasis).

80. Georges-Louis Leclerc, Comte de Buffon, *Histoire Naturelle, Générale et particulière, avec la description du Cabinet du Roi*, cited in Helmut Müller-Sievers, *Self-Generation*, 32–33.

81. The intellectual reasons may have to do with the influence of Leibniz's thought, and in particular with his idea of the monad as a complex yet closed system (a unity in multiplicity) that transforms itself according to an inner principle, and in this sense is self-active and desiring. See *Monadology*, § 11–15. The political and social reasons have to do with Germany's lack of centralization, which makes its small principalities a good laboratory for experimenting with new forms of governmental controls, such as the use of statistics and the implementation of rudimentary forms of health care. On the birth of health care see Foucault, "The Birth of Social Medicine"; on statistics in Germany, see Ian Hacking, *The Taming of Chance* (Cambridge, MA: Cambridge University Press, 1990), 16–46.

82. Reill, *Vitalizing Nature*, 7.

I will briefly sketch the structure of this vitalism by reference to writings by Johann Friedrich Blumenbach (1752–1840) and Johann Gottfried Herder (1744–1803). I choose these texts not merely because they were extremely influential in their time but also because they allow us to highlight, with the help of Thomas Khurana, a structural feature of *all* modern thinking about life. Khurana has argued that the modern concept of life is built around "a dialectics of force and form operative in the living."[83] On the one hand, "it might seem distinctive of living phenomena that they possess form in an eminent sense. Seen from the viewpoint of form, a specific unity and directedness of the living comes to the fore: the way in which it reaches and sustains a complex form that possesses an inherent necessity."[84] The paradigm of this view of the living is the organized integrity of the organism. On the other hand, however, living processes also appear to be manifestations of a force productive of form and thus not reducible to it. "Living processes as such seem to have a generative productivity, an openness and undirectedness, that not only generates form but supercedes and transgresses them in the course of development."[85] Khurana's model is very helpful in understanding shifts in the German discourse of life from the late eighteenth to the mid-twentieth century. For the moment, however, I want to sketch how eighteenth-century vitalism both opens up and occludes a view of the living in terms of a dialectic of force and form.

Blumenbach's concept of a *Bildungstrieb* illustrates this double movement most clearly. In the manner of the eighteenth-century naturalist, Blumenbach introduces his theory by way of two observational anecdotes. His first narrative relates how, during a summer vacation in the country, he came across a many-armed green polyp which he took home for experimentation. Cutting off some of its limbs, he noticed the growth of new, albeit shorter, arms in place of the amputated ones. His second narrative tells that, back in Göttingen, he visited a patient with an abscess in his knee which, after

---

83. Thomas Khurana, "Force and Form," *Constellations* 18, no. 1 (2011): 21.
84. Ibid., 22.
85. Ibid.

healing, left behind a scar and a slightly depressed area of flesh. According to Blumenbach, both cases testify to the organism's tendency to return, albeit in diminished form, to its previous shape. This suggests an activity, even productivity, of organic matter, on the basis of which Blumenbach formulates a general theory of animate nature:

> That in all living creatures, from man down to maggot and from the cedar down to mold, there is a peculiar, innate, lifelong active and effective drive [*Trieb*] to take a particular form in the beginning, then to maintain it, and, even when it has been destroyed, to repair it whenever possible. A drive (or tendency or endeavor, however one wants to call it) that is completely different both from the common properties of the body in general as well as from the other characteristic powers [*Kräfte*] of the organized body in particular; and for which I, in order to anticipate any misinterpretation and to distinguish it from other natural powers, reserve the name "formative drive [*Bildungs-trieb*]" (*Nisus formativus*).[86]

Blumenbach's repeated insistence that the *Bildungstrieb* is "completely different" from common bodily properties or powers highlights its new and peculiar status. For while the *Bildungstrieb* is said to be a property of matter, it is also that which forms and organizes this matter. Thus, unlike the new polyp arm or the new flesh beneath the knee, which can be observed and localized, the drive that produces them is both ubiquitous and hidden, everywhere and nowhere: everywhere, because it gives bodies their specific form and directs their development; and nowhere, because it is an invisible force operating beneath the bodily surface. Yet it is precisely this *"qualitas occulta,"*[87] as Blumenbach came to call the *Bildungstrieb* in 1789, that defines "all living creatures, from man down to maggot and from the cedar down to mold"—defines, that is, life itself.

Blumenbach's notion of the *Bildungstrieb* is clearly meant to emphasize the dynamic character of living things and thus to account for the changeability of natural forms. The *Bildungstrieb* is a *vis* or

---

86. Johann Friedrich Blumenbach, *Über den Bildungstrieb und das Zeugungsgeschäfte* (Göttingen: Johann Christian Dieterich, 1781), 12–13.

87. Blumenbach, *Über den Bildungstrieb und das Zeugungsgeschäfte*, 2nd ed. (Göttingen: Johann Christian Dieterich, 1789), 26.

nisus, a vital force that drives the organism from within, fueling the three kinds of activity—generation, nutrition, and reproduction—that distinguish it from mechanical objects. But Blumenbach is silent about the destructive side of this force. Change entails the transgression of already established boundaries, the supersession and discarding of previous forms. In Blumenbach's description, however, the force of formation is fully regulated by the lawful unity of the form it brings about. Change is conceived as the stabilization and maintenance of the *same* form—a form that is there from the beginning and that directs all material changes toward a predetermined goal, as the preceding quote unambiguously states: "in all living creatures . . . there is a peculiar, innate, lifelong active and effective drive [*Trieb*] to take a particular form in the beginning, then to maintain it, and, even when it has been destroyed, to repair it whenever possible." Thus in Blumenbach's model, force is no longer in tension with form but becomes its temporal and material manifestation; it is the "source or generative medium" of form.[88] For all its emphasis on dynamics and change, Blumenbach's theory of the living rests on an utterly orderly vision of nature.

Things become more complicated with Johann Gottfried Herder, a philosopher, historian, theologian, and literary critic whose writings exerted an enormous influence not just on contemporary thinkers such as Goethe, Fichte, Hegel, Humboldt, and Schleiermacher, and later thinkers such as Nietzsche and Dilthey, but on German culture at large. Herder came to prominence in the early 1770s as the leader of *Sturm und Drang*, a literary and artistic youth movement that rebelled in the name of the immediacy of "life" against the cultural and political petrification of contemporary society. His wide-ranging work inspired later academic developments in biblical studies, anthropology, and historiography, and his theories of culture and *Volksgeist* (spirit of the people) influenced nationalist movements inside and outside Germany. Herder's vitalism is thoroughly expressivist, both conceptually and stylistically: conceptually, in that Herder conceives of all reality—whether biological,

---

88. Khurana, "Force and Form," 28.

mental, or cultural—as the manifestation of vital forces; and stylistically, because his rhapsodic and metaphorical writings are designed to express and invoke, rather than merely describe or analyze, this interior force. With Herder and the writings of *Sturm und Drang*, we enter the modern aesthetic paradigm, according to which art does not so much imitate as *express* life. For our purposes, we can distinguish two strands within his vitalism: a dominant holistic one that emphasizes the dynamic *unity* of cultural and natural forms, and a differentialist strand that highlights the *excess* of force over form.

The holistic strand is clearly in evidence in Herder's most famous text, the *Ideen zur Philosophie der Geschichte der Menschheit* (*Ideas on the Philosophy of the History of Mankind*, 1784–1791). Herder, who was very familiar with contemporary developments in natural history and had read Blumenbach's *De generis humani varietate nativa* (in which the naturalist had introduced his concept of the *Bildungstrieb*[89]), essentially transfers Blumenbach's idea of purposeful vital forces to the historical realm. Starting from the axiom that "nothing in nature stands still, everything strives and moves forward,"[90] Herder sets out to write a "pure natural history of human powers, actions, and drives in space and time."[91] What unites human and natural history into a single whole is the unity of the *Kraft*—the vital force—that propels all change. As with Blumenbach, Herder conceives of transformation in developmental and teleological terms, as the purposeful unfolding of a unified form. But whereas Blumenbach was content with applying this idea to individual organisms, Herder expands it to compose an evolutionary history of the earth:

> In the creation of our earth a sequence of ascending forms and forces prevails. From a stone to a crystal, from crystals to the metals, from these to plant creations, from the plants to animals, and from these to humans,

---

89. See Richards, *The Romantic Conception of Life*, 225.

90. Johann Gottfried Herder, *Ideen zur Philosophie der Geschichte der Menschheit*, in *Werke in zehn Bänden*, ed. Martin Bollacher et al. (Frankfurt am Main: Deutscher Klassiker Verlag, 1985), 6:176.

91. Ibid., 568.

we see the *form of organization ascend*. Along with them the forces and drives of the creature become more varied until finally all unite in the form of the human [*Gestalt des Menschen*], to the extent that the human can contain them.[92]

Note that nothing gets lost in Herder's temporalized chain of being. Force and matter combine to create organized wholes, which over time give rise to more complex and advanced forms of life, until history finally reaches man, in which nature's drive for perfection attains its spiritual and moral apotheosis—the "noble measure [*das edle Maß*]" of humanity.[93] Here, too, a certain conservativism underlies the overt language of force; put differently, Herder shrinks back from the more radical implications of his own vitalism. Despite its dynamic character, his conception of nature is ultimately harmonious: force creates order and organization at every step of the evolutionary ladder. There is a metaphysical reason for this. If the vital force always operates in the service of a unifying form, this is because *Kraft*, for Herder, is a spiritual principle acting at the heart of matter. In fact, *Kraft* is Herder's name for what he considers the absolute principle of unity: God. Building on Spinoza's identification of God with nature, Herder drafts the biological notion of an organic *Bildungstrieb* onto the metaphysical concept of a single infinite substance: "Nature is not an independent being; but God is *Everything in his Works*. . . . He to whom the name 'nature' has become meaningless or base through writings of our time, should imagine instead that *almighty force, goodness, and wisdom*, and should name in his soul the invisible being that no earthly language is able to name. It is the same thing when I speak of the *organic forces* of creation."[94]

In much of his work, Herder uses the term "force" in this metaphysical sense, as an idea that unites natural and moral life into a single, teleologically conceived whole—a view that, as some argue,

---

92. Ibid., 166.
93. Herder, *Vom Erkennen und Empfinden der menschlichen Seele*, in *Werke in zehn Bänden*, ed. Martin Bollacher et al. (Frankfurt am Main: Deutscher Klassiker Verlag, 1985), 4:360.
94. Herder, *Ideen*, 17 (Herder's emphasis).

strongly influenced Hegel's dynamic understanding of concept formation.[95] But there is another, more submerged strand in Herder's
writing that complicates this metaphysical model by drawing attention to a different kind of force—a *force of signification* that is
specific to human life and cannot be understood in organic and teleological terms. One of the first instances of this strand occurs in
Herder's celebrated treatise *On the Origin of Language.* Though
ostensibly intended to emphasize the naturalness of human language, Herder's account highlights a crucial difference between
humans and animals. Humans, Herder suggests, are in certain ways
inferior to animals in that they lack strong instincts capable of regulating their interactions with their environment. However, language
more than compensates for this instinctual weakness by enabling
human beings to focus their attention, distinguish between inner and
outer sensations, and consciously and intentionally intervene in the
world. Thus, precisely because the use of words is not determined
by fixed automatisms of instinctual behavior—is not in that sense
natural—language opens up a world of possibilities unavailable to
animals. True, Herder immediately reterritorializes human linguistic creativity, conceiving it as a mere refinement of nature's inven-
tiveness, but his reflections nonetheless open up another line of
thinking. If the creation of individual words is already uncon-
strained by instinctual automatisms, how much more expansive
does this freedom become through the production of *chains* of
articulation? And if so, do speaking and writing not generate a
kind of force—a force of *signification*—that is very different from
the vital force operating within the body? In short, is not human
life much more conflict-ridden, broken, and unpredictable than
Herder admits?[96]

Christoph Menke recently argued that Herder's aesthetic writings articulate a nonteleological conception of force that anticipates

---

95. On Herder's influence on Hegel, see Charles Taylor, *Hegel* (Cambridge:
Cambridge University Press, 1975) and Michael Forster, *Hegel's Idea of a Phenomenology of Spirit* (Chicago: University of Chicago Press, 1998).

96. For a very different reading of Herder's work that emphasizes the politically critical potential of his organicism, see John Noyes, *Herder: Aesthetics against
Imperialism* (Toronto: University of Toronto Press, 2015).

Nietzsche's dictum that it is "only as an aesthetic phenomenon that existence and the world are eternally justified." According to Menke, Herder's theory of human creativity rests on an understanding of imagination as the continuous production of new images out of older ones.[97] Because this metamorphic force of the imagination knows no norm, law, or telos, it is the source of an aesthetic mode of life that is radically different from biological and social forms of life. Despite its powerful argumentative drift, Menke's interpretation willfully separates Herder's understanding of aesthetics from the broader ontological and metaphysical claims on which it rests. Rather than reading Herder as Nietzsche's precursor, I understand the various strands within his thinking as articulating the tension between force and form that lies at the heart of eighteenth-century vitalism. It is because Herder extends Blumenbach's idea of vital force beyond nature into the aesthetic and cultural realm that the limits of early vitalism's teleological containment become particularly visible. As with Blumenbach, Herder is unable to see in "life" anything other than a formative and unifying force.

Nor does the tension between form and force disappear with Herder and Blumenbach. In 1790, Kant, who had praised Blumenbach's theory but written a scathing review of Herder's *Ideen*, sought to integrate both their insights into his own critical framework. While the first part of the third *Critique* explores the "purposiveness without purpose" of mental life engaged in aesthetic experience, the second part draws on contemporary natural research, including Blumenbach's *Bildungstrieb*, to develop a regulative conception of biological organisms as purposeful wholes and "natural ends [*Naturzwecke*]." The overall intention behind Kant's concept of purposiveness is to bring cognitive and natural life in closer proximity, and ultimately to think of the history of nature and culture as a single directed process culminating in the cultivation of humanity. In this sense, the book is an attempt to conceive of Herder's project in the *Ideen* without the latter's metaphysical baggage. But as we shall see, no matter how much Kant tries to contain the tension between force and form, its dialectic remains productively

---

97. Menke, *Kraft*, 60.

unresolved, and the *activity* of formation continues to put pressure on the bounded forms it nonetheless produces. There is an excess within life that resists its movement toward a "kingdom of ends."

Foucault

To an English reader versed in political theory, the semantic reach of the German term *Kraft*, which can be rendered as either "force" or "power," is bound to be confusing. English-speaking political scientists distinguish sharply between "power" and "force," reserving the latter to designate the mostly *physical* means of coercion authorities turn to as a final resort when other modalities of power have failed. But force as violence is very different from Herder's notion of *Kraft*, the energetic connotation of which is understandable only in the context of the modern conception of life. *Kraft* is *vital* force. It will be helpful to keep this eighteenth-century meaning of *Kraft* in mind as I turn in more detail to Foucault's theory of biopower. To be sure, Foucault hardly ever uses the term *puissance*, the closest French equivalent to German *Kraft*, and on the few occasions he does it is precisely to distinguish his own relational conception of power from vitalist models of force.[98] But things become more complicated once we remember that the emergence of biopower Foucault analyzed in the late 1970s is coextensive with the rise of the modern concept of "life" he had discussed in 1966 in *The Order of Things*. The operations of biopower, in other words, take as their object a reality understood in vitalist terms; that is, in terms of *force*. Biopower is a mode of power that seeks to regulate, channel, and exploit a *dynamically conceived nature*. Foucault's observation in the *History of Sexuality* that biopolitics marks the "entry of phenomena peculiar to the life of the human species into the order of knowledge and power"[99] is therefore somewhat misleading

---

98. Michel Foucault, *The History of Sexuality: Volume 1: An Introduction* (New York: Vintage Books, 1980), 93. "Power is not . . . a certain force [*puissance*] we are endowed with; it is the name that one attributes to a complex strategical situation in a particular society."

99. Ibid., 141–42.

in that it seems to suggest that these phenomena had always been there, awaiting comprehension and realization within a new epistemo-political framework. Against this formulation, it needs to be stressed that the entry of life into politics affects not only the structure of politics but also the scope and meaning of what counts as "life." The following comments seek to bring out more clearly this interplay between structures of life and structures of power. Rather than reiterating Foucault's programmatic statements, I will read them against some of his descriptions of the operations of bio-power, suggesting that the latter reveal a more complex and dynamic picture of Foucaultian biopower than his more abstract pronouncements imply.

In a much quoted passage in *History of Sexuality*, Foucault argues that the modern power over life unfolds along two axes of development "linked together by a whole intermediary cluster of relations": "One of these poles—the first to be formed, it seems—centered on the body as a machine [*machine*]: its disciplining, the optimization of its capabilities, the extortion of its forces . . . all this was ensured by the procedures of power that characterized the disciplines: *an anatomo-politics of the human body*. The second, formed somewhat later, focused on the species body, the body imbued with the mechanics of life [*mécanique du vivant*] and serving as the basis of the biological processes: propagation, births and mortality, the level of health, life expectancy and longevity. . . . Their supervision was effected through an entire series of interventions and *regulatory controls*: a *bio-politics of the population*."[100] Modern biopower operates through the "subjugation of bodies" on the one hand and the "control of populations" on the other.[101] There is general agreement in the critical literature that the first of these axes is the subject matter of *Discipline and Punish*, while biopolitics proper is at the center of Foucault's work on population control between 1977 and 1979. What is rarely noticed, however, is that Foucault's mechanical imagery in the above passage ("the body as machine," "mechanics of life") is at odds with the

---

100. Ibid., 139.
101. Ibid., 140.

thrust of his argument in his earlier works. Consider, for instance, the following passage from *Discipline and Punish*, in which Foucault describes the emergence of disciplinary practices explicitly in terms of a *break* with the mechanical conception of the body:

> Through this technique of subjection a new object was being formed; slowly it superseded the mechanical body—the body composed of solids and assigned movements, the image of which had for so long haunted those who dreamt of disciplinary perfection. This new object is the natural body, the bearer of forces [*forces*] and the seat of duration; it is the body susceptible to specified operations, which have their order, their stages, their internal conditions, their constituent elements.[102]

Disciplinary power brings into focus a new and nonmechanical kind of body—the ʼnatural body conceived as a dynamic "bearer of forces." Thus for discipline to impose itself *on* the body, it must to some extent adapt its own operations *to* the body's intrinsic structure and power. The "docile body," Foucault writes, is "a body of useful training and not of rational mechanics, but one in which, by virtue of that very fact, a number of natural requirements and functional constraints are beginning to emerge. This is the body that Guilbert discovered in his critique of excessive artificial movements. In the exercise that is imposed upon it and which it resists, the body brings out its essential correlations and spontaneously rejects the incompatible."[103] Natural requirements, functional constraints, spontaneity, essential correlations: this is a considerably more dynamic picture of body and body politics than in the passage from the *History of Sexuality*. According to *Discipline and Punish*, then, disciplinary operations convert a previously mechanically conceived body into a *natural* body more susceptible to its operations. This implies that biopower's productivity is intimately bound up with the productivity of the life it molds; there can be biopower only because the body is addressed as a congeries of forces.[104] And the *form* such

---

102. Michel Foucault, *Discipline and Punish: The Birth of the Prison*, trans. Alan Sheridan, 2nd ed. (New York: Vintage Books, 1995), 155.

103. Ibid.

104. This is also the claim of Maria Muhle's excellent *Eine Genealogie der Biopolitik. Zum Begriff des Lebens bei Foucault und Canguilhem* (Munich: Wilhelm

a biopolitically shaped body can take will follow the redirection of its forces to specific ends, the ultimate aim of which is the extraction of a vital surplus.

The object of anatomo-politics, thus, is not the body itself but the forces it harbors. One of the axioms of Foucault studies is that his work, and *Discipline and Punish* in particular, discovers the body as the true site of power operations, and many passages from *History of Sexuality* and *Discipline and Punish* seem to corroborate this reading. But a closer look shows that *Discipline and Punish*, in Jeffrey Nealon's words, "charts power's increasing movement away from the literal, individual body as the primary site of its intervention."[105] Moreover, this movement beyond the literal body blurs the very boundary between the physical and the mental. Take the most celebrated chapter of *Discipline and Punish*, the description of the panopticon. The function of the panopticon is clearly not to control the prisoner's physical body but to induce in him a particular form of *self-relation*, and while the success of this operation depends on the placement of the physical body within a space of perfect visibility, it also depends on the prisoner's *awareness* of his visibility. The panopticon is only an apparatus of surveillance insofar as those within its purview are reflective and self-conscious beings seeing themselves as exhaustively available to its panoptic gaze. The ultimate target of the panopticon, in other words, is not the body as such but a specifically *human form of life*: a life susceptible to the (real or imagined) gaze of the other.

Let us turn to the second pole of biopower, the "biopolitics of population," which Foucault studies after *Discipline and Punish* and whose historical emergence he locates in eighteenth-century Germany. Unlike anatomo-politics, which imposes itself on the individuated body, the biopolitics of a population targets the "species-body, the body imbued with the mechanics of life and serving as the basis of the biological processes: propagation, births and mortality,

---

Fink, 2013), who reads Foucault's writings of biopolitics through the prism of Canguilhem's rich conception of "vital normativity."

105.   Jeffrey T. Nealon, *Foucault beyond Foucault: Power and Its Intensification since 1984* (Redwood Hills, CA: Stanford University Press, 2008), 27.

the level of health, life expectancy and longevity."[106] But here too, the language of "the body" is somewhat misleading. Populations are not natural entities; they are the product of technologies of enumeration and statistical classification.[107] Strictly speaking, the body of biopolitics is not a body but a cluster of measurements, an artifact of information. The emergence of this artifact has two important implications. The first is that it changes the understanding of what counts as an individual. From the point of view of population politics, the individual is at best a "case" and at worst a point on a statistical curve. The second implication is that the statistical picture changes our understanding of what counts as "life." The target of biopolitics is neither the individual nor even necessarily the biological processes of a group of people but the reality of dynamic systems, which are understood to have a "life of their own" precisely insofar as their logic, movement, and force are irreducible to the potencies and dynamics of individual intentions or bodies.

Read along these lines, we can think of Foucault's theoretical trajectory in the 1970s in terms of his increasing desubstantialization of the target of biopower; that is, his exploration of the development of instruments and subjects of biopower, from their more concrete, corporeal expressions to their realization in configurations of force, susceptibility, etc., regardless of their material substrate. This line of inquiry culminates in Foucault's analysis of the liberal art of government in the late 1970s. The latter's uniqueness consists in its ability, made possible by new styles of probabilistic thinking,[108] to devise forms of regulation that are in accordance with, rather

---

106. Foucault, *History of Sexuality*, 139.

107. See Hacking, *The Taming of Chance*, and more recently Colin Koopman, "Michel Foucault's Critical Empiricism Today: Concepts and Analytics in the Critique of Biopower and Infopower," in *Foucault Now: Current Perspectives in Foucault Studies*, ed. James D. Faubion (Cambridge: Polity Press, 2014), 88–111, who puts the informational character of populations succinctly: "Before one has techniques in place for counting a population, there just is no population in a meaningful sense, and certainly not as an object of biopolitical intervention" (103).

108. Hacking, *The Taming of Chance*, and, with a stronger view to the connection of statistics to literature, Rüdiger Campe, *The Game of Probability: Literature and Calculation from Pascal to Keist* (Redwood Hills, CA: Stanford University Press, 2013).

than merely imposed upon, the "stubbornness of things."[109] Seen through the lens of statistics, seemingly random natural and social events—birth, death, epidemics, and reproduction, but also price fluctuations and the spirals of labor and wealth—reveal patterns of regularity that can be tracked, measured, stimulated, and channeled. Liberal arts of government thus go hand in hand with a new conception of "nature"—the "second nature" of the population which, precisely insofar as it is granted a certain autonomy and intrinsic dynamic, opens up as a field of possibilities for political and economic forms of intervention. As we saw in the previous section, these new techniques of governing coincide with the emergence of vitalism and, ultimately, biology, which abandon the classificatory and causal-mechanical paradigms of natural history in favor of a dynamic understanding of living beings as self-regulating organisms. But they are also accompanied by new liberal concepts of autonomy and freedom that transform both politics and morality and the very understanding of what it means to be a subject.

It is in this context that Foucault widens his analytical lens and begins to pay greater attention to processes of subjectivation and self-constitution. The two previously identified vectors of biopower—the anatomo-politics of bodies and the biopolitics of populations—are now supplemented by a third form of power having to do with subjectivity. Yet even now Foucault conceives of subjectivity in essentially vertical terms, as the self's identification with an impersonal regime of truth imposed on it from above: "This form of power that *applies* itself to immediate everyday life *categorizes* the individual, *imposes* a law of truth on him that he *must recognize* and others *have to* recognize in him. It is a form of power that *makes* individual subjects."[110] Note the verbs, which locate all relevant activity outside the subject, thus neatly circumscribing the vitality of subjective life. Far from marking a break in his work, Foucault's explicit turn to processes of subjectivation in the late 1970s continues and refines the trajectory of *Discipline and Punish* and the *History of Sexuality, Volume 1*. The Foucaultian liberal subject

---

109. Foucault, *Security, Territory, Population*, 344.
110. Foucault, "Subject and Power," in Faubion, *Power*, 331.

is only another, perhaps intensified, version of the panoptic and confessional subject that has internalized the gaze of the Other, continually and spontaneously correcting his own potential for deviation. Foucault can thus claim with some reason that he had all along been focused on analyzing "the genealogy of the subject in Western civilization," a genealogy that now, at the end of the 1970s, leads him back to early Christian conceptions of pastoral power and "truth-telling." The modern reflexive self—the subject who must know itself and say what it is—is the product of a particular Christian regime of government that constitutes the self by binding it to the imperative of telling the truth about itself.

It is against this background, as John Forrester suggests, that we must place Foucault's last theoretical turn, his interest in the ethics of self-care:

> Having located in the Christian pastoral tradition the roots of that Western violence which he implied gave rise both to imperialism and to the private self, [Foucault] now addressed full frontal the possibility of finding an alternative way of being a modern individual. This alternative way had, of necessity, to be non-Christian; it had to escape from the hermeneutics of the self, from the pastoral injunction to singularize. It had to be not only a genealogy of power but also of ethics.[111]

Foucault's so-called turn to ethics is a continuation of his earlier inquiry into the biopolitical constitution of life. If the latter suggested that human life is the effect of a network of technological, political, and epistemological operations, the turn to ethics is driven by the search for a mode of self-relation that cuts through this network, thus escaping the normalizing matrix of modern individuality. It is therefore no accident that at the core of the various ancient practices of self-care that Foucault studies are techniques of detachment. The ethical subject must first of all learn to unlearn; it must extricate itself from the internalized gaze of the other, undo the web of habits and beliefs that have shaped it, severing the attachments that dispose it to governance by others and liberating it from everything outside

---

111. John Forrester, "Foucault's Face: The Personal Is the Theoretical," in Faubion, *Foucault Now*, 125.

its own practice of self-care. Although Foucault discusses these ascetic practices in the context of Greek and Roman society, their real target is the panoptic (seeing oneself exclusively as *seen*) and hermeneutic (searching one's inner truth and hidden secrets) mechanisms that hold the modern self in place. The ethics of self-care is intended as an antidote to technologies of corporate individualization.

It is not difficult to see what Foucault finds so attractive about this model. Classical self-care treats the subject as a product of practices, dispensing with ideas of authenticity or a substantial self that are crucial to conceptions of modern individuality. As such, self-care promises to provide a technology of self that is on par with the institutional production of the modern private self, whose real insubstantiality, according to Foucault, the received language of subjectivity conceals. Yet the rather strong conceptual and historical distinction between classical Greek and Roman technologies of the self and modern processes of subjectivation poses at least two problems. First, and most obviously, it is not clear how the various phases of Foucault's work relate to each other; that is, what form classical practices of self-care would assume within modern regimes of truth or the biopolitics of population. Given the ease with which neoliberalism has adopted the language of self-fashioning and self-care, some skepticism is surely in order. In fact, the two research projects not only never meet in Foucault's work but have grown even further apart in the writings of his followers, with research on biopolitics focusing increasingly on the biomedical manipulation of living matter and questions of ethics dominating the analysis of subjective life. Second, the Foucaultian notion of individualization as normalization—as the self's internalization of a truth imposed on it from above—rests on an overly restricted notion of human life, one that, in failing to account for the latter's mode of vitality, also fails to capture the full reach and violence of its political manipulation. Foucault's famous opposition to psychoanalysis, phenomenology, and the "philosophy of the subject" comes at a heavy price, in that it deprives him of an important perspective on power.[112] Note

---

112. On Foucault's engagement with and avoidance of psychoanalysis, see John Forrester, "Foucault and the History of Psychoanalysis," in *The Seductions of*

that there is very little in Foucault's work that explores how modern subjects *experience* their biopolitical colonialization. What happens to my body, sensations, and desires when they are framed as living matter, or when my life becomes a "vital resource"? What kinds of normative pressures do modern biopolitical technologies produce in human life, how do these pressures register on the level of psychosomatic experiences (as anxiety, fantasy, bodily excitations, etc.), and how do these conscious and unconscious experiences shape the subject's libidinal economy or its relationship to itself, others, language, and the world? I point here to a region of subjective life that lies, as it were, between normalization and ethical self-constitution, yet is structurally implied by the latter. Put simply, if the self is capable of working on itself, as Foucault claims, then it must also register, in its body and psyche, that others are working on *it*. There is no biopolitical organization of human life without the recognition of fragmentation, splitting, derealization, psychic deadness, madness, etc.

Yet Foucault never addresses himself to these issues, nor does he develop a complex notion of experience that incorporates processes of normalization but is not limited to them. In this context we should note Foucault's complete disinterest in aesthetics after 1966, even though he had authored some brilliant essays on avant-garde literature in the early 1960s. When Foucault returned to aesthetic questions at the end of his life, it was with a view to recuperating the classical idea of an "aesthetics of existence," which he explicitly opposed to the modern system of art, claiming that "in our society, art has become something that is related only to objects and not to individuals or to life."[113] We only have to recall Friedrich Schlegel's claim that the modern novel is about the "art of all arts, the art of

---

Psychoanalysis: Freud, Lacan, and Derrida (Cambridge: Cambridge University Press, 1990), 286–316 and Joel Whitebook, "Against Interiority: Foucault's Struggle with Psychoanalysis," in *The Cambridge Companion to Foucault,* ed. Gary Gutting, 2nd ed. (Cambridge: Cambridge University Press, 2005), 212–347.

113.   Michel Foucault, "On the Genealogy of Ethics: An Overview of Work in Progress," in *Ethics: Subjectivity and Truth,* ed. Paul Rabinow, vol. 1 (New York: The New Press, 1997), 261.

living"[114] to cast some doubt on Foucault's statement, and in chapter 1 I will show in detail that Kant's invention of modern aesthetics coincides precisely with a *turn toward* experience and subjectivity. What matters for us at the moment is that Foucault's analysis of modern biopower disregards the critical, ethical, and diagnostic resources of modern literature and art. Put differently, the notion of an "aesthetics of existence" undertheorizes the complexity of both aesthetics and human existence, neither of which is reducible to the work of self-fashioning and the ethics of self-care. Hence my claim that we need to draw on the aesthetic archive to grasp the interplay of ethical, political, and existential life. Art, and especially literature, most comprehensively articulates the pathologies of biopolitics, explores the link between modern forms of domination and subjectivation, and experiments with alternative ways of living and being alive.

The following chapters' task is to make good on this claim that literature provides insights into the political organization of human life not available in contemporary theories of biopolitics. To give some idea of what this amounts to, let me turn briefly to a passage from Robert Musil's novel *The Man without Qualities*, which I will discuss in greater detail in chapter 6. In the following scene, Ulrich, the protagonist of Musil's novel, is arrested and taken to the police station for interrogation:

> He felt as though he had been sucked into a machine that was dismembering him into impersonal, general components before the question of his guilt or innocence came up at all. His name, the most intellectually meaningless yet most emotionally charged words in the language for him, meant nothing here. His works, which had secured his reputation in the scientific world, a world ordinarily of such solid standing, here did not exist. His face counted only as an aggregate of officially describable features. . . . His own feeling was that he was tall and broad-shouldered, with a chest curving like a filled sail on the mast, and joints fastening his muscles like small links of steel whenever he was angry or fighting or when Bonadea was clinging to him; but that he was slender, fine-boned, dark, and as soft as a jellyfish floating in the water whenever he was read-

---

114. Friedrich Schlegel, "Über Goethes Meister," in *Schriften zur Literatur*, ed. Wolfdietrich Rasch (Munich: Carl Hanser Verlag, 1970), 275.

ing a book that moved him or felt touched by a breath of that great homeless love whose presence in the world he had never been able to understand. Thus he could, even at such a moment as this, himself appreciate this statistical demystification of his person and feel inspired by the quantitative and descriptive procedures applied to him by the police apparatus as if it were a love poem invented by Satan. (MoE 159; MwQ, 168–69; changes to the translation are mine)

Ulrich's statistical demystification condenses several aspects of Foucault's analysis of biopower into a single scene. While focused on the body (Foucault's anatomo-political pole), the police investigation identifies Ulrich using the statistical methods Foucault associates with the biopolitics of population. Ulrich is transformed into "Ulrich"—an artifact of legalistic and statistical categorization. Moreover, in juxtaposing the mechanisms of surveillance with processes of (self) identification, the scene also recalls what I earlier described as the panoptic dynamic of modern individualization in Foucault. The passage therefore not only depicts how the police see Ulrich; it also asks if and to what extent Ulrich succumbs to the perspective of the *seen*, seeing himself in the statistical details through which he is made politically visible. And it is here, in its handling of the interplay between third- and first-person perspective, that Musil's novel is significantly more complex than Foucault's account of modern individualization. In one way, Ulrich, himself a mathematician, is clearly fascinated by his statistical identification, whose precision and impersonal elegance he admires. This delight points to Ulrich's dissatisfaction with the received humanistic language of subjectivity and authenticity, whose hollow ideology the novel analyzes in great detail. Like Foucault, Ulrich acknowledges the insubstantiality of the self, whose constructedness out of impersonal qualities the police machinery displays. But unlike Foucault's depiction of the panopticon, Musil's handling of perspective and imaginative language articulates an incalculable remainder, a dimension of psychic, erotic, and linguistic life not captured in the statistical identification of the subject. It is the brilliance of Musil's text, here and elsewhere, that it avoids resubstantializing this surplus of sense and subjectivity, hinting at it instead through metaphorical language and the feeling of loss the violence of biopolitical identification produces in Ulrich. As we shall see, Musil's exploration of this surplus enables him not only to analyze the fantasmatic and libidinal effects of the subject's social and institutional determination; it also becomes the source of the novel's experimental search for alternative ways of feeling and speaking, and for modes of being and living that overcome the ossification of both the old models of subjectivity and the new forms of biopolitical identification.

Forms of Life

It is time to address the title of my book, and with this its larger theoretical ambitions. I have suggested that literature and aesthetics capture crucial aspects of the transformations of human life in modernity that tend to evade both standard biopolitical theories and social scientific work focused on the science and politics of living matter. This is so because literary texts are repositories of cultural interaction, meaning that they draw on and reflect their *entire* environment, registering not only changes in the organization of power and knowledge but also shifts in the fine-grained texture of experience. Exploring the way such texts refract and shape the political, epistemic, and phenomenological transformations of their time is of historical as well as theoretical interest. Part of the aim of this book is to derive from the texts I examine a model of human life that more properly reflects its plasticity and complexity. I am not claiming, of course, that this model is already present as such in the texts. It is very much a model—that is, a theoretical construct—and one informed by a number of contemporary critics whose thinking I have found useful. But I do want to insist that the model is derived from the unique perspective on human life these texts articulate, which is to say that it emerges both from the modes of thinking that are specific to aesthetic forms and from the close reading of such forms.

I will call this model "forms of life," drawing on a phrase that was coined in the context of Romantic philosophy and biology in the 1820s[115] and became a popular term of conservative cultural-political criticism after World War I, but is perhaps best known in relation to Wittgenstein, who uses it in his *Philosophical Investigation* to highlight the embeddedness of language in broader social practices. Although I will broaden the notion to emphasize more strongly its aesthetic and political implications, what follows is deeply indebted to Wittgenstein's understanding of human life and its intertwinement with language and form. That questions of form—and indeed of aesthetics—are important in the *Philosophical Investigation* is already evident from its *mode* of presentation. As has often been noted, Wittgenstein's writing eschews the impersonal style of philosophical argumentation in favor of an intricate weave of voices that express divergent views on the issues at hand. Moreover, since these voices are neither named and personified, as in drama or narrative fiction, nor asymmetrically structured, as in Socratic dialogue, the reader is deprived of any clear-cut way of orienting her reading of the text or determining its basic shape and argument. The difficulty of this task is compounded by another distinctive feature of Wittgenstein's text: his invention of short philosophical fictions, often represented as the language games of "primitive" tribes, that ask readers to imagine unfamiliar forms of life. For "to imagine a language is to imagine a form of life" (PI §19).

Style is anything but ornamental here. Wittgenstein's play with literary and ethnographic genres is directed against the prevailing propositional conception of truth. Polyphonic texture and fictional fables combine to foil the reader's search for abstract truths and redirect her attention to the intricate tangle of words, thoughts, and contexts. Wittgenstein's language games thus serve an eminently philosophical task: they help us see that the standard philosophical view of concepts as fixed universals or meanings is an illusion, an intellectual fantasy that reifies cognition and human life. On Wittgenstein's view, concepts are not abstract rules that impose order *on* our life; they are part of this life, an expression of it, and as such

---

115. Helmreich and Roosth, "Life Forms," which also shows that the phrase remained central to nineteenth-century biological and evolutionary debates.

much blurrier and more malleable than we like to think: "For in the flux of life, where all our concepts are elastic, we couldn't reconcile ourselves to a rigid concept" (LWPP I, §246).

Hence also Wittgenstein's most famous notion, that of "language games," which blurs the boundaries between the linguistic and the nonlinguistic. "The word *language-game* is used here to emphasize the fact that the *speaking* of language is part of an activity, or of a form of life" (PI §23, Wittgenstein's emphasis). The relevant point here is not that speaking is an activity but that it is constitutively interwoven with other, *nonlinguistic* activities. Meaning arises from a zone of indistinction between language and nonlanguage: "Our talk gets its meaning from the rest of our activities [*Unsere Rede erhält durch unsere übrigen Handlungen ihren Sinn*]" (*Über Gewißheit*, §229). From this perspective, any theory that conceives of meaning in mentalist or representational terms—as an idea or object—misses that which imbues speaking and thinking with vitality. Concepts acquire life in the to-and-fro of ordinary speech and action, which in turn is bound up with bodies and things in motion: "Words have meaning only in the stream of life [*Nur im Fluß des Lebens haben die Worte Bedeutung*]" (LWPP I, §913).

It should be obvious that the metaphor of *Strom* (stream, river, flux), which recurs throughout Wittgenstein's later work, complicates the traditional understanding of form. If words acquire meaning in the context of language games, and if language games are in turn interwoven with nonlinguistic activities (i.e., embedded in a "stream of life"), then the boundaries of language games and meaning cannot be rigidly determined by rules or conventions but are instead loosely governed by the exigencies of context and historicity. "If a pattern of life is the basis for the use of a word then the word must contain some amount of indefiniteness. The pattern of life, after all, is not one of exact regularity" (LWPP I, §211). Note that the critical impulse of these lines cuts two ways: Wittgenstein's rejection of an overly logical view of language and meaning goes hand in hand with his critique of an irrational understanding of life, one that would oppose life and concept, as in contemporary *Lebensphilosophie*. "Life," for Wittgenstein, is not some formless Dionysian vortex but contains recognizable patterns. Its flowing motion displays *some* kind of order and regularity—just not the "exact" and immutable one we are inclined to imagine.

In sum, for Wittgenstein the meaning of linguistic or bodily expressions is a function of their use within the context of a system of more or less regular activities, or "patterns," of life. Wittgenstein refers to these patterns variously as "use" (*Gebrauch*; PI §30, 43, 138, 556), "convention," (*Gepflogenheit*; PI §198, 199, 205, 337), "institution" (*Institution*; PI §199, 337, 380), or "practice" (*Praxis*; PI §7, 21, 51, 54,197, 202), and the whole of these patterns he calls *Lebensform*.[116] This expression is used only five times in the *Philosophical Investigations*, and only once in its plural form. Three of these occurrences emphasize the close connection between the notion of *Lebensform* and that of language games. Wittgenstein writes, as previously quoted, that to imagine a language is to imagine a form of life (PI §19), that the term language game is meant to emphasize that "the *speaking* of language is part of an activity, or of a form of life" (PI §23), and that "human beings agree in the *language* they use" where this is "not agreement in opinions but in form of life" (PI §241). In the (incomplete) second part of the book, we read that "phenomena of hope are modes of this complicated form of life," namely the form of life of creatures that have "mastered the use of language" (PPF §1; PI, Part II, 148), and, perhaps most enigmatically: "What has to be accepted, the given, is—so one could say—*forms of life* [*Das Hinzunehmende, Gegebene—könnte man sagen—seien Lebensformen*]" (PPF §345; PI, Part II, 192).

Despite Wittgenstein's penchant for ethnography, the term refers not to empirically distinct cultures but, more broadly, to the "general form of those social activities that make phenomena of meaning and understanding possible."[117] *Lebensform*, in other words, is Wittgenstein's name for the *human* form of life, for a life that is shaped by signification and normative pressures. Yet calling this general form <u>*Lebensform*</u> rather than "culture" or "the social"

---

116. See also the helpful discussion in Khurana, "Gesellschaft und 'menschliche Lebensform'. Zum Verhältnis zweier Fundamentalbegriffe," *Soziale Systeme* 13, nos. 1 and 2 (2007): esp. 445–47.

117. Khurana, "Gesellschaft und 'menschliche Lebensform,'" 446.

highlights an important dimension of Wittgenstein's thought. In using a phrase that has clear biological connotations, Wittgenstein is drawing attention to what Stanley Cavell has called the "mutual absorption of the natural and the social." On the one hand, *Lebensform* points to the fact that our life with words is embedded in a certain physical reality, which includes laws of physics such as gravity. On the other, it points to the peculiar kind of naturalness that shapes many of our linguistic and social practices: "Commanding, questioning, storytelling, chatting, are as much part of our natural history as walking, eating, drinking, playing" (PI §25). Human life is not natural *and* symbolic, as if meaning-making was added onto a distinct biological substrate; rather, language and meaning-making are natural to humans, the "medium" through which humans assume vital form. Implicit in this emphasis on the natural history of cultural forms is a rejection of any narrowly conventionalist or contract-theoretical explanation of language and social order. "Patterns of (human) life" are not the result of explicit agreements or rules to which individual actors have consented and which they could freely change. Rather, speech and society rest on some deeper background agreement, some prior and mostly unconscious attunement among speakers of a language, that must already be in place for any discussion about social and political arrangements to take off. "If language is to be a means of communication there must be agreement not only in definitions but also (queer as this may sound) in judgments" (PI §242).

There are several aspects of Wittgenstein's philosophy that will be important throughout this book. First, the notion of *Lebensform* highlights the paradoxical "groundless ground" of human linguistic life.[118] Speech and meaning are groundless in that they lack any absolute or transcendent foundation; yet they are grounded in the sense that we do, in fact, mostly understand one another, thus revealing that we are attuned, share a *common* ground. Second, this common ground—our shared form of life—is not available to empirical description. Our *Lebensform* cannot be described or ob-

---

118. See Braver Lee, *Groundless Grounds: A Study of Wittgenstein and Heidegger* (Cambridge, MA: MIT Press, 2012).

served as a neutral fact since any such description is already a part of this life, hence included in what it seeks to articulate.[119] There is no external standpoint, no privileged position outside our form of life from which to determine its content and boundaries. Third, this undercuts not only any scientific or biological definition of *Lebensform* but also points to an important political implication of Wittgenstein's thought. What counts as a human form of life can only be articulated by *us*, in the first-person plural. Transferred to the political realm, this means that "the public community exists in its presentation by us—a presentation that is always vulnerable to your and my repudiation," hence open-ended.[120] Compare this to the status of sovereignty in Carl Schmitt's work. Whereas for Schmitt the unity of society is the result of a sovereign *decision* that puts an end to all talk, from a Wittgensteinian point of view such an act would count as a violent *imposition* of form, as an attempt to curtail both the "river of life" that runs through communal speech and practices and the political expressiveness of each individual, her capacity to shape society and make claims to community. Fourth, Wittgenstein's insistence on the open-endedness of our practices runs counter to any traditional organicist understanding of culture. Wittgenstein's *Lebensform* is not a neatly bounded organic whole but "a very complicated filigree pattern" [RPP II, §624]. It is composed of countless language games and the shared life of a community, which, while providing the tacit background that validates or invalidates judgments and distinctions, is nonetheless a messy and constantly transforming network of activities and practices— "the whole hurly-burly [*Gewimmel*] of human actions" (Z §567). Finally, Wittgenstein's claim that the meaningfulness of individual speech-acts depends on a shared form of life points to what Jonathan

---

119. See Jonathan Lear, "Transcendental Anthropology," in *Open Minded: Working Out the Logic of the Soul* (Cambridge, MA: Harvard University Press, 1998), 247–81.

120. See Andrew Norris, "Introduction: Stanley Cavell and the Claims to Community," in *The Claim to Community: Essays on Stanley Cavell and Political Philosophy*, ed. Andrew Norris (Redwood Hills, CA: Stanford University Press, 2006), 2.

Lear has called a "peculiar form of human vulnerability."[121] If my speech is intelligible only in the context of a communal form of life, then the radical contingency of this communal life—its "groundless ground"—exposes me to the constant danger of losing the concepts that structure my life and of becoming incomprehensible to myself and others. This loss can assume collective and historical-political proportions, as when, in Lear's example, white American settlers destroyed the traditional way of life of the Crow people, causing their leader to declare that after the disappearance of the buffalo "nothing happened" any longer (i.e., no further meaningful event occurred); but the loss of concepts and intelligibility can also happen gradually or in more intimate settings. There is no human *Lebensform* without the existential possibility of becoming formless and inhuman.

Wittgenstein is very much alive to this danger. Whether reflecting on animals, imagining speaking automata, or inventing surreal language games and bizarre tribes, his writings constantly probe the bounds of our attunement, the limits of what we are able to recognize as shared forms of life. Far from being merely episodic, Wittgenstein's reflection on the unfamiliar and strange points to the dialectic of the ordinary and the uncanny within human life. It is precisely because the intelligibility of our words rests on our participation in a web of shared ordinary practices that the seams suturing our existence can rip open at any moment, unraveling the perceived coherence of both bodies and words, somatic and symbolic life. The reach and integrity of human life forms, including the forms of "life" and "the human" themselves, depend on acts of imaginative investments that are subject to disturbances from within and without: from the public world of communication and language games, and from the "private" world of imagination and consciousness.

Let me briefly sketch two ways in which such disturbances can impinge on an individual's or community's sense of vitality. One threat, widely felt at the beginning of the twentieth century, was cap-

---

121. Jonathan Lear, *Radical Hope: Ethics in the Face of Cultural Devastation* (Cambridge, MA: Harvard University Press, 2006), 6.

tured in metaphors of petrification and exhaustion. Consider the following lines from Oswald Spengler's enormously successful *Decline of the West* (1918), which Wittgenstein recognized as an important influence on his work:

> Civilization is the inevitable destiny of the Culture. . . . Civilizations are the most external and artificial states of which a species of developed humanity is capable. They are a conclusion. . . . Death following life, rigidity following expansion, petrifying world-city following mother-earth. They are an end, irrevocably, yet by inward necessity reached again and again. . . . *Pure* Civilization, as a historical process, consists in a progressive exhaustion of forms that have become inorganic or dead.[122]

Spengler harks back to Goethe's morphology but inverts its valences. Rather than emphasizing the formative creativity of life, he invokes laws of organic transformation to evoke the inevitable death of Western culture, the exhaustion of its forms. Spengler's organic rhetoric of cultural decline is echoed in Freud's contemporaneous theory of life as directed in part toward the inorganic (1920).[123] Driving both theories is the sense that the iteration of forms results in the progressive dissolution of the vital-creative impulses that gave rise to them; repetition hollows out expression, turning culture into a mausoleum of dead forms. A similar logic underlies Weber's famous metaphor of the iron cage (1905) and Simmel's account of the tragedy of modern culture (1911),[124] both of which in turn influenced Lukács's theory of reification (1923).[125] Framed in Wittgensteinian terminology, Simmel's and Weber's worry is that language games and cultural practices come to operate *too* smoothly, sealing themselves off from the lives of their practitioners. The life

---

122. Oswald Spengler, *Decline of the West: Form and Actuality*, trans. Charles Francis Atkinson (New York: Alfred A. Knopf, 1926), 31–32; changes to the translation are mine. Spengler's emphasis.

123. Freud, "Beyond the Pleasure Principle," 1–64.

124. Max Weber, *The Protestant Ethics and the Spirit of Capitalism* (London: Routledge, 1992), 123–24; Georg Simmel, "Der Begriff und die Tragödie der Kultur," in *Aufsätze und Abhandlungen, 1909–1918*, ed. Rüdiger Kramme and Angela Rammstedt (Frankfurt am Main: Suhrkamp, 1993), 385–416.

125. György Lukács, *History and Class Consciousness: Studies in Marxist Dialectic* (Cambridge, MA: MIT Press, 1972).

of a culture dies when its forms begin to run on their own, assuming a quasi-mechanical autonomy and automaticity. In such historical moments, our games and practices lose their expressiveness, their capacity to shape and channel the desires and thoughts of the community.

The dynamics of petrification are diametrically opposed to another disturbance in the dialectic between consciousness and communication that is captured in metaphors of *woundedness* and *flesh*. Like all forms, language games have limits, and under certain conditions the experience of these limits can provoke feelings of panic and heightened vulnerability. In a penetrating essay, Cora Diamond has analyzed moments in which what she calls the "difficulty of reality" shoulders us out of our familiar language games, leaving us speechless, without words or concepts to comprehend what lies before us.[126] Diamond's examples are taken from a poem by Ted Hughes and J. M. Coetzee's novel *Elizabeth Costello*. Each text depicts situations in which a poetic "I" or fictional character, confronted with the death or suffering of living creatures, experiences "the inability of thought to encompass what it is attempting to reach,"[127] not merely as an intellectual problem but as a bodily feeling of being wounded. This feeling, though painful, is accompanied by a widening empathy that upsets our familiar hierarchies of "life." The "awareness we each have of being a living body, being 'alive to the world,' carries with it exposure to the bodily sense of vulnerability to death, sheer animal vulnerability, the vulnerability we share with them. This vulnerability is capable of panicking us."[128] In pushing us beyond what we can think, Diamond suggests, certain realities both dislodge us from our ordinary cultural practices and expose us to the creaturely life on which these practices rest. For a vivid depiction of these mechanisms in the writings of a contemporary author whom Wittgenstein admired, consider the fol-

---

126. Cora Diamond, "The Difficulty of Reality and the Difficulty of Philosophy," in *Philosophy and Animal Life*, ed. Stanley Cavell, Cora Diamond, John McDowell, Ian Hacking, and Cary Wolfe (New York: Columbia University Press, 2008), 43–91.

127. Ibid., 58.

128. Ibid., 74.

lowing scene from Rilke's *The Notebooks of Malte Laurids Brigge*, in which the protagonist, an impoverished Danish aristocrat, encounters a beggar on the streets of Paris:

> But that woman, that woman: bent forward with her head in her hands, she had completely fallen into herself. . . . The street was too empty; its emptiness was bored with itself and it pulled away the sounds of my footsteps and clattered around all over the place with them like a wooden clog. Out of fright the woman reared up too quickly, too violently, so that her face was left in her two hands. I could see it lying there, the hollowness of its shape. It cost me an indescribable effort to keep looking at those hands and not at what they had torn away from. I dreaded the inside of her face, but I was much more afraid of the exposed rawness of the head without a face.[129]

This is an extreme instance of Diamond's "difficulty of reality." Our encounter with poor people is ordinarily regulated by more or less conventionalized practices, from denial or the dispensing of pennies on one side of the spectrum, to moral outrage or even political activism on the other. Malte's reaction is entirely different. Rather than ignoring or practically responding to the beggar, he is undone by her, shouldered out of reality. In fact, the encounter quite literally unhinges him. Can there be any doubt that the scene depicts a hallucinatory disturbance of vision? What Malte sees in the woman's horrifying *Gestalt* is not simply an empirical fact but the imaginative projection of his own terrifying woundedness, which the beggar's destitution provokes in him. Her faceless face, in other words, is a fantasmatic expression of the flesh of creaturely life that sustains our ordinary practices and constitutes the uncanny underside of our cultural *Lebensform*. Moreover, as in Diamond's discussion of Coetzee's novel, this flesh carries a distinct political charge. As Diamond makes clear, what terrifies and panics Elizabeth Costello is both the suffering of animals *and* the knowledge of her own implication in this suffering, the realization that this is what *we*, through practices like industrialized farming of animals, do to animals. Similarly, Malte's horror is fueled by his superior social

---

129. Rainer Maria Rilke, *Die Aufzeichnungen des Malte Laurids Brigge* (Frankfurt am Main: Suhrkamp, 1976), 10.

position—he is, after all, an aristocratic male—which implicates him, however indirectly, in the mechanisms that have marginalized the beggar woman. Malte is also wounded by the realization of his *own* biopolitical violence.

I have cited Spengler and Rilke to bring into relief the cultural and discursive context in which Wittgenstein's later philosophy took shape. Wittgenstein's well-documented interest in Goethe's morphology and his vision of culture as a form of nature were widespread in the early decades of the twentieth century, as was his heightened sense of the fragility and vulnerability of human life. As we shall see, the early twentieth-century rhetoric of exhaustion, petrification, and formless flesh rests on, but reverses, the ontology of earlier German vitalism. Whereas the late eighteenth century coined the concept of the organism to depict life as the harmonious *interplay* of force and form, early twentieth-century vitalism dramatizes the *dissociation* of life's "organic" dialectic, depicting the excess of form over force (metaphors of petrification, exhaustion) or force over form (images of formless flesh). Wittgenstein's later philosophy belongs to this vitalist tradition, but it also articulates a set of concepts and models (language games, family resemblance, *Lebensform*, etc.) that allows us to reflect more clearly on vitalism's aesthetic, existential, and political implications. For this reason, Wittgenstein occupies a unique position within the present book, as both a significant exponent of the vitalist discourse I am concerned with and a theoretical resource for understanding it.

Seeing-As

Among Wittgenstein's most instructive concepts is his notion of aspect seeing, derived from contemporary Gestalt psychology (yet another movement of the time inspired by Goethe's morphology),[130]

---

130. On the influence of Goethe on Gestalt psychology, see Mitchell G. Ash, *Gestalt Psychology in German Culture, 1890–1967: Holism and the Quest for Objectivity* (Cambridge: Cambridge University Press, 1996), 84–102. On Wittgenstein's relation to Gestalt psychology, see Nicole Hausen and Michel ter Hark, "Aspect Seeing in Wittgenstein and in Psychology," in *A Wittgensteinian Perspective*

which he introduces in the second part of the *Philosophical Investigations*. In its basic meaning, "aspect seeing" refers to the psychological experience of seeing an object not just differently but as a different object, such as when we see the same drawing first as the picture of a duck and then as a picture of a rabbit, or when we suddenly discern in a collection of puzzle pieces the contours of a face. But the notion is not restricted to perception, narrowly understood: Wittgenstein himself used it to explore the phenomenology of reading and what he calls aspect blindness (PPF §257), and his readers have developed his scattered comments to bring out internal connections between aesthetics, ethics, and politics. Aspect seeing is "pertinent to describing and thinking through the central conundrum of aesthetic judgment—namely, how can an aesthetic experience that is not only prompted by, but (we feel) *attached to*, a publicly available object be had in full recognition that others may not, or will not, have it?"[131] As in Goethe's scientific writings, aspect change exemplifies a form of vision that undermines the strict dichotomy between sensibility and cognition: it is both subjective event and objective disclosure, inner *Erlebnis* (a term Wittgenstein uses throughout his writings on psychology) and epistemic insight. As such, the notion points to an extended mode of thinking that conceives of thinking as accompanied by inner change, knowledge that is transformative experience. This emphasis on the link between thinking, sensibility, and inner change is, of course, a defining feature of the anti-Cartesian orientation of modern aesthetics since Kant, but it also opens up the notion of aspect seeing to ethical and political questions. In certain contexts, aspect change bears on the subject's relation to itself and others. More precisely, it bears on the self's ability to *acknowledge* its relation to others. And acknowledgment and recognition are, of course, eminently political categories.

Think again of Diamond's discussion of Coetzee's novel. Costello is haunted by a complex set of realities: the reality of her "sheer

---

on the Use of Conceptual Analysis in Psychology, ed. Timothy P. Racine and Kathleen L. Slaney (Houndmills, UK: Palgrave Macmillan, 2013), 87–109.

131.   William Day and Victor J. Krebs, "Introduction: Seeing Aspects in Wittgenstein," in *Seeing Wittgenstein Anew*, ed. William Day and Victor J. Krebs (Cambridge: Cambridge University Press, 2010), 9.

animal vulnerability, the vulnerability we share with them";[132] the reality of what we do to animals; and the fact that in the face of this "crime of stupefying proportions,"[133] most people continue to live their ordinary lives. What sets Costello apart and shoulders her out of ordinary language games is not new information—knowledge of the practices of animal production facilities is widespread, as Costello herself highlights. What distinguishes her from those around her is that she sees something different in these facts. This is so because she does not draw the traditional line between man and irrational beast that allows her interlocutors to protect themselves from the full meaning of reports about large-scale animal slaughter. Costello is struck by her deep kinship with animals, by her recognition of them as capable of joy and suffering, alive to the world, like herself. In the face of this knowledge, which is not strictly speaking conceptual but nonetheless extends the scope of what can be seen, our implication in the suffering of animals becomes a bewildering fact, a "difficulty of reality" that dislodges her from the familiar coordinates of intelligibility, thus pushing her to the limits of the *Lebensform* she shares with others. This is where Coetzee's story, like Rilke's novel, far exceeds the complexity of ordinary perceptual aspect seeing. While the switch from seeing a drawing as the picture of a duck to that of a rabbit is also accompanied by a momentary sense of recognition—now I see!—the recognition at stake in Coetzee is much more radical in that it bears on a sense of shared being that affects the subject's understanding of itself and its relations to others. Costello recognizes her *internal* relation to animals; in looking at what we do to them, she sees a shared form of being, the being of embodied souls, sentient life. As the singularity of her response shows, there is nothing necessary or automatic about this acknowledgment. And just as it is possible *not* to recognize our connection to animals, deny our shared aliveness, it is possible not to see other people *as* human, exclude them from our form of life. From animal to Jew to beggar to intimate partner, the possibilities of failed acknowledgment and soul blindness are endless.

---

132. Diamond, "The Difficulty of Reality," 74.
133. J. M. Coetzee, *Elizabeth Costello* (New York: Penguin, 2003), 114.

This is precisely what Coetzee's fictional framing—the setting of Costello's speech at a college in upstate New York—brings out, for Costello's words meet with a chorus of outrage and bewilderment. The difficulty of recognizing the suffering of animals is thus linked, in Coetzee's novel, to the difficulty of recognizing the wounded animal that is Elizabeth Costello herself. As Diamond emphasizes, this is not a failure of rationality but the result of its excess. Whereas Costello speaks from a desire to "save [her] soul,"[134] her listeners take her to be arguing for animal rights and vegetarianism. And while Costello describes herself as "an animal exhibiting, yet not exhibiting, to a gathering of scholars, a wound, which I cover up under my clothes but touch on in every word I speak,"[135] her interlocutors, deaf to the wound in her words, only attend to their propositional content and consistency. Earlier we saw that aspect seeing is not a matter of rational argument: you cannot prove to the other that he is seeing a duck. Coetzee goes further by showing that rational argument can serve as a *defense* against recognizing what is beyond concept in the expression of others. Yet without such recognition, living beings fail to come alive to us *as* animals or humans. True, Costello's interlocutors do not literally deny that she is a human being. But they do dismiss her speech as the ramblings of an old woman who has lost her wits, or as proof that she is not quite up to the rigors of philosophical argumentation. In doing so, they avoid acknowledging *why* she is speaking, and so what she is speaking about; they ignore the horror that haunts her, screen out the stirrings of her embodied soul. While this might not amount to denying that Costello is a human being, it is a hardness that protects them from being unsettled by existence, hers as well as their own. To those around her, Costello is not a wounded human being but an annoyance that disturbs their established forms of life. As John says to his wife Norma on the morning of her mother's departure, "a few hours and she'll be gone, then we can return to normal."[136]

---

134. Ibid., 89.
135. Ibid., 71.
136. Ibid., 114.

Let me connect these comments to my earlier discussion of Wittgensteinian *Lebensform* and the broader concerns of this book. First, I want to suggest that the dynamics of aspect seeing point to the ontological status of "forms of life." Forms of life are not empirical facts but depend for their identification on a mode of seeing that is bound up with imagination and recognition. Aspect seeing thus draws attention to a nonbiological understanding of notions like "human," "animal," even "life" itself. On this view, recognizing something in the world as human, animal, or living is not to subsume it under a concept but to acknowledge our internal relation to it: as Cavell writes, it is not "merely an identification *of* you but *with* you" (CPR, 421).[137] Second, aspect seeing is pivotal to both Wittgenstein's conception of philosophy and his vision of human life. Rather than developing a new set of theories, his writings seek to induce in his readers a new way of seeing their lives with words. Part of this involves facing up to the countless ways in which we are driven to use language to *deflect* life, to protect us from exposure to our bodily vulnerability and the historical contingency of our words and meaning. Against this ultimately metaphysical desire to ground our existence in rational rule or fantasies of absolute authority, Wittgenstein's writings constantly return our attention to the particular role words play in our lives, asking us to look in new ways at what is already there. Moreover, it is this disposition to see anew what is already there that gives language and language games their vitality. Lacking any fixed rules, the patterns that constitute our *Lebensform* are in perpetual flux, and moves within it are, as a matter of principle, open to variation and invention. Without the imaginative capacity both to project old words into new contexts and to recognize such projections, our lives with words would turn into the mechanical repetition of already established patterns of meaning—it would petrify. Aspect blindness, in short, is a form of emotional and cognitive deadness. Hence, third, the very

---

137. What counts for us as internal relation is not fixed once and for all. If Cavell's talk of "identification" restricts the range of internal relations to other humans, our age of ecological disaster increasingly impresses on us the interconnection between human and nonhuman life, making us recognize internal relations we didn't see before.

form of Wittgenstein's writing. Wittgenstein's use of philosophical fictions and bizarre thought experiments is an integral part of his view of the essential role of imagination and exhibition in human life. It reflects, in fact performs, not only the belief that proper thinking—thinking as reorientation and acknowledgment—requires an imaginative extension of our concepts and our sensibility but also that such change cannot be accomplished through rational-logical argument and instead must be exhibited by way of careful arrangements of phenomena—what Wittgenstein calls "perspicuous presentation [*übersichtliche Darstellung*]" (PI §121). Proper thinking contains an irreducibly *aesthetic* dimension.

Which brings us back to my earlier claim that any account of the transformation of life in modernity must draw on the aesthetic archive. This is so, I now want to say, because aesthetic media reflect—that is, show and exhibit—the unregulated singularities of human life that defy the ordered terrain of theoretical discourse. No theoretical account can grasp the infinite complexity of the "stream of life" that makes phenomena of meaning possible: the intricate tangles of words, thoughts, and bodies; the oscillation of perspectives and aspectual shifts; the play of recognition and its avoidance; and the dynamic intertwinement of these and other layers of experience with the political institutions and apparatuses that seek to shape and frame them. To be sure, aesthetic media also reduce the overcomplexity of life through the circumscription of details in aesthetic forms. But as in Wittgenstein, the goal of these organizing frames is not to provide a theory of life but a *picture* of it, one that, if successful, throws into relief new patterns of intelligibility, thus expanding the range of what is given to the senses to make sense of.[138]

Nor is art's imaginative power limited to the level of content and theme.[139] One example connected to aspect seeing that Wittgenstein

---

138. On aesthetics as a way of making sense of what is given to the senses, see Jacques Ranciere, *The Politics of Aesthetics*, trans. Gabriel Rockhill (London: Continuum, 2004), esp. 12–19.

139. For the following, see also Joachim Schulte, "Das Leben des Zeichens," in *Wittgenstein und die Literatur*, ed. John Gibson and Wolfgang Huemer (Frankfurt am Main: Suhrkamp, 2006), 215–41.

touches on in his late writings on psychology bears on two different modes of reading:

> But how about this: when I read a poem, or some expressive prose, especially when I read it out loud, surely there is something that is going on as I read it which isn't going on when I glance over the sentences only for the sake of their information. I may, for example, read a sentence with more intensity or with less. I take trouble to get the tone exactly right. Here I often see a picture before me, as if it was an illustration. And may I not also utter a word in such a tone as to make its meaning stand out like a picture? A way of writing might be imagined, in which some signs were replaced by pictures and so were made prominent. This does actually happen sometimes, when we underline a word or positively put it on a pedestal in the sentence. (RPP I, §1059)

Unlike the superficial and automatic reading, in which one scans for information, the tactile and imaginative reading attends to the form and physiognomy of words and sentences: their tone and rhythms, the physical shape of the letters (PI §§167–69), phonological and rhetorical patterns, and so on. As with regular aspect change, this shift in attention transforms both object and perception. The text begins to "sing" and "taste," the words release "an aroma" (RPP II, §465) and reveal a "strong musical element" (RPP I, §888). What is at stake here is what Wittgenstein, in the *Philosophical Investigations*, describes as "the experience [*das Erleben*] of the meaning of a word" (PI II, §234). And while the possibility of such heightened experience of words is intrinsic to all language use, poetic texts, through their use of formal devices that put words and phrases "on a pedestal," foreground this expressive aspect of language more strongly than ordinary communicative speech.[140] In short, literature, by concentrating our attention, amplifies the texture of meanings in ordinary life that get ignored, even repressed, in other kinds of language use.

These considerations point back to what I earlier called *aesthetic life*—the peculiar kind of animation (*Belebung*) Burke and Kant identified as a hallmark of aesthetic experience. But the contrast be-

---

140. This is of course very similar to Jacobson's notion of the "poetic function."

tween imaginatively engaged and disengaged reading also illumi-
nates the complicated link between aesthetics, ethics, and politics.
As we saw, the seemingly rational response of Costello's interlocutors is both an instance of deflection and blindness and an act of
exclusion that pushes Costello to the margin of a community intent on maintaining its status quo. Faced with the "difficulty of reality" presented by Costello, her interlocutors retreat to the seemingly firm conventions of the language game of philosophical
argumentation, thus occluding both her message and her voice. To
her fellow-citizens, Costello falls short of the criteria of rational discourse, and thus recedes from its community. Though seemingly
idiosyncratic, Costello's case points to the irreducibly aesthetic and
ethical dimensions of politics. Political power involves the production of regimes of aspects that circumscribe what counts as intelligible reality; it involves what Jacques Ranciere has called "the distribution of the sensible."[141] To challenge the status quo, it is thus
necessary not only to articulate new claims but also to open up new
possibilities of seeing and saying. What is necessary, in Wittgensteinian terms, is aspect change, an expansion of what is given to the
senses to make sense of. Wittgenstein's writings suggest that such
change cannot be achieved by rational argumentation alone but requires an aesthetic-ethical shift; that is, an imaginative expansion of
our concepts that in turn rests on attention and receptiveness to
what is already in front of us yet unacknowledged. The problem
is not necessarily that we know too little; in fact, in some cases
we know more than we can tolerate and are willing to acknowledge. The causes that hold us back from seeing all that there is to
be seen range from inattention and impatience, to lack of imagination, to our unwillingness to face up to our implication in the
existing system of violence and injustices. But they also have to
do with resistance to acknowledging the ultimate groundlessness
of norms, to conceding that the meaningfulness of our words and
practices, and hence the consistency of both individual life and
communal *Lebensform*, lack any absolute or transcendent foundation but rest instead on our fragile attunement to one another.

---

141. Ranciere, *The Politics of Aesthetics*.

In the face of this lack, which is always there but becomes palpable whenever our habitual modes of seeing and speaking run into a "difficulty of reality," we shrink back from our vulnerability, insisting instead on the presumed fixity of convention, logical rule, or biological essences, or worse yet, on the brute force of sovereignty.

The polemical upshot of these observations should be clear: Such existential avoidance is at work in biopolitical discourse itself. Biopolitical theories share the fundamental concerns of Wittgenstein's late philosophy—the ultimate groundlessness of normative claims, the limits of rational rule, the relation between life and form—yet develop these problems in often diametrically opposed directions. In the work of Giorgio Agamben, for instance, the critique of rationalist formalism gives rise to a highly formalistic theory of "*the* political" that explains political order in terms of what Agamben, following Schmitt, calls the "paradox of sovereignty." The paradox consists in the fact that the sovereign lies outside the law he imposes. The entire political-legal order thus rests, in the first and last instance, on an act of sheer positing—a decision—that is itself without legal or rational support: order and normativity are based not on law and reason, as liberalism holds, but on violence and force. Moreover, Agamben projects Schmitt's state of exception onto Foucault's notion of the biopolitical, thus equating the political with biopolitics. The sovereign decision that creates order also produces its outside, and with it, a type of person unprotected by law—*homo sacer*, or "bare life," whose paradoxical status, produced *by* law as excluded *from* it, constitutes the "originary political element, the *Urphänomen* of politics."[142] *Urphänomen* is, of course, a crucial concept of Goethe's natural philosophy, and Agamben's use of it to describe the figure of the *homo sacer* underscores the ontological character of his argument. Where Goethe's *Urphänomen* promises the symbiosis of noumenon and phenomenon, intellect and nature, Agamben's *homo sacer* embodies the violent displacement of life by law. As in Kafka's "In the Penal

---

142. Agamben, *Homo Sacer*, 109.

Colony,"[143] law is a machine that extracts life from the body and converts it into an expression of legality:

> Law is made of nothing but what it manages to capture inside itself through the inclusive exclusion of the *exceptio*: it nourishes itself on this exception and is a dead letter without it. In this sense, the law truly "has no existence in itself, but rather has its being in the very life of men."[144]

The exceptional case of the *homo sacer* thus merely makes visible a mechanism that permeates the juridical order as a whole. Whether naked or qualified, as *homo sacer* or ordinary citizen, the moment law and politics impose their forms onto human life, submitting it "to the original ban-structure of sovereignty," life is abandoned to a logic that captures and exploits it.[145]

Given this highly abstract and totalizing analysis of "the political," it is not surprising that Agamben's alternative to the existing order veers toward an "empty utopianism."[146] To the bare life produced by sovereignty, Agamben opposes what he calls, without reference to Wittgenstein, a "form-of-life" that, while structurally almost identical to the former,[147] somehow transforms the subjugation of life by law into a messianic state of exception in which human life is granted its full potentiality. This "solution" entails not only a theoretical shift from the political to the ethical—from the world of institutions and social structures to the question of how to relate to the existing structures and systems[148]—it also rests on problematic ontological and metaphysical premises that cast doubt on

---

143. See my "Lessons of the Cryptograph: Revelation and the Mechanical in Kafka's 'In the Penal Colony,'" *Modernism/Modernity* 8, no. 2 (2001): 295–302.

144. Agamben, *Homo Sacer*, 127.

145. Ibid., 43, 28.

146. I borrow this formulation from Dominick LaCapra's critique of Agamben in his *History and Its Limits: Human, Animal, Violence* (Ithaca, NY: Cornell University Press, 2009), 165.

147. On the structural similarity between bare life and form-of-life in Agamben, see Eva Geulen, "Form-of-life/Forma-di-Vita: Distinction in Agamben," in *Literatur als Philosophie—Philosophie als Literatur*, ed. Eva Horn, Bettina Menke, and Christoph Menke (Munich: Wilhelm Fink, 2005), 363–74, and Khurana, "Desaster und Versprechen."

148. Khurana, "Desaster und Versprechen."

Agamben's conception of both ethics and politics. Note, for instance, that Agamben's explanation of the political in terms of the paradox of sovereignty empties the social world of all agency but that of the sovereign who, in deciding on the state of exception, establishes the political order ex nihilo. In fact, Agamben follows Schmitt in claiming that the sovereign act does not merely lay down the law but determines, in fact institutes, normality: "The sovereign," he writes, " decides not the licit and illicit but the originary inclusion of the living in the sphere of law or, in the words of Schmitt, 'the normal structuring of life relations,' which the law needs."[149] Leaving aside the obvious theological implications of an act that creates order out of nothing (or out of chaos), what would it mean to *decide* the normal structuring of life relations? Can one—anyone—found normality?[150]

The difference with Wittgenstein should be obvious. For Wittgenstein, every act—including a "foundational" political one—is intelligible only in relation to a web of existing linguistic and other regularities. This is not to deny that political actions can alter existing frames of intelligibility but merely to insist that even revolutionary events do not emerge from an historical vacuum. Whatever is said or done arises out of the messy, though *not* utterly chaotic, "hurly-burly [*Gewimmel*] of human actions" (Z §567). While such a view may lack the pathos of Agamben's theory, it makes for a much richer conception of ethics and politics. Since no fixed rule or supreme authority determines the meaning of words or actions, each one of us is responsible for evaluating what counts as normal and abnormal, and thus for determining the bounds of intelligibility—politically speaking, the scope of existing law. "The subject of responsibility," Andrew Norris writes with respect to Cavell's interpretation of Wittgenstein, "is always *us*, here and now,"[151] and this applies to all human action, from the ordinary to the political. In short, Agamben, and Wittgenstein as interpreted by Cavell, respond to a shared

---

149. Agamben, *Homo Sacer*, 26.
150. See, with respect to Schmitt, Andrew Norris, "Sovereignty, Exception, and Norm," *Journal of Law and Society* 34, no. 1 (2007): esp. 35ff.
151. Norris, "Introduction," 12.

insight into the ultimate groundlessness of norms in diametrically opposed ways: where Agamben argues that order is the product of brute force, Wittgenstein and Cavell suggest that "human speech and activity, sanity and community"[152] depend on a fragile web of agreement, a shared form, a *Lebensform*, that is both beyond individual control *and* constantly transformed by practices of making ourselves and others intelligible.

These seemingly lofty philosophical distinctions have considerable implications for our understanding of historical events. Take, for instance, one of Agamben's favorite examples, the concept of "life unworthy of living" (*lebensunwertes Leben*) that was at the core of the Nazi program of euthanasia. Instead of analyzing this juridical concept as the "necessary" and logical outcome of the biopoliticization of politics that begins with Aristotle and culminates in the concentration camps of the Nazis, as Agamben does, a Wittgensteinian (and for that matter, Foucaultian) approach would dwell more systematically on the prehistory of this term, mentioned but then quickly forgotten by Agamben. Coined in 1920,[153] the concept of *lebensunwertes Leben* points to the complex set of conditions that made Nazi eugenic politics possible: on the one hand, the emergence of new biomedical discourses and normativities dating back to the *Kaiserreich*; on the other, the erosion of the state of law in favor of a totalitarian conception of unfettered sovereign decisionism, as formulated in Schmitt's theory of *the* political from the 1920s, on which Agamben himself draws heavily. Placed in this broader historical context, Nazi biopolitics results not from the "paradox of sovereignty" but rests instead on a host of discourses, practices, and distinctions that took shape prior to 1933, and outside the conventional sites of political power, in laboratories, universities, and public discussions. Moreover, each of these genealogical lines can be understood, from a Wittgensteinian and Cavellian

---

152. Stanley Cavell, "The Availability of Wittgenstein's Later Philosophy," in *Must We Mean What We Say? A Book of Essays* (Cambridge: Cambridge University Press, 1976), 52.

153. Karl Binding and Alfred Hoche, *Die Freigabe der Vernichtung lebensunwerten Lebens. Ihr Mass und ihre minderwertige Form* (Leipzig: Felix Meiner, 1920).

point of view, as rational or scientific attempts to *deflect* from the groundlessness of the social order by defining it either in biological terms, or in the quasi-theological framework of absolute sovereignty. This denial of the insubstantiality of society culminates in the Nazi state, which combines the biopolitical and sovereign strands in its conception of the *Führer* as the physical embodiment of a racially homogenous *Volk* with whom he shares the same biological "substance." Finally, a Wittgensteinian understanding of the social allows us to see more clearly the historical and political importance of literature and other aesthetic modes of cultural expression. As I will endeavor to show, the literary archive, through its far more fine-grained presentation of social and subjective life, suggests, for example, that the biopolitical distinction between the life worthy and unworthy to be lived is symptomatic not of an abstract "paradox of sovereignty," nor merely of changes in scientific and governmental discourses, but of a more thoroughgoing crisis of normativity that permeates early twentieth-century German culture.

This crisis is also at the core of the most sustained and intelligent work on the biopolitical dimension of German modernism; that is, that of Eric Santner. Santner's framework, refined over a period of almost two decades, is broadly Lacanian and Heideggerian. Human life is *Dasein*, life inscribed in a normative social space and subject to the operations of signifiers that charge psychic and somatic expression with an energetic excess, a constitutive too-muchness, that "opens up the possibilities of distinctively human forms of wretchedness and joy, of misery and jouissance."[154] The political implications of this psychosomatic surplus are most obvious in situations where the subject is explicitly tasked with speaking on behalf of the law, thus assuming the position of sovereignty. This predicament underlies the psychotic breakdown of Judge Schreber, analyzed in *My Own Private Germany*, which Santner reads as illustrating a general "crisis of investiture" permeating German-speaking culture around 1900. Santner's more recent work expands on this psychoanalytical account of human-mindedness to

---

154. Eric Santner, *Royal Remains: The People's Two Bodies and the End-games of Sovereignty* (Chicago: University of Chicago Press, 2011), 4.

argue for the unacknowledged theological undercurrents of modern biopolitics. The conceptual link between subjectivity and politics is provided by the notion of "flesh," which Santner borrows from Merleau-Ponty but extends considerably. On the one hand, Santner's "flesh" refers to the "semiotic—and somatic—vibrancy generated by the inscription of bodies into a normative social space";[155] on the other, it names the "sublime somatic materiality . . . produced by the logic of sovereign presentation."[156] According to Santner, the great achievement of the medieval theory of the king's two (natural and sacred) bodies, as analyzed by Ernst Kantorowicz, was to symbolically contain this sublime "flesh" of sovereignty, which becomes desymbolized and ubiquitous with the deconsecration of the king. More precisely, whereas the medieval imaginary tied the vital surplus of sovereignty to the figure of the monarch, whose "sacral soma was seen to embody a 'vertical' link to a locus of transcendence—to divine authorization,"[157] modern secular politics disperses this surplus across the entire social body, among the "people," thereby fundamentally altering its psychosomatic form. "The new bearers of the principle of sovereignty are in some sense stuck with an excess of flesh that their own bodies cannot fully close in upon and that must be 'managed' in new ways."[158] And it is this enigmatic object, Santner suggests, that drives modern biopolitics:

> My claim is that biopolitics assumes its particular urgency and expansiveness in modernity because what is at issue in it is not simply the biological life or health of populations but the "sublime" life-substance of the People, who, at least in principle, become the bearers of sovereignty, assume the dignity of prince.[159]

Note that Santner's fusion of psychoanalysis and existential ontology with political theory reads all manifestations of "flesh"—from individual feelings of joy and misery to Nazi racism—as political.

---

155. Ibid., 4.
156. Ibid., xxi.
157. Ibid.
158. Ibid.
159. Ibid., xi.

This is possible, I want to suggest, because Santner fuses two problematic conceptions of the political, one that is too narrow, and another that is too broad. On the one hand, Santner draws no distinction between the political and the social, insisting that the former be understood as the primary domain of meaning and normativity. The political here is conceived extremely broadly, and is in fact identified with what Santner calls "normative social space." On the other hand, this social space is also said to be structured by the logic of sovereignty, with the sovereign functioning as a master-signifier that represents, as Santner, following Lacan, writes, the "subject for all other signifiers, all other bearers of symbolic value."[160] Taken together, the two definitions suggest that (a) all social relations and symbolic phenomena are political because (b) they are all structured by the logic of sovereignty—and that this is true for both early modern and modern societies. Accordingly, even when the master-signifier can no longer be embodied in a concrete person, *the logic of sovereignty*, which rests on this master-signifier, remains in force and continues to function as a *master-code* that structures (Santner's interpretation of) all psychic, social, and political life. With or without a king, we are always under the spell of political sovereignty.

Is this a plausible model of the relations between meaning, sociality, and politics? Are all social relations political? Is meaning always grounded in a master-signifier? Conversely, is what we call "political" reducible to the logic of sovereignty? And what about psychic phenomena? Should we claim, with Santner, that psychic life as a whole—*all* "human forms of wretchedness and joy, of misery and jouissance"[161]—are the product of (*bio*)*political* pressures? Given my earlier discussion of Wittgenstein, it should be clear that I believe Santner fails to make an important terminological distinction between "normative social space"—Wittgenstein's *Lebensform*—and "the political." While human life is indeed *always* subject to normative pressures, not *all* of these pressures are political. Before, or at least apart from the fact that, human life falls

---

160. Ibid., xx.
161. Ibid., 4.

under the institutionalized sway of law and political authority, it is subject to a force of determination that derives from the regularities of speech, habits, and practices. Making explicit this distinction allows us to bring into sharper focus a theoretical counterargument to Santner's theory embedded in his own employment of the notion of "ontological vulnerability." Santner borrows the term from Jonathan Lear, who uses it, as we saw, to describe the fact that human life assumes meaning only within contingent and fragile collective forms of life. But he then goes on to argue, beyond Lear, that the "defense mechanisms cultures use to protect against a primordial exposure—to 'cover' our nudity—serve in the end to redouble this exposure and thereby to 'fatten' the flesh of creaturely life."[162] This formulation implies a distinction that Santner's conflation of the social and the political elsewhere obscures: the political organization of society is a normative *response* to the inexorable contingency of psychic and social life. We are ontologically vulnerable not because we are exposed to the logic of sovereignty but because *there is no sovereign* in the requisite sense of a transcendent symbol, law, or being. In a famous and haunting passage, Stanley Cavell offers a Wittgensteinian account of this more fundamental, prepolitical fragility of human life:

> We learn and teach words in certain contexts, and then we are expected, and expect others, to be able to project them into further contexts. Nothing insures that this projection will take place (in particular, not the grasping of universals nor the grasping of books of rules), just as nothing insures that we will make, and understand, the same projections. That on the whole we do is a matter of our sharing routes of interest and feeling, modes of response, senses of humor and significance and of fulfillment, of what is outrageous, of what is similar to what else, what a rebuke, what forgiveness, of when an utterance is an assertion, when an appeal, when an explanation—all the whirl of organism Wittgenstein calls "forms of life." Human speech and activity, sanity and community, rest upon nothing more, but nothing less, than this. It is a vision as simple as it is difficult, and as difficult as it is (and because it is) terrifying.[163]

---

162. Ibid., 6.
163. Cavell, "The Availability of Wittgenstein's Late Philosophy," 52.

Cavell points to two primarily philosophical strategies (universals and rules) of disavowing the terrifying frailty of human life, but the variety of individual and collective denials is endless, ranging from narcissism and rational deflection to psychosis and racism. Santner's identification of normativity with sovereignty not only elides these differences; it also obscures the indeterminacy of individual and collective responses to human vulnerability. Does talk of "forced choice"[164] and the inexorable "logic of sovereignty" not reintroduce, on the level of theory, the very thing whose existence this theory rightly denies: foundations, rules, logic? Yet, for example, Costello's interlocutors do not face a forced choice; nor is their failure of empathy and imagination determined by the logic of sovereignty. Quite the opposite—if there is a political dimension to their behavior, it has precisely to do with the way they *use* the authoritative appeal to the sovereignty of logic and rational discourse both to marginalize Costello and to avoid taking responsibility for this act. As Cavell repeatedly points out, appeals to the explanatory power of logic and sovereignty—let alone of the "logic of sovereignty"— often function to *deflect* from the terrifying realization that "human speech and activity, sanity and community" lack any foundation in rule or authority. Santner's claim that human beings' reaction to their ontological vulnerability *necessarily* traps them in the biopolitical defense mechanism of sovereignty, thus "'fattening' the flesh of creaturely life," ignores the variety of individual and collective responses to the contingency of human life, and with it, its full frailty.

---

164. Santner, *Royal Remains*, 21.

PART I

LIFE AS FORMATION

1

THE LIFE OF COGNITION AND THE
COGNITION OF LIFE (KANT)

> Forming concepts is a way of living and not a way of killing
> life.
>
> —MICHEL FOUCAULT, "LIFE: EXPERIENCE AND SCIENCE"

Kant's *Critique of the Power of Judgment* has the rare distinction
of having shaped not one but two discursive traditions. While Kant's
explication of the concept of organism in the second half of his book
provided a crucial "contribution to the constitution of biology as
an autonomous science,"[1] his analysis of the judgment of taste in
the first half is widely seen as helping to inaugurate modern aesthetics.

---

1. Camilla Warnke, "Naturmechanismus und Naturzweck: Bemerkungen zu
Kants Organismusbegriff," 45, cited in Toepfer, "Wechselseitigkeit—Organisation—
Teleologie: Die Bestimmungsstücke und die Einheit von Kants Organismusbeg-
riff," in *Kant und die Philosophie in weltbürgerlicher Absicht. Akten des XI. Inter-
nationalen Kant-Kongresses*, ed. Stefano Baccin, Alfredo Ferrarin, Caludio La
Rocca, and Margrit Ruffing (Berlin: de Gruyter, 2013), 5:278.

But if the *Critique of the Power of Judgment* opened up the conceptual space for a new thinking about nature and art, the institutionalization of this thinking, in turn, transformed the conceptual space that made it possible. With the differentiation of the university system in the nineteenth century, Kant's third *Critique* was increasingly carved up along disciplinary lines: scientists read the second ("biological") part of the book, while humanists focused on its first ("aesthetic") part. What got lost in this division of disciplinary labor was the most radical novelty—the true foundational act—of Kant's book: the way it draws organic life and aesthetic experience into a single overarching framework. Kant's contemporaries, unencumbered by disciplinary blinders, immediately discerned this common thread connecting the seemingly incongruous parts of Kant's great book, and even assigned it a rubric. Here is Goethe, reflecting in 1820 on the discursive event that was Kant's book:

> Then the *Critique of Judgment* fell into my hands, and with this book a wonderful period arrived in my life. Here I found my most disparate interests brought together; products of art and nature were dealt with alike, aesthetic and teleological judgment illuminated one another. . . . The inner life of art and nature, their respective effects as they work from within—all this came to clear expression in the book. ("Einwirkung der neueren Philosophie," FA 24:444)

"The inner life of art and nature": in what follows, I shall focus on this simple, if charged, phrase, suggesting that it points to the systematic and historical heart of Kant's book. My claim is that, contrary to Kant's own philosophical commitments, the *Critique of the Power of Judgment* inaugurates a new discourse of vitalism, the defining feature of which lies in its undercutting the boundary between cognitive and biological life. Hence the title of my chapter, which is meant to encapsulate the systematic connection between the new model of thinking and the new model of nature Kant develops in the two parts of the third *Critique*.

Scholarly discussions of "life" in the *Critique of the Power of Judgment* are usually restricted to the second part of the book, focusing on Kant's new concept of the organism. But the term "life" makes its appearance much earlier, in the opening paragraph of the book, where Kant describes the pleasure evoked by beautiful objects in terms of *Lebensgefühl* (feeling of life). This is no isolated occurrence: of the roughly seventy instances of the word or its compound forms *(lebendig, Lebenskraft, Lebensgefühl,* etc.), more than half occur in the first part of the *Critique of the Power of Judgment.* These numbers not only highlight the book's thematic unity, they also point toward a different interpretation of Kant's theory of aesthetic judgment. Kant's book articulates a new theory of beauty, but it also introduces a new model of thought. Beauty matters to Kant because it provides us with unique access to the *vitality* of the mind, a vitality at work in every judgment—in every act of thinking—but one ordinarily overlooked in the routines of cognition. Aesthetic experience brings to light this extraconceptual energetic dimension at the heart of our cognitive processes. It allows us to feel the organizing and purposive *activity* of our mind, its dynamic and "living" nature, which both generates and exceeds our use of concepts.

My goal in the following chapter is thus twofold. On the one hand, the aim is to articulate this new, dynamic image of thought that underlies Kant's discussion of aesthetic experience. On the other hand, I want to bring out the structural connections between Kant's new model of thought and his new model of nature and organic form. I claim that these two tasks are interwoven, and that Kant develops an overarching framework that allows him to describe thought and nature as two sides of a single, if merely speculative, unity. Kant never called this unity "life," and indeed seemed to believe that the only possible name for it would be "God." But many of Kant's readers, seizing on the explanatory thread he himself had laid out, derived from his book a vitalism that traversed thinking and organism, affect and body, politics and biology. It is from Kant's new naturalism, what we might call a *second* naturalism, that the vitalist discourse of subsequent centuries will draw some of its defining principles.

A Feeling of Life

Kant highlights the connection between aesthetic experience and "life" from the very beginning of the *Critique of the Power of Judgment*. The "Analytic of the Beautiful" opens as follows:

> In order to decide whether or not something is beautiful, we do not relate the representation by means of understanding to the object for cognition, but rather relate it by means of the imagination (perhaps combined with the understanding) to the subject and its feeling of pleasure or displeasure. The judgment of taste is therefore not a logical one, but is rather aesthetic, by which is understood one whose determining ground *cannot* be *other than subjective*. Any relation of representations, however, even that of sensations, can be objective (in which case it signifies what is real in an empirical representation) but not the relation to the feeling of pleasure and displeasure, by means of which nothing at all in the object is designated, but in which the subject feels itself as it is affected by the representation.
>
> To grasp a regular, purposive structure with one's faculty of cognition (whether the manner of representation be distinct or confused) is something entirely different from being conscious of this representation with the sensation of satisfaction. Here the representation is related entirely to the subject, indeed to its feeling of life [*Lebensgefühl*], under the name of the feeling of pleasure or displeasure, which grounds an entirely special faculty for discriminating and judging that contributes nothing to cognition but only holds the given representation in the subject up to the entire faculty of representation, of which the mind becomes conscious in the feeling of its state. (KU §1, 5:203–4; CPJ 89–90)

Our aesthetic encounter with the object sets into motion another encounter within ourselves. Instead of grasping an external object, we turn our attention inward and, in sensing the effect of the presented object on body and mind, feel ourselves. The feeling aroused in this process is not simply pleasure or displeasure but something more profound. Pleasure and displeasure are only modifications of the more basic sensation that forms the affective core of aesthetic experience: the "feeling of life" (*Lebensgefühl*). The experience of beauty thus draws attention to what would appear to be most basic about us: the sense of our own aliveness. What could be more ordinary and less philosophical than this feeling? And why does Kant, of all people, assign to the murky term *Lebensgefühl*, which had been coined only a few years earlier in literary texts of the *Sturm und Drang*,[2] such a prominent place at the beginning of his third *Critique*? As we shall see, the notion of *Lebensgefühl* carries enormous philosophical weight within Kant's argument. Coupled with the proper kind of awareness and framed within the context of an inquiry into the human ability to form judgments, the feeling of life provides the "basis of a very special power of discriminating and judging"—the basis, that is, of aesthetic taste and its underlying operation of reflective judgment, which is the central topic of Kant's entire book. It can do this because the sort, or rather the *form*, of life in question here is not the bare fact of existence or animation, whatever this might amount to, but what Kant takes to be the defining condition of being human—the condition of being at once perceptually and conceptually *engaged*.

Kant was, of course, not the first to associate beauty with life. His description of aesthetic pleasure as *Lebensgefühl*—or as he will specify, as *"Gefühl der Beförderung des Lebens"* (KU §23, 5:244)—echoes an older rhetorical tradition that had emphasized the power of specific tropes to create lively locutions and images.[3] In the poetics of the Renaissance, which in turn drew on Roman reflections on *ekphrasis*, "vividness" referred to the expressiveness of successful aesthetic representation. Alexander Baumgarten's *Aesthetica* (1750) redefined the trope for philosophical discourse.[4]

---

2. The term appears first in writings by Friedrich Müller, Gottfried August Bürger, and Goethe. See Jacob and Wilhelm Grimm, *Deutsches Wörterbuch* (entry *Lebensgefühl*).

3. Frank Fehrenbach, "'Das lebendige Ganze, das zu allen unsern geistigen und sinnlichen Kräften spricht.' Goethe und das Zeichnen," in *Goethe und die Verzeitlichung der Natur*, ed. Peter Matussek (Munich: C. H. Beck, 1998), 128–56; Fehrenbach, "Lebendigkeit," in *Metzlers Lexikon Kunstwissenschaft. Ideen Methoden, Begriffe*, ed. Ulrike Pfisterer (Stuttgart: Metzler, 2003), 222–27. See also Gottfried Boehm, "Der Topos des Lebendigen. Bildgeschichte und ästhetische Erfahrung," in *Dimensionen ästhetischer Erfahrung*, ed. Joachim Küpper and Christoph Menke (Frankfurt am Main: Suhrkamp, 2003), 94–112.

4. On Baumgarten, see John H. Zammito, *The Genesis of Kant's Critique of Judgment* (Chicago: University of Chicago Press, 1992), 19–21; Paul Guyer, "Origins of Modern Aesthetics: 1711–1735," in *The Blackwell Guide to Aesthetics*, ed. Peter Kivy (Malden, MA: Blackwell, 2004), 15–44; Menke, *Kraft*, esp. 46–66; and the older but still informative books by Alfred Bäumler, *Das Irrationalitätsproblem*

Located between the clear, formal, and potentially "empty" language of universal concepts and the vibrant but "blind" intuitions of the senses, the *representatio vivida* of art provided an intermediary type of representation that, due to its extensive, detailed clarity, was uniquely capable of picturing the specificity of individuals and singularities. Baumgarten thus began to carve out an epistemological rather than rhetorical space for the legitimacy of art, whose vividness he contrasted with the "selectivity, abstractness, feature-poverty and normative non-affectivity of theoretical cognition."[5]

Important though Baumgarten's writings are for Kant, his appropriation of the language of aesthetic life marks a fundamental break with tradition. For Kant, *Leben* is not a quality of the sign but of the aesthetically engaged subject, and *Lebensgefühl* is a feeling that brings the subject into contact with her own existence. Kant inaugurates modern aesthetics by directing the reflection on beauty to a specific mode of (human) experience. And at the heart of this experience he places the mysterious notion of "life," no longer understood as the making vivid of what is dead—as artistic *Verlebendigung*, a term Kant tellingly does not use—but as the subject's joyful awareness of her own rational vitality.

This reworking of the rhetorical tradition goes hand in hand with another momentous semantic shift: Kant's recalibration of the concept of *aesthesis*.[6] In the tradition stemming from Aristotle and culminating in medieval philosophy, *aesthesis* referred to the role of sense perception. Framed by Aristotle's injunction that no knowledge is possible without sensual perception, without *aesthesis*, the

---

in der Ästhetik und Logik des 18. Jahrhunderts bis zur Kritik der Urteilskraft (Darmstadt: Wissenschaftliche Buchgesellschaft, 1974; original publication 1915), esp. 198–231 and Ernst Cassirer, *The Philosophy of the Enlightenment* (Boston, MA: Beacon Press, 1962), 338–57.

5. Winfried Menninghaus, "'Ein Gefühl der Beförderung des Lebens.' Kants Reformulierung des Topos 'lebhafter Vorstellung,'" in *Vita aesthetica. Szenen ästhetischer Lebendigkeit*, ed. Armen Avanessian, Winfried Menninghaus, Jan Völker (Zürich: diaphanes, 2009), 79.

6. For a good overview of the history of the concept, see Joachim Ritter, "Ästhetik, ästhetisch," in *Historisches Wörterbuch der Philosophie*, ed. Joachim Ritter and Karlfried Gründer (Basel: Schwabe, 1972), 1:555–81.

notion was squarely placed within the context of questions of epistemic access. This was still its place in the *Critique of Pure Reason,* where, under the heading "Transcendental Aesthetics," Kant outlines the pure forms of intuition (space and time) that determine and shape inner and outer experience. The redefinition of aesthetic life in the *Critique of the Power of Judgment* breaks with this traditional epistemic context. Rather than being a faculty or power of cognitive reception, *aesthesis* is now seen to operate outside the epistemic frame of knowledge and truth. Yet this separation of beauty from truth, as we shall see, is only the first move in a complex argument that reconnects sensibility with thinking, albeit on a radically new and systematically elevated level. It is in our perceptual encounter with beauty, and *only* there, that we become fully aware of the creativity of our minds, of thinking as vital activity rather than product. Kant's separation of *aesthesis* from knowledge does not signify a rejection of cognition but a surprising expansion of what it means to think. The two lines of Kant's appropriation of the traditional language of aesthetic experience—the trope of aesthetic vividness and the notion of *aesthesis*—meet in his conception of beauty as the experience of what I will call *the life of cognition.*

Kant approaches the task of bringing out the vitality of thinking through an analysis of aesthetic judgments. His approach in the opening sections resembles the procedures of twentieth-century ordinary language philosophy. What, he asks, do we really mean when we say "this is beautiful," what kinds of claims, assumptions, and commitments are implied in this statement? Kant's analysis amounts to showing that a judgment of taste ("this is beautiful") really contains *two* judgments. What looks at first sight like an ordinary, empirical judgment about an object—Kant speaks of "logical" judgments (AA 20:223; CPJ 26)—yields on closer inspection a second judgment that points in the opposite direction. In Beatrice Longuenesse's words, "This second judgment, imbedded, as it were, in the first (or in the predicate of the first), and which only the critique of taste brings to discursive clarity, is a judgment no longer about the object, but about the judging subjects, namely the subjects that pass the judgment: 'this rose is beautiful,' 'this painting is beautiful', and so on."[7] In other words, even though a judgment of taste assumes the logical form of ordinary predication, in which an object (the grammatical subject: "this rose," "this painting," etc.) is brought under a concept (the predicate: "beautiful"), it turns out to be something entirely different: rather than attributing a property to a thing, it is a *report on the feeling* that the attempted cognition of the thing generates in the beholder.

This double structure of aesthetic judgment highlights a crucial feature of aesthetic experience. Aesthetic experience begins with the subject's inability to bring the object in front of it under an adequate concept; it begins with a cognitive stumble.[8] Something in the object resists conceptualization and overwhelms our understanding. Moreover, this resistance is not merely a temporary glitch on the path to conceptual accomplishment; the incomprehensibility is structural, an essential, indeed insurmountable, dimension of our experience with beautiful objects. Yet here the phenomenological puzzle begins. For instead of experiencing our failure of understanding as frustrating or unpleasant, or as occasioning disinterest or distraction, we draw enjoyment from it. Beauty throws us, shoulders us out of our epistemic and practical routines—*and* it exhilarates us. This pleasure is unlike any other pleasure we know. Unlike ordinary pleasant objects, such as apples or hot showers, beautiful objects get our mind going, make us think, reflect, speculate about them; yet, unlike ordinary objects of cognition, they remain at bottom incomprehensible, thus thwarting the satisfaction

---

7. Béatrice Longuenesse, "Kant's Leading Thread in the Analytic of the Beautiful," in *Kant on the Human Standpoint* (Cambridge: Cambridge University Press, 2005), 265.

8. There is disagreement in the literature on this point. Whereas Longuenesse claims that aesthetic judgments "fail" in their attempt at concept formation, Henry Allison argues that they cannot fail because concept formation is not their goal. I think both are right and that Longuenesse, in her response to Allison, puts the matter nicely by saying that "aesthetic judgments *start* where the search for concepts collapses" (Longuenesse's emphasis). See Henry Allison, *Kant's Theory of Taste: A Rereading of the Critique of Judgment* (Cambridge: Cambridge University Press, 2001), 354, and Béatrice Longuenesse, "Kant's Theory of Judgment, and Judgments of Taste: On Henry Allison's *Kant's Theory of Taste*," *Inquiry* 46, no. 2 (2003): 146.

of conceptual understanding. So why do we enjoy what looks like an intellectual failure? What is the source and nature of this other kind of enjoyment? And what does it, or our capacity for it, say about the kind of creatures that we are?

Kant's answer to these questions involves nothing less than a new model of thought. The fact that we remain cognitively engaged with beautiful objects even though we are unable to assign adequate concepts to them reveals the true breadth of thinking, which exceeds cognition as traditionally understood. Beauty pushes us beyond, and in this sense exposes, the limitations of *conceptual* knowledge. It shows that there is more to thinking than the assignment of concepts; there is the spontaneous *activity* of thinking itself, which highlights what might be called the imaginative mobility of the mind. Moreover, as we shall see in more detail, aesthetic cognition, which is characterized by the mind's desire to prolong and reproduce its pleasurable state—"We *linger* in our contemplation of the beautiful, because this contemplation reinforces and reproduces itself" (AA 5:222; CPJ 107)—exhibits thinking as a self-regulating and self-fulfilling activity, a "purposiveness without a purpose," freed from practical and theoretical goals. And in making us feel this self-reproductive dynamic of the mind, which both resembles and differs from the self-reproduction of biological life, aesthetic contemplation grants us experiential access to the *life of cognition*, and thus to the form of life that we, as human beings, are.

Statistics of the Mind

The model of thought that emerges from Kant's discussion of beauty is no longer centered on the labor of conceptualization, on subsuming particulars under general concepts; it is a more dynamic and energetic model of thinking as creative synthetic activity, as the mind's power to forge connections, draw distinctions, construct form.

To gauge the dynamism of this model, we must first get a clearer sense of Kant's picture of ordinary cognition, which aesthetic experience both begins with and transcends. A short detour through the

Critique of Pure Reason will help. According to the first *Critique*, empirical knowledge depends on the interplay of three faculties: intuition, imagination, and understanding. Intuition (*Anschauung*) receives sensual data and organizes it in terms of space and time, thus making possible the apprehension of singular objects, while understanding (*Verstand*) subsumes and unifies the intuitively represented singular object under general concepts and rules. However, it is the imagination (*Einbildungskraft*) that does the crucial work of bridging the gap between intuition and understanding.[9] This mediation is necessary because the singular representations provided by intuition and the general rules furnished by understanding are epistemically incongruous. To give a simple example: my intuition of a dog is bound to the perceptual presence of *this* spatial configuration in front of me, at this particular moment in time.[10] That dogs come in different sizes and colors, that they sometimes run and often sleep, that some have long tails and others cropped ones—all of this, and much more that belongs to particular dogs or the accident of my encounter with them, is absent from the concept "dog," which is scarce in content and thus incongruous with particulars and their qualitative complexity. Thus few of the details of my current intuition pass the threshold of conceptual abstraction: the peculiar way my dog responds to his name, the smell of his wet fur, his precise markings—these "accidental" features are not part of the concept "dog." Even if we leave aside the still more vexing problem of how the categories—that is, the *pure* concepts of understanding as opposed to empirical concepts—are related to sensibility, it is clear that the operations of understanding and intuition are too incongruous to produce, by themselves, empirical cognitions.

This is where imagination enters the picture. In Kant's model, imagination acts as a go-between that connects the disparate faculties of intuition and understanding. The faculty of imagination is able to accomplish this task because it is a kind of mental nomad, trafficking between sensibility and rationality without being be-

---

9. See in particular the chapter "On the Schematism of the Pure Concepts of the Understanding" (A 137/B 176–A 147/B 187).

10. See A 141/B 181.

holden to either. Unlike understanding, it produces images rather than concepts; yet, unlike intuition, these images do not depend on immediate sensory contact. The German word *Einbildungskraft* aptly captures this ambiguity. Understood as fancy or fantasy, *Einbildung* points to the power of imagination to see more than what is before the eyes; whereas intuition is bound to perceptually present objects, the images of the *Einbildungskraft* are composed of past and possible representations. However, understood according to its other, literal sense—as the power to coin images—the term highlights imagination's productive nature, the fact that it *creates* images rather than simply mirroring them. "Imagination," Kant writes in the *Critique of Pure Reason*, "has to bring the manifold of intuitions into the form of an image," (A 120), and in the *Critique of the Power of Judgment* he specifies this formative labor as imagination's "power of exhibition [*Vermögen der Darstellung*]" (KU §49, 5:314; my translation).

How exactly this production of images and its interplay with understanding work is rather obscure, as Kant himself admits in the *Critique of Pure Reason*, where he calls imagination "a blind but indispensable power of the soul, without which we should have no knowledge whatsoever, but of which we are scarcely ever conscious" (A 78/B 103). But in a seemingly marginal comment in the *Critique of the Power of Judgment*, Kant speculates about this "blind but indispensable power" of the imagination in ways that illuminate its contribution to conceptual thought. In the context of a critique of the traditional notion of "ideal beauty," Kant writes:

> It should be noted that the imagination does not only know how to recall for us occasionally signs of concepts, even after a long time, in a way that is entirely incomprehensible to us; it also knows how to reproduce the image and shape of an object out of an immense number of objects of different kinds, or even of one and the same kind; indeed, when the mind is set on making comparisons, it even knows how, by all accounts actually if not consciously, as it were to superimpose one image on another and by means of the congruence of several of the same kind to arrive at a mean [*ein Mittleres*] that can serve them all as a common measure [*gemeinschaftlichen Maß*]. Someone has seen a thousand grown men. Now if he would judge what should be estimated as their comparatively normal size, then (in my opinion) the imagination allows a great

number of images (perhaps a thousand) to be superimposed on one another, and, if I may here apply the analogy of optical presentation, in the space where the greatest number of them coincide and within the outline of the place that is illuminated by the most concentrated colors, there the average size [*mittlere Größe*] becomes recognizable, which is in both height and breadth equidistant from the most extreme boundaries of the largest and smallest statures; and this is the stature for a beautiful man. (One could get the same result mechanically if one measured all thousand men, added up their heights, widths (and girths) and then divided the sum by a thousand. But the imagination does just this by means of a dynamic effect, which arises from the repeated apprehension of such figures on the organ of inner sense.) (KU §17, 5:234; CPJ 118–19)

The passage provides an account of the work of schematization in ordinary empirical cognition. The work of imagination here is completely mundane, in fact so mundane that even "the most common experience would not be possible without it" (AA 5:187; CPJ 74), as Kant writes in the introduction. Yet something rather wondrous happens at the heart of the ordinary. Far from being a passive act of taking in a fully formed world, "the most common experience" is the result of a complex act of mediation and data processing performed by the imagination, which reconciles two "realities": the irregular appearances of the senses on the one hand, and the lofty regularities of abstract concepts on the other. If imagination functions as a bridge between intuition and understanding, between the multifariousness of experience and the austerity of the concept, this is because it presents the particular in such a way as to prepare it for its placement under concepts. The passage describes this preparation in terms of visual standardization. To stick with our earlier example, superimposing past representations of dogs, the imagination produces an average image—a standardized dog—which, due to its schematic nature, is sufficiently abstract to generate in the understanding a definition or rule, as it were, for doghood, that can subsequently be summoned when an appropriate intuition presents itself. Imagination thus effects a kind of figurative synthesis: faced with countless details, it extracts and combines select common features, creating an empirically saturated image of something that exists neither in appearance nor understanding—the average dog or man.

What should we make of this fantastic translation of the particular into the average? Two interpretations suggest themselves. One places imagination's labor in a kind of master-slave matrix, stressing not only imagination's hidden character—doing invisible cognitive work while the understanding gets all the credit—but also its socializing nature. This reading highlights the fact that the formation of images unfolds under the auspices of the understanding, which provides the principles of unity and selection that guide the imagination's combinatory work. Under ordinary cognitive circumstances, it would seem, the imagination is only allowed to generate images of things for which there are concepts, that is, combinatory rules. The average image thus appears as the product of an imagination that has thoroughly "internalized" the norms of rationality.

However, while not inaccurate, this reading only tells part of the story. It downplays the slave's contribution, as it were, ignoring the dialectical interplay characteristic of the master-slave model. The averaging of the singular is not simply a matter of flattening the multiplicity of experience; it also refashions and organizes it. Faced with innumerable variants and details, the imagination extracts their common features and combines them into a single image. It condenses and compresses, transforming, through a process of imagistic welding, disparate bits of information into a gestalt that is neither found nor merely invented. So conceived, far from being a mere mechanical leveling, standardization is the creative translation of the pure particulars into an exemplar, an operation we might liken to the distillation of an essential form. To be sure, Kant limits the range of imaginative creativity, insisting that the work of schematization, or *picturing*, unfolds under the oversight of the understanding and in the service of cognition and concept formation. But while the labor of imagination is subservient to the rule of the understanding, understanding is also dependent on the imagination's capacity for unifying the diverse contours of appearances, which capacity it neither possesses itself nor is capable of governing. The imagination is free and self-determined in the sense that it alone can synthesize appearances into images.

Note that in Kant's model, imagination's power to transcend the immediacy of perception is not opposed to that which counts for the subject as empirical reality but is in fact a necessary condition of it. The average man or dog exists in the imagination alone, a fictional image without immediate empirical referent. Yet it is precisely such fictional images that, in bridging sensibility and understanding, make possible the identification of something *as* something, thereby constituting phenomenal reality as a site of experience and empirical knowledge. In other words, our experience of the world as a universe of *kinds* of things and beings, as well ordered and comprehensible, would seem to depend crucially on the imagination's power of standardization.

Let me widen the lens for a moment and place Kant's comments in a larger historical and political context. Recent studies have drawn attention to the development and explosive proliferation of statistical knowledge in the eighteenth century, in particular in Germany. Ian Hacking's *The Taming of Chance*, which begins with developments in Prussia around 1800, and more recently Paul Fleming's *Exemplarity and Mediocrity* and Rüdiger Campe's *The Game of Probability*, which track statistical thought within eighteenth- and nineteenth-century literature, have convincingly shown that from the mid-eighteenth century onward statistical reasoning played a pivotal role in areas as diverse as health policy, economics, and novel writing.[11] Kant, to whom Fleming and Campe devote illuminating pages, was part of this trend. He was familiar with contemporary work on statistics and made use of it,[12] for instance, in the opening page of his "Idea for a Universal History from a Cosmopolitan Standpoint" (1784).[13] Arguing that the regularity of birth, death, and marriage suggests the workings of a law that operates independently of will and intention, Kant proposes to conceive of historical development in terms of the "play of freedom in the human will *in the large*"[14]—

---

11. Ian Hacking, *Taming of Chance* (Cambridge: Cambridge University Press, 1990); Paul Fleming, *Exemplarity and Mediocrity: The Art of the Average from Bourgeois Tragedy to Realism* (Stanford, CA: Stanford University Press, 2009); Rüdiger Campe, *The Game of Probability: Literature and Calculation from Pascal to Kleist* (Stanford, CA: Stanford University Press, 2013).

12. See Campe, *Game of Probability*, 338–68.

13. AA 8:15–32; *On History*, 11–26.

14. AA 8:17; *On History*, 11; my emphasis.

that is, as a type of (historical) causality that works behind the scenes of personal agency. But the use of the statistical language of standardization in the *Critique of the Power of Judgment* is different and perhaps more intriguing. Here Kant seems to extend statistical analysis into the seemingly subjective operations of the imagination. Rather than applying statistical models to empirical facts (births, deaths, etc.), Kant suggests that our very processing of experience is the result of the mind's own quasi-statistical calculations. The law of large numbers operates at the heart of the subject, and moreover at a level that precedes consciousness and reflection. One effect of this shift is to highlight the creative character of standardization. The production of standards is an imaginative act, the making of something new. A standard, so conceived, is the mind's active response to an environment characterized by an excess of perceptual detail and stimuli on the one hand, and to a faculty of understanding that demands unity and generality on the other. However, since imaginative standardization works in the service of creating empirical concepts, the former's dynamism extends to the latter, highlighting knowledge production as a vital activity, as the mind's dynamic engagement with a constantly changing world.

This claim is not meant to dehistoricize the rise of statistics but to reframe the historiographic narrative. Hacking and, before him, Foucault have linked the rise of statistical knowledge to developments in governmental technologies, and in particular to the emergence of new "biopolitical" arts of governance. According to Foucault, in extracting regularities from the contingent and fleeting facts of empirical reality, governmental techniques that make use of statistical reasoning bring "life and its mechanisms into the realm of explicit calculations."[15] Statistical knowledge thus helps to replace an older model of power in which subjects are held in check primarily through physical force and prohibitive law with a more adaptive system of power, which conceives of the citizenry as a vital resource, and of politics as the art of stimulating and regulating this resource. The principal goal of biopolitical power, Foucault writes, is not the "repression of disorder, but an ordered maximization of

---

15. Foucault, *The History of Sexuality, Volume 1*, 143.

individual and collective forces."[16] While Foucault, like the Kant of the *Idea* essay, focuses on the physical and biological life of populations, Kant's reflections in the *Critique of the Power of Judgment* apply probability to the *interior*—cognitive, psychical, imaginative—life of human beings. But note the fundamental structural similarities between the two models. Like biopolitical normativity, Kant's imaginative standardization, rather than superimposing abstract laws on reality, extracts order and regularity from it. Moreover, in both cases this reality is emphatically understood as fleeting and dynamic—as "living." The crucial difference is that the account in the *Critique of the Power of Judgment* extends the dynamism of the Real beyond empirical reality into the very heart of the subject, and in so doing reframes empirical thinking in ways that highlight its creative and productive character. Imagination emerges as the vital kernel of the mind, as the driving force in thinking, which in its totality is now conceived of as a particular *form of life*, that is, as *cognitive life*.

To be clear, I am not suggesting that Kant's account of imaginative standardization is "biopolitical" in the sense that it applies the new logic of power to subjectivity. Rather, my point is to place Foucault's account in a broader historical context and make visible connections between developments in economics and politics on the one hand, and changes in epistemology, aesthetics, and the conception of subjectivity on the other. The rise of statistical models to measure birth rate, longevity, fluctuations of prices, and so on goes hand in hand with an increasingly dynamic understanding of the mind. What links the seemingly disparate discourses on health policies and the imagination is the attempt to devise models that take account of a reality conceived as active and productive, as a "living" force. Thus if we want to gain a more fine-grained picture of what Foucault describes as the "entry of life into history,"[17] we need to go beyond the study of biology and populations and track the emergence of, and interplay between, multiple forms of "life": organic and biopolitical, but also cognitive and psychic life. And to

---

16. Ibid., 24–25.
17. Ibid., 142.

do this is to reintroduce into Foucault's account of modernity a dimension of social practice that disappears from his writings after 1970: literature, arts, and aesthetics.

A Play of Faculties

Let me return to Kant's text itself. Imaginative standardization tells us something interesting about the mind, but it does not yet tell us much about *aesthetic* perception. In fact, the discussion of the average image in §17 serves the negative purpose of highlighting the *difference* between beauty and knowledge: "An ideal of beautiful flowers, of beautiful furnishings, of a beautiful view, cannot be conceived" (KU §17, 5:233; CPJ 117). Beauty and average image thus stand in a complex relation to each other. On the one hand, they exclude each other. An object appears beautiful only when the imagination *fails* to picture it as a visual type, as an average image. Faced with an object that gives the mind as it were *too much* to see, the process of coordinating image and concept remains incompletable, thwarting the attempt to identify and cognize the object. On the other hand, this failure of cognition throws into relief the *activity* of cognizing, and in particular imagination's creative work in extracting form from reality. It is precisely because beauty provides us with no determinable knowledge that it gives us access to the formative nature of thinking, thus enabling us to recognize, indeed feel and bodily experience, a drive within us that we also recognize in external nature: the drive toward the realization of kinds and the articulation of form.

But let us go slowly and spell out in more detail how aesthetic cognition draws on and inflects ordinary cognition. Kant makes two claims: First, the beautiful object cannot be subsumed under a concept. This is not to say that in contemplating it the beholder forms no concepts, but merely that the process of reflection never resolves into a final judgment and propositional claim—into a "this is that (kind of object)." Radically singular, the beautiful object is, strictly speaking, inconceivable, outside the grasp of concept and imaginative standardization. Second, beauty is not merely outside received knowledge but actively disturbs our ordinary ways of thinking. Aesthetic experience owes the vibrancy of its mental and affective structure to the *disruption* of the quasi-statistical mechanisms at work in ordinary cognition. The inadequacy of concepts to which beauty exposes us stimulates our mind and thrills us.

As we saw, cognition involves the interplay of three faculties, intuition, imagination, and understanding: Intuition gathers sense-data and unifies it into temporally and spatially localizable representations; imagination reproduces previous or possible perceptions, combining them into more abstract (average) images; and understanding subsumes this schematic image under a concept, thus making possible its recognition as a certain kind of thing. In ordinary, or propositional, cognition, the relation between (2) and (3) is structured hierarchically; the synthesis of multiple perceptions into the average image (2) is governed by the concept of the object (3), which means that imagination operates according to a rule given to it by the understanding. In the case of beautiful objects, the understanding fails to provide such an organizing concept, so that the imagination is no longer bound to a particular rule—a particular concept[18]—that prescribes the synthesis of multiple intuitions into a single average image. As a result, the faculties involved in the act of grasping the object—imagination and understanding—engage in a constant back-and-forth, reciprocally stimulating one another, a mental activity that communicates itself to the subject as a feeling of intellectual vitality:

> The powers of cognition that are set into play by this representation are hereby in a free play, since no determinate concept restricts them to a particular rule of cognition. (KU §9, 5:217; CPJ 102)
>
> Only where the imagination in its freedom arouses the understanding, and the latter, without concepts, sets the imagination into a regular play is the representation communicated, not as a thought, but as the inner feeling of a purposive state of mind. (KU §40, 5:296; CPJ 175–76)

---

18. For Kant, a concept articulates a rule for subsuming particulars. See for instance his formulation that the "concept of a dog signifies a rule in accordance with which my imagination can specify the shape of a four-footed animal in general, without being restricted to any single particular shape" (A 141; B 180).

The repeated emphasis on the "freedom" of the imagination is crucial. The imagination is free not only from the understanding but also from its own regulative routines. Lacking a rule that tells it what *kind* of thing to look for, the imagination cannot draw on the record of its own activity and model its current task of imaging the object on its stock of past images. Aesthetic experience, we might say, allows the imagination to let go of its own protorational mechanisms of standardization, inviting it to engage the object in front of it in new and fresh ways.[19] And this freeing of imagination from its own past allows it to enter into a new and stimulating dialogue with the understanding. Forming images for which there are not yet any concepts, the imagination *spurs on* the understanding to grasp what is put before it, setting into motion a mental play that Kant, drawing on a musical metaphor, describes as a self-tuning of the faculties, or as a "reciprocal subjective attunement between the cognitive powers [*einer wechselseitigen subjektiven Übereinstimmung der Erkenntniskräfte untereinander*]" (KU §9, 5:218; my translation).

Note that there is no technician or musician that tunes the strings of the mind. Rather, the intuition of an external object sets into motion an activity whereby the parts of the mind, through a feedback loop, tune *one other*. The result of this reciprocal attunement is a pleasing mental "chord"; a mood—or *Stimmung*[20]—in which, as in consonant musical chords, the simultaneous interplay of different tones, or in this case, faculties, produces a complex yet harmonious effect. And Kant's musical taste is distinctly classical. The well-balanced and agreeable "chord" is based on the properly proportional attunement of the powers of the mind. Beauty puts us in a sound mood (*Stimmung*).

---

19. We can discern here a line of argument that runs straight from Kant to the Russian Formalists and their influential concept of "defamiliarization" (*ostranenie*). See Viktor Sklovsky, "Art, as Device," *Poetics Today* 36, no. 3 (2015): 151–74.

20. German *Stimmung* can be translated as both "mood" and "attunement," and clearly Kant's term is meant to cover both. In addition, the term calls up *Stimme* (voice) and thus language, speech, and communication. For an excellent study of the concept of *Stimmung*, see David Wellbery, "Stimmung," in *Ästhetische Grundbegriffe*, vol. 5, ed. Karlheinz Barck et al. (Stuttgart: Metzler, 2003), 703–33, who credits Kant with introducing the term into aesthetic discourse.

The polysemy of *Stimmung* obviously reaches into yet another semantic field, that of voice and speech. But before we can fully gauge the communicative and political dimension of aesthetic life, we must first get a clearer sense of the subjective character of "attunement." *Stimmung* names something that, prior to the *Critique of the Power of Judgment*, is unthinkable within Kant's system: a *nonconceptual* unity, or, perhaps better, an activity of unification without unity. For the Kant of the first two *Critiques*, unification (of perception, object, action, consciousness) depends on conceptual synthesis, whether by empirical concept, category, or idea.[21] In fact, although Kant's table of categories assigns to the concept of "unity" a subordinate place, the notion functions as a kind of metaconcept of rationality in that *all* operations of understanding and reason involve unification, and all achieve formal unity by way of concepts.[22] The unity of "attunement" in aesthetic experience is different. Not only is it horizontal rather than vertical, based on the proportion *between* understanding and imagination rather than on their hierarchical arrangement; the attunement of the mind also occurs freely and spontaneously, without intervention of concepts. Aesthetic experience thus allows Kant to develop a new model of unity: a unity not of concept and object but of the free association of voices.

From this perspective, objects of beauty are not, strictly speaking, "objects." Recall that for Kant, "an object is that in the concept of which the manifold of a given intuition is united" (B 138). Concepts synthesize a motley array of phenomenal features into fixed and circumscribed "objects." Object and concept are thus, for

---

21. For a good account of the conceptual status of unity in Kant's philosophy, see Susan Neiman, *The Unity of Reason: Rereading Kant* (Oxford: Oxford University Press, 1997).

22. As for the distinction and connection between the unity of understanding and the unity of reason, see the following concise comment from the first *Critique*: "The understanding may be considered a power of providing unity of appearances by means of rules; reason is then the power of providing unity of the rules of understanding under principles. Hence reason initially never deals with experience or any object, but deals with the understanding in order to provide the understanding's manifold cognitions with a priori unity through concepts" (A 302). The concepts through which reason achieves this meta-unity are, of course, the ideas.

Kant, two sides of the same coin: no concept without object, and no object without concept. This means that aesthetic judgments, which lack a determining concept, are neither objective nor objectifying. Instead of combining multiple impressions into identifiable things, aesthetic experience throws into relief the activity of the mind itself. It is in this strong sense that the attunement of the mind in aesthetic experience is nonobjective and indeed subjective. Foucault, juxtaposing the ancient idea of an aesthetics of existence to the modern conception of art, wrote that "what strikes me is that, in our society, art has become something that is related only to objects and not to individuals or life."[23] Nothing could be further from Kant's theory. For Kant, the relevant dimension of the apprehension of beauty, of aesthetic judgment, resides not in the object of apprehension but in the formative powers of the subject; aesthetic experience discloses, not the fixed unity of an object, but the dynamic coherence of the mind.

A simple objection might be raised at this point: is not insight into the spontaneous and sense-making character of the human mind the hallmark of Kant's *entire* transcendental philosophy? After all, Kant's main juggling act in the first *Critique* was to "preserve a full-blooded sense of objectivity, but to give a philosophical account which revealed it as dependent upon mind."[24] On the transcendental picture, as we saw, what it is to be an "object" cannot be understood without reference to the synthetic activity of our mind that structures a heterogeneous array of intuitions *as* an object. So what is it that aesthetic judgments reveal about our mind that regular veridical judgments cannot? The answer, once again, has to do with the availability of standardized images. Even though in principle every cognitive act involves an element of constructive unification, in ordinary circumstances this labor of synthesizing, due to the availability of an archive of ready-made prior schematizations (average images), occurs so quickly as to remain unnoticed. This is what Kant

---

23. Michel Foucault, "On the Genealogy of Ethics," in *Ethics: Subjectivity and Truth*, ed. Paul Rabinow (New York: New York Press, 1997), 261.

24. Jonathan Lear, *Open-Minded: Working Out the Logic of the Soul* (Cambridge, MA: Harvard University Press, 1998), 254.

means by pointing out, in a remarkable passage in the introduction, that we no longer feel "any noticeable pleasure resulting from our being able to grasp nature" (AA 5:187; my translation). We have become cognitively jaded, insensitive to the complex inductive work we undertake to generate concepts of everyday objects. Thus we have lost touch with an archaic sense of wonder that "must certainly have been there in its time, and only because the most common experience would not be possible without it has it gradually become mixed up with mere cognition and is no longer specially noticed" (AA 5:187; CPJ 74). It is this wonder at our mind's ability to grasp reality, and at the equally wondrous fact that reality somehow accommodates our mind, fits our ways of understanding it, that aesthetic experience revives once again. Resisting its schematization via the average image, the irreducible singularity of the beautiful object redirects the beholder from the object to the cognitive processes involved in attempting to grasp it, and to the pleasures of cognition itself. Aesthetic experience upends our cognitive routines and revives a sense of wonder that has been buried under the crust of repetition.

The connection between beauty and knowledge is thus complicated. On the one hand, beauty defies the cognition of the object that instantiates it. On the other hand, it allows us to experience the cognitive purposiveness of our mind, its fitness for "cognition in general [*Erkenntnisvermögen im Allgemeinen*]," a formulation that Kant uses no fewer than thirteen times in the first part of the *Critique of the Power of Judgment*. Beauty provokes our cognitive expansiveness, the power of our mind to illuminate the world and give shape to it. And it is precisely in relation to this world-disclosing power of our mind' that Kant's use of the language of "life" becomes most pronounced. The purposive activity of the mind, without which no world and hence no objects could be known, can itself never become an object of knowledge, but must be felt. And what is felt is nothing other than the dynamic vitality—the life—of the mind:

The judgment of taste must rest on a mere sensation of the reciprocally animating imagination in its *freedom* and the understanding with its *lawfulness*, thus on a feeling. [*So muß das Geschmacksurteil auf einer bloßen Empfindung der sich wechselseitig belebenden Einbildungskraft* *in ihrer <u>Freiheit</u> und des Verstandes mit seiner <u>Gesetzmäßigkeit</u>, also auf einem Gefühl beruhen.*] (KU §35, 5:287; CPJ 167; Kant's emphasis)

Thus that subjective unity of the relation [between the cognitive powers] can make itself known only through sensation. The animation of both faculties (the imagination and the understanding) to an activity that is indeterminate but yet, through the stimulus of the given representation, in unison, namely that which belongs to a cognition in general, is the sensation whose universal communicability is postulated by the judgment of taste. [*Die Belebung beider Vermögen (der Einbildungskraft und des Verstandes) zu unbestimmter, aber doch vermittelst des Anlasses der gegebenen Vorstellung, einhelliger Tätigkeit, derjenigen nämlich, die zu einem Erkenntnis überhaupt gehört, ist die Empfindung, deren allgemeine Mittelbarkeit das Geschmacksurteil postuliert.*] (KU §9, 5:219; CPJ 104)

The Life of Cognition

Why depict aesthetic pleasure as a *"Gefühl der Beförderung des Lebens"* (KU §23, 5:244)? And why describe the contemplation of beauty in terms of a *"Belebung"* of the mind? Most commentators pay scant attention to Kant's talk of *Lebensgefühl*, presumably on the assumption that it represents a mere rhetorical flourish that has no bearing on the logic of the argument.[25] This indifference to

---

25. This has changed somewhat over the last twenty years or so. The main texts on the relation between Kant's discussion of life and his theory of aesthetic judgments are: Rudolf Makkreel, *Imagination and Interpretation in Kant: The Hermeneutical Import of the Critique of Judgment* (Chicago: Chicago University Press, 1995), 88–110; Menninghaus, "Ein Gefühl der Beförderung"; Longuenesse, "Kant's Leading Thread in the Analytic of the Beautiful"; Howard Caygill, "Life and Aesthetic Pleasure," in *The Matter of Critique: Readings in Kant's Philosophy*, ed. Andrea Rehberg and Rachel Jones (Manchester: Cinamen, 2000), 79–92; Michel Chaouli, *Thinking with Kant's Critique of Judgment* (Cambridge, MA: Harvard University Press, 2017), esp. 4–6 and 242–69; Ross Wilson, *Subjective Universality in Kant's Aesthetics* (Bern: Peter Lang, 1997), 109–46; and James Porter, "Beauty, Value, and the Aesthetics of Life in Kant and Aristotle," *Republics of Letters* 5, no. 1 (January 2017), https://arcade.stanford.edu/rofl/beauty-value-and-aesthetics -life-kant-and-aristotle. My own argument is closest to those of Menninghaus, Longuenesse, and Porter, all of whom emphasize the importance of Kant's use of the term "life" for an extended conception of what Kant calls *Gemüth*. On the other hand, Eckart Förster, in his otherwise excellent chapter on Kant's third *Critique* in his *Twenty-Five Years of Philosophy*, does not even mention Kant's notion

Kant's wording goes hand in hand with the claim that questions of life are central only to the second part of the *Critique*, where Kant discusses natural organisms and engages contemporary biological theories. But this view ignores not only the actual order of Kant's book; it makes the overall architecture of its argument incomprehensible. Kant's discussion of aesthetic and cognitive life—*Lebensgefühl*—prepares the ground for his analysis of organic form; it is only because thinking is a form of (nonbiological) life that we are capable of grasping nature as (biological) life.

Models of "life" structure Kant's depiction of the core of aesthetic contemplation, the "free play of the faculties." Kant's description of aesthetic play already touched upon in the above passages introduces and prefigures the new autopoietic model of natural life fleshed out in part 2—the theory of natural things as "*self-organizing* being[s]" endowed with a "self-propagating formative power [*eine sich fortpflanzende bildende Kraft*]" (KU §65, 5:374; CPJ 245–46; Kant's emphasis).[26] Thus before he introduces the idea of natural organisms, Kant describes the mind as a kind of living organism, and both the play of the faculties in aesthetic contemplation and the pleasure to which this play gives rise are self-organizing. We have already encountered the first instance of autopoiesis, pertaining to the play of faculties:

> *Spirit* [Geist], in an aesthetic significance, means the animating principle in the mind [*das belebende Prinzip im Gemüte*]. That, however, by which this principle animates [*belebt*] the soul, the material which it uses for this purpose, is that which purposively sets the mental powers into motion, i.e., into play that is self-maintaining and even strengthens the powers to that end. (KU §49, 5:313; CPJ 192; Kant's emphasis)

"Purposiveness" refers not, in this instance, to the fit between mind and world but applies to the mind's inner movement. The aesthetic

---

of a "feeling of life," even though his entire book is devoted to the attempt of philosophers around 1800 to intuit an underlying unity between nature and culture. See Förster's *The Twenty-Five Years of Philosophy: A Systematic Reconstruction*, trans. Brady Bowman (Cambridge, MA: Harvard University Press, 2012).

   26. See Menninghaus, "Ein Gefühl der Beförderung," 86. This part of my argument closely follows Menninghaus's excellent discussion.

play of the faculties is autopoietic for the obvious reasons that it "sustains itself on its own." It is purposive because it aims at sustaining *aesthetic play*, which is why it keeps going even though it does not result in conceptual cognition. In fact, precisely because it does not culminate in the cognition of an object, aesthetic contemplation throws into relief the *inner* organization and movement of the cognizing mind, whose parts (imagination and understanding) reciprocally strengthen one another. This autopoietic model also informs Kant's phenomenological description of aesthetic pleasure, which is distinguished from other forms of pleasure by its active and self-stimulating character:

> This pleasure is also in no way practical, neither like that from the pathological ground of agreeableness nor like that from the intellectual ground of the represented [moral] good. But yet it has a causality in itself, namely that of *maintaining* the state of [having] the representation of the mind and the occupation of the cognitive powers without a further aim [*nämlich den Zustand der Vorstellung selbst und die Beschäftigung der Erkenntniskräfte ohne weitere Absicht zu erhalten*]. We *linger* over the consideration of the beautiful because this consideration strengthens and reproduces itself [*Wir* weilen *bei der Betrachtung des Schönen, weil diese Betrachtung sich selbst verstärkt und reproduciert*], which is analogous to (yet not identical with) the way in which we linger when a charm in the representation of the object repeatedly attracts attention, where the mind is passive [*da ein Reiz in der Vorstellung des Gegenstandes die Aufmerksamkeit wiederholentlich erweckt, wobei das Gemüt passiv ist*]. (KU §12, 5:222; CPJ 107; Kant's emphasis)

Despite the hint at analogy, the passage is built on the contrast between aesthetic and nonaesthetic pleasure. Whereas the continuity of ordinary pleasure results from the mind's repetition of an external stimulation—"where the mind is passive"—aesthetic pleasure is the effect of a contemplation that "reinforces and reproduces itself." Kant's description of aesthetic contemplation is the site of a highly compressed discursive reappropriation. On the one hand, drawing on the new biological language of self-formation, Kant appropriates and recasts the traditional topos of aesthetic vividness. Understood as self-stimulation, "vividness" refers no longer to the quality of signs but to the activity of the subject: it is a form of

"*Selbst-Belebung*," and hence an example of the capacity of living things to organize and shape themselves. But on the other hand, Kant employs this biological language to highlight a feature of *cognitive* life. It is the play of mental faculties in aesthetic contemplation, not the interplay of organs in a biological organism, that is at issue. Furthermore, this self-stimulation of the mind displays an orientation toward the world—a pleasant lingering in the contemplation of the beautiful, without practical goals—that is qualitatively different from the reproductive and nutritive orientation of biological life as such. Winfried Menninghaus captures the logic of Kant's intervention concisely: "In conformity with his transcendental perspective, Kant shifts the focus from the vividness of representations themselves and their mechanically conceived effect on the beholder to a self-strengthening—and above all self-feeling—activity within the subject. The causality of aesthetic pleasure in the autopoietic 'lingering' points to a temporally indefinite space-time ecstasis of heightened vitality. Thus Kant employs the autopoietic model for the description of a particular sensual-mental state, a state which, for all its connection to the biology of living material, nonetheless captures a highly specific and qualitatively distinct mode of a 'feeling of life of the subject.'"[27]

Kant's use of the language of life thus cuts two ways. On the one hand, it functions to emphasize the continuity between nature and mind, suggesting that thinking and judging are natural to the human form of life, activities through which we, the human species, express our vitality. On the other hand, terms like *Belebung* and *Lebensgefühl* are employed to highlight the difference between human and (merely) biological life; that is, the mere maintenance of organismic existence and integrity. The cognitive "life" whose self-reflection constitutes aesthetic pleasure is the exclusive and distinctive possession of a being that enjoys its ability to intelligently and imaginatively cognize the world around it.

As yet another marker of this difference between aesthetic and biological life, consider Kant's use of the term *Erhaltung* (preservation) in the preceding passage. *Erhaltung* calls up *Selbsterhaltung*, a

---

27. Menninghaus, "Ein Gefühl der Beförderung," 93–94.

word that began its career as a biological term in the second half of the eighteenth century, occupying a central place in the description and explanation of living beings.[28] Kant, who reserves the term for sentient beings, emphasizes its instinctual and thus biological meaning whenever he uses it with respect to human beings: "The first, though not the most noble, duty of a human being to himself as an animal being is his self-preservation in his animal nature [*die Selbsterhaltung in seiner animalischen Natur*]."[29] *Selbsterhaltung* is, for Kant, closely connected with both life and pleasure. If life can be understood as the functioning of an organism to maintain itself, in creatures endowed with desire any act that accomplishes this goal will be experienced as pleasurable. The pleasures of self-preservation are thus, for nonrational as well as rational creatures, dependent on the faculty of desire that strives to obtain its objects; they are interested pleasures, satisfactions associated with a hardwired drive to stay alive. But the tendency of the mind to perpetuate the play of its faculties is different. While here, too, pleasure results from the capacity of an entity to maintain the dynamic state that it is in, the entity at issue is not the biological organism as such but the mental faculties, and the goal is not to survive but to keep feeling, and contemplatively attending to, the mind's capacity to accommodate phenomena. Hence Kant's (in)famous definition of aesthetic pleasure as "disinterested": the object of aesthetic contemplation is not desirable in view of its potential consummation, as a means to secure the organism's interests with respect to its environment, but is enjoyable because it stimulates the harmonious and self-stimulating play between understanding and imagination. But why, we might still ask, is it pleasurable to become aware of our mind's capacity for harmonious interaction? Why get a kick out of an activity that serves no

---

28. See, for instance, the definition of the eighteenth-century Scottish anatomist and physician William Hunter (1718–1783): "The first, and most simple idea of life . . . is the principle of self-preservation, preventing matter of falling into dissolution," cited in Georg Toepfer, *Historisches Wörterbuch der Biologie. Geschichte und Theorie der biologischen Grundbegriffe* (Stuttgart: Metzler, 2011), 2:257. According to Toepfer, in Germany the term *Selbsterhaltung* was first used in an explicitly biological context by J. S. Haller in 1757.

29. AA 6:421 (*Metaphysik der Sitten*).

practical or epistemic purpose? The answer, Kant suggests, is that in aesthetic contemplation we experience in a particularly strong way our mind's intrinsic purposiveness, *its capacity to do what it is designed to do*: think, cognize, apprehend the world. We linger in the beautiful because the interaction between imagination and understanding—their attunement to each other—allows us to feel the fitness of our mind for "cognition in general."

To sum up, Kant's frequent use of the term "life" to describe features of aesthetic contemplation is not a mere rhetorical flourish, nor is it a metaphor derived from a biological usage, the soft use of a hard term. To be sure, words like *Lebensgefühl* and *Belebung* are rhetorically important, but they are important because they crystallize and condense a multitude of *systematic* threads in Kant's argument. First, *Belebung* points to the autopoietic dimension of aesthetic contemplation, to a self-strengthening and self-feeling activity within the subject. Second, insofar as the causality of aesthetic pleasure is akin to the self-organizing causality that we ascribe to organic beings, aesthetic contemplation highlights the *natural* character of the mind. It shows that thinking is natural to us, that everything in the mind is geared toward and made for making sense of experience. Aesthetic experience draws our attention to the naturalness of thinking precisely because, in blocking the work of imaginative standardization, it redirects cognitive activity from its extrinsic goals to its intrinsic vitality. In suspending our interest in the reality of the object, aesthetic experience allows us to attend to the interior purposiveness of rational life without the further exterior epistemic, social, and cultural purposes and projects it normally serves. Third, in anticipating the discussion of living organisms in the second part of the book, terms like *Lebensgefühl* and *Belebung* signal the systematic ambition of Kant's book to articulate a conceptual framework that brings out the connection between the *life of cognition* (part 1) and the *cognition of life* (part 2). Finally, the analogy between cognitive and biological life points to a common ground uniting both. The mind's intrinsic purposiveness opens up the possibility of an extrinsic fit. Beauty strengthens our belief that mind and world are fitted to each other—that we are up to the task of knowing the world, *and that the world accommodates our ways of knowing it.*

Excursus: De-formation and Communal Life

Before we turn to Kant's theory of organic life, I want to highlight two aspects of his text that have become particularly important in their twentieth-century reception. The first has to do with the constraints Kant places on imaginative freedom, which come under attack in modernist writings, resulting in a radically different picture of the relation between cognitive and biological life. The second aspect concerns the communal and communicative dimension of aesthetic experience, which is taken up in explicitly political readings of Kant, providing the ground for what might be called a political aesthetics of democratic life.

Let us first revisit the "freedom" of the imagination, which is not as absolute as it might seem. The problem, from a Kantian perspective, is that a truly free imagination generates not beauty and harmony but chaos and disfigurement: "For all the richness of the former produces, in its lawless freedom, nothing but nonsense [*Unsinn*]" (KU §50, 5:319; CPJ 197). To prevent this drift toward non-sense, the imagination must be reined in. In aesthetic experience, the imagination is therefore free only to the extent that it subsumes itself under the general operations of the understanding, which are geared toward the articulation of unities:

> Taste, as a subjective power of judgment, contains a principle of subsumption, not of intuitions under *concepts*, but of the *faculty* of intuitions or presentations (i.e., of the imagination) under the *faculty* of concepts (i.e., the understanding), insofar as the former *in its freedom* is in harmony with the latter *in its lawfulness*. (KU §35, 5:287; CPJ 167–68)

Though no longer subject to a particular law of the understanding, or a particular concept, the imagination is still bound to what might be called the understanding's supreme law of laws: that everything presented to it be *capable* of being unified under a law.[30] Hence the holistically disciplined character of aesthetic imagination: liberated from the tyranny of concepts, though not conceptualization, the imagination is "free" to produce forms which, due to their integrated gestalt, delight reason's innate drive toward the unity of the concept. This is precisely what Kant means when he links aesthetic experience to cognition *in general*.

For Kant, the cognitively bound play of the imagination—its function as an instrument of approximation and accommodation—is clearly not a problem. But from the point of view of later writers sensitive to the effects of social conformity and (bio)political normalization, Kant's emphasis on accommodation and agreement highlights a problematic region in his thought: his unwillingness to conceive of imagination as a force of *dis*figuration. Kant's rather flippant aside on the nonsensical effects of an imagination let loose gives us an inkling of what is at stake here, for the freedom of the imagination can easily devolve into a rogue autonomy that undoes the coherence of the world that imagination is called upon to help create. Kant had already touched on the pivotal role of the imagination in the first *Critique*, where he described the transcendental synthesis of imagination as "a blind but indispensable function of the soul, without which we should have no cognition" (A 78; B 103). In expanding on imagination's dynamic creativity, the *Critique of the Power of Judgment* opens up a door into madness and disorder, only to drape a beautiful curtain over it. On one hand, imagination emerges as the pivotal cognitive faculty in that it sutures the manifold of appearances to concepts, thus giving rise to a coherent world. Without the creativity of imagination, we would have no objects, no memory, no experience, and no world of meaningful signification; imagination is thus world-disclosing. On the other hand, this world-disclosing power is also what imbues imagination with a potentially terrifying force. Since imagination has no law of its own, it is intrinsically unruly, constantly threatening to dissever and disrupt the mind's syntheses, turning sense into non-sense. Thus the

---

30. Förster makes this point very clearly. See his *Twenty-Five Years of Philosophy*, 130.

very imaginative faculty that permits the disclosure of the world as a universe of meaningful connections also threatens to rip it apart. Madness, on this model, occurs precisely when imagination, freed from the operative constraints of understanding, undoes the suture it has itself sown.

The rogue autonomy of imagination, its potentially mad freedom, may be thought of as a zero point of subjectivity, the moment when consciousness separates itself from the animal world. Kant touches on this dimension in his allegorical rewriting of Genesis in "Conjectures on the Beginning of Human History," first published in 1786, where imagination, giving rise to "artificial desires" that disrupt the automatisms of natural instinct, inaugurates human freedom and catapults man into the openness of history.[31] But there, as in the *Critique of the Power of Judgment*, the freedom of imagination remains ultimately tied to a teleological conception of history and cognition. It is this double—cognitive and teleological—containment of the imagination that modernism will attack. Writers like Rilke, Benn, Kafka, and Hofmannsthal, and before them Kleist and Büchner, explore a possibility that Kant was unwilling to entertain, yet one that his own account of imagination had made conceivable: the possibility that the mind uses its freedom not to create meaningful wholes but to *disrupt* its own capacity for meaning-making. When Benjamin, in a fragment written shortly after World War I, claims that "imagination has nothing to do with forms or formations" but instead brings about "the deformation [*Entstaltung*] of what has been formed,"[32] he highlights precisely this other—destructive and anti-organic—side of imagination, its potential as a force of dismemberment and disfiguration. The point not to miss is that this modernist destruction of organic unity does not constitute a fantasmatic relapse into nature—the return to some

---

31. In Immanuel Kant, *On History*, ed. Lewis White Beck (New York: Macmillan, 1963), 55–56. See also Dorothea E. von Mücke, *Practices of the Enlightenment: Aesthetics, Authorship, and the Public* (New York: Columbia University Press, 2015), 36–38.

32. Walter Benjamin, *Selected Writings, Volume 1: 1913–1926*, ed. Marcus Bullock and Michael W. Jennings (Cambridge, MA: Harvard University Press, 2004), 280.

presymbolic life—but rather the aesthetic celebration of an imagination set free to undo both the organic unity of biological *and* the
symbolic unity of sociopolitical forms of life. Kleist's and Benn's
seemingly inhuman literatures do not revoke Kant's distinction between biological and cognitive life; they merely attack the latter's
teleological appeasement, turning the powers of the imagination
against the very humanistic culture that imagination's controlled liberation helped found.

The second connection I want to discuss between Kant and
twentieth-century discussions of modernity bears on Kant's famous
comments on the communicative and communal character of aesthetic experience. Aesthetic judgments may be subjective—grounded
in feeling rather than rule—but they are nonetheless universal, de-
manded of everyone.[33] Kant expresses this by saying that such judgments are governed by a specific kind of common sense, the *sensus
communis aestheticus*, and that they are "public," as opposed to the
"merely private" judgments of ordinary senses (KU §8, 5:214; CPJ
99). Given its basis in feeling, the universality of aesthetic judgment
is very different from the kind of universality that attaches to theoretical or moral judgments, which are objective and binding for all
rational creatures. When we claim to find something beautiful, Kant
says, we are in no position to *demand* the assent of others to our
judgment but instead are "suitors for agreement from everyone else
[*Man wirbt um jedes anderen Bestimmung*]" (KU §19, 5:237; my
translation). Lacking any (theoretical or moral) rule on which to
base our claims that something is beautiful or ugly, all we can do is
present our aesthetic judgment as *exemplary* (KU §22, 5:239; CPJ
123), and ask others to share it. As Kant puts it, in a formulation
that is inconceivable within the framework of his first two *Critiques*,
aesthetic judgments carry "*subjectively universal validity* [subjek-
tiven Allgemeingültigkeit]" (KU §8, 5:215; CPJ 100).

Beginning with Hannah Arendt's later lectures on Kant, contemporary political theorists have found in this notion of subjective

---

33. The following paragraph closely follows Andrew Norris's lucid discussion
of Kant in his *Becoming Who We Are: Politics and Practical Philosophy in the
Work of Stanley Cavell* (Oxford: Oxford University Press, 2017), 31–32.

universality the nucleus of a genuinely democratic model of community.[34] According to this model, the existence of a democratic community rests not merely on obedience to law but also on the readiness of citizens to impart their thoughts, judgments, and feelings to one another. Democratic sovereignty, so understood, resides in a dynamic and constantly transforming "we," a plurality of citizens demanding public recognition for their beliefs and convictions, in a bid for an authority that speaks for all. I want to align myself with this democratic reading but keep in view the conceptual link between community and "life," a link that, while clearly present in Kant, is largely ignored by most contemporary theorists, perhaps to avoid any association with organicist models of politics. To gauge this vitalist dimension, we must first grasp the depth of the connection between communication and pleasure. Kant does not simply say that beauty induces in us a pleasure that we *then* want to communicate to others; he claims that the "others" are there from the beginning, built into the pleasure. Aesthetic pleasure and aesthetic judgments are intrinsically communal and public. This is the claim embedded in a much-disputed sentence from §9:

> Thus it is the universal capacity for the communication [*die allgemeine Mitteilungsfähigkeit*] of the state of mine in the given representation which, as the subjective condition of the judgment of taste, must serve as its ground and have the pleasure in the object as a consequence. (KU §9, 5:217; CPJ 102)

Most critics take this sentence as an aberration, suggesting that pleasure in the beautiful that results from the recognition of its universal

---

34. Hannah Arendt, *Lectures on Kant's Political Philosophy* (Chicago: University of Chicago Press, 1989); Ronald Beiner, "Interpretive Essay," in *Lectures on Kant's Political Philosophy* (Chicago: University of Chicago Press, 1989), 89–157; Kennan Ferguson, *The Politics of Judgment: Aesthetics, Identity, and Political Theory* (Lanham, MD: Lexington Books, 1999), 3–12; Linda M. G. Zerilli, "'We Feel Our Freedom': Imagination and Judgment in the Thought of Hannah Arendt," in *The Aesthetic Turn in Political Thought*, ed. Nikolas Kompridis (New York: Bloomsbury, 2014), 29–60; Norris, *Becoming Who We Are*. Zerilli and Norris in particular approach Kant's idea of *sensus communis* from a theoretical framework that is informed by Wittgenstein and Cavell. Cavell's reflections on aesthetic judgment can be found in his "Aesthetic Problems of Modern Philosophy." This is the line of thought that I pick up here as well.

character would make the feeling derivative of the judgment rather than the other way around. But the confusion disappears, or is at least lessened, once we recognize that aesthetic pleasure is multilayered. Beatrice Longuenesse makes this point lucidly:

> The pleasure we experience in apprehending the object we judge to be beautiful is twofold. It is a first-order pleasure we take in the free play of our own mental capacities (imagination and understanding). But this pleasure on its own would not yet be sufficient to constitute our experience of what we call aesthetic pleasure, pleasure in the beautiful. What makes the specificity of the aesthetic pleasure is the sense that our first-order pleasure could, and should, be shared by all. This sense of a possible universal shareability of a pleasure is the source of the second order pleasure that is characteristic of aesthetic judgment. As such, it elicits the peculiar kind of longing (the demand we make upon others, says Kant) that is characteristic of the aesthetic experience.[35]

Aesthetic pleasure is public in the strong sense that it is caused by the consciousness of its communicability. We enjoy beauty not only because it stimulates our mind but also because we realize that we are not alone in feeling this way, that our specific, interior emotion, rather than enclosing us in the privacy of our body and mind, opens us to a potentially universal community. What Kant tries to think under the heading of an aesthetic common sense, in other words, is a feeling of human kinship that precedes any empirical judgment, and a sense of shared attunement that is based not on explicit agreements but built into, and disclosed through, the feeling of vitality beauty elicits. Although Kant would not put it this way, his argument seems to be based in a kind of transcendental anthropology. Since aesthetic judgments rest on the pleasurable feeling of heightened vitality, and since this feeling is elicited by the free play of imagination and understanding, it follows that all beings endowed with these two cognitive powers are, in principle, open and receptive to the pleasures aroused by beauty. Note that this implies a sense of community that is both inclusive and exclusive. *All* beings endowed with imagination and understanding share in the *sensus communis*, but, also, *only* these beings. Hence Kant's often overlooked claim

---

35. Longuenesse, "Kant's Theory of Judgment," 153.

that aesthetic sensibility is the defining feature of human beings: "Agreeableness is also valid for nonrational animals; beauty is valid only for human beings, i.e., animal but also rational beings, but not merely as the latter (e.g., spirits), rather as beings who are at the same time animal; the good, however, is valid for every rational being in general" (KU §5, 5:210; CPJ 95).

This is the first, quasi-biological sense in which the idea of a *sensus communis* is connected to questions of life: Kant's argument about aesthetic receptivity appeals to the *species* of human beings, which is constituted by the possession of specific cognitive and emotional qualities. However, the appeal to a shared natural disposition does not say anything about the form in which this disposition articulates itself—which is to say, it does not say much about the open-ended and internally differentiated form of the communal "we" that articulates itself in and through the subjective universality of aesthetic judgments. Since aesthetic judgment rests on feelings rather than concepts, its universality remains bound up with the particularity of those who appeal to it. Unlike moral judgments, judgments of taste, in Stanley Cavell's words, are "the expression of a conviction whose grounding remains subjective—say myself—but which expects or claims justification from the (universal) concurrence of other subjectivities, on reflection."[36]

Cavell and, after him, Andrew Norris have brought out the democratic implications of Kant's model of aesthetic judgment. Lacking any determined rule yet demanding assent from all, aesthetic judgments are *claims to community*, meaning that they express an open and "insubstantial" form of community, a "we" that exists only "in its presentation by us—a presentation that is always vulnerable to your and my repudiation."[37] The language of "claims" and Norris's term "presentation" highlight an important feature of aesthetic judgments. Judgments of taste do not end with the declaration "this

---

36. Stanley Cavell, *Conditions Handsome and Unhandsome: The Constitution of Emersonian Perfectionism*, The Carus Lectures, 1988 (Chicago: University of Chicago Press, 1979), xxvi.

37. Andrew Norris, "Introduction: Stanley Cavell and the Claims to Community," in *The Claim to Community: Essays on Stanley Cavell and Political Philosophy* (Redwood City, CA: Stanford University Press, 2004), 2.

is beautiful" but plead their case. They are "suitors for agreement from everyone else" (*"werben um jedes anderen Bestimmung"*), which is to say that aesthetic pleasure gives rise to linguistic activity, to speech that seeks to spell out and support the judgment and solicit assent from others.[38] The political dimension of the aesthetic resides in the fact that this kind of articulation is not restricted to judgments of taste but highlights a constitutive feature of *all* evaluative judgments, including moral and political ones. Like judgments of taste, moral and political rationality rests on the capacity of individuals both to judge reflectively, in the absence of any determinate concept, and to solicit assent from others for their convictions. This is not to erase the differences between aesthetics and politics but to highlight the "groundless" ground that pertains to both. The subjective universality of aesthetic judgments points to an extended conception of thinking, and with it, to an extended conception of communal life. According to this model, reason and community do not rest on fixed rules or laws but instead consist in the ongoing articulation of reflective judgments that seeks to *produce* the support of others. It is because no rule fully determines the articulation of aesthetic and political judgments that the expression of reason in both areas takes the form of claims that can do no more, and must do no less, than appeal to the agreement of others. And because these claims, lacking the ultimate authority of a logical rule, "are always vulnerable to your and my repudiation," the community that emerges through the exchange of political and aesthetic judgments is always subject to revision and transformation, hence open-ended and insubstantial. There is no ultimate authority that stands outside the community—no sovereign or law—that guarantees its existence and determines its form.

Kant's notion of *sensus communis* points to a model of community that is based on dynamic agreement rather than fixed law. But the idea of universal claims grounded in feelings also highlights an irreducibly affective and aesthetic dimension of politics. This intertwinement of thinking and affect, speech and pleasure, in aesthetic

---

38. On the linguistic dimension of aesthetic experience and *Stimmung*, see also Chaouli, *Thinking with Kant's Critique of Judgment*, 62–64.

judgments encourages me to read in Kant's theory of aesthetic life the intimation of a theory of political vitality. Two loci of political vitality must be distinguished. One belongs firmly to the public realm and has to do with the activities in which citizens, engaged in the work of soliciting assent, give rise to a dynamic "we" that is actualized in the expressions of those that speak on its behalf, one by one, one against the other. The type of animation at stake here may be understood on the model of Kant's conception of *Stimmung*, or subjective attunement. If the encounter with the beautiful object gives rise to a reciprocal stimulation of faculties within the subject, the political deliberation over the shape of the common good un- leashes a dynamic in which citizens, through their competing claims to speak on behalf of all, reciprocally stimulate one another, thus increasing the affective *and* rational power of the community. Po- litical vitality, so conceived, contains an important, extrapersonal dimension in that it operates through a communicative and affec- tive circuit that passes through and beyond the autonomous sub- jects it binds to communal ends. But this extrapersonal vitality is simultaneously sustained by subjective acts of investment. For the circuit to work, citizens must be willing and able to plug into it. This means, first, that I must treat at least some of my feelings and thoughts as potentially universalizable, as claims to community. To experience myself as fully alive, I must have the courage to stake myself publicly in my words and gestures, mean what I say. But it also requires that I live in a culture whose forms and institutions are flexible enough to make room for my expressions. Hence the dialec- tic character of political vitality, which both animates those caught in its extrapersonal movement, and is animated by their willingness to voice their feelings and thoughts as communal claims. As we shall see, it is the *breakdown* of this dialectic between communal and subjective life that becomes a central theme in modernist writings.

The Life of Nature

Let us return to the *Critique of the Power of Judgment*. I have argued that the first part of Kant's book—the "aesthetic" part—explores the peculiar vitality of mental life, experienced most powerfully in our encounter with beauty, and that Kant, in discussing aesthetic experience, articulates an expanded model of thinking. According to this new model, thinking is not restricted to concept formation but is understood more dynamically and holistically as the mind's active generation of meaningful relations, as the power (*Vermögen*) of sorting and selecting sensual data, forging connections, constructing forms. But this is only half the story. This new dynamic model of thinking is complemented by a new dynamic model of nature developed in the second half of his book. To understand how the *Critique of the Power of Judgment* places mind and nature in an analogical relation to one another, we must therefore turn, if briefly, to Kant's discussion of natural form in the "Critique of Teleological Judgment." [39]

At the core of Kant's reflections is his account of natural objects as "organized beings [*organisierte Wesen*]" (KU §65). Although Kant never talks of organisms as *living* creatures—the term "life" appears only once in the second part—the connection between the two concepts is evident from his examples and is made explicit in a remark from his *Opus postumum*: "That an organized body is alive [*belebt*], is an identical proposition" (AA 21:66). Kant's discussion of organisms thus contains his theory of life. The theory takes as its starting point an observation about the unusual character of natural forms. Nature presents us with a plethora of highly articulated forms that lack any necessity when viewed in terms of our ordinary

---

39. Like the criticism on Kant's aesthetics, the literature on Kant's theory of nature and natural purposiveness is immense. The most extensive survey of Kant's discussions of life is still Reinhard Löw's *Die Philosophie des Lebendigen. Der Begriff des Organischen bei Kant, sein Grund und seine Aktualität* (Frankfurt am Main: Suhrkamp, 1980). I have also found particularly useful Hannah Ginsborg's *The Normativity of Nature: Essays on Kant's* Critique of Judgment (Oxford: Oxford University Press, 2014), 225–346; Toepfer, "Wechselseitigkeit"; Georg Toepfer, "Kant's Teleology, the Concept of the Organism, and the Concept of Contemporary Biology," in *Philosophiegeschichte und Logische Analyse* 14 (2011): 107–24; and Chaouli, *Thinking with Kant's Critique of Judgment*, 199–248, who rightly emphasizes not only the ambivalences in Kant's accounts of the organic world but also the inconclusiveness of his talk of "life."

notion of (mechanical) causality: "For if one adduces, e.g., the structure of a bird, the hollowness of its bones, the placement of its wings for movement . . . one says that given the mere *nexus effectivus* in nature, without the help of a special kind of causality . . . i.e., that nature, considered as a mere mechanism, could have formed itself in a thousand different ways without hitting precisely upon the unity in accordance with such a rule" that it did in fact develop (KU §61, 5:360; CPJ 233–34). Treating natural forms as utterly contingent leaves us with "such an *infinite multiplicity* of empirical laws and such a *great heterogeneity of forms* of nature" as to thwart any systematic, unified explanation of diversity (AA 20:203; CPJ 9; Kant's emphasis). To explain the plurality of natural forms we must operate with a concept of a *single* nature that we cannot derive from mechanical causality. Yet (efficient) causal physical laws cannot generate, for example, the formal concept of a tree or bird. True, we are capable of identifying trees or birds, but this identification grasps them merely as spatiotemporal objects of experience, not as natural kinds. What makes a bird a bird remains inexplicable in terms of the efficient causality used to explain the diverse facts about it (i.e., that it hatches from eggs, uses wings to fly, eats worms, emits certain sounds when in danger, etc.). And yet bones and feathers and worm-eating and flying do add up to something that we perceive and treat as a single bird. So how account for the laws that make a bird a bird?

To answer this question, Kant argues, we must resort to teleological explanation. In other words, we must consider natural forms in view of the functions they serve. Seventeenth- and eighteenth-century naturalists and philosophers frequently invoked a type of functionalist explanation that Kant calls "relative" purposiveness (KU §63 5:366; CPJ 239). According to this model, natural forms exist in order to serve purposes that lie outside them. Nature as a whole is thus viewed in terms of a pervasive adaptation of means to ends; it is a beautifully arranged machine, designed by a divine intelligence and serving our—human—needs. This is the watered-down Leibnizian view that Voltaire caricatured in *Candide*: "Since everything was made for a purpose, it follows that everything is made for the best purpose. Observe: our noses were made to carry spectacles, so we have spectacles."[40] Kant's idea of "*inner* purposiveness" (KU §66 5:376; CPJ 248; my emphasis) is very different from this anthropocentric teleology. Natural purposes are neither designed by God nor do they serve human needs. Instead,

> For a body . . . to be judged as a natural end in itself and in accordance with its internal possibility, it is required that its parts reciprocally produce each other, as far as both their form and their combination is concerned, and thus produce a whole out of their own causality, the concept of which, conversely, is in turn the cause (in a being that would possess the causality according to concepts appropriate for such a product) of it in accordance with a principle. (KU §65 5:373; CPJ 245)

As Kant makes clear, this definition specifies two requirements. "For a thing as a natural end it is requisite, *first*, that its parts (as far as their existence and form is concerned) are possible only through their relation to the whole" (KU §65, 5:373; CPJ 244–45; Kant's emphasis). Viewed teleologically, a natural being is a functional whole composed of interdependent parts. We have an approximate model for such an entity in man-made objects, what Kant calls artifacts. The wheels and hands of a watch, for instance, acquire their identity as wheels and hands only in relation to one another and to the whole of which they form a part. Machines are functional unities in which the parts exist for that unity, and so derivatively for one another. But in the case of the watch, the cause of its functional unity lies outside itself, in the mind of the watchmaker who made it. Machines are products of design and intention, the result of organizing concepts. But since organisms are as such neither rational beings nor made by them, we have to conceive of them, as it were, as their own watchmakers, and of their organizing idea as somehow intrinsic. Thus to speak of *natural* purposes, a second requirement must be met:

> But if a thing, as a natural product, is nevertheless to contain in itself and its internal possibility a relationship to ends, i.e., is to be possible

---

40. Voltaire, *Candide: Or Optimism*, translated by John Butt (London: Penguin, 1950), 20.

only as a natural end and without the causality of the concepts of a rational being outside of it, then it is required, *second*, that its parts be combined into a whole by being reciprocally the cause and effect of their form. For in this way alone is it possible in turn for the idea of the whole conversely (reciprocally) to determine the form and combination of all the parts: not as a cause—for then it would be the product of art—but as the ground for the cognition of the systematic unity of the form and the combination of all of the manifold that is contained in the given material for someone who judges it. (KU §65, 5:373; CPJ 245; Kant's emphasis)

Organic beings are not only organized but *self-organizing*; they are *dynamic* wholes, the products and causes of their own structure, which is thus somehow active and formative. Hence even the comparison to artifacts cannot do justice to the kind of intelligence that seems to be at work in natural objects:

One says far too little about nature and its capacity in organized products if one calls this an *analogue of art*: for in that case one conceives of the artist (a rational being) outside of it. Rather, it organizes itself, and in every species of its organized products, of course in accordance with some example in the whole, but also with appropriate deviations, which are required in the circumstances for self-preservation. (KU §65, 5:374; CPJ 246; Kant's emphasis)

Viewed teleologically, which is the view we must assume in order to make sense of the peculiar form and behavior of organic beings, natural objects appear, as it were, hyperpurposive. Their organization seems intelligent and bound to concept down to the smallest interstices of their material makeup, to the very cells of their being. Nothing is superfluous or wasted, everything serves a function and is integrated. Whereas artifacts have their rationality outside of them, in the mind of their maker, organisms seem to embody an intrinsic intelligence that is, strictly speaking, incomprehensible and "not analogous with any causality that we know" (KU §65, 5:375; CPJ 246f). Moreover, organisms sustain their functional unity over time. An organism, Kant writes in a letter to Soemmering, is a "purposeful and as regards its form *persistent* organization of parts [*eine zweckmäßige und in ihrer Form beharrliche Anordnung der*

Theile]."⁴¹ To capture the unity and identity of an organism, therefore, it is necessary to look at the "wider context" of its existence,
which includes both its environment and its development over time.
The "form" of an organism is thus no longer conceived in terms of
spatial extension but as the dynamic unity of a life: it is a *Lebensform* (form of life).

Note that there is a tension in Kant's account of natural purposiveness. On the one hand, Kant's stress on reciprocity ("*second*,
that its parts be combined into a whole by being reciprocally the
cause and effect of their form") explains the peculiar unity of natural objects in terms of its *circular* causality. On the other hand, Kant
insists that our understanding of organisms as functional wholes
must be modeled on the causality of human actions and artifacts.
To grasp natural organisms, we must conceive them "as if" they
were the products of design and planning, as the result of an intelligent creator that intended their form and function. But circular
causality is clearly very different from the linear causality of goal-
oriented rationality. So what is at stake in explaining system-
theoretical teleology in terms of intentional teleology?⁴² I think
there are two answers to this question. In the first place, Kant remains committed to upholding the Newtonian conception of matter
as lifeless and inert:

> One says far too little about nature and its capacity in organized prod-
> ucts if one calls this an *analogue of art*; for in that case one conceives
> the artist (a rational being) outside of it. Rather, it organizes itself. . . .
> Perhaps one comes closer to this inscrutable property if one calls it an
> *analogue of life*: but then one must either endow matter as mere matter
> with a property (hylozoism) that contradicts its essence, or else associ-
> ate it with an alien principle *standing in communion* with it (a soul), in
> which case, however, if such a product is to be a product of nature, or-
> ganized matter as an instrument of that soul is already presupposed, and
> thus makes that product not the least more comprehensible, or else the
> soul is made into an artificer of this structure, and the product must be
> withdrawn from (corporeal) nature. Strictly speaking, the organization

---

41. Toepfer, "Wechselseitigkeit," 277, my emphasis.
42. The terms "system-theoretical" and "intentional teleology" are Toepfer's.
See his "Kant's Teleology," 122.

of nature is therefore not analogous with any causality that we know. (KU §65, 5:375; CPJ 246; Kant's emphasis)

The idea of circular causality puts pressure on the dualism between lifeless matter and animating spirit, which Kant is not willing to surrender. Hence this characterization of self-organization in terms of the demands of cognizability; the functional unity of organisms is a purely regulative principle of our judgment about nature, which we generate by conceiving of organisms on the model of our own practical activities.

And yet as Kant both recognizes and disavows, the causality of intentional actions cannot produce the schema for understanding a system in which the parts are "combined into a whole by being *reciprocally* the cause and effect of their form" (KU §65, 5:373; CPJ 245; my emphasis). If Kant nonetheless insists on explaining circular-natural teleology in terms of linear-rational purposiveness, this is owing to a second, and more profound, systematic philosophical commitment to the subordination of natural to moral teleology. Kant's conception of natural teleology is designed to bridge the gap between freedom and nature that his first two critiques had opened up, and his claim that the structure of organisms can be understood by reference to the causality of voluntary goal-setting allows him to marshal nature as support for his argument about the *moral* directedness of human history. Natural organisms, reflectively judged as if produced by design and intention, point to "the ultimate end of nature here on earth" (KU §83, 5:429; CPJ 297), which is nothing other than the unique capacity of humans, founded in freedom, to set ends for themselves and transform nature into culture (KU §83, 5:429–30; CPJ 297).

The irony is of course that Kant had already identified a type of human activity that resembles much more closely the circular causality of natural organisms than do voluntary moral actions: aesthetic experience. In aesthetic contemplation, as we saw, pleasure becomes the cause of its own effect, giving rise to a kind of auto-affection of the mind. Aesthetic pleasure is its own "determining ground," its own raison d'etre, divorced from all practical, moral, and epistemic purposes. Thus, like the "intrinsic purposiveness" we ascribe to natural organisms, the "merely formal purposiveness" (KU §12, 5:222; CPJ 107) of the play of the cognitive faculties in aesthetic contemplation has a causality that is "strictly speaking, not analogous with any causality that we know." To repeat the relevant passage:

> This pleasure is also not practical in any way, neither like the one aris-ing from the pathological basis of agreeableness, nor like the one arising from the intellectual basis of the conceived [moral] good. Yet it does have a causality in it, namely, to *preserve* the state of [having] the presenta-tion and the activity of the cognitive powers without any further aim. We *linger* in our contemplation of the beautiful, because this contem-plation reinforces and reproduces itself. (KU §12, 5:222; CPJ 107; Kant's emphasis)

"We *linger* over the contemplation of the beautiful because this con-templation strengthens and reproduces itself": it is the autopoiesis of aesthetic pleasure, and not moral action, that closely resembles Kant's model of self-organizing biological life.

But this is not all, for Kant also emphasizes the nature-like char-acter of the beautiful artwork:

> In a product of art one must be aware that it is art, and not nature; yet the purposiveness in its form must still seem to be as free from all con-straint by arbitrary rules as if it were a mere product of nature. . . . Na-ture was beautiful, if at the same time it looked like art; and art can only be called beautiful if we are aware that it is art and yet it looks to us like nature. (KU §45; 5:306; CPJ 185)

The work of art is unlike nature because it is the product not of nature but of imagination, understanding, and sensibility. In this sense, the artwork is an expression of the creativity of human free-dom, of its capacity to work outside the bounds of mechanical cau-sality. Yet the artwork also looks like nature in that its organization is "free from all constraint by arbitrary rules"—that is, inexplica-ble in terms of an underlying determinate concept. The form of a work of art, in other words, is not a means to an end but an ex-pressive totality in which every element stands in a reciprocal, rather than a mechanical or instrumental, relationship to all other elements.

It is the artwork, not ordinary goal-oriented action, that resembles most clearly the circular causality of natural organisms.

And yet, Kant appears to forget about his own argument in the second half of his book, insisting instead that intentional actions provide the best model for understanding the form of natural organisms. Neither the peculiar vitality of aesthetic pleasure nor the "second" nature of aesthetic artworks plays a significant role in the second part of the book. Moreover, even though Kant's discussion of the form of artworks points to a significant difference between natural and artistic beauty, Kant neglects to expand on this distinction and instead continues to treat natural beauty as the paradigm of aesthetic experience. The reason for these elisions and displacements, as already suggested, has to do with Kant's broader philosophical commitment to moral teleology, which becomes explicit toward the end of his book. On the one hand, the self-organizing powers we ascribe to nature are now framed as part of a larger teleological design that culminates in man as the "final purpose" or "ultimate end of nature," (KU §83, 5:429; CPJ 297), without whom "the whole of creation would be a mere desert" (KU §86 5:442; CPJ 308). From this perspective, the possibility of nature's intelligibility is important not primarily because it accommodates our scientific need to know it but because it satisfies our moral need to create a human world built on rational principle, that is to say, on moral law. Kant thus inscribes his system-theoretical account of natural organisms into a progressivist narrative that conceives of nature and culture as a "directed process that aims at the cultivation and civilization of mankind."[43] On the other hand, this philosophical-historical framework also recasts the conception of aesthetic experience. From the perspective of moral teleology, aesthetic freedom and pleasure matter not primarily because they allow us to experience the vitality and creativity of our mind but because, in cultivating our senses and aligning them with aesthetic ideas, they contribute to the task of establishing a moral universe.

---

43. Toepfer, "Kant's Teleology," 122. Toepfer also stresses the tension between this broader historical-philosophical teleology and his more limited account of natural purposiveness.

Beautiful arts and sciences, which by means of a universally communicable pleasure and an elegance and refinement make human beings, if not morally better, at least better mannered for society, very much reduce the tyranny of sensible tendencies [*Tyrannei des Sinnenhanges*], and prepare humans for a sovereignty [*Herrschaft*] in which reason alone shall have power [*in welcher die Vernunft allein Gewalt haben soll*]. (KU §83 5:433–34; CPJ 301).

Much of the literary and aesthetic discourse after Kant will attack his philosophical commitment to moral teleology, and, with it, fundamental tenets of Kant's theory. As they chip away at the philosophical system that enabled Kant to conceive of natural, aesthetic, and moral-political life as elements of a single, if speculative, directed process, authors from Kleist to Musil will flesh out in great detail the dynamics within, and conflicts between, these diverse forms of life. Yet insofar as it was Kant's new vision of mind and nature that made visible these forms as *forms of life* in the first place, Kant's *Critique of the Power of Judgment* can be said to open up the conceptual horizon that allowed much of the nineteenth- and twentieth-century German aesthetic and philosophical discourse on life to go beyond it.

2

METAMORPHOSES OF FORM (GOETHE)

In an enigmatic scene from Goethe's novel *Wilhelm Meister's Apprenticeship* (the placement of which at the exact midpoint of the text emphasizes its importance), the protagonist is taught a painful lesson:

> [Aurelie] made a motion with her right hand so that he thought she was about to grasp his; but she quickly plunged it into her pocket and in a flash pulled out the dagger and swept over his hand with it. He withdrew his hand quickly but blood was already dripping from it.
>
> "You men must be marked sharply if you are to take notice [*Man muß euch Männer scharf zeichnen, wenn ihr merken sollt*]," she cried in wild excitement. . . .
>
> The cut went across the ball of the hand just below the thumb, separated the lifeline [*teilte die Lebenslinie*], and ran out toward the little finger.[1]

---

1. Goethe, WML, 280; Goethe, WMA, 168. If only the German edition is referenced, the translation is mine.

Cutting, marking, noting—what is impressed upon Wilhelm here is not only the violent character of inscription but also the requirement of a break with his belief in the unity of biological and biographical life, expressed in the notion of the *Lebenslinie*. Drawn from the medieval vocabulary of chiromancy, the term suggests that it is possible to foretell the fortunes and dispositions of persons by inspecting their hands. It thus articulates a worldview in which biography is organically contained in the body. Aurelie's knife severs this natural unity of *bios* and *zoe*. Unlike biological form, the passage suggests, human life is marked by the incisions of artificial signs into the natural. Aurelie's cut thus explicitly enjoins Wilhelm "to take notice" (*zu merken*)—that is, to become conscious of the inscriptions and representations that have shaped his life from the beginning.

The scene encapsulates the central problem of Goethe's novel: the *extrabiological* form of human life. The novel suggests that human life is riven and composite, which is to say that its unity is the unity of a heterogeneous multiplicity, one shaped and traversed by the more or less incongruous boundaries between overlapping forms and dimensions of life. On the one hand, the novel constantly highlights the biological determination of human life, its irreducibly organic and corporeal nature. Images of wounds, blood, and sickness recur throughout *Wilhelm Meister*,[2] and no fewer than five of the book's main characters die, most of them violently and dramatically. On the other hand, death and physical injury in Goethe's novels are always complexly interwoven with psychological and social factors. Thus in the above scene, Aurelie's attack, which is motivated by jealousy, recasts rather than denies the unity of body and biography implicit in the chiromantic model. The encounter with Aurelie, an important event in Wilhelm's life, does indeed imprint itself on his body, yet the imprinted sign of this event is no longer innate and organic but contingent and artificial. Aurelie's cut therefore draws

---

2. See A. G. Steer, "The Wound and the Physician in Goethe's *Wilhelm Meister*," in *Studies in German Literature of the Nineteenth and Twentieth Centuries: Festschrift for Frederic E. Coenen*, ed. Siegfried Mews (Chapel Hill: University of North Carolina Press, 1970): 11–23.

attention not merely to the biological vulnerability of human life but to its fundamental historicity and plasticity; that is, to its openness to other (social, psychological, political, aesthetic) forms.

From this perspective, *Wilhelm Meister's Apprenticeship* can be seen to mark a crucial event in the German discourse of life around 1800. That Goethe was actively involved in delineating the new biological conception of "life" is well known. During the very years in which he rewrote his *Wilhelm Meister* novel, having abandoned it in 1785, he was also busy rethinking his own theory of organic form, the first version of which appeared in 1790 under the title *The Metamorphosis of Plants*. Goethe's botanical studies, which exerted a deep influence on Wittgenstein,[3] address themselves to the problem of understanding the principles of formation underlying dynamic, yet organized, wholes: principles of form*ation*, not of form. Goethe relentlessly emphasizes the dynamic character of life, its metamorphic drive, and his newly developed morphological method is explicitly designed to capture the formative laws not of stable structures but of self-modifying processes. The pertinence of these reflections to the aesthetic realm, already clear to Goethe in the 1780s, was thrown into sharp relief with the publication of Kant's *Critique of Judgment* in 1790, which centers philosophical reflection on the question of the relation between aesthetic and natural form, culture and nature. And it is this question, sharpened now by Kant's transcendental articulation, that prompts Goethe's return both to his pre-1790 botanical studies and his older *Wilhelm Meister* fragment, and drives his scientific and novelistic writing of the 1790s. Here again is Goethe's reflection on the third *Critique* from 1820:

> Then the *Critique of Judgment* fell into my hands, and with this book a wonderful period arrived in my life. Here I found my most disparate interests brought together; products of art and nature were dealt with alike, aesthetic and teleological judgment illuminated one another. . . . The inner life of art and nature, their respective effects as they work from

---

3. See Joachim Schulte, *Chor und Gesetz: Wittgenstein im Kontext* (Frankfurt am Main: Suhrkamp, 1990) and M. W. Rowe, "Goethe and Wittgenstein," *Philosophy* 66, no. 257 (1991): 283–303.

within—all this came to clear expression in the book. ("Einwirkung der neueren Philosophie," FA 24:444)

In what follows, I shall analyze Goethe's *Wilhelm Meister's Apprenticeship* as a self-reflexive inquiry into the relation between sociopolitical, biological, and aesthetic form. Note that the *form* in which Goethe explores this relation—the form of the novel—already complicates the Kantian picture. The Kantian subject of aesthetic experience is a philosophical abstraction. A generic locus of capacities without concrete existence, it is a theoretical construct without gender, family, and history. Goethe's novel, by contrast, places the subject of aesthetic experience in a richly textured lifeworld and charges it with desires, memories, and attachments. Wilhelm, too, is constantly drawn to art and aesthetic form, but his experience of these media (puppet theater, paintings, epic tragedy, drama), far from being an expression of "disinterested pleasure," is passionate and partial, even fantasmatic. Where Kant's *Critique* outlines an ideal model of aesthetic experience, Goethe's novel, which begins, not by chance, with Wilhelm's memories of his earliest childhood, explores a primordial and archaic dimension of the human responsiveness to aesthetic form, one that bears on the very formation of subjectivity and character. That Wilhelm's biography is fundamentally shaped by his erotically charged engagement with theater, epics, and paintings points to what Goethe's novel presents as the defining feature of human as opposed to biological life: its aliveness to, dependence on, and obsession with forms. This is also why Goethe's novelistic inquiry into the formation of life is simultaneously a self-reflexive exploration of the life of form and representation; that is, a meditation on the vital role of aesthetic experience.

The relevance of questions of life to Goethe's novel and the genre as a whole has of course not escaped notice. A coming-of-age story that traces its hero's transition from childhood to fatherhood, *Wilhelm Meister's Apprenticeship* already signals through its plot its concern with articulating an aesthetic form attuned to the developmental arc of the human life-form. This interlacing of biography with novel has given rise to a long tradition of reading *Wilhelm*

Meister as the paradigm of the bildungsroman genre (in view of the concept of organic formation, or *Bildung*), whether to praise it, in conservative fashion, for modeling human growth in terms of the "natural" integration of expressive self-formation with social responsibility, or to deconstruct it as the prime example of an organicist ideology that veils the normative violence of socialization.[4] Moreover, from Friedrich Blankenburg to Friedrich Schlegel and György Lukács, the most ambitious philosophies of the novel have emphasized the relation between life and novelistic form. "The innate drive of this organized and organizing work to form itself into a whole [*Der angeborene Trieb des durchaus organisierten und organisierenden Werks, sich zu einem Ganzen zu bilden*],"[5] writes Friedrich Schlegel in his 1798 review of *Wilhelm Meister*, all but citing Kant's description of natural organisms in the third *Critique*. One hundred years later, Lukács, drawing on Schlegel as well as Bergson and Weber, places the tension between life and meaning— the "refusal of the immanence of meaning to enter into empirical life"[6]—at the center of his theory of the novel. For Schlegel and Lukács, the novel is unique among literary forms in that it is intrinsically—by its very form—bound to life: the form of the novel is the form of life.[7] And therein lies both its promise and its problem, for in opening itself to the immediacy of life the novel also invites

---

4. The idea that organicism is the master trope of ideology is perhaps most influentially developed in Paul de Man's work on English and German Romanticism. De Man essentially defines Romanticism in terms of its tendency to veil the mechanical character of language through "organic" tropes such as prosopopoeia. See his essays in *Allegories of Reading: Figural Language in Rousseau, Nietzsche, Rilke, and Proust* (New Haven, CT: Yale University Press, 1982) and *The Rhetoric of Romanticism* (New York: Columbia University Press, 1984).

5. Friedrich Schlegel, "Über Goethes Meister," in *Schriften zur Literatur*, ed. Wolfdietrich Rasch (Munich: Carl Hanser Verlag, 1970), 265.

6. György Lukács, *The Theory of the Novel* (Cambridge, MA: MIT Press, 1971), 71.

7. On the interrelationship between life and the novel in Lukács, see Eva Geulen, "Response and Commentary (Sara Guyer, Marc Redgield and Emily Sun)," *Romantic Circles*, 2012, http://www.rc.umd.edu/praxis/biopolitics/HTML/praxis .2012.geulen; Rüdiger Campe, "Form und Leben in der Theorie des Romans," in *Vita aesthetica. Szenen ästhetischer Lebendigkeit*, ed. Armen Avanessian, Winfried Menninghaus, and Jan Völker (Zürich, Berlin: diaphanes, 2009), 193–212.

contingency and impermanence, thus jeopardizing its own formal unity. Hence the repeated complaints about the "formlessness" of the novel, with Lukács going so far as to call it a "half-art."[8]

Rüdiger Campe has recently expanded on this line of thought, arguing that modern theories of the novel mark a "turning point in the relationship between literature and knowledge."[9] As long as rhetorically codified poetic forms regulate the presentation of content, Campe suggests, life as *zoe* does not enter the realm of aesthetic articulation. It is only with the disintegration of the older rhetorical system that the relationship of art and life moves to the center of both literature and its theory. Thus, as "with the (modern) novel, literary form becomes a matter no longer of poetical forms but of the form of life,"[10] there emerges alongside the new genre, and in reflective engagement with it, a new type of knowledge: a *theory* of the novel that is simultaneously a theory of life. While I am sympathetic to much in Campe and the authors he analyzes, my own discussion of the link between novel and life follows a different direction. First, while Campe focuses on the theory of the novel, I am interested in Goethe's novel itself, which I believe provides us with a richer model of "life" than do the philosophical reflections of Schlegel or Lukács. Second, whereas Campe is concerned with a new type of knowledge about literature, I place Goethe's novel in the context of a broader transformation of the understanding of natural and social life. *Wilhelm Meister* is interesting to me because it crystallizes a variety of contemporary discourses and models of life, ranging from aesthetics and biology to economy and politics. Thus, third, while Campe claims that the novel is concerned with giving form to biological life (*zoe*), my reading emphasizes the text's engagement with *multiple and conflicting* forms of life. From this perspective, the novel's supposed "formlessness" becomes readable as a function of its new subject matter, which is not life as such but a particular conception of *human life*. If the genre of the novel is formally heterogeneous to the point of seeming "formless," as it ap-

---

8. Lukács, *Theory of the Novel*, 73.
9. Campe, "Form and Life in the Theory of the Novel," 53.
10. Ibid., 54.

peared not only to Schlegel and Lukács but also to Goethe himself, this is because the novel in general, and Goethe's *Wilhelm Meister* in particular, seek to give form to a strangely riven and multifarious phenomenon: to human life understood as a *form of forms*.

One upshot of this emphasis on heterogeneity is that Goethe's novel complicates the Foucaultian account of "liberal" subjectivity. Building on Foucault's lectures from the late 1970s, Miguel de Beistegui has recently argued that the eighteenth-century emergence of liberal governmentality involves a "rehabilitation of desire as a natural or vital feature" of human life.[11] "From an object of mastery and domination, desire progressively became the necessary mechanism for the production of the greater good" and thus "the very engine and energy of political life, the instrument of a new sovereignty and the object of a new political science."[12] De Beistegui bases his argument on readings of Locke, Hume, Smith, and Bentham, who derive from their redefinition of the subject in terms of vital needs and desires a new conception of socioeconomic life understood as a self-regulating order driven rather than threatened by the impetus of self-interested passions. What de Beistegui fails to mention is that this new appreciation of "desire" goes hand in hand with a radical flattening of its content. As Albert O. Hirschman has shown, the eighteenth-century notion of "self-interested" desire functioned to contain and tame an older and much darker discourse of unruly and violent "passions."[13] Unlike the latter, "self-interest" is a "calm"[14]—steady and methodical—passion that can be aligned with, in fact provides the affective basis for, a new model of economic and sociopolitical rationality. But what gets eliminated in this recodification of passions as self-interest is the particular color and

---

11. Miguel de Beistegui, "Desire Within and Beyond Biopolitics," in *The Care of Life: Transdisciplinary Perspectives in Bioethics and Biopolitics*, ed. Miguel de Beistegui, Giusseppe Bianchi, Marjorie Gracieuse (London: Rowman & Littlefield, 2015), 242.

12. Ibid., 243.

13. Albert O. Hirschmann, *The Passions and the Interests: Political Arguments for Capitalism before Its Triumph* (Princeton, NJ: Princeton University Press, 2013; orig. pub. 1977).

14. Ibid., 63.

irrational force of passions and desire, including erotic desire. It is here that Goethe's novel—and for that matter psychoanalysis, whose model of desire is irreducible to the logic of self-interest[15]—provides a helpful corrective to the Foucaultian account of (liberal) subjectivity. While not harking back to the seventeenth-century notion of passions, Goethe's novel explores the tension between new models of erotic and economic desire, between lack of being and self-interest, and between romantic subjectivity and liberal governmentality. The consequences of this exploration are twofold. On the one hand, the novel shows that Wilhelm's accession to bourgeois, liberal existence rests on a therapy of desire that is carried out through the careful orchestration of narratives and imagery: liberal subjectivity involves a fundamental aesthetic dimension. On the other hand, this aesthetic therapy is shown to be unable to tame the entirety of human passions and desires, which contain an irreducibly unruly and formless kernel that must be violently excluded from liberal subjectivity. The included exclusion of this formless limit of human life, artfully rendered in the figure of Mignon, complicates not only Foucault's notion of liberal subjectivity but also Goethe's own model of organic and human *Bildung*.

Organic Form

Aimed at explaining the growth and transformation of natural forms, Goethe's botanical studies of the 1780s and 1790s were part of the emerging life sciences, which replaced, as we saw, the older static and spatial models of natural history with an emphasis on development and force.[16] In fact, more than any author at his time,

---

15. On the relation between psychoanalysis and the older discourse of the passions, see John Forrester, *Dispatches from the Freud Wars: Psychoanalysis and Its Passions* (Cambridge, MA: Harvard University Press, 1997), 13–43, esp. 34–43.

16. "Vorarbeiten zu einer Physiologie der Pflanzen," in FA 24:357. On Goethe's scientific writings, see Frederick Amrine, *Goethe and the Sciences: A Reappraisal*, Boston Studies in the Philosophy of Science 97 (Dordrecht: D. Reidel, 1987); Olaf Breidbach, *Goethes Metamorphosenlehre* (Munich: Fink, 2006); Eckart Förster, "Die Bedeutung von §§ 76, 77 der 'Kritik der Urteilskraft' für die Ent-

Goethe places the idea of transformation (i.e., change, movement, impermanence) at the center of his reflections on nature. Form is formation, a dynamic process rather than a static, determinate structure. Morphology, a term Goethe introduced into natural history, is concerned with the "formation *and* transformation of organic bodies [*Bildung* und *Umbildung der organischen Körper*]" ("Betrachtung über Morphologie" (ca. 1795), FA 24:365, my emphasis). Hence also Goethe's grafting of the new and more technical notion of morphology onto another term with deep mythological pedigree: "The *Gestalt* is mobile, becoming, passing away. The doctrine of *Gestalten* is a doctrine of transformation. The doctrine of metamorphosis is the key to all signs of nature [*Die Gestalt ist ein bewegliches, ein werdendes, ein vergehendes. Gestaltenlehre ist Verwandlungslehre. Die Lehre der Metamorphose ist der Schlüssel zu allen Zeichen der Natur*]" ("Betrachtung ueber Morphologie" (ca. 1795), FA 24:349). It is with respect to this metamorphic character of form that Goethe explicitly motivates his use of the term *Bildung*. The concept of *Gestalt* is inadequate to capture the specific form of living beings in that it "abstracts from their changeability" and veils the fact that "nothing in them is permanent, nothing is at rest or complete—everything is in a flux of continual motion" ("Die Absicht eingeleitet" (1806–7), FA 24:392). Goethe continues: "This is why German frequently and fittingly makes use of the word *Bildung* to describe the end product and what is in process of production as well" (ibid.).

To understand the form of living things, then, it is necessary to identify the law of *Bildung* underlying their development. But how does one determine the concept of a thing that is in perpetual

wicklung der nachkantischen Philosophie," *Zeitschrift für Philosophische Forschung* 56, no. 3 (2002): 321–45; Eckart Förster, "Goethe und das 'Auge des Geistes,'" *Deutsche Vierteljahrsschrift für Literaturwissenschaft und Geistesgeschichte* 75, no. 1 (March 2001): 87–101; Dorothea E.von Mücke, "Goethe's Metamorphosis: Changing Forms in Nature, the Life Sciences, and Authorship," *Representations* 95 (Summer 2006): 27–53; Eva Geulen, *Aus dem Leben der Form. Goethes Morphologie und die Nager* (Berlin: August Verlag, 2016); and Jocelyn Holland, *German Romanticism and Science: The Procreative Poetics of Goethe, Novalis, and Ritter*, Routledge Studies in Romanticism 13 (New York: Routledge, 2009), 19–56.

transformation? On the one hand, it is clear that the law of *Bildung* cannot be read off the immediate empirical phenomenon, say that of a plant, for all we can encounter directly is the appearance of the plant at this or that particular moment of its development, not its developmental arc as a whole. On the other hand, knowing what set of phenomena is relevant to defining the concept of a particular plant would seem to require having its organizing principle, its law, already in hand.[17] Goethe's answer to this dilemma involves a complex and shifting array of terms—morphology, metamorphosis, archetype, idea, type, etc.—whose meanings and significance undergo subtle shifts over time. To simplify a complicated story, in the 1780s, Goethe is primarily concerned with questions of classification, and the notion of an *Urpflanze*, understood as a kind of primal form diversifying itself into empirically diverse plants, is called upon as a model for description and comparison. After 1790, and partly in response to his reading of Kant, Goethe increasingly reflects on the phenomenology and technology of observation, articulating more clearly the subjective and experimental conditions that make knowledge of living things possible. Put simply, Goethe begins to realize that the fluidity of life requires a newly fluid mode of knowing. The metamorphosis of the organism is mirrored, in Goethe's scientific writings, in a metamorphic model of thought that culminates in the liquefaction and animation of the concept.[18]

The shift is initiated in Goethe's remarkable essay "The Experiment as Mediator of Object and Subject" from 1792. The link between subject and object (hence, knowledge) requires an experimental mediation that interrupts and recalibrates our habitual modes

---

17.   The problem of knowing plants is further complicated by their generic fluidity, which makes the traditional classificatory method look hopelessly schematic. If "*das Geschlecht sich zur Art, die Art zur Varietät, und diese wieder durch andere Bedingungen ins Unendliche sich verändern kann*," (HA 13:163), then the bio-logic underpinning natural history, the notion of static *and* fixed natural classes, evaporates.

18.   For a very persuasive but different account of Goethe's development that stresses the influence of Spinoza, see Frederick Amrine, "Goethean Intuitions," *Goethe Yearbook* 18, no. 1 (January 2011): 35–50.

of seeing and intuiting. Our ordinary perceptual engagement with the world both opens up and obscures the richness of phenomena: overpowered by the plentitude of detail, color, variation, and change, we get in our own way, clip, distort, censor, compress, overlook, and exaggerate what we see. There is always too much, and too little, to be seen. Goethe tells the story of friends who, after being told by him about his optical theories, "make quick note of phenomena I was unaware of or had neglected to observe. Thus they may be able to correct ideas developed in haste, and even produce a break-through by transcending the inhibitions in which exacting research traps us" (HA 13:12). The idea that "exacting research" can blind us as to what is in plain sight may seem trivial, but Goethe's point is complex and rich; it is not just that the friends, unburdened by theoretical preconceptions, have fresh eyes that naively take in what the scientist entrenched in his own ideas can no longer acknowl-edge (although that is one part of the story) but rather that the friends' vision, while capturing significant bits and aspects of phe-nomena, is also partial and incomplete. Freud depicts the psyche as shielded from the too-muchness of life by a deadened surface (the skull) that fends off and filters an otherwise unbearable onslaught of stimuli.[19] Goethe suggests a similar discrepancy between the complexity of life and our resources for processing it; yet unlike Freud, for whom psychic life outside the protective skull is unliv-able, Goethe's essay works toward closing, or at least minimizing, the complexity gap: it works toward creating an "experience . . . of a higher sort" that is equal to the richness of life.[20]

To achieve this enhanced experience, work on the subject is needed. Goethe's essay articulates the problem of scientific knowl-edge in terms of the education of the scientist. The techniques and technologies captured under the term "experiment" are first of all spiritual and cognitive practices designed to slow down our habitual

---

19. Sigmund Freud, "Jenseits des Lustprinzips," in *Gesammelte Werke*, vol. 13 (Frankfurt am Main: Fischer Tacshenbuch, 1999) XIII:26–27.

20. "*Eine solche Erfahrung, die aus mehreren andern besteht, ist offenbar von einer höhern Art*" (HA 13:18).

modes of cognition.[21] The problem of knowledge is deeply embedded in our human condition: our perceptual encounter with the world is always orchestrated within the context of a complex cognitive apparatus that tends to overburden our intuitions and prematurely eclipse the visible. Our distinctly human capacity for theorizing, for imaginatively constructing a whole out of something that presents itself only in part, is both a blessing and a curse. Kant describes knowledge production in terms of the intellectual synthesis of inchoate sense data; Goethe suggests that synthetic cognition must be subordinated to experimental compilation, which postpones the act of unification and creates room for the articulation of differences between the compiled elements.[22] Thus the experiments are designed to arrest our cognitive syntheses and to expand the temporal and spatial range of our intuitions. We must learn to enlarge our capacity for attentiveness, to leave appearances alone, to let them grow in our mind until they achieve, in us, their full phenomenal richness. Only then do we gain the "higher intuition" that is capable of grasping what Goethe would call, six years later, "*das reine Phänomen*" ("Erfahrung und Wissenschaft" (1798), HA 13:25).

Goethe's 1792 essay offers a first stab at this new conception of scientific observation, which consists of three phases. In a first, analytic and countersynthetic phase, our ordinary modes of synthesis are suspended in favor of amplifying our cognition in three ways: (1) multiplication of perspectives—"We will find that the greatest accomplishments come from those that never tire in exploring and working through all aspects and modifications of a single experience, of every experiment, in all its possibilities" (HA 13:17); (2) multiplication of observers—"The interest of many focused

---

21. Pierre Hadot devoted an entire book to Goethe's relationship to ancient spiritual practices; see his *N'Oublie Pas de Vivre: Goethe et la tradition des exercises spirituels* (Paris: Albin Michel, 2008). However, Hadot does not mention Goethe's essay or even his scientific work, even though he had discussed the latter in a previous study, *Veil of Isis: An Essay on the History of the Idea of Nature*, trans. Michael Chase (Cambridge, MA: Harvard University Press, 2008).

22. On the importance of internal differentiation and postponement of cognitive syntheses in particular, see Eva Geulen's excellent *Aus dem Leben der Form*.

on a single point can produce excellent results" (HA 13:12); (3) multiplication as iteration and cross-linking—"Thus when we have done an experiment of this type . . . we can never be careful enough in studying what lies next to it or derives directly from it. . . . The multiplication of experiments thus is the real task of the scientific researcher" (HA 13:18).

In a second, constructivist phase, multiple experiments are organized into a *series*. The relevant element of scientific observation is not the momentary experience but the experimental system conceived as the arrangement of interrelated snapshots. "In the first two parts of my optical contributions I sought to set up a series of contiguous experiments derived from one another in this way which, studied thoroughly and surveyed in their entirety [*wenn man sie alle genau kennt und übersieht*], make up as it were one single experiment, one single experience, represented in its manifold perspectives" (HA 13:18). Recall the problem of capturing the form of something subject to perpetual transformation: since all we can directly perceive is the thing at a particular moment of its development, we must somehow transcend ordinary perception and capture the developmental arc as a whole, grasp the elusive law underlying the chain of transformations. The creation of an experimental series is meant to prepare the ground for this apprehension by providing a synoptic overview of the plant in its developmental stages. As such, the experiment functions as a new kind of cognitive engagement, constructed in the laboratory, that enables the scientist to surmount the pitfalls of empirical perception and reach an "experience of a higher sort."

The experiment thus ideally culminates, in a third and final phase, in the synthetic apprehension of the "pure phenomenon" in its vital richness (HA 13:25). Sometime after 1792, Goethe spelled out in more detail this higher experience. Thus he wrote in 1798: "At first I am inclined to think certain steps, but since nature makes no leaps, I am finally obliged to intuit the succession of an uninterrupted activity as a whole [*mir die Folge einer ununterbrochenen Tätigkeit als ein Ganzes anzuschauen*] by sublating the singular without destroying the impression. . . . If one thinks of the results of these experiments, one sees that in the end experience must stop, the intuition of a becoming begin [*die Anschauung eines Werden-den eintreten*], and finally the idea be articulated" ("Ordnung des Unternehmens" (1798), FA 24:352–53). The *Anschauung eines Wer-denden* requires a nonmaterial form of vision, what Goethe calls the "mind's eyes" ("Entwürfe zu einem osteologischen Typus" (1795–96), FA 24:248).[23] This adds two other fundamentally imagined layers of visuality to the empirical images of ordinary perception: it pictures the invisible transitions from one form to another, and it intuits the entire sequence of transformations as a unified form in which simultaneity and succession coincide. In the higher experience, that is, the mind both sequentializes the various stages of plant growth *and* grasps these stages in their totality, as a nondiscursive, nonsequential unity, a unity that is not a mere intellectual concept but the object's own unity and essence. In a remarkable passage from 1824, Goethe depicts the interplay of perception, imagination and cognition involved here in some detail:

> Of the productivity of such inner images that are called upon the eyes I can say a lot. I had the capacity to conjure up, eyes closed and head down, a flower in the middle of my eyes, such that it did not stay fixed in its first gestalt for a moment but instead unfolded, with new flowers emerging from its interior, even green leaves; these were no natural flowers but fantasized ones, yet regular like the roses of sculptors. It was impossible to arrest the gushing creation; it lasted as long as I pleased, did neither slacken nor intensify. . . . It did not occur to me to do these experiments with other objects; why they emerged so freely may have to do with the fact that through many years of observing the metamorphoses of plants . . . I had fully immersed myself in them. . . . [In these visual experiments] the appearance of the after-image [*die Erscheinung des Nachbildes*], memory, productive imagination, concept and idea are all in play at once, manifesting themselves in the vitality of the organ with perfect freedom and without intention and direction. ("Das Sehen in subjektiver Hinsicht, von Purkinje," MA 12:353)

Eckart Förster has drawn attention to the relation between Goethe's model of scientific observation and Kant's third *Critique*. According to Förster, Goethe takes his cue from Kant's discussion of the

---

23. See Förster, "Goethe and the 'Auge des Geistes.'"

antinomies of teleological understanding in the *Critique of Judgment*, taking "Kant's merely problematic notion of an 'intellectual intuition' as an invitation to develop an extended, not only discursive, but at the same time intuitive thinking, one that leads from the general to the particular, from the particular to the general, and which becomes, in the intuition of the whole, an experience of a higher order."[24] Whether or not one follows Förster's characterization of Goethean observation as intellectual intuition—and there are good reasons to think that Förster underplays the aesthetic and constructive dimension of Goethe's writings[25]—it is clear that Goethe breaks with the Kantian framework. Where Kant conceives of organic form as a regulative idea, Goethe develops an organic mode of cognition that dissolves the (Kantian) opposition between concept and intuition, thought and object. Faced with a world that is in constant flux, thought surrenders itself to the mutability of its object and develops along with it. It becomes as supple as the life it observes: "That which is formed is immediately being transformed [*Das Gebildete wird sogleich wieder umgebildet*]. If we wish to arrive at some living intuition of nature [*lebendige Anschauung der Natur*], we ourselves must remain as flexible and formative [*beweglich und bildsam*] as nature and follow the example by which she leads us" ("Die Absicht eingeleitet" (1806–7), FA 24:392). In short, Goethe extends the fluidity of *Bildung* to the inner workings of the mind. Instead of arresting and freezing the object, as does conceptual thinking according to Kant and the philosophical tradition, proper thinking models its inner movement on nature's metamorphic rhythm. Mobile, fluid, and supple, the *anschauendes Denken* no longer fixes and separates, and thus no longer carries the air of the mechanical associated with discursive thinking. Instead, it has achieved a kind of second-order organicism; it has become "living thought."

---

24. Förster, "Bedeutung," 186.

25. See for instance Geulen, who suggests that the demand on the observer to oscillate between two countervailing perspectives on his (non)object is mirrored in the style of Goethe's text, which "first postulates a principle and simultaneously reduces this prinicple to a mere hint/interpretation [*zur bloßen (An)Deutung reduziert*]." *Aus dem Leben der Form*, 63.

Art, Life, and the Novel

Kant's transcendental inquiry shows that our judgments about living things differ from judgments about other kinds of things. Goethe adds that our ability to so judge and single out living things shows up something about our mind: it shows that, given proper training, we are capable of a mode of thinking that is attuned to the metamorphic dynamics of living things. The question of vital form thus poses itself in Goethe on two interrelated levels: on the level of the self-forming natural object; and on the level of its proper description. Turning now to *Wilhelm Meister*, this double perspective implies that any discussion of life in Goethe's novel must engage both (a) the form of the represented content, and (b) the aesthetic form of its novelistic enframement.[26] And there is a further complication, one that distinguishes the novelistic representation of human life from the botanical description of natural life. A short plot summary will give us an initial inkling of this difference.

Wilhelm, in love with the actress Marianne, narrates in detail to her the story of his childhood infatuation with the puppet theater, as well as with an epic poem by Tasso and a painting owned by his grandfather (book 1). After recovering from a mental breakdown brought about by his discovery of Marianne's unfaithfulness, Wilhelm is sent by his father on a business trip, where he soon uses his father's money to form a theater company (book 2). Attracted to the actress Philine, deeply fascinated by the mysterious and androgynous Mignon, and accompanied by a melancholic musician known as Harper, Wilhelm is introduced by Jarno to the work of Shakespeare, whose *Hamlet* he plans to stage with the theater director Serlo and his sister Aurelia, yet another actress (books 3–4). As he is preparing for the role of Hamlet, Wilhelm learns of his father's death. On the night following the performance, during which Wilhelm is puzzled by an unknown actor playing the ghost, the theater burns down, marking a turning point in Wilhelm's life.

---

26. The notion of life-form, in other words, complicates the traditional narratological distinction between fabula (content) and sjuzet (organization).

Shortly thereafter Wilhelm and his group are attacked by robbers, and the wounded Wilhelm meets for the first time the "beautiful amazone" and his future wife, Natalie. The company disbands, Mignon and the Harper suffer breakdowns, and Aurelie dies, asking Wilhelm to communicate news of her death to her former lover, Lothario (book 5). Before Wilhelm meets Lothario, Goethe inserts into the narrative a religious autobiography, the *Confessions of a Beautiful Soul*, written by Lothario's aunt, who tells of her dedication to God and her withdrawal from the everyday world (book 6). Wilhelm meets Lothario and is introduced to the aristocratic Tower society, a secret society engaged in economic, social, and pedagogical reforms. He learns that he had fathered a child (Felix) with the late Marianne, decides to marry the homely Therese, and is presented with an account of his life, written by the Tower, which reveals that its members (Jarno, Abbé, the ghost, etc.) have overseen and influenced his life all along (book 7). Wilhelm again meets Natalie, Lothario's sister, who had dressed his wounds after an earlier accident, and whom he had since sought in vain. Mignon dies of a sudden heart attack and is embalmed by the Tower's doctor and laid to rest during an elaborate ritual, while the Harper, after a report revealing that he had incestuously fathered Mignon with his sister, commits suicide. Finally, Wilhelm inherits his father's business, adopts Felix, and, thanks to the intervention of Lothario's brother Friedrich, is united with Natalie, while Lothario marries Therese (book 8).

Even this cursory summary should highlight the twisted plot character of Goethe's novel and caution against any straightforwardly organicist reading. But the synopsis also points to a crucial reason for this formal complexity. Wilhelm's biography is shot through with and shaped by his engagement with forms of representation, and in particular with *aesthetic* form (puppet theater, epic poetry, paintings, Shakespeare, dance, songs, confessional narrative, funeral rites, embalmment, etc.). Human life, Goethe's novel suggests, is irreducibly representational, marked and delineated through symbolic forms that overwrite their organic substrate. Hence the paradigmatic significance of Aurelie's cut discussed at the outset of this chapter. Moreover, the various uses of art within the novel point to the ambiguous role of aesthetic representation within the economy of human life: while the subject (Wilhelm) is involved in acts of aesthetic self-fashioning, larger social forces (the Tower) make use of art to orchestrate their normative interventions. If we add to this that artificial marks, as emblematized in Aurelie's cut, are shown to cut into biological life, we get a first inkling of the novel's stance on the form of human form: the suggestion that it is through art, the medium of form's self-reflection, that the incorporation of artifice, power, and nature proper to individuals shaped by community and symbols can be fully apprehended. Observing observers, representing representations, Goethe's novel self-reflexively depicts the formation of human life—its *Lebensform*—as a function of aesthetic development. Aesthetics is bioaesthetics. To flesh out this equation, I will focus on four aspects of the novel in which aesthetic representation, biology, and power intersect: (a) Wilhelm's obsession with the puppet theater; (b) the relation between art and life; (c) Mignon; and (d) the work of the Tower Society.

Puppets, Theater, and the Mystery of Animation

It seems that the canonization of Goethe's novel in terms of *Bildung* and bildungsroman has systematically obscured one of its most intricate features: its exploration of the place of the *mechanical* in human life. This is all the more surprising since from the outset the novel places this theme squarely in front of us. Wilhelm's story begins, after all, with his fascination with puppets, and the link forged in this primal scene between human desire and the secret life of physical bodies remains of central concern throughout the book. In beginning the story of Wilhelm's life with his infatuation with puppetry, the novel frames the birth and formation of the subject in terms of his fascination not just with artifactual or representational form but more disturbingly and precisely with their vitality. For what draws Wilhelm to the puppets is the mystery of their animation, the undisclosed life encrypted in the motion of mechanical limbs.

Late eighteenth-century aesthetic discourse associated marionettes with the low and popular—vulgar enjoyments drawn from lifeless objects without interiority.[27] Goethe's depiction of the puppet theater is diametrically opposed to this discourse. Instead of the noisy openness of the marketplace, the puppets make their appearance in the intimate setting of the nuclear family. And instead of mocking the bourgeois pretense of psychological interiority, their enigmatic fusion of inanimate artifacts with lifelike motion elicits in Wilhelm a quintessentially hermeneutic desire: the desire to decipher the hybrid code, to discover the hidden cause, to unveil the life beneath the machinery of the symbolic. Tropes of unveiling pervade Wilhelm's obsession with the theater from the very beginning:

> The first time I had the joy of surprise and astonishment; at the second performance I was intensely curious and observant. This time I wanted to find out exactly how everything was done. I had decided on that first evening that it couldn't be the puppets themselves that were speaking. I had even suspected that they could not move by themselves. But why it was all so agreeable, and why the puppets themselves seemed to speak and move . . . these mysteries disturbed me [*diese Rätsel beunruhigten mich*]. (WML 18; WMA 7)

Intent on unmasking the source of the puppet's motion, Wilhelm "lifts the curtain" of the theater, only to face a second, equally mysterious scene:

> I lifted the lower curtain, and looked through the framework. My mother noticed me and pulled me back; but I had already seen how my friends and foes, Saul and Goliath, and whoever all the others were, were being put away in a drawer [*Schiebkasten*]. This was fresh nourishment for my half-satisfied curiosity. To my great astonishment I saw the lieutenant busy in this sanctuary [*im Heiligtume sehr geschäftig*]. (WML 19; WMA 7)

The Lieutenant's busy movement in the *Heiligtume*, the mother's intervention, the disappearance of little creatures in the *Schiebkasten*— Wilhelm's lifting of the curtain opens a view onto a scene that is, as

---

27. See Christopher J. Wild, *Theater der Keuschheit, Keuschheit des Theaters. Zu einer Geschichte der (Anti-)Theatralität von Gryphius bis Kleist*, Reihe Litterae 113 (Freiburg im Breisgau: Rombach, 2003).

David Wellbery has pointed out,[28] itself structured as a screen memory, that is, as a representational veil that reveals at the same time as it hides its underlying fantasmatic content. For what Wilhelm believes to have witnessed in the activity behind the curtain is nothing other than the act of creation itself. The riddle of the inanimate puppets promises to hold the answer to the origin of animation, and thus ultimately to Wilhelm's own origin. Behind the puppet theater, and radiating through its manifest contents, lies the fantasy of the primal scene. This fantasy is intimately connected to another riddle that fascinates Wilhelm: the question of sexual difference. This is made abundantly clear in the novel's earlier version, *Wilhelm Meisters Theatralische Sendung*, where the above passage is followed by the following sentences:

> Just as at certain times children become aware of the differences of the sexes, and their gazing through the veils that conceal these secrets evoke strange commotions in their nature [*und ihre Blicke durch die Hüllen, die diese Geheimnisse verbergen, gar wunderbare Bewegungen ihrer Natur hervorbringen*], so it was for Wilhelm with this discovery. (WMTS; MA 2.2:15)

To return to the later version, his curiosity both thwarted and intensified, Wilhelm combs through the house, in the manner of "children [who] like rats and mice . . . seek out cracks and crannies to find their way to forbidden dainties" (WML 19; WMA 7). He eventually gains access to another forbidden *Heiligtume*, the maternal sanctuary of the pantry:

> One Sunday morning the special key was left in the keyhole as my mother was caught unawares by the bells ringing for the church service. . . . As soon as I noticed it, I crept gingerly along the wall, moved quietly to the door, opened it, and with one stride was in the midst of so many long-desired delights. I rapidly scrutinized all the chests, sacks, boxes, cases and jars and, wondering what to take, I finally picked up some of my

---

28. See David Wellbery, "Die Enden des Menschen. Anthropologie und Einbildungskraft im Bildungsroman (Wieland, Goethe, Novalis)," in *Das Ende. Figuren einer Denkform*, ed. Karlheiz Stierle and Rainer Warning (Munich: Wilhelm Fink, 1996), 619 ff.

beloved prunes, some dried apples and some preserved pomegranate skin, and was about to slip out with my loot when I noticed some boxes with wires and hooks hanging out of the lids, which had not been properly closed. I had an idea what these might be, fell upon them and discovered to my delight [*überirdischen Empfindung*] that here packed away was the whole world of my joys and heroes. I tried to pick up the ones on top to look at them, and then those underneath, but soon I had tangled up all the wires and got very upset and frightened, especially since I heard the cook moving in the adjoining kitchen. (WML 20; WMA 8)

Curtain, pantry, chests, boxes, cases, jars—the mystery of mechanical motion draws Wilhelm into a labyrinth of enclosures in which, in the manner of Russian dolls, boxes contain boxes, veils hide other veils, and revelation releases, not a hidden truth, but another secret demanding disclosure. The secrecy, excitement, and anxiety involved suggest an illicit engagement with boxes encountered not simply as vessels of containment but as metonyms of the maternal womb: disclosure, in other words, is framed as an erotic exploration into the mysteries of sexuality, which are in turn invested with metaphysical and religious significance (*überirdische Empfindung, Heiligtume*, etc.). But the passage also introduces to us, in compressed form, the problematic dialectic of desire and appearance that permeates Goethe's depiction of human representational life. If, in the case of the biological, "metamorphosis" describes a teleological process according to which matter's *immanent* development yields to the articulation of form, human life is shaped by the encounter with external forms that simultaneously promise and defy the revelation of hidden meaning, thus eliciting a desire for disclosure that is unsatisfiable and hence open-ended.

The contrast with Goethe's scientific writings could not be greater. As we have seen, Goethe's model of scientific observation is decidedly phenomenological. The search for a higher intuition aimed at capturing the unity of metamorphic change remains committed to the observation of the surface. Form is *Gestalt*, a visual constellation located in the interplay of shifting shapes, rather than behind them. Thus time and again, Goethe the scientist warns against the ruse of depth and hiddenness: "Nature has neither kernel nor shell" (HA 1:359); or, "One must not look behind the phenomena; they are themselves the teaching," (FA 13:49), a phrase Wittgenstein cited approvingly.[29] Since for Goethe (as for Wittgenstein) the search for underlying causes is a prime example of our problematic human propensity for symbolic and conceptual closure, we might say that Goethe's entire model of scientific observation is designed to *counter* the hermeneutic impulse to penetrate the phenomenological surface. The scientific creation of an experimental series is an antidote to our obsession with interiority and depth.

Thus when Wilhelm lifts the curtain of the puppet theater, he looks for answers in the wrong places. Tellingly, Wilhelm's theatrical obsessions unfold under the spell of the very faculty Goethe as scientist sought to curb through the empirical constraints of serial observation: unbridled imagination.[30] What makes imagination so seductive is its power to make present and whole what is hidden and inchoate, specifically in this instance, its power to *animate*[31] (thus to bridge mind and matter, interior and exterior, concept and intuition). This power of animation is nowhere more active than in (Wilhelm's perception of) the puppets, whose paradoxical vitality draws his mind beyond the phenomenological curtain, toward the fantasmatic scene of life's origin.

Let me push the link to biology a bit further and suggest that Wilhelm's fantasies are intimately connected to contemporary scien-

---

29.   Wittgenstein, RPP 1, §889.

30.   Just as young Wilhelm's "*Einbildungskraft brütete über der kleinen Welt* [my imagination brooding over that little world]" (WML 23; WMA 9) of the puppet theater, so the adult Wilhelm falls in love with the actress Marianne on "*den Flügeln seiner Einbildungskraft* [wings of imagination]" (WML 14; WMA 4). On the pathology of imagination in Goethe's novel, see Wellbery, "Die Enden des Menschen."

31.   Consider the language of animation in the following passage, which depicts the adult Wilhelm musing over his marionettes. "*Und mit diesem erbat er sich die Schlüssel, eilte, fand die Puppen und war einen Augenblick in jene Zeiten versetzt, wo sie ihm noch* belebt *schienen, wo er sie durch die* Lebhaftigkeit *seiner Stimme, durch die Bewegung seiner Hände zu* beleben *glaubte* [He then asked for the keys for the room where the puppets were kept, rushed off, found the puppets, and for a moment was transported back to the time when they seemed to him *animated*, when he thought he could bring them *alive* by his own *lively* voice and the movements of his own hand]" (WML 14; WMA 4, my emphases; translation modified).

tific discussions. The increasing emphasis on the dynamism of natural organisms opened up the conceptual space for vitalist inquiries into the origins of life. As Blumenbach suggested, what animates natural beings and holds them together is a hidden yet ubiquitous formative energy. Vitalism thus introduced a new type of causality, what might be called a causality of revelation, in which observable forms were seen as surface expressions of an underlying, invisible cause. While Kant framed his inquiry in transcendental terms, as a condition of our possibility of cognizing natural organisms, thus barring all investigation into the mystery of life itself, more vitalist thinkers such as Blumenbach sought to identify the expressive force *behind* organic form. One offshoot of this is the link between the new conception of organic form and a new, so-called epigenetic theory of development and generation.[32] Unlike its precursor model, preformationism, which held that the offspring already preexists in earlier generations, theories of epigenesis maintained that the development of the organism is directed by a generative force that is most powerfully at work at the moment of conception. Though seemingly esoteric, epigenetic theories exerted a strong attraction beyond the field of natural research. Put broadly, with the turn to vitalism, questions of origin and reproduction, and thus of sexuality, came to exert a new and heightened fascination, and in fact became focal points for intense biometaphysical fantasy.[33]

Goethe's novel dramatizes this new kind of vitalist fantasy. Wilhelm's search for the source of the puppets' movements, which leads him to boxes contained in boxes, stages the emergence of the new vitalist model of revelatory causality out of the failure of the older mechanical theory of generation, the theory of preformation. Theories

---

32. See Helmut Müller-Sievers, *Self-Generation: Biology, Philosophy, and Literature Around 1800* (Stanford, CA: Stanford University Press, 1997) and Justin E. H. Smith, ed., *The Problem of Animal Generation in Early Modern Philosophy* (Cambridge: Cambridge University Press, 2009), 235–417. On preformation, see Clara Pinto-Correia, *The Ovary of Eve: Egg and Sperm and Preformation* (Chicago: University of Chicago Press, 1997).

33. See Ludmilla Jordanova, "Interrogating the Concept of Reproduction in the Eighteenth Century," in *Conceiving the New World Order*, ed. Faye D. Ginsburg and Rayna Rapp (Berkeley: University of California Press, 1995), 369–87.

of preformation maintained that the adult organism was already fully formed, in miniature, in either the maternal egg or the male sperm, such that the shape of each offspring was already contained in the earlier generation, following a strict line of descent ultimately originating in the first parents. Natural history, on this model, was conceived as a mechanical series of encapsulations, of one generational box enclosed in the previous one, all the way down to the first parents. Hence the somewhat ironic German name for preformation: *Einschachtelungstheorie* (literally: theory of emboxment). Wilhelm's inquiry into the mystery of mechanical motion leads him straight into this preformationist world of infinite encapsulations, of boxes containing boxes. Yet in searching for the animating principle *behind or within* these boxes, Wilhelm asks the very question that preformationist theories excluded from the realm of natural science: the question of the origin of life, which performationism had relegated to a supposed divine act that fell outside the properly scientific—that is, mechanical—framework of explanation.[34]

Goethe was not a proponent of preformationism, but he also kept his distance from epigenetic theories.[35] The reason for this dual indifference has to do with Goethe's insistence on the epistemic primacy of intuition. As we saw, questions of origin inevitably lead the mind beyond the realm of the visible, toward ideas of beginning and absent cause. Whereas preformationism either bracketed the question of first cause or associated it with an incomprehensible divine act, epigeneticism, as Goethe critically remarks, "anthropomorphizes the word of the riddle" (FA 24:451). In other words, as soon as it is framed in epigenetic terms, the question of origin becomes the mystery of all mysteries, a biometaphysical riddle endlessly fueling the human mind's problematic propensity for theoretical spec-

---

34. But see the intriguing account of mechanism by Georges Canguilhem, *Knowledge of Life*, trans. Stefanos Geroulanos and Daniela Ginsburg (New York: Fordham University Press, 2008), 75–97, which argues that machines are not quite as mechanical as one might think, insofar as they presuppose a maker, and thus include elements of nonmechanical spontaneity and irrationality. Mechanistic thought tends to bracket this dimension, but cannot rid itself of it.

35. For a critique of both, see his short text "Bildungstrieb" (FA 24:452; also, FA 24:361).

ulation, thus threatening to derail the kind of phenomenological observation Goethe championed. Hence his unambiguous opposition to any "theory" of generation: "The concept of origination [*Entstehung*]," Goethe declares apodictically, "is completely denied to us" (FA 13:170).

This is clearly not what Wilhelm thinks. Wilhelm's investigations are infantile versions of an epigeneticist's theory of procreation, investigations that bring to the fore the latter's underlying and highly problematic *fantasmatic*—and thus psychological and cultural—dimension. Goethe's novel shows that once the question of life is asked, the causality of desire, as opposed to instinct or drive, assumes a more central and complex role. As long as generation is seen in mechanistic terms, as in preformation, desire plays no explanatory role in biological reproduction and thus is free, as it were, to roam outside the natural realm of reproduction, in the spectatorial and cultural world of banter, seduction, and disguise. This is the world of the aristocratic salon, of *Liasons Dangereuses* and *Così fan tutte*, of sartorial experimentation and cross-dressing. Terri Castle, Dror Wahrman, and others have written about "the mystery of the masquerade's cultural death" in the final decades of the eighteenth century, the "historical enigma," as Castle puts it, that the previously ubiquitous themes of transvestism and cross-dressing suddenly disappear from literature and culture.[36] I want to suggest that the reason for this historical enigma is a change in the character of enigma itself, which, in the context of the vitalist turn, acquires an existential dimension that it lacked in the visual illusion game of the eighteenth-century masquerade. As the genealogical question of origin imposes itself, it becomes necessary to explain the relation of the biological *Bildungstrieb* to the motivational force of desire. The role of desire is thus extended beyond the cultural realm and into accounts of reproduction, life, and existence. But this extension is neither unproblematic nor easy. Given the idiosyncrasy

---

36. Terry Castle, *Masquerade and Civilization: The Carnivalesque in Eighteenth-Century English Culture and Fiction* (Redwood Hills, CA: Stanford University Press, 1986), 330; Dror Wahrman, *The Making of the Modern Self: Identity and Culture in Eighteenth-Century England* (New Haven, CT: Yale University Press, 2004), 163ff.

of erotic attraction, it becomes necessary to connect the intrinsic mutability of desire with the brute facts of reproduction: to explain how desire both shapes the choice of reproductive partners and is in turn shaped by the forms of cultural representation it is expressed in, but also how the fickle play of desire can be aligned with the essentially teleological trajectory of a formative drive. Human sexuality thus emerges at the end of the eighteenth century as a profound and puzzling point of convergence between nature and culture, biological and symbolic life; a position, we might add, that it still occupies in Freud's definition of the sexual drive as a border concept between the somatic and the psychological, between body and representation.[37]

Art and Life

The theater is the first and formative site of a fantasy of depth that arrests Wilhelm's attention and orients the direction of his desire. As we saw, in its most extreme form, this fantasy centers on the spectacle of Wilhelm's own conception. But the primal scene only marks the extreme articulation of a search that shapes Wilhelm's life throughout the novel, and the question it raises points beyond the mystery of life's origin to another even more intractable and important mystery: the humanness of human life. Wilhelm's obsession with origins is part of his larger question concerning the unity, direction, and purpose—the characteristically human form—of (his) life. And it is in works of art, rather than in nature, that Wilhelm looks for answers.

Consider Wilhelm's engagement with his favorite book, Tasso's *Jerusalem Liberated*, which he discovers as a ten-year-old, stages as a director of children's theater, and fondly retells to Marianne in the novel's opening chapters. Wilhelm's interest in Tasso's sprawling poem is limited to a single story line: the tragic love of Tankred, a Christian warrior, for Chlorinda, an Ethiopian Amazon fighting for the Muslim armies. Tasso's epic poem ties war and love, desire

---

37. See for instance *Three Essays on the Theory of Sexuality: The 1905 Edition* (Brooklyn, NY: Verso, 2017), 168.

and death, into an inextricable knot. After encountering Chlorinda, "all clad in armor" (I, 47),[38] Tankred is consumed by both love and melancholy, the image of her androgynous beauty "in his heart and memory" (I, 48); he is stricken by the impossibility of his love, walking around "with every sign of sorrow in his face" (I, 49). Chlorinda is also torn. Hostile to all "feminine manners [*ingegni feminili*]" (II, 39) since childhood, she cannot yield to her desire for Tankred without losing her identity as a warrior. The two eventually meet during a night battle during which Tankred, not realizing that he is fighting Chlorinda, kills her. Grasping his mistake, Tankred tries to commit suicide and eventually falls into depression, which is only alleviated after Chlorinda appears to him in his dreams. But Tankred's suffering is not yet over. In the coda of the epic, set in a forest bewitched by a Muslim magician, Tankred plunges his sword into an animated tree only to hear Chlorinda's voice accusing him of having killed her yet another time. Overwhelmed by what the poem presents as Tankred's hallucinatory vision of Chlorinda's blood, he flees the woods and dies shortly thereafter.

Desire and death, blood and wounds, melancholy and suicidal ideation—Tasso's epic casts its tragic shadow on Wilhelm's life. Chlorinda's androgyny shapes Wilhelm's attraction to the important women in his life (Mariane, Mignon, and Natalie), while Tankred's melancholy returns in Wilhelm's frequent self-accusations and his tendency to "torment himself" (WML 77; WMA 42). Moreover, the tragic repetition structuring Tankred's love extends to Wilhelm's life, convincing him that he too is "destined to harm unwittingly everything he ever loved" (WML 27; WMA 12). And indeed, Marianne, Aurelie, and Mignon all die as a result of Wilhelm's love, while the Baronesse, accidentally wounded by him during an amorous embrace, sinks into hypochondria and melancholy. Tasso's text thus literally imprints itself on Wilhelm's and his lovers' lives, marking them physically as well as psychologically. As Wilhelm himself puts it in strikingly organic terms: "Now I see that an early, deep damage

---

38. All references are to Torquato Tasso, *Jerusalem Delivered*, ed. and trans. Anthonly M. Esolen (Baltimore: Johns Hopkins University Press, 2000). Roman numbers refer to the numbers of the canto, Arabic numbers to the strophe.

can never grow out, can never heal [*daß ein tiefer, früher Schade sich nicht wieder auswachsen, sich nicht wieder herstellen kann*]" (WML 84).

Art that damages, causes illness, endangers life—Wilhelm's fantasmatic identifications draw attention to an existential and pathological dimension of aesthetic experience absent from Kant's account. For Kant, aesthetic experience is both pleasurable and free from identification. We enjoy beautiful objects because their form perpetually engages our intellect and senses, making us reflect on the mysterious correspondence between the internal resources of our mind and the external resources of the object. Whereas the Kantian subject experiences the *structural* fit between mind and world as a life-enhancing pleasure, Wilhelm's passionate absorption in the diegetic content of Tasso's poem produces lethal effects. Under the pressure of Wilhelm's overactive imagination, aesthetically mediated reality assumes a hallucinatory hyperpresence that eclipses and overtakes empirical reality: "I still see it at this moment in front of me" (WML 12), Wilhelm says to Marianne about his childhood puppet theater, highlighting imagination's power to annul time and make sensually and affectively present what is empirically absent. Hans-Jürgen Schings has argued that *Wilhelm Meister* is a novel of healing, and David Wellbery has identified the imagination as the seat of disease in the early bildungsroman.[39] On Wellbery's reading, Wilhelm's theatrical obsession highlights the "phenomenological form of the imagination,"[40] its capacity, as a mode of seeing, to both cause and assuage desire through the imaginary production of visual scenarios of fullness.[41] The desired object whose presence imagination hallucinates is, in the last instance, not an empirical but an essentially imaginary one: the self-identity and completeness of the subject. Wilhelm's desire for art is driven by a fundamental "anthropological" lack.

---

39. Hans-Jürgen Schings, "Wilhelm Meisters schöne Amazone," *Jahrbuch der deutschen Schillergesellschaft* 29 (1985): 141–206; Wellbery, "Die Enden des Menschen."

40. Wellbery, "Die Enden des Menschen," 618.

41. Ibid., 607.

Whether theatrically orchestrating his own identity or emulating the desire of the characters of Tasso's poem—Wilhelm treats art as an instrument of self-fashioning. What Wilhelm looks for in theater, paintings, and songs, beyond mere aesthetic pleasure, is an answer to the fundamental questions of origin and identity: Who am I? What does it mean for me to be a properly human being? It is in view of these existential questions that the fictional and mimetic power of representational art asserts its crucial importance. For what Wilhelm finds in art is not simply clearly circumscribed objects or characters but their immersion in an internally differentiated world. Tasso's poem, for instance, shows Wilhelm what it means to love and to suffer, what is noble and base, what is worth dying for, what is a man and what is a woman, what generosity, despair, understanding, and blindness are—and it models a world in which all these and countless other phenomena interconnect, shaping the lives of those entangled in them. Tasso's poem initiates Wilhelm into a *form of life*.

And therein lies the true seductiveness of art in Goethe's novel. Aesthetic media are essential for Wilhelm because they provide him with a model of unity that holds the promise of coherence and comprehension. On the one hand, theater, painting, and epic poetry conjure up a world of vital activity and human drama, of characters in conflict with themselves and each other, existing in time and space, driven by desire and subject to despair and loss; they offer a slice of what Wittgenstein called "the whole hurly-burly [*Gewimmel*] of human actions" (Z, §567). On the other hand, aesthetic media enframe and organize this chaotic slice of human life, arranging it in a surveyable form that imparts to it a measure of completeness and finitude: a unity. The Russian semiotician Yuri Lotman has argued that art is a "secondary system" that uses pre-existing signs as building blocks for the creation of a more complex and unified sign.[42] Aesthetic media combine multiple signs and phenomena into a synoptically available, articulable form. Goethe's narrative highlights the existential implications of this synoptic

---

42. Yuri M. Lotman, *Die Struktur literarischer Texte* (Munich: Wilhelm Fink, 1972), 39–43.

power of art. In beginning the story of Wilhelm's life with his child-hood infatuation with art, the novel dramatizes the essential *and* problematic role of aesthetic form in the formation of human life. Wilhelm is drawn to theater, epics, and paintings because they of-fer him aesthetically demarcated models of life that, through their formal coherence, enable him to disavow his "anthropological lack" and imagine his life as a coherent and purposeful unity.

The novel clearly depicts this attitude as pathological. Pathology arises because in Wilhelm's engagement with art imagination oc-cludes the roles of intellect and intuition. As we have seen, both Kant's aesthetics and Goethe's morphology, while assigning a cru-cial cognitive role to imagination, also limit its power, either through the empirical constraints of serial observation (Goethe) or by sub-suming imagination "under the power of concepts (the understand-ing)" (Kant).[43] Wilhelm's engagement with art, by contrast, subor-dinates the role of understanding to the process of fantasmatic identification. Wilhelm is absorbed by the drama, the theatric repre-sentation, of desire, which his imagination imbues and identifies with reality. While from a Kantian perspective such an attitude clearly represents a skewed engagement with the aesthetic, I want to suggest that Goethe highlights an aspect of aesthetic experience that is markedly absent from the Kantian picture: the immersive power of mimesis. Kant's account of the aesthetic attitude is focused entirely on the *form* of the beautiful object, which explains his priv-ileging of natural—nonrepresentational—objects as paradigms of beauty. But unlike natural objects, art in general and narrative in particular are also fictions, and part of the pleasure we derive from them stems from our immersion in the imaginary worlds they con-jure. Under "normal" circumstances, imaginative immersion is an intentional stance accompanied by the awareness of fiction *as* fiction—"*seeing* the represented object while *knowing* that one sees a mimeme."[44] But the ability to differentiate between simulation and reality is itself an achievement that depends on the development

---

43. KU § 35.
44. Jean-Marie Schaeffer, *Why Fiction?*, trans. Dorrit Cohn (Lincoln: Univer-sity of Nebraska Press, 2010), 134 (emphases in the original).

of consciousness and ego structure. Kant may have had something like this in mind when he stressed that the capcity for disinterested aesthetic pleasure is a cultural achievement. It is against this background that the relevance of Wilhelm's *childhood* infatuation with art becomes visible. In highlighting the ambiguity of the immersive power of mimesis, Goethe's novel deepens and complicates Kant's inquiry into the relationship between art and life.

On the one hand, aesthetic experience is vital to human beings because it shows them something essential about both life and form: it shows them that life in general, and human life in particular, *can* have an articulate form. Art's synoptic power brings human life into a formal unity, imparting to it a boundedness and clarity that is inaccessible to individuals immersed in the midst of their lives. This synopticism of aesthetic media is a major source of their emotional power, which asserts its pull on human life, as Wilhelm's story shows, prior to and independent of any developed and "cultivated" aesthetic taste. Moreover, aesthetic fascination derives its intensity from what I described in the introduction as human life's "ontological vulnerabity." Due to its essential dependence on language and symbols, human life is open and incomplete, thus in need of receiving its form and "identity" from outside itself, from the world of culture. Hence the intrinsic plasticity of the human life-form, which makes human life particularly responsive to the force of aesthetic form. But this is also where the darker side of aesthetic experience enters the picture. Goethe's novel frames the ontological vulnerability of human life—its dependence on external forms—as a matter of a potentially lethal aesthetic susceptibility. Wilhelm's search for identity lures him into an artistic hall of mirrors. The problem is that the very source of art's appeal—its coherence and completeness—blinds Wilhelm to the discordant nature of his actual life. We have already touched on the hermeneutic dimension of the aesthetic lure. Theater's synoptic presentation of human life elicits in Wilhelm the promise of revelation, thus fueling his problematic desire to look behind the theatrical curtain and discover the source of life. Here as always, Wilhelm falls prey to the ordered veil of representation precisely because he seeks to penetrate it. Art's capacity to frame human life and arrange it in a surveyable form draws him *into* the represented frame, leading him to mistake the aesthetic orchestration of life for life itself. Yet life is unlike its aesthetic orchestration. In ignoring the difference between the two, Wilhelm represses the dimension of otherness within both: the contingent and flawed character of actual life, and the differential and open-ended play of the aesthetic. The consequence of this repression is a problematic aestheticization of life. Wilhelm does not simply immerse himself in fiction; he models internal and external reality after it, thus stifling his capacity to learn from experience—including, ironically, *aesthetic* experience. Kant's strict separation of aesthetic from ordinary experience was intended to highlight the freedom of the former but also to allow this freedom to inform and enrich the latter. It is because aesthetic engagement is freed from cognitive and moral demands that it gives rise to the reflective experience of a structural fit between mind and world that encouraged both scientific inquiry and ethical behavior, cognitive and moral life, without reducing aesthetic life to either of them. Wilhelm's absorptive stance flattens the distinction between these different regions and forms of human life. In making of art an instrument of identification, Wilhelm ignores both the artificiality of art and the heterogeneity of life.

Mignon

Nowhere are the dangers of art and the seductions of depth more pointedly concentrated than in the figure that became the darling of Romantics and nineteenth-century *Bildungsbürger*: the vexed, and in fact uncanny, figure of Mignon.[45] Explicitly introduced as a "*Rätsel* [riddle]" (WML 96), Mignon is the embodiment of the enigmatic, the unreadable sign that becomes the seductive focus of Wilhelm's and the reader's desire for revelation. Mignon's profound allure is the result of her polymorphic form. Oscillating between male and female, living being and mechanical contraption, child and adult, Mignon's heterogeneity both confounds the ordinary patterns of sense-making and brings her into conflict with the existing so-

---

45. On the history of Mignon, see Michael Wetzel, *Mignon. Die Kindsbraut als Phantasma der Goethezeit* (Munich: Wilhelm Fink, 1999).

cial forms of human life. And yet this heterogeneous and liminal figure is also the source of the novel's most poetic passages. While unable to speak and write coherently, Mignon expresses herself effortlessly in songs and poems that are among the most beautiful in Goethe's oeuvre. This confluence of beauty and liminality famously prompted Novalis and Schlegel to celebrate Mignon as the embodiment of poetry and denounce Goethe for sacrificing her, and poetry itself, to the prosaic world of the Tower Society. But this Romantic binary of art and power fails to capture Mignon's ambiguity and the complex status of art and biology within the novel. The conflict that defines Mignon runs not simply between her and the Tower but also through Mignon's very being. Mignon does not so much embody poetry as demonstrate the *impossibility* of embodying it—of living, being, existing as poetry. The stark duality of Mignon's existence—suffering and broken creature on the one hand, source of flawless poetry on the other—raises Wilhelm's problematic identification of art and life to a heightened level. Mignon is indeed, as the Romantics realized, the symbolic center of the novel, the figure around which the biological, existential, aesthetic, and political implications of its new model of human life are most clearly on display. If Goethe's novel conceives of human life as a form of forms, as I have claimed, then Mignon's unredeemed heterogeneity, which as we will see is given a *biological* explanation, places her at both the heart and limit of what the novel articulates as the human *Lebensform*.

But let us slow down and first analyze in more detail the link between Mignon's ambiguity and what I earlier described as the hermeneutics of vitalist desire. Mignon evokes in compressed and existential form all aspects of Wilhelm's obsession with secrecy. Thus, the riddle of sexual difference, first raised in Wilhelm's infantile investigation of the puppet theater and sounded throughout the novel in the form of cross-dressing, becomes in Mignon a veritable conundrum of gender identity:

Reflecting on this pleasant episode, [Wilhelm] was going upstairs to his room when a young creature [*ein junges Geschöpf*] jumped out at him and immediately attracted his attention. . . . He looked at the figure with amazement, uncertain whether it was a boy or a girl [*ob er sie für einen Knaben oder für ein Mädchen erklären sollte*]. But he finally decided in favor of the latter and stopped her . . . and asked to whom she belonged, although he could easily see that she was a member [*ein Glied*] of the group of acrobats and dancers. (WML 90; WMA 50)

Suspended between the grammatically neutral gender of descriptive categories—*das Geschöpf* (the creature), *das Glied* (the member), even *das Mädchen* (the girl)—and the masculine form of a foreign name, Wilhelm's "explanation" (*ob er sie für einen Knaben oder für ein Mädchen* erklären *sollte*) of Mignon's gender remains a matter of decision rather than biological determination. In Mignon, sexual hybridity is no longer a play with surfaces, as it is, say, in Mozart's roughly contemporaneous *Così fan tutte*, in which the characters' strategic use of cross-dressing never impinges on their "real" sexual identity. Whereas the play of illusion of eighteenth-century masquerade locates hybridity at the level of cultural forms, for Mignon the distinction between man and woman acquires an ontological and existential (and in fact, as we shall see, biological) indeterminacy: it points to a vital essence that withdraws into the depth of her mysterious being. It is precisely this withdrawal that piques Wilhelm's hermeneutic desire and rekindles his earlier bio-metaphysical fantasies of origin and generation.

Hence Wilhelm's obsession with Mignon. Like the ambiguous veil of theatrical representation, Mignon's sexual indeterminacy functions as a seductive entryway to an imagined interior locus of ontological truth and vitality. A similar intensification of ambiguity occurs in the other distinction that vitalism introduces—that between the mechanical and the organic. Once again Mignon is the uncanny embodiment of both conceptual distinction and its dissolution. Rather than a marionette mimicking life, Mignon seems to embody the paradox of a human android in which life and mechanical motion are conjoined:

She blindfolded herself, gave a sign for the music to begin, and started to move like a wound-up mechanism [*Räderwerk*], beating the time of the melody with the clap of her castanets. . . . Relentlessly, like a clockwork [*Uhrwerk*], she pursued her course, and the strange music gave a new jolt, with every repetition, to the movement of the continuously recommencing and surging dance. Wilhelm was absolutely transported by this strange spectacle; forgetting all his worries, he followed every movement of the beloved creature, amazed to see how supremely her character developed in the dance [*wie in diesem Tanz ihr Charakter sich vorzüglich entwickelte*]. . . . Severe, sharp, dry, violent, and in more tender positions more solemm than pleasing, she showed herself. (WML 113–14)

The mimicry of traditional marionettes is akin to the masquerade of cross-dressing: established distinctions are mixed up in ways that remain recognizable as a play of forms that supervene upon an unchanging material substrate. Masquerade and puppetry celebrate a certain freedom of cultural expression, establishing an autonomous realm in which representation is liberated both from the constraints of moral convention and from the efficient causality of natural bodies. As such, they represent an aesthetic suspension of normative categories anchored in a mimetic paradigm that leaves the distinction between (cultural) appearance and (natural) essence intact. The play is one of pure surface, of representations as opposed to things. Mignon's dance explodes this paradigm. In presenting her as a human being whose essence (*Charakter*) is paradoxically realized in a series of mechanical movements, her dance confounds the established criteria underpinning the distinctions between culture and nature, life and machine, animate and inanimate. More precisely, with Mignon the very idea of animation undergoes an uncanny conversion. To borrow a description aimed at a radically different context (that of twentieth-century racist depictions of black hyperexpressivity), animation "loses its generally positive associations with human spiritedness or vitality and comes to resemble a kind of mechanization."[46] In Mignon, Wilhelm's inquiry into the essence of "life" encounters a truly enigmatic object, one that, precisely because it undercuts traditional distinctions between the animate and the inanimate, seems to *embody* life's mysteriousness. Mignon captures Wilhelm's imagination, and our own, because she poses an ontological rather than a merely representational riddle.

---

46. Sianne Ngai, *Ugly Feelings* (Cambridge, MA: Harvard University Press, 2007), 32.

And there is another crucial feature of Mignon's hybridity: her incomplete grasp of language. Chopped and disjointed, Mignon's speech displays the machine-like character of a language at the boundaries of communicative and semantic function:

> [Mignon] began to recite what she had learnt and in her own special way asked the strangest questions. Once again it became apparent that, for all her energy, her comprehension was slow and laborious. So too was her handwriting, though she took great pains over it. She still spoke a broken German; and only when she opened her mouth to sing, or played the zither, did she reveal the one organ she had to express her innermost self. (WML 261; WMA 156)

Mignon neither entirely inhabits nor is inhabited by language, as her very first words in the novel already highlight. When asked for her name, she evades the use of the first-person singular and reports her name in the alien, objective register of the third person: "They call me Mignon [*Sie heißen mich Mignon*]" (WML 97; WMA 54). The formulation harks back to the topic of sexual difference. Just as Mignon's ambiguity highlights the discriminatory force of sexual-symbolic distinctions, so her inability to identify with her name draws attention to the inescapability of society. Mignon's third-person formulation gets things just right: naming is a social act in which we are imposed upon by the society of those who name us. The problem with Mignon is not that she is named by others— we all are—but that she is unable to appropriate this ascription, and thus develop a voice in language. In this sense, Mignon's first sentence foreshadows her fate in the novel, which culminates, as we shall see, in the Tower Society's violent orchestration of her death. Before we can fully appreciate the politics of Mignon's death, we must better understand how her ambiguity troubles the very thinking of life and form—and thus the models of *Lebensform*—in 1800. For Mignon does not fit any of the notions of form and causality that Kant and Goethe developed in their attempt to conceptualize the relationship between nature and culture, *bios* and *zoe*, human freedom and natural life.

Kant in particular develops his conceptions of form in terms of causality. Prior to the third *Critique*, he operates with a sharp opposition between two types of causality: the efficient, mechanical causality of nature, and the free and spontaneous causality of reason. The third *Critique* complicates this opposition by introducing the idea of a teleological causality as a necessary schema or "maxim" for our understanding of living beings (KU §66, 5:376; CPJ 248). The form of "organized products of nature," in which "everything is an end and reciprocally a means as well" (ibid.) points to a causality that is "strictly speaking . . . not analogous with any causality that we know" (KU §65, 5:375; CPJ 246). Although Kant goes on to conceive of teleological causality on the model of "our own causality in accordance with ends" (that is, in accordance with goal-directed and intentional action) (ibid.), the form of organisms is, as we saw, most akin to the "purposiveness without purpose" characteristic of works of art (KU §15, 5:226, my translation). The organization of a work of art is not a means to an end but an expressive totality in which every element stands in a reciprocal, rather than a mechanical or instrumental, relationship to all other elements. Because an artwork's "purposiveness in its form" seems to be "free from all constraint by arbitrary rules," the work of art appears as "if it were a mere product of nature" (KU §45, 5:306; CPJ 185). Thus in art, freedom manifests itself not in the form of will or intentional action but "through an order in which that which is ordered seems to be natural."[47] As for Mignon? Her problem is that she fits none of these models of causality and form. Neither machine nor plant, her behavior also lacks the ordinary structure of intentional action or the "purposiveness without purpose" of an artwork. The single most characteristic feature of Mignon's existence is a persistent stutter that reveals, not a coherent form, but the friction between incongruous systems and causalities.

This is why attempts at interpreting Mignon in view of contemporary biological or aesthetic models of form miss the mark. In a book-length study, Michael Wetzel has analyzed Mignon in terms of Goethe's theory of organic form, arguing that she represents "the

---

47. Thomas Khurana, "Die Kunst der zweiten Natur. Zu einem modernen Kulturbegriff nach Kant, Schiller und Hegel," *WestEnd—Neue Zeitschrift für Sozialforschung* 1 (2016): 41.

transitional stage of a metamorphosis, a snapshot that compresses before and after into a moment of seemingly perfect development."[48] But Mignon's ambiguity never coheres into an individual whole, let alone into the individual universality of a Goethean type. Mignon represents precisely the *failure* of developmental unification. Whereas in Goethe's scientific model the mind's eye synthesizes the series of snapshots into a single image-concept that captures the living being in its developmental unity, as a dynamic life-form, in the case of Mignon any such attempt at synthetic unity is clearly frustrated. Mignon's chopped and machinelike movement reveals, if anything, the disruption of formal development. Nor is it very convincing to understand Mignon according to the model of a work of art, as the Romantics have done. While her songs are indeed utterly beautiful, her *being* clearly lacks the immanent coherence of an "order in which that which is ordered seems to be natural." What is striking about Mignon is not the harmonious fusion of freedom and materiality that Kant saw articulated in the artwork but the various *conflicts*—between mouth and speech, desire and body, inner and outer, mechanical and organic—expressed in her disjointed being. In short, Mignon's brokenness places her in radical opposition to the two paradigmatic models of form—organisms and artworks— used to rethink the relationship between human and biological life, first and second nature, in nineteenth-century German science and philosophy.

And this is precisely the significance of Mignon's ambiguity. Kant's description of the artwork as a purposive whole reconceptualized the relationship between nature and culture. Following the third *Critique*, the work of art was seen as a model of human freedom that realized itself not against nature but in and through it. Just as the artist creates new, artificial, yet seemingly natural orders out of existing material, so culture and morality were to be conceived as free and creative extensions of an underlying biological substrate—as a second nature that, while carried out by embodied creatures bound to natural laws, had its own kind of *non*biological vitality. This is why the beautiful artwork, in Kant's famous phrase,

---

48. Wetzel, *Mignon*, 165.

is the "symbol of morality" (KU §59, 5:351; CPJ 225)—that is, the sign of man's supersensible freedom. Mignon's split nature—broken creature and sublime poet—casts a twofold doubt on this symbolic model. While her inability to dance, speak, or write fluidly highlights the mechanical side of cultural forms (and thus the unavailability of a second-order automaticity proper to nature), the rift between her perfect poetry and her imperfect speech undercuts the moral symbolism of art. Kant's argument rests on the claim that aesthetic and moral freedom are continuous with each other. Art's freedom of expression functions as a paradigm—a symbol—that discloses the possibility of moral-political progress. But what if art and life, aesthetic and social expression, have become discontinuous, as the fissure between poetry and existence that runs through Mignon's being implies? Mignon, I want to suggest, if a symbol at all, signifies neither the aesthetic nor the moral but the formal impossibility of both. Her function is not to represent a higher artistic or moral-political life but to mark out the *limits* of human and social form in Goethe's novel. Put differently, Mignon's symbolic homelessness, her inability to settle into the world of familiar categories, highlights the normative and ultimately violent dimension of what counts as a form of life in *Wilhelm Meister*.

Liberalism and the Art of Power

It is a commonplace of Goethe criticism that the appearance of the Tower Society marks a significant break in the narrative, with the loose and meandering episodic structure of the first four books giving way to a more straightforward movement toward closure and a happy ending. Yet the explicit interventions of the Tower Society only accentuate a dimension of the text that had been present from the very beginning. Not only does Wilhelm learn at the end that the Society has overseen and on occasion intervened into his life since childhood, the narrative itself is punctuated by auctorial directives. Passages such as the following emphasize the demiurgic character of narration, its power to forge the represented world, dropping characters once they have fulfilled their narrative duties and inserting others when the logic of the text requires it: "So we will not treat our readers to a detailed account of Wilhelm's woes and sorrows . . . but rather jump forward to join him again when we shall hope to find him more pleasurably employed" (WML 75). Narrative, in such passages, is shown to orchestrate and arrange rather than merely intuit, and the aesthetics of the novel draws closer to the mechanics of the puppet theater than to the "tender empiricisim" of Goethe's botanical laboratory. The operations of the Tower Society thus highlight an element of human life that is emphatically absent from the aesthetic and biological discourse of self-organization: power. This raises a number of crucial questions: To what extent is form, in Goethe's novel, *imposed onto* human life rather than emerging from within it? What broader forces and institutions are shown to shape and determine human life? What is the relationship between these trans-individual factors and the subjective forces of human life (desire, imagination, aesthetic sensibility, etc.) explored in the first half of the novel? In sum: what is the politics of the novel's conception of *Lebensform*?

The Romantic critique of *Wilhelm Meister's Apprenticeship* points in the direction I would like to follow: "The economic nature," Novalis writes about Goethe's novel, "is the truth—the one that remains."[49] The increasing importance of economic themes and considerations toward the end of the novel is unmistakable. It is not just that Wilhelm, by the close of the novel, inherits his father's business and becomes a merchant; with the appearance of the Tower, conversations on art and theater give way to decidedly more pragmatic issues. The Tower is involved in concrete economic and social reforms. Lothario advocates the abolishment of feudal rights, the capitalization of estates, a common system of taxation, and the end of old "hereditary privileges" such as primogeniture and entailment (WML 509–10; WMA 311). The goal is to free individuals from restrictive laws and traditions and to release "everybody into

---

49. Novalis, "Die Oeconomische Natur ist die Wahre—*Übrig-Bleibende*"; Novalis, "Fragmente und Studien. II. 1799–1800," in *Werke, Tagebücher und Briefe Friedrich von Hardenbergs*, ed. Hans-Joachim Mähl and Richard Samuel (Darmstadt: Wissenschaftliche Buchgesellschaft, 1999), 806; Fragment 320.

lively, free activity [*um alle in eine lebhafte freie Tätigkeit zu verset-zen*]" (WML 509). This emphasis on mobility and interdependence is raised to a global level by the Society's plan to organize its economic operations in the form of a kind of securities and exchange commission.[50]

One needs to know only little about the present state of the world trades [*Welthändeln*] to notice that we are on the brink of great changes, and that property is no longer safe anywhere. . . . The balance in human actions can, unfortunately, only be maintained through oppositions. At the present moment it is highly inadvisable to entrust all one's property and money to *one* place, yet it is difficult to oversee them in different places. We have therefore come up with an idea: from our ancient Tower a Society shall emerge, which will extend into every corner of the globe, and people from all over the world will be allowed to join in. We will ensure one another our existence [*Wir assekurieren uns untereinander unsere Existenz*], in case some political revolution should displace one of our members from the land he owns. I am now going to America to take advantage of the connections our good friend has established there, the Abbé will go to Russia, and you will have the choice, if you want to join us, to stay with Lothario in Germany or to come with me. (WML 564)

As an economic agent, the Tower Society is anything but a providential force. Like everybody else, it is also subject to circumstances it cannot control, a strong but limited actor in an unsurveyable and unpredictable field of opposing forces. What it can do, however, is to take this uncertainty into account, assess its probabilities, and arrange its own actions accordingly. It can *calculate* contingency, not in order to dispel it, but to make the best of it, either by buffering its effects or by bending contingency to its own purposes. This is the reasoning behind the Society's geographical diversification of its assets. A form of risk management, the strategy is built on the

---

50. On the economics of Goethe's novel, see Stefan Blessin, "Die radikal-liberale Konzeption von 'Wilhelm Meisters Lehrjahren,'" *DVJS* 49 (1975): 190–255; Joseph Vogl, *Kalkül und Leidenschaft. Poetik des ökonomischen Menschen* (Zurich: diaphanes, 2002); and Bernd Mahl, *Goethes ökonomisches Wissen. Grundlagen zum Verständnis der ökonomischen Passagen im dichterischen Gesamtwerk und in den "Amtlichen Schriften"* (Frankfurt am Main: Peter Lang, 1982).

Tower Society's awareness of its own limited powers and on the recognition of a complex reality that eludes human control.

Thus, changing laws is not enough. The new conception of reality—complex, contingent, irreducible to individual intention—calls not only for new laws and institutions but also for a new attitude toward the world: a willingness to confront, even highlight the dangerous and unpleasant aspects of reality in order to manage them in a systematic fashion. We get a first inkling of this attitude in a famous passage from the first book. "What advantage accrues to the businessman by double-entry bookkeeping!" raves Wilhelm's childhood friend Werner, himself a merchant:

> This is one of the finest inventions of the human mind, and every serious housekeeper should introduce it into his business [*und ein jeder guter Haushalter sollte sie in seiner Wirtschaft einführen*]. . . . Order and clarity increase the desire to save and to acquire. A man who doesn't keep good accounts, who doesn't reckon up what he owes, easily finds himself in a foggy state, whereas a good manager knows no greater pleasure than watching his fortunes mounting daily. A setback may be an unpleasant surprise for him, but it does not scare him; he can balance this out with the gains he has made elsewhere. (WML 37; WMA 18)

If double-entry bookkeeping is "one of the most beautiful inventions," this is not merely for economic reasons but also for moral ones. It is, as Franco Moretti comments, "because the precision of double-entry bookkeeping forces people to face facts: all facts, including—and in fact, *especially*—unpleasant ones."[51] Double-entry bookkeeping is not merely an economic practice but an ethos, a way of doings things that, while trained on economic operations, also engages the self's relation to itself. In recording his expenses and returns, the good housekeeper learns to acknowledge not what he wants to see but what is actually there. He learns to pay attention to what is in plain sight, be precise and systematic, weigh his desires, and control his imagination. Lorraine Daston and Peter Galliston have argued that the rise of nineteenth-century scientific

---

51. Franco Moretti, *The Bourgeois: Between Literature and History* (London: Verso, 2013), 86.

objectivity goes hand in hand with the development of what they call "epistemic virtues"—dispositions and attitudes such as precision, regularity, patience, and impartiality that inform the creation of a scientific self and shape the practice of science.[52] Something similar can be said about the practice of double-entry bookkeeping, which teaches, together with a model of fiscal transparency and a method for establishing it, a new set of ethical and psychological dispositions.

It is in this broader context that we must place the Tower's economic endeavors. What Novalis called the novel's "economic nature" is not limited to financial operations but encompasses a new conception of external reality in general, and of human life and ethics in paricular. We have already touched on the ethical implications of the Tower Society's economic vision, whose call for legal reform rests on a specific image of how human beings *ought* to live. Designed to unleash "lively, free activity," the reforms of the Tower Society reflect a belief in the economic *and* moral superiority of a society in which people get what they need through market exchange rather than through the goodwill of their masters. The primary role of the state, from this perspective, is to create and protect a solid framework for the free play of mutual self-interests; government must safeguard freedom of movement and implement a system of law and taxation that transforms all members of society into formally equal economic agents (WML 432, 509). The Tower Society's positions here reflect key aspects of eighteenth-century liberalism; in particular, they echo the work of Adam Smith, whose German followers Goethe had studied carefully from the 1780s onward.[53] For Smith, too, commercial society is both materially and morally superior to feudalism.[54] This is because economic transactions within feudalism depend on asymmetrical relationships between individuals, making the majority

---

52. Lorraine Daston and Peter Galison, *Objectivity* (New York: Zone, 2010).

53. Mahl, *Goethes ökonomisches Wissen*, esp. 354–91.

54. My reading of Smith draws heavily on Elizabeth Anderson, "Lecture I. When the Market Was 'Left,'" in *Liberty, Equality, and Private Government: The Tanner Lectures in Human Values* (Princeton University: March 4–5, 2015).

of people dependent on the "good pleasure" of the "great proprietor."[55] But to "depend on the good will of another for one's own subsistence puts one at the mercy of the other, and under his subjection. Gifts are not free: 'hospitality' is given in return for obedience."[56] Moreover, feudalism's form of private government is both degrading and ineffective. Not only does feudalism reduce most people to a state of "servile dependency," the feudal lords, constantly at war with one another, also leave the country "a scene of violence, rapine, and disorder."[57] Smith's argument for market economy in his *Wealth of Nations* builds on this dual critique of feudalism. Commercial society, Smith maintains, introduces a measure of equality among individuals while creating a dynamic network of interdependencies that increase prosperity and productivity. In appealing to the self-interest of others rather than to their benevolence, free and independent workers both raise their respectability and increase their own and their fellow-citizens' material well-being. Contrary to common perceptions, Smith does not oppose all state interference but charges politics with the task of creating the conditions that support this "natural system of liberty." Good government requires a strong legal framework, impartiality in enforcing laws, the removal of monopolizing constraints on trade, and even support of public education. Like the members of the Tower Society, Smith rails against institutions such as primogeniture and entails that keep land ownership in the hands of the few;[58] and like them, he advocates for free trade and holds up America as a kind of utopia in which the principles of equality and freedom are most perfectly developed.

Smith's seemingly paradoxical idea that government ought to create a "natural system of liberty" points to what Foucault has identified as the biopolitical core of eighteenth-century liberalism. Liberalism, which Foucault understands not merely as an economic

---

55. Adam Smith, *An Inquiry into the Nature and Causes of the Wealth of Nations*, vol. 1, ed. R. H. Campbell and A. S Skinner (Indianapolis: Liberty Classics, 1981), 414–15.

56. Anderson, "When the Market Was 'Left,'" 75.

57. Ibid.

58. Ibid., 76.

theory but as a novel model of governing human beings, introduces a new conception of both politics and nature.[59] "For political economy, nature is not an original and reserved region on which the exercise of power should not impinge, on pain of being illegitimate. Nature is something that runs under, through, and in the exercise of governmentality. It is, if you like, its indispensable hypodermics."[60] Nature enters the calculation of liberal government in two ways: as the spontaneous and "natural" mechanism of the market which, if framed correctly, organizes itself into a vibrant and dynamic system; and as the ensemble of vital processes and natural factors (weather, growth cycles, the physicality of working bodies, etc.) that enters into economic and social activity. Put differently, and in terms that hark back to my earlier discussion of masquerade, with liberalism, nature ceases to be conceived as an unchanging given and instead becomes the material correlate of culture and politics, its vital and "natural" field of articulation.

Two aspects of Foucault's analysis of eighteenth-century liberalism are of particular importance to our discussion. First, political economy conceives of the market in autopoietic terms. The market is a complex dynamic system that cannot be ruled from above but must be governed indirectly and with respect to its *internal* laws. Composed of myriad self-interested microoperations, it generates an order that is beyond individual consciousness and intention. No sovereign will—no head—directs the movement of Smith's "invisible hand." And yet this trans-individual hand miraculously imparts continuity and order to the ceaseless movements of the social body. Smith's "invisible hand" is a teleological figure that resembles Kant's conception of organic causality. Second, liberalism's emphasis on

---

59. See also Thomas Lemke's succinct description of this new link between nature and politics. "Foucault conceives of liberalism not as an economic theory or a political ideology but as a specific art of governing human beings. Liberalism introduces a rationality of governing that differs both from medieval concepts of domination and from early modern state reason: the idea of a nature of society that constitutes both the basis and the border of governmental practice." Thomas Lemke, *Biopolitics: An Advanced Introduction* (New York: New York University Press, 2011), 45.

60. Michel Foucault, *The Birth of Biopolitics: Lectures at the College de France, 1978–79* (New York: Palgrave Macmillan, 2008), 15f.

self-regulation goes hand in hand with an extension and fine-tuning of governance. If the market is a self-regulatory organism, it will be necessary to know its inner laws to organize political measures accordingly. Specialized knowledge of the market—of economic mechanisms, but also of the vital processes involved in them—thus becomes a crucial element of good governance. Like a doctor who studies the physical body in order to protect its health and vitality, specialists study the population's sociobiological body to free its natural movement and identify dangers that might interfere with that movement. Liberalism's production of freedom is thus accompanied by the development of a "security apparatus" designed to protect the free play of self-interests from destroying itself.

> The liberalism we can describe as the art of government formed in the eighteenth century, entails at its heart a productive/destructive relationship [with] freedom. Liberalism must produce freedom, but this very act entails the establishment of limitations, controls, forms of coercion, and obligations relying on threats, etcetera. . . . [61]
>
> In short, strategies of security, which are, in a way, both liberalism's other face and its very condition, must correspond to all these imperatives concerning the need to ensure that the mechanism of interests does not give rise to individual or collective dangers. The game of freedom and security is at the very heart of this new governmental reason.[62]

The new technologies of security differ from both traditional juridical models of power and modern disciplinary mechanisms. Power as law prohibits; discipline introduces prescriptive norms that distinguish between the normal and the abnormal. Security technologies, by contrast, take as their starting point the empirically normal—the statistical average—that "serves as a regulative norm and allows for further differentiations and variations. Rather than adjusting reality to a predefined 'should-be' value, the technologies of security take reality as a norm."[63] Furthermore, unlike Foucaultian

---

61. Ibid., 64.
62. Ibid., 65.
63. Lemke, *Biopolitics*, 47; Michel Foucault, *Security, Territory, Population: Lectures at the College de France, 1977–78* (New York: Palgrave Macmillan, 2007), 45ff.

disciplines, which are primarily focused on body politics, the concept of governmentality is meant to extend the domain of politics to include questions of subjectivity and self-constitution. "Biopolitics," in this broader sense, is the name for a new, "liberal," form of governing that bears on humans as legal persons, biological beings, and moral selves.

This, at least, was the claim underlying Foucault's research project. In reality, Foucault never explored in detail the relation between biopolitics and subjectivity, which instead separate in his work into two historically and conceptually distinct clusters: *modern* biopolitics (his lectures from 1977 to 1979), and *ancient* forms of self-government (1981 to his death in 1984). The reasons for this shortcoming are complex and can only be touched upon briefly. They have to do with Foucault's belief in the enduring and disastrous heritage of Christian thought in modernity,[64] his resulting tendency to conceive of modern subjectivization in terms of disciplinary individualization, and his decision to analyze biopolitics through the framework of political economy, which limits his notion of subjectivity in two interrelated ways: motivation and desire. Motivation and desire enter the description only in the anemic form of economic *interests*; and, given political economy's focus on "population," individuals come to be thematized only as statistical and quantifiable "*series* of individuals."[65] Whatever Foucault's exact reasons for separating practices of subjectivization and modern conceptions of life, the result is that modern subjective life tends to be reduced to an effect of structuring forces located *outside* this life. It is against this background that Goethe's treatment of the Tower assumes its full significance. Goethe's novel maps the production, not of a liberal population, but of the liberal self. It shows what the liberal "art of governing humans" would look like when applied to

---

64. See for instance *Security, Territory, Population*, 148, in which Foucault emphasizes that "we have still not freed ourselves" from Christian pastoral forms of governing human beings.

65. "The population is pertinent as the objective, and individuals, the *series* of individuals, are no longer pertinent as the objective, but simply as the instrument, relay, or condition for obtaining something at the level of the population." Foucault, *Security, Territory, Population*, 42 (my emphasis).

individuals as passionate and self-conscious actors engaged in their own constitution.

This returns us to the "ethos" of double-entry bookkeeping. Crucially, this ethos is not enough, is in fact problematic, as the novel suggests when it reintroduces Werner at the beginning of book 8:

> Werner claimed that his friend had become taller, stronger, more upright, more cultivated and in his manner more pleasant. . . .
>   The impression that Werner made on him was by no means so favorable. The good fellow seemed to have regressed rather than advanced. He was much thinner than back then, his pointed face seemed finer, his nose longer, he was bald on front and temple, his voice loud, high, and strident, and his flat chest, dropping shoulders, pallid cheeks left no doubt that a hypochondriac with a mania for work was present. (WML 500–501)

The message is clear: Werner's rigorous ethos of double-entry bookkeeping did not enhance his life but caused it to contract and wither, whereas Wilhelm's confused theatrical and erotic adventures fostered his inner and outer growth. Note the vitalist rhetoric of the scene, which articulates, through its physiognomic imagery, both a broad organic vision of life—life conceived as a set of powers and capabilities that can grow and shrivel, flourish and decay—and a more specific understanding of the essence of human, as opposed to merely biological, life. If Werner's life did not flourish, the passage suggests, this is because the ethos of double-entry bookkeeping does not reach deep enough into the *subjective* fabric of human life. To develop proper human beings, and not just interest-driven and calculating machines, one must go beyond epistemic and economic virtues and engage human existence at its vital core: at the level of desire and imagination.

This is why Wilhelm, not Werner, is the focus of Goethe's novel and the Tower's governmental activity. Modern liberal society requires the structured development not just of rational and cognitive but also of imaginative and libidinal powers. Thus, rather than posing an obstacle to the Tower's broader political vision, Wilhelm's earlier erotic and aesthetic adventures constitute a necessary stage within it. For it is through his engagement with aesthetic media that Wilhelm has cultivated the aptitudes—imagination, empathy, desire, flexibility of mind—that will infuse his adult commitments to family and work with an intensity and depth unavailable to people like Werner. Accordingly, Wilhelm's education, in the last chapters of the book, takes the form of an *aesthetically* mediated reorchestration of his fantasies and libidinal attachments. The Romantics' claim that the last chapters of Goethe's novel depict the end of art and the birth of economic existence undertheorizes the complex interwinement of liberalism and aesthetics. Instead of repressing or correcting Wilhelm's erotic and theatrical obsessions by way of harsh disciplinary measures, the Tower Society uses aesthetic media— paintings, images, (auto)biographies, music, spectacles—to channel the affective and imaginative powers driving these obsessions into socially productive venues. Under the Tower's expert hands, governmentality becomes the art of making subjective life count.

The first application of this art of governing targets Wilhelm's erotic fantasies. Natalie, Lothario's sister and as such intimately connected to the Tower Society, is the iconographic condensation of images, texts, and paintings that have imprinted themselves on Wilhelm's youthful mind and shaped his libidinal attachments. If in their first encounter Wilhelm loses consciousness, this is because her appearance stirs up in him, and subtly rearranges, all the unconscious fantasies that have shaped his life since infancy. Injured from a gunshot wound inflicted by robbers, Wilhelm gazes transfixed at Natalie, the "beautiful amazon" who, dressed in a man's coat but endowed with "*sanften, hohen, stillen, teilnehmenden Gesichtszüge[n]* [gentle, distinguished, calm, and compassionate features]," has come to his rescue (WML 224; WMA 134).

> Wilhelm, captivated till then by the healing power of her eyes, was now, once the coat was off, amazed at the beauty of her figure. She came up and gently put the coat over him. In this moment, as he was about to open his mouth and murmur some words of thanks, the vivid impression of her presence so strangely affected his already impaired senses, that it appeared to him all of a sudden that her head was surrounded by shafts of light, and a radiating light was spreading across her entire image. The surgeon, intent on extracting the bullet that was still lodged in his wound, touched him at that moment rather heavily. The saint [*die Heilige*] disappeared from his fainting sights; he lost all consciousness,

and when he came to again, horsemen and carriage, the beautiful lady
and her attendant had all vanished into thin air. (WML 226)

Note the tableau-like structure of this arrangement which cites, and
condenses into a single image, all of the paintings and poems that
have shaped Wilhelm's erotic and theatrical adventures throughout
the novel: Chlorinda's manliness and the theme of bisexuality;
Tankred's wounds; Tasso's melancholic association of love with
death; Hamlet's ill-fated fight with Laertes; and, above all, Wilhelm's
favorite childhood painting of the "sick prince." Yet while in their
first appearance these aesthetic sources exerted a problematic influence on Wilhelm, the new tableau rearranges them in such a way
as to radically transform the direction of Wilhelm's desire. With
Wilhelm's love for Natalie, dark eroticism gives way to familial
commitment; homoeroticism to heterosexual love; self-destructive
melancholy to productive empathy; and oedipal struggle to fatherhood, inheritance, and investment in the larger socioeconomic projects of the Tower Society.

Hans-Jürgen Schings, who has done more than any other scholar
to reconstruct the dense iconographic fabric of this scene, has spoken of Goethe's "morphological method, which almost impercepti-
bly integrates the literary citation into the novel."[66] At the core of
this method, Schings argues, is the subtle transformation of genet-
ically older images into similar yet different, new ones. Rather than
disabusing Wilhelm of his earlier, aesthetically mediated attachments, as would have been typical of earlier novels of disillusion-
ment, *Wilhelm Meister* narrates the subtle metamorphosis of the
hero's formative impressions, thus creating a deeper, symbolically
enriched psychology that "makes palpable in the present moment
always the past that continues to exert its effects" (WMA 122–23).
Note, however, that in order to achieve this higher symbolic perspective, the text must transcend the first-person perspective of its
character. What happens to Wilhelm occurs, to a large extent, beyond his understanding. He is largely unaware of the dense narrative and symbolic network into which the text and its intertextual

---

66. Schings, "Wilhelm Meisters schöne Amazone," 157.

operator—the Tower Society—has inserted him.[67] Wilhelm's revelation—manifest in the shafts of light he sees radiating across Natalie's image—is the effect of an aesthetic arrangement that has been constructed for him. We should thus be skeptical of Schings's overly harmonious description of Goethe's symbolism in terms of a "morphological reciprocity that portrays the psychology of interiority in external relations."[68] The higher symbolic operation underlying Wilhelm's encounter with Natalie carries a political dimension: the tableau is a carefully arranged picture—an aesthetic framing—that transforms Wilhelm's desires and directs them toward socially acceptable objects. It is a means of reorganizing Wilhelm's subjectivity.

What is at stake here is more than a minor interpretive squabble. Schings's talk of "metamorphosis" and "morphology" obscures the crucial difference the novel itself establishes between biological and human life. Goethe's morphological method was intended to capture the fluid transformations internal to plants and other natural organisms. The point was to suspend premature conceptual intervention in favor of a mode of observation that was capable of grasping, in a single image, the formative laws operating within living things. Goethe's novel shows that intrinsic biological laws are inadequate to account for the development of subjectivity. Wilhelm's story demonstrates that human life is, from its inception, shot through with and shaped by *non*organic forms (images, words, paintings, poems, etc.) that direct desire and draw it into a labyrinth of imaginary constellations and identifications. In certain respects, the ways aesthetic forms serve human beings are analogous to how natural resources such as water, light, and food serve biological organisms: they allow humans to grow and flourish by developing their subjective (imaginative, affective, cognitive) powers. But unlike organisms, whose metabolic exchange with the environment is regulated by internal and biologically determined programs,

---

67. See also Albrecht Koschorke's comments on Schings in "Die Textur der Neigungen. Verwandtschaft und Attraktion in Goethes 'Mann von fünfzig Jahren,'" *Deutsche Vierteljahrschrift für Literaturwissenschaft und Geistesgeschichte* 73 (1999): 592–610, esp. 599.
68. Schings, "Wilhelm Meisters schöne Amazone," 152.

these subjective powers are undetermined as to their objects, and thus highly vulnerable to what Foucault, in his discussion of liberal freedom, described as "individual and collective dangers." Hence the need for social institutions to intervene and reshape the imaginary scripts that drive the subject's free actions. Goethe's novel extends liberalism's "productive/destructive relationship with freedom" into the fantasmatic heart of subjectivity. Natalie's carefully orchestrated appearance is less a mechanism or moment of natural development than a sociopolitical redistribuiton of Wilhelm's libidinal and aesthetic energies, a narrative recalibration that directs his desire toward a properly liberal form of life—in short, a *security measure*. But note that the text figures this security measure as joyful and healing. Unlike Aurelie's violent physical cut, which inflicts wounds and causes pain, Natalie's aesthetic-symbolic intervention is framed as a therapeutic and even redemptive event that saves Wilhelm from mortal danger and initiates his organic and psychic recovery.

I will return to the conception of "health" underlying this passage, but first I want to discuss another scene in which the Tower Society co-opts the human need for aesthetic self-fashioning. At the beginning of book 8, Wilhelm is presented with a narrative of his life as composed by members of the Tower Society:

> He found the detailed description of his life depicted in large and incisive traits. Neither individual events nor narrow emotions confused his gaze, general sympathetic comments enlightened him without embarrassing him, and he saw for the first time his picture outside himself, not like a second self in a mirror, but a different self, as in a portrait. One never approves of all traits, but one is glad that a thinking mind was able to grasp us, a great talent has wanted to represent us thus. [*Er fand die umständliche Geschichte seines Lebens in großen scharfen Zügen geschildert, weder einzelne Begebenheiten, noch beschränkte Empfindungen verwirrten seinen Blick, allgemeine liebevolle Betrachtungen gaben ihm Fingerzeige, ohne ihn zu beschämen, und er sah zum erstenmal sein Bild außer sich, zwar nicht, wie im Spiegel, ein zweites Selbst, sondern wie im Portrait, ein anderes Selbst; man bekennt sich zwar nicht zu allen Zügen, aber man freut sich, daß ein denkender Geist uns so hat fassen, ein großes Talent uns so hat darstellen wollen.*](WML 507)

David Wellbery has described this scene as the culmination of Wilhelm's development from a form of "self-positing that unfolds in the medium of scenic experiences of presence [*im Medium szenischer Präsenzerfahrungen*] to a narratively mediated identity."[69] This is correct, but only half the truth. The shift from first- to third-person perspective is mediated not just by narrative but also by external authorities. Wilhelm's biography is written by members of the Tower Society, and in embracing the *denkender Geist* ("thinking mind") that composed it, he is in fact identifying with what Lacan calls the gaze of the big Other. The moment of truth is thus also a moment of ideological interpellation, a shift from one problematic model of self-relation (imaginary identification) to another (symbolic identification). This narrative interpellation, moreover, goes hand in hand with processes of normalization and averaging. Wilhelm's biography, while based on empirical details drawn from his life, is part of a larger archive of confessions, letters, diaries, and biographies that the Tower Society has collected. "We wanted to see with our own eyes, and to build up our own archive of world knowledge [*und uns ein eigenes Archiv unserer Weltkenntnis bilden*]," Jarno explains to Wilhelm, "therefore the many confessions were produced, which we partly wrote ourselves, partly inspired others to write, and from which later the apprenticeship [*die Lehrjahre*] was put together" (WML 550). Thus what Wilhelm joyfully embraces as the truth of his life is distilled from, and shaped by, a large narrative data bank. The very structure of Wilhlem's *Lehrjahre*—of a proper formative *Bildung*—is the product of the superimposition and condensation of countless narrative details. It is a biographical script.

We encounter again, albeit with an important difference, the appeal to "nature" understood as a distribution of empirical differences that Foucault has identified as the distinctive feature of liberal normativity. Rather than imposing a static and prescriptive norm *onto* reality, the Tower Society takes the empirical norm—in this case, the actual experiences, feelings, aspirations, and life events of individuals—as a starting point for its interventions and regulatory efforts. But whereas the security technologies of political economy derive their norms from statistical averages centered on the biological and economic lives of populations, the Tower Society

---

69. Wellbery, "Die Enden des Menschen," 617.

produces *narrative averages* that coalesce into stories and scripts that self-conscious individuals, engaged in their own self-fashioning. can identify with. In short, the Tower regulates Wilhelm's life by modeling its possibilities on the lives of others. And like all normalizing scripts, Wilhelm's new biography contains an element of violence that reaches both inward and outward. Inward in that it circumscribes the open-ended play of human desire and language around a narrative average, thus flattening both life and art; and outward, because it draws a border where the proper biographical form of life ends and its abnormal deformation begins. Goethe's novel thus confirms the biopolitical dialectic analyzed by Foucualt, according to which the production of liberal forms of life goes hand in hand with the creation of security mechanisms directed against threats to their perpetuation. The fate of the Harper and of Mignon take us into the biopolitical heart of Goethe's conception of *Lebensform*. Mignon's treatment in particular highlights the violence of security technologies deployed to preserve historically established patterns of human freedom and development.

Inititally, these measures take the relatively soft form of efforts to reform Mignon's strangeness. The Tower Society submits Mignon to a battery of psychological, pedagogical, and medical technologies whose historical emergence coincides with the rise of modern liberal biopolitics. Under the gaze of Natalie and the doctor, Mignon's nomadic life is given biographical shape and turned into a psychiatric case history.[70] Despite Mignon's determination, following an early experience of abduction, "not to tell her story to anybody but instead live and die in the hope of immediate divine help," Natalie pieces together her life story from unconscious confessions— "isolated comments, songs and hasty childish remarks that betray precisely that which they want to conceal" (WML 524). Natalie's new analytical technique of listening rests on Mignon's prior placement within a larger institutional and affective apparatus. Shortly

---

70. On the invention of psychiatric case histories in the late eigheteenth century, see my "A Case of Individuality: Karl Philipp Moritz and the Magazine for Empirical Psychology," *New German Critique: An Interdisciplinary Journal of German Studies* 79 (2000): 67–105.

after arriving at the Tower Society, Mignon is transferred to Natalie's recently created home for girls. It is within this closed and controlled environment, and under the loving care of Natalie's maternal authority, that Mignon, coaxed into wearing female dresses and confessing her life story, is subjected to the pedagogical and symbolic labor of disambiguation. This first attempt at normalization reaches its climax and turning point with Mignon's theatrical performance as an angel in a Christmas carol:

> I first thought I would omit the wings, but the women who dressed her insisted on a pair of big golden wings with which she could demonstrate her skill. And so this miraculous vision appeared, a lily in one hand and a little basket in the other, right in the midst of the girls, and surprised me as well. "Here comes the angel!" I said. All the children made as if to withdraw, but then finally shouted: "It's Mignon!" though still not venturing any closer to the wondrous sight. [*Anfangs wollte ich die Flügel weglassen, doch bestanden die Frauenzimmer, die sie anputzten, auf ein Paar große goldene Schwingen, an denen sie recht ihre Kunst zeigen wollten. So trat, mit einer Lilie in der einen Hand, und mit einem Körbchen in der andern, die wundersame Erscheinung in die Mitte der Mädchen, und überraschte mich selbst. Da kommt der Engel, sagte ich. Die Kinder traten gleichsam alle zurück! Endlich riefen sie aus: es ist Mignon, und getrauten sich doch nicht, dem wundersamen Bilde näher zu treten.*] (WML 516–17; WMA 315)

Natalie's surprise at her own arrangement leaves no doubt that mere pedagogical reforms will not suffice. Mignon's transcendence of the theatrical frame signals a wondrous (*wundersames*) surplus of subjectivity that cannot be contained within the forms and norms of ordinary life. Yet at the same time, the theatrical transformation of Mignon's actual existence into a "*wundersames Bild*" already suggests the way out of the sociopolitical dilemma she poses. Where psychology and pedagogy fail, art steps in to offer an alternative mode of normative reform. Mignon's song immediately following the carol spells out the trajectory the Tower Society will follow:

> So let me seem till I become:
> Take not this garment white from me!
> I hasten from the joys of earth
> Down to that house so fast and firm.

There will I rest in peace a while,
Till opens wide my freshened glance.
Then I will cast my dress aside,
Leaving both wreath and girdle there.

For all those glorious heavenly forms,
They do not ask for man or wife,
No garments long or draperies fine
Surround the body now transformed.

[*So laßt mich schein bis ich werde,*
Zieht mir das weiße Kleid nicht aus!
Ich eile, von der schönen Erde
Hinab in jenes feste Haus.

Dort ruh ich eine kleine Stille,
Dann öffnet sich der frische Blick,
Ich lasse dann die reine Hülle,
Den Gürtel und den Kranz zurück.

Und jene himmlische Gestalten
Sie fragen nicht nach Mann und Weib,
Und keine Kleider, keine Falten
Umgeben den verklärten Leib.]

(WML 517; WMA 316)

The angel iconography offers a ready-made system for absorbing Mignon's troubling androgyny as well as an aesthetic answer to the threat of the free play of desire she embodies. Angels are typically characterized as incorporeal beings, and thus free from bodily desire of any kind. What follows, accordingly, is Mignon's aesthetic petrification. When Wilhelm sees Mignon again, her wish to shine rather than be has all but consumed her erotic desire and biological life (WML 527; WMA 322). Once again the novel showcases the aesthetic delineation of human life, except that here art is employed in the service of death rather than life. Nowhere is the machinery of narrative orchestration more violently at work than in the Tower Society's deanimation of Mignon.

Natalie stood gazing in front of her, when all of a sudden Mignon shot up, clasped her heart with her left hand, flung out her right arm, and fell with a cry at Natalie's feet, as if dead. Everyone was greatly alarmed. There was no sign of any movement in heart or pulse. Wilhelm took her into his arms and quickly lifted her up, her body [*schlotternde Körper*] hanging lifeless over his shoulders. The doctor came but gave little hope, though he and the young surgeon whom we already know did all they could—but in vain. The poor dear creature could not be brought back to life. (WML 545; WMA 333)

In a few sentences, the "riddle" is transformed into a lifeless thing. Goethe's choice of verb is telling. While *schlottern* usually denotes the intense trembling of the body as a result of fear or cold, and is thus predicated of living beings, the word is used here to describe the dangling of limbs deprived of consciousness and expressiveness. This minute semantic shift, which approximates Mignon to a puppet, signals the beginning of the final phase of her aesthetic reification.

Stay away from this sad thing [*traurigen Gegenstande*] and let me use my art [*meine Kunst*] to impart some permanence to the remains of this strange being. I will at once employ the beautiful art [*schöne Kunst*], not just of embalming the body but of imparting to it an appearance of life [*ein lebendiges Ansehn*], on this beloved creature. Since I foresaw her death, I have made all preparations. . . . Grant me a few days and don't ask to see the dear child until we have brought her into the Hall of the Past. (WML 546–47)

And shortly thereafter, at Mignon's burial:

"The child that we bury here, we know little about. . . . Its firmly locked heart gave us no inkling of what was going on inside it; nothing was clear or apparent about her except her love for the man who rescued her from the clutches of a barbarian. . . . But if art [*Kunst*] could not give permanence to her spirit, it could employ every skill to preserve her body and save it from decay. Balsam has been introduced into all her veins and, instead of blood, this color those cheeks that faded so early. Draw near, my friends, and observe the wonders of art and solicitude [*die Wunder der Kunst und Sorgfalt*]!"

He lifted the veil, and there lay the child in its angel costume, as if sleeping, in the most pleasing position. They all stepped up, and marveled at this semblance of life [*diesen Schein des Lebens*]. (WML 577; WMA 353)

Art as embalmment: the physical replacement of blood with chemicals, a procedure widely used in eighteenth-century practices of anatomical preservation and display,[71] vividly illustrates the novel's own use of "beautiful art" to transform the fragile temporality of embodied life into an unchanging image of its eternality. For what remains of Mignon is only a "*semblance* of life"—that is, an artificial thing that preserves the appearance of life by removing it from the organic process of decay. This devitalizing trajectory culminates in the operatic staging of Mignon's burial, complete with costumes, singing, and theatrical sets.

> In the evening the Abbé summoned everyone to the funeral rites for Mignon. The whole company repaired to the Hall of the Past, and found it strangely decorated and illuminated. The walls were almost entirely draped with tapestries of azure blue, so that only the base and the frieze remained uncovered. Huge wax candles were burning in the four big candelabras at the corners of the room, and others of appropriate size in the four smaller ones surrounding the sarcophagus in the center. Four boys were standing beside the bier, dressed in silver and blue, fanning with sheaves of ostrich feathers a figure that lay on top of the sarcophagus. The assembled company all took their seats, and two invisible choruses intoned in gentle strains: "Whom do you bring to those at rest?" The four boys answered, with love in their voices: "A weary comrade we bring unto you; here let it stay and rest till joyful comrades in heaven shall wake it once more." (WML 575; WMA 352)

Novalis's claim that Mignon's fate marks the novel's programmatic turn from art to commerce and philistinism obscures the intertwinement of those realms. What Goethe's novel highlights in its last chapters is the crucial role of aesthetic media in what Foucault describes as liberalism's "productive/destructive relationship [with] freedom." The Tower uses art to sanitize Mignon's strangeness and secure the boundaries of freedom and human expression. Thus, the only freedom left to Mignon is the freedom of the work of art. Transfigured into an angelic sign, Mignon now embodies not the

---

71. See Christine Lehleiter, *Romanticism, Origins, and the History of Heredity* (London: Bucknell University Press, 2014), 133–50.

plasticity of human desire and form but the triumph of art over life, and of static form over dynamic force.

But what kind of art is at work here? Can there be any doubt that Mignon's museumization in the Hall of the Past differs from the novel's own mode of aesthetic reification? The Tower Society employs the resources and media of the aesthetic for purely sociopolitical ends, as a way of protecting the normative boundaries of the new "liberal" forms of life. In this sense, Mignon's elaborate burial arrangement merely completes the anatamo-political process of normalization that began with Natalie's pedagogical efforts. In fact, from Natalie's female dresses, to the doctor's draining of Mignon's blood, to her monumentalization in the Hall of the Past, Mignon's devitalization takes the form of what we might call an aesthetic-political transfiguration. The result of these operations is an increasingly sanitized aesthetic sign whose rigid form is determined not by an interior aesthetic principle but by political regulation of the laws of appearance and beauty. What the novel depicts through the Tower's treatment of Mignon, in other words, is the reification not only of Mignon but also of art. Mignon's kitschy burial represents the political appropriation of the aesthetic. More precisely, it represents the transformation of aesthetic force into what Walter Benjamin, looking back at the history of bourgeois art, will call "exhibition value."

Incest

But Mignon's treatment does not end at this point. While Goethe may be critical of the Tower's political instrumentalization of art, he seems to be backing the novel's final narrative twist in explaining Mignon's eccentricity in explicitly biological terms. I am referring to the revelation of Mignon's incestuous origin. After her burial, we are told that Mignon is the product of an incestuous relationship between Mignon's father, Augustin, and his sister, Sperata, who conceived Mignon out of love, unaware of their biological ties. Once apprised of their kinship and urged by his brothers to abandon his sexual relation with his sister, Augustin defends his actions through

a botanical analogue, claiming that since the lily, symbol of innocence, is an androgynous plant that reproduces through the union
of its male and female parts, he and his sister should be equally free
to consummate their relationship. Goethe's initial suggestion here
seems to be that Augustin's argument, which echoes contemporary
positions of natural law philosophers in favor of the liberalization
of incest prohibitions,[72] is itself a kind of perversion, and that Augustin, like Wilhelm, looks for explanations in the wrong places. If
incest is prohibited, the text seems to be saying, this is not due to
organic or biological proscription but because incest expresses a
narcissistic denial of social norms, and thus a failure to acknowledge the difference between nature and culture. Yet the novel does
not stop at this culturalist position, as becomes clear as soon as Augustin insists not merely on the naturalness of incestuous love but
also of incestuous reproduction. "Nature clearly indicates," he continues, "what it abhors: a creature that should not exist, cannot
exist, develops wrongly, or is soon destroyed. The marks of her
curse, the signs of her severity are: barrenness, stunted growth, premature decay" (WML 584; WMA 357). The irony is of course that
Mignon's existence—her difficulty learning to speak and write, her
androgyny, her weak heart and early death—confirms what Augustin vociferously denies: that nature does indeed "abhor" incestuous
reproduction. Goethe's novel thus explains Mignon's strangeness in
biological terms. Incest has deleterious organic consequences, which
also means that the incest prohibition, while clearly a cultural law,
has some basis in nature.

What is the significance of this narrative twist for our discussion
of Goethe's place in the discourse of life around 1800? To begin
with, Goethe's treatment of incest provides further evidence of his
deep involvement with the science of his time. Christine Lehleiter
has convincingly argued that Goethe's biological framing of Mignon
is informed by contemporary experiments in animal husbandry,

---

72. On the liberalization of incest prohibitions in the late German Enlightenment, see Koschorke, "Die Textur der Neigungen"; Isabell V. Hull, *Sexuality, State,
and Civil Society in Germany, 1700–1815* (Ithaca, NY: Cornell University Press,
1996); and especially Lehleiter, *Romanticism*, 113–22, who discusses in detail
Goethe's treatment of incest in *Wilhelm Meister's Apprenticeship*.

which had shown that inbreeding can have problematic organic consequences.[73] As Lehleiter emphasizes, the very existence of these experiments is the result of the broader liberalization of laws regulating sexuality during the eighteenth century. The "discovery of biological laws becomes possible precisely at that moment in which animal breeders were willing to *ignore* the incest taboo. . . . Only when animal breeders freely started to use inbreeding as a main form of reproduction, did they start to discover the biological laws of how traits are transmitted from one generation to the next."[74] Goethe's treatment of Mignon thus corroborates my earlier claim that her eccentricity must be understood in view of the contemporary realignment of the relation between nature and culture. Mignon is a product of the new discourse of life. Read along these lines, Goethe's novel helps to shed light on a broader cultural phenomenon, namely the explosive rise of incest narratives at the end of the eighteenth century throughout Western Europe, but above all in Germany, where roughly one in five fictional texts written between 1770 and 1815 deals with incest.[75] The character of Mignon suggests that incest narratives moved to the center of the cultural imagination because they provided ready-made metaphors with which to articulate anxieties associated with the new disourse of life. Incest became fascinating because it figured, in compressed narrative form, the new coordination of nature and culture under the rubric of "life."

Second, Goethe's peculiar intervention into this discourse adds an important dimension to our understanding of the novel's reflection on the human *Lebensform*. Unlike any other incest narrative of the time, Goethe frames incest in terms of the intersection of different systems of *form*. To claim that Mignon's incestuous origin makes her incapable of linguistic mastery, as Goethe does, is to suggest that cultural expressions are shaped, at their outer boundaries,

---

73. Lehleiter, *Romanticism*, 122–24.
74. Ibid., 152.
75. Michael Titzmann, "Literarische Strukturen und kulturelles Wissen. Das Beispiel inzestuöser Situationen in der Erzählliteratur der Goethezeit und ihrer Funktionen im Denksystem der Epoche," in *Anthropologie der Goethezeit. Studien zur Literatur und Wissensgeschichte*, Studien und Texte zur Sozialgeschichte 119 (Berlin: De Gruyter, 2012), 373–432.

by biology. Biological laws circumscribe the articulation of cultural forms. Underlying the novel's figuration of incest is thus a specific model of biological life. Instead of being formless matter or mere material substrate, the biological is shown to have its own autonomy, its own forms and laws, which culture mobilizes but which also constrain the production of social and psychological forms. Culture and biology are both distinct *and* interlocking systems of form. Incestuous reproduction becomes epistemologically and politically interesting in this context because it represents the interface between these two systems, the point of intersection between biological and cultural organization, between *zoe* and *bios*. To be clear, this is *not* a matter of grounding culture in nature. Biological processes, while circumscribing the range of cultural expression, do not determine the content of the latter. This antideterminism is explicitly highlighted in the novel's second, happy ending, which serves as a mirror image of Mignon's terrible fate. Wilhelm's education culminates in a life that is emphatically shaped by *cultural* ties. He adopts Felix, who might not be his son; marries Nathalie, who is not Felix's biological mother; and buys a house financed by Werner's investments of Wilhelm's inheritance. A financial economy built on debt and interest (Werner is a moneylender)[76] is joined to a familial economy rooted in adoption and benevolence. Though interwoven, the forms of cultural and biological reproduction are irreducible to each other.

Illuminating the complex interplay of biological and cultural form is the first function of the incest motif. The second function has to do with the dynamic force that expresses itself through incest. In *Wilhelm Meister,* the incest prohibition is directed not only against incestuous reproduction but also, and above all, against incestuous *desire*. The real danger to the cultural order is not biological deformation but the transgressive formlessness of the free play of desire, which finds in sibling incest its paradigmatic expression. Consider in this context a crucial change in the figuration of

---

76. According to Anderson, the capitalist transformation of creditor-debtor relations is at the heart of Smith's claims about capitalism's moral superiority.

the incest motif around 1800. Whereas incest narratives prior to 1770 overwhelmingly focus on intergenerational incest (father-daughter, mother-son), between 1770 and 1815, 80 percent of all fictional German texts dealing with incest center on the relation between brothers and sisters. The reason for this dramatic shift, I would surmise, is that the horizontal axis of sibling incest better suits the symbolic expression of anxieties associated with the new democratic forms of power and intimacy than the vertical, hierarchical order of the older, oedipal model of incest, which served to highlight transgressions of patriachical authority and sovereignty. Sibling incest casts light on a fundamental tension between political, legal, and moral principles of freedom on the one hand, and the anomic force of desire on the other. As Isabel Hull and others have shown, with the secularization of the legal system in the late eighteenth century, the extensive network of prohibitions that had regulated incest up to this point is increasingly weakened and reduced to a single concern: coercion versus consensuality. In this context, the love between brothers and sisters poses a conundrum. On the one hand, for an emerging society presumably grounded in self-determination and the rejection of tradition and convention, the consensual love between siblings, equal in all but sexual difference, might be said to express the very ideal of a radical democratic bond. This is what Herman Melville will indeed claim fifty years later for his protagonist's incestuous union with his sister in *Pierre, or The Ambiguities*: "And believe me you will pronounce Pierre a thoroughgoing Democrat in time; perhaps a little too Radical altogether to your fancy."[77] On the other hand, the genetic proximity between siblings intensifies the principle of equality to the point of approaching identity, thus undercutting the other foundation of democratic self-determination—the notion of individuality. This is the constellation in which we must place Mignon's enigmatic monstrosity. Born from the passionate love between Augustin and Sperata, Mignon is the product of desire operating outside the bounds of cultural and

---

77. Hermann Melville, *Pierre, or The Ambiguities* (Evanston, IL: Northwestern University Press; Chicago: The Newberry Library, 1971), 13.

legal constraint. Yet as with Wilhelm's love affairs, this free desire is shown to threaten the integrity of the form of life it inhabits. Just as Wilhelm's narcissistic blurring of self and other produces death and trauma, so Augustin and Sperata's sexual union generates a being whose ambiguity derails the mechanisms of cultural and biological formation. Mignon must die not just because she is biologically or culturally incoherent but because her incoherence—her fusion and confusion of all established distinctions—embodies the ultimate formlessness of desire, and with it, a dimension of human life that cannot be converted into liberal forms of life.

Yet while exiled from the biological and social worlds, this unruly dimension of desire does not disappear entirely. Can there be any doubt that Goethe's novel turns Mignon's incoherence into the locus of a heightened aestheticism? It is precisely her enigmatic fusion of established distinctions (male and female, mechanical and living) that makes Mignon an object of endless allure for both Wilhelm and the reader. Put differently, the formless force of desire survives in Goethe's novel in the controlled and sublimated form of aesthetic fascination. This allows us to make three final observations. First, in placing desire at the center of his novel, Goethe eroticizes the Kantian definition of the aesthetic in terms of the free play of the imagination. Art is crucial not because it highlights the vitality of *cognitive* life but because it reminds us of, and gives articulation to, the vital role of desire in the formation of human life. Second, in doing so, art must avoid two dangers: the suppression of desire through the instititions of politics and morality, and its anarchic reign in transgression and jouissance. While the first danger leads to the sterile art of the Tower Society, the second pushes the work of art toward disarticulation and formlessness. Third, to claim that aesthetic form situates itself between the law and desire is also to say that art keeps both reigns actively apart. In this sense, Goethe's decision to ban Mignon's eccentricity from communal life and channel it into the aesthetic realm is, in the end, a political decision. One can think of incoherence or deformity as the end of human life, the impossibility of biological and social reproduction, as Goethe does. But the anomalous can also be seen as the beginning of a new species, the creation of a new form of (post)human life. This is the path that Nietzsche will take when he defines the task of philosophy as the breeding of a new race. And it is also, and more clearly in response to Goethe's model of human *Bildung*, the trajectory Musil follows in *The Man without Qualities*, when his protagonist Ulrich and his sister Agathe enter an erotic union to inaugurate what the novel calls a "New Millenium."

Part II

The Conflict of Forms

3

ENTER THE HYBRID (KLEIST)

As we saw in the previous chapters, philosophical, scientific, and literary discussions of life around 1800 revolve around the idea of self-organization. The elements of this discourse are first given explicit theoretical expression in Kant's *Critique of the Power of Judgment*. Living beings are not just functionally organized entities in which the "parts . . . are possible only through their relation to the whole" (KU § 65, 5: 373; CPJ 244–45); they are actively self-organizing. To put this in contemporary terms, a living being is a unified ensemble of homeostatic (or homeodynamic)[1] mechanisms that regulate and maintain the unity and identity of the whole, differentiating it from an ever-changing environment. It is in this paradigmatic sense that a living being is an *organism*.

---

1. See Steven Rose, *Lifelines: Biology beyond Determinism* (Oxford: Oxford University Press, 1997).

As we saw, Kant draws on contemporary naturalist research but integrates its findings into an ambitious conceptual framework that brings mind and nature into close proximity. In order to make sense of living beings, he claims, we must conceive of them teleologically, as "natural purposes." To understand living beings as purposes means to think of their organization and behavior as directed toward a singular, characteristic function: the life of the individual organism. While purposiveness remains a reflective concept for Kant—one that makes intelligible the otherwise incomprehensible complexity of living things—its introduction nonetheless allows him to soften the stark opposition between natural necessity and intellectual freedom that had characterized his earlier writings on morality. Conceived teleologically, as goal-oriented processes, the dynamics of nature can be reconciled with the moral-political task of establishing a just society, and nature's drive toward complex organic forms cast as part of an evolutionary process that culminates in the cultivation of mankind. Thus, biological and moral-political self-organization converge.

Moreover, Kant uses the language of self-organization to highlight homologies between the *internal* operations of mind and organic nature. This is the function of the first—aesthetic—part of the *Critique of the Power of Judgment*, which explores the characteristic vitality of mental life, articulating a newly dynamic model of thinking that prepares the ground for the book's subsequent discussion of biological organisms. Kant inaugurates the modern discipline of aesthetics by conceptualizing it as a window to broad epistemological and ontological issues: it is in our encounter with beauty that the vitality of the mind and its homology with the vitality of organic nature becomes most palpable. On the one hand, aesthetic perception, unfolding without the guidance of an organizing concept, gives rise to an open-ended and self-regulating play of the mental faculties that is experienced as a "feeling of the promotion of life [*ein Gefühl der Beförderung des Lebens*]" (KU § 23, 5: 244; CPJ 128). Kant's emphasis on the autopoietic character of aesthetic experience, which prefigures his later description of organisms, paints the mind as a self-organizing system, as a dynamic, and in this sense living, machine whose various parts reciprocally stimulate one another to produce forms. On the other hand, the aesthetic object, conceived as a complex system of relations rather than as an aggregate of independent parts, appears as a man-made analogue of a living being, an organism. Mirroring one another, nature and art glow in the light of reconciliation: "Nature was beautiful, if at the same time it looked like art [*als Kunst aussah*]; and art can only be called beautiful if we are aware that it is art and yet it looks to us like nature [*als Natur aussieht*]" (KU § 45, 5: 306; CPJ 185).

This analogy rests on an implied third term: autonomy.[2] Biological self-organization, the *Critique of the Power of Judgment* suggests, is structurally akin to moral self-legislation. Unlike complex artifacts such as watches, which are caused by an idea that exists outside of them in the mind of the watchmaker, living beings shape themselves: they are self-determined. Considered as organisms, in other words, natural beings are free not only in that they obey the laws of their own nature but in that these "laws are the living beings' own in the deeper sense that they are brought about by this very being."[3] To be sure, biological autonomy differs from moral autonomy, which rests, in Kant's conception, on the freedom of the will and hence on our transcendental freedom as rational creatures. But the two are nonetheless operationally analogous, and it is this analogy that Kant's idea of biological self-organization is meant to bring out. In short, the "living" matters for Kant not just as a distinct class of entities but as an exemplar of a peculiar type of order and process. Bridging structure and change, order and creativity, mind and matter, the idea of a self-organizing life allows Kant, and much of German literature and philosophy around 1800, to imagine the harmonious continuity of nature, art, and politics.

It is this continuity—this assimilation of culture to nature under the name of "life"—that Kleist's textual machines relentlessly attack. No reader can fail to notice the recurrent scenes of bodily violence in his texts, and several commentators have drawn attention to

---

2. Regarding the following, see Thomas Khurana, "Life and Autonomy: Forms of Self-Determination in Kant and Hegel," in *The Freedom of Life: Hegelian Perspectives*, ed. Thomas Khurana (Cologne: August 2013), 155–94.

3. Khurana, "Life and Autonomy," 167.

Kleist's critique of the organicist aesthetics of his time. The two observations are connected. Kleist's anti-organicism is a matter not of theory but of poetic practice, one that articulates itself in and through the infraction of boundaries and the breaking of organic wholes. The smashed skulls and lacerated bodies that populate Kleist's texts are not just gory accidents of narrative; they are the climactic expression of Kleist's systematic attack on the conception of life as organic, unifying self-organization.

Yet destruction is not an end in itself. Kleist's attack on the idea of self-organization goes hand in hand with his articulation of a competing model of life, a model I will call "hybrid." My use of the notion of hybridity draws on but ultimately differs from its employment in postcolonial and science studies, where it has come to designate the dynamics of intercultural contact[4] or, nearer to my argument, the inextricable link between nature and culture[5] or between bodies and machines.[6] While authors such as Bhabha, Haraway, and Latour use "hybridity" to highlight the combination of diverse orders or elements into something new, "the figuration of a third kind,"[7] I employ the term primarily to capture Kleist's singularly agonistic conception of the relationship between system and environment.

In the self-organization model, the system-environment relationship is tipped in favor of the system and figured in terms of assimilation: the living system takes up the environment and converts it into something that is formative of it*self*. To live is to grow, and to grow is to transform the outside into a resource of self-expression and reproduction. (Think of a tree converting sun and water, or of the nineteenth-century novelistic hero's recruitment of

---

4. Homi K. Bhabha, *The Location of Culture* (New York: Routledge, 1994).

5. Bruno Latour, *We Have Never Been Modern*, trans. Catherine Porter (Cambridge, MA: Harvard University Press, 1993).

6. Donna Haraway, *Simians, Cyborgs, and Women: The Reinvention of Nature* (New York: Routledge, 1991), 149–82.

7. Uwe Wirth, "Between Hybrid and Graft," in *From Literature to Cultural Literacy*, ed. Naomi Segal and Daniela Koleva (New York: Palgrave Macmillan, 2014), 239.

"opportunities.")[8] Kleist inverts this power dynamic. It is not just that his stories and dramas revolve around moments of crisis in which outside forces overwhelm established orders; this destruction of the status quo is celebrated as the very condition of any life worth living. For Kleist, the true danger to life comes not from outside but from within; not from a hostile environment that disrupts an established order and upsets its internal operations but from the system's own drive toward order, its propensity to regulate its activities around an inner norm. Thus the very thing that Kant and Goethe hail as the essence of life—the capacity of living beings to organize themselves as autonomous, differentiated forms—Kleist identifies as the source of life's depletion. Hence the relentless transgressiveness of Kleist's narratives, in which boundaries exist only to be violated, bodies to be injured, paradise to be spoiled. For Kleist, the essence of vitality is hybridity.

The following pages will flesh out these rather abstract remarks and prove useful as reading guides to Kleist's textual universe. Given my emphasis on hybridity, it should be clear that I do not intend to treat the term as a neatly circumscribed concept that anticipates its articulation in diverse (con)texts. The notion of hybridity is itself hybrid, and thus irreducible to a singular form or type. But while the following readings do not amount to a theory of hybridity, they are also not meant as mere hermeneutic exercises. Rather than producing the richest possible interpretation of a single text, I hope to show how Kleist's oeuvre as a whole articulates a distinct heteropoietic logic of the living that stands in sharp contrast to the dominant biological, political, and, above all, aesthetic discourses of his time. With the "aesthetic turn" inaugurated in Kant's *Critique of the Power of Judgment*, art comes to occupy a newly reflective relationship to reality. Rather than representing a world of preexisting forms, art now increasingly focuses on depicting the human act

---

8. The image of the tree converting water is Kant's (see CPJ §64). On the use of situations as "opportunities" in the modern novel, starting with Goethe's *Wilhelm Meister*, see Franco Moretti, *The Way of the World: The Bildungsroman in European Culture* (London: Verso, 2000), 45ff.

of world-making itself, the drive to impose form on life. "In art," Thomas Khurana writes, "life exceeds itself in a distinctive way; as such, art becomes the privileged site of reflection on the self-difference and self-transcendence of life."[9] But this reflection proceeds along two opposing axes. One axis is represented by Kant, Goethe, and most of the Romantics, who conceive of art as the perfection of life, as "aesthetic education." Kleist's work takes the opposing turn. In highlighting the divided and irreducibly conflicted nature of life, Kleist holds on to the idea of aesthetic perfection but gives it a radical twist: art exceeds ordinary life, not by providing it with a beautiful form but by extracting and magnifying life's capacity to exceed itself, to break its own form, to become hybrid.

Of Bears and Puppets

Like his fictional narratives, Kleist's most famous "theoretical" text, the short essay *On the Marionette Theater*, has a precise setting and semidramatic form. The time is 1801, the place M . . . , a German city big enough to afford an opera house. The narrator, surprised to see C., "the first dancer of the opera,"[10] at the lowly spectacle of a puppet theater staged in the marketplace, engages him in a conversation that touches, over the course of just seven pages, on such seemingly disparate topics as the mechanics of puppeteering, the pitfalls of consciousness, fencing bears, and man's return to paradise. No part of this dialogue is more famous than C.'s opening gambit, his claim that dancing marionettes are capable of achieving a level of kinetic and aesthetic grace that is unavailable to human beings. Most critics have read the marionette as a purely mechanical contraption and seen in the text's apparent celebration of the machine, Kleist's countermodel to the organicist aesthetics of his time. Yet the puppets are not mere machines. Rather, they are cyborgs of a

---

9. Thomas Khurana, "Reflexives Leben: Biologie und Ästhetik um 1800," *Texte zur Kunst* 10 (2010): 181.

10. Kleist, MT (dtv, 2011), 2:425. (All citations from Kleist hereafter will come from this edition.) Unless otherwise noted, English translations are mine.

sort, mechanic-human hybrids, and it is the mixing of natural and mechanical causality, not their simple opposition, that underlies Kleist's anti-organicist stance. To highlight this notion of hybridity in Kleist's aesthetics, I want to begin by reading the essay from its end, looking first at its final and least discussed anecdote.

The anecdote, which is told by C., takes the story to Russia. A young aristocrat challenges C. to a fencing match, loses swiftly, and "half joking, half annoyed," vows to introduce C. to a fencing opponent who will be his master (MT 431). C. is led to a shed, where he finds himself opposite a bear, shackled to a pole, which the young man's father "was rearing in the yard" (MT 431):

> I didn't know if I was dreaming when I saw myself confronted by such an opponent; but "Go on, go on" said Herr von G., "and see if you can land a hit on him." Recovering a little from my astonishment, I thrust at the bear with my rapier: he made a very slight movement with his paw and parried the thrust. I tried to mislead him with a feint; the bear made no move. I thrust at him again, swiftly and shrewdly, beyond any doubt had it been a human breast I would have hit: the bear made a very slight movement with his paw and parried the stroke. Now I was almost in the position of the young Herr von G. The bear's seriousness did its part to discompose me, thrust and feint followed one another, the sweat was dripping off me: all in vain! Not only did the bear, like the foremost fencer in the world, parry all my thrusts; when I feinted—no fencer in the world could follow him in that—he did not even react: eye to eye, as if he could read my soul in it, he stood, with his paw lifted in readiness, and when my thrusts were not seriously intended he did not move. (MT 432)[11]

---

11. ["*Ich wußte nicht, ob ich träumte, da ich mich einem solchen Gegner gegenüber sah; doch: stoßen Sie! stoßen Sie! sagte Herr v. G . . . , und versuchen Sie, ob Sie ihm Eins beibringen können! Ich fiel, da ich mich ein wenig von meinem Erstaunen erholt hatte, mit dem Rapier auf ihn aus; der Bär machte eine ganz kurze Bewegung mit der Tatze und parierte den Stoß. Ich versuchte ihn durch Finten zu verführen; der Bär rührte sich nicht. Ich fiel wieder, mit einer augenblicklichen Gewandheit, auf ihn aus, eines Menschen Brust würde ich ohnfehlbar getroffen haben: der Bär machte eine ganz kurze Bewegung mit der Tatze und parierte den Stoß. Jetzt war ich fast in dem Fall des jungen Hr. von G. . . . Der Ernst des Bären kam hinzu, mir die Fassung zu rauben, Stöße und Finten wechselten sich, mir triefte der Schweiß: umsonst! Nicht bloß, daß der Bär, wie der erste Fechter der Welt, alle meine Stöße parierte; auf Finten (was ihm kein Fechter der Welt nachmacht) gieng er gar nicht einmal ein: Aug' in Auge, als ob er meine Seele darin*

It is clear from the outset that what C. faces is no mere bear. Fencing is not an instinctual or natural expression of ursine behavior; it is not an activity bears develop in nature. For a bear to fence, it must have been captured and forcibly submitted to an arrangement that includes the bear but is not reducible to it. While the shackles that tie the bear to the pole are the most visible marks of this violent imposition, the bear's capture does not end with its literal enchainment but extends to the countless hours of training to which it has been submitted. It is this ensemble of chains, drills, foil, pole, and bear that constitute Kleist's fencing bear, the progeny of technology and animality.

This is not a matter of "cultivating" nature. When, through a process of grafting and hybridization, the wild pear tree is transformed into a species that produces edible fruits, the nature of the tree is altered but not fundamentally changed: trees grow fruit. Cultivation, so understood, implies the perfection of a tendency that is already latent in nature. To quote Georg Simmel, to whom I also owe the pear tree example:

> Cultivation presupposes the prior existence of an entity in an uncultivated, i.e. "natural" state. It also presupposes that the ensuing change of this entity is somehow latent in its *natural structures or instincts* [*irgendwie in dessen natürlichen* Strukturverhältnissen oder Triebkräften *latent sei*], even if it cannot be achieved by the entity itself but only through the process of culture. That is to say, cultivation develops its object to that perfection which is predetermined as a potential by its proper and ingrained tendency of its essence [*dass die Kultivierung ihren Gegenstand zu dem für ihn determinierten, in der eigentlichen und wurzelhaften Tendenz seines Wesens angelegten Vollendung führe*].[12]

The contrast to Kleist's anecdote could not be stronger. Kleist's bear is not a refined bear, nor is fencing the cultural perfection of its natural,

---

lesen könnte, stand er, die Tatze schlagfertig erhoben, und wenn meine Stöße nicht ernsthaft gemeint waren, so rührte er sich nicht."] (MT 432).

12. Georg Simmel, *Simmel on Culture: Selected Writings*, ed. David Frisby and Mike Featherstone (London: SAGE, 1997), 41 (translation modified). German text: Georg Simmel, "Vom Wesen der Kultur," in *Aufsätze und Abhandlungen, 1901–1908*, ed. Alessandro Cavalli and Volkhard Krech, vol. 2 (Frankfurt: Suhrkamp Taschenbuch Wissenschaft, 1993), 365–66 (emphasis Simmel's).

let alone *wurzelhaften* (ingrained, literally, root-like), tendency. In fact, the true object of perfection in Kleist's anecdote is not the bear but the activity of fencing, and the achievement of this perfection requires the violent imposition of a rational will, that is, the *undoing* of the bear as a nonrational animal. To capture the logic at work here, Simmel's humanist vocabulary will not do. Kleist's bear, I will say, is not so much cultivated as it is "enframed," inserted into and made part of an "apparatus" that both uses and binds its animality.

I borrow the terms "enframing" (*Gestell*) and "apparatus" (*dispositif*) from Heidegger and Foucault. Heidegger introduced the notion of "enframing" in 1953 to describe the way in which technological modernity reorganizes nature.[13] Modern technology, he argues, gives humans the power to transform natural objects with fixed properties into flexible resources that can be controlled and manipulated for specifically human purposes. Technological framing, on this view, is not just an extension or refinement of tool use: it is an entirely new way of seizing the real, one that considers reality only in terms of its potential for human use and exploitation. Foucault's conception of the "apparatus" builds on Heidegger's account.[14] An "apparatus" is an ensemble of practices, institutions, and bodies of knowledge that captures and frames living beings in order to manage and govern them. The notion, first used by Foucault in 1975 and partly inspired by the work of his teacher Georges Canguilhem on socio-organic normativity,[15] is closely connected to the concept of "biopower," which Foucault introduced in his lectures at the Collège de France in the following year. A means of capturing life, the "apparatus" provides the conceptual and operational grid—the *Gestell*—for a mode of power that seeks to "incite,

---

13. See Martin Heidegger, "The Question Concerning Technology," in *The Question Concerning Technology, and Other Essays*, trans. William Lovitt (New York: Harper & Row, 1977), 3–35.

14. This link was first pointed out by Agamben. See Giorgio Agamben, *"What Is an Apparatus?" and Other Essays*, trans. David Kishik and Stefan Pedatella, Meridian: Crossing Aesthetics (Redwood City, CA: Stanford University Press, 2009).

15. See Matteo Pasquinelli, "What an Apparatus Is Not: On the Archeology of the Norm in Foucault, Canguilhem, and Goldstein," *Parrhesia* 22 (2015): 79–89.

reinforce, control, monitor, optimize, and organize the forces under it: a power bent on generating forces, making them grow, and ordering them, rather than one dedicated to impeding them, making them submit, or destroying them."[16]

Herr G. uses the bear in much the same way as the engineers of the electrical power plant use the Rhine, according to Heidegger. If the engineers redirect the natural currents of the river into turbines in order to extract energy from them, Herr G. channels the bear's innate capacities (fast reflexes, agility, eye and arm coordination, etc.) into an activity and purpose that is no longer proper to its nature. Attached to the pole, its instincts fashioned to the technology of fencing, the bear is, functionally speaking, no longer a bear but an organic machine: a hybrid. As in Heidegger and Foucault, the apparatus that captures and transforms the living creature is both destructive and productive: destructive in that it submits the bear to an arrangement that exceeds the design of its organism; and productive in that this imposition increases the power of its living support, generating a supremely effective fencing machine. But note that Kleist is not at all critical of the violence against the bear: enframing is clearly celebrated as a way of going beyond organic life, which by itself seems to carry no value whatsoever. Animal rights activists will find little support in Kleist's text, but neither will humanists, for the power of the newly created hybrid exceeds not just biological but also received human life. While the apparatus that disrupts the bear's animality is a human invention—a product of culture—its ultimate goal is to transcend the limits of human capacity and culture. Indifferent to feints, Kleist's bear raises the cultural technology of fencing to a level of perfection that "no fencer in the world"—no human—could ever attain.

What prevents humans from achieving the perfection of culture, Kleist suggests, is the very capacity that German philosophy and literature around 1800 hail as the defining feature of man's superiority: reflection.[17] Why does the bear not react to feints? In a feint,

---

16. Foucault, *History of Sexuality, Volume 1*, 136.

17. The notion of reflection is, for instance, at the heart of Herder's influential "Essay on the Origin of Language" (1771). On Herder and his importance for the

appearance and intention split; a feint has the meaning of an attack without being one. But this split exists only for a creature that reads physical movements as the visible expression of an invisible interiority. It is precisely because the bear lacks this hermeneutic perspective that feints do not work on him. C.'s own interpretation of the bear's superiority thus misses the point. If the bear outfences him, this is not because it reads C.'s soul ("eye to eye, as if he could read my soul in it [*Aug in Aug, als ob er meine Seele darin lessen könnte*]"), but because it has no notion of the soul's existence and thus no need to decipher it.

The bear anecdote introduces us to some characteristic features of Kleistian hybridity. Hybridity, in Kleist, cuts across different species and kinds of beings. Unlike the contemporary holistic thinking of "life" in terms of self-organization, which emphasizes the systemic integrity of living things, juxtaposing them to merely mechanical aggregates, Kleist favors a logic of (re)combination and heterogeneity: assemblages are superior to organisms. Driving this valuation is Kleist's utterly functional conception of perfection: the object of perfection is not the individual or class of beings (pear trees, persons, mankind) but the art, function, or activity to which human beings devote themselves, such as fencing. Moreover, "perfection" entails an energetic dimension: the hybrid is the bearer of a heightened intensity, a being that exceeds in power the established biological and cultural forms of life it modifies. But this heightened vitality comes at a price: the path to perfection is intrinsically violent in that it subordinates the organism to a transcendent purpose, sacrificing its integrity to the requirements of an artificial or, as I will argue, *aesthetic* project. This is also why Kleistian hybridity is necessarily and characteristically agonistic: imposing itself on already established orders, hybridity always takes the form of a struggle for domination and a clash of competing systems.

project of *Bildung* in German Classicism and neo-humanism, see Dorothea E. von Mücke, *Virtue and the Veil of Illusion: Generic Innovation and the Pedagogical Project in Eighteenth-Century Literature* (Redwood Hills, CA: Stanford University Press, 1991), 161–206.

In fact, Kleist's essay is itself an instance of the agonistic hybridity it talks about. As de Man and others have pointed out, *On the Marionette Theater* is not a sustained theoretical essay but a succession of three anecdotes "encased in the dialogic frame of a staged scene."[18] This generic polyglossia—narrative, drama, philosophical essay—is heightened by the fact that both the embedded narratives and the dramatic frame are centered on scenes of combat and persuasion. Just as C., within the narrative, loses his composure when faced with the superior bear, so the narrator, within the dramatic frame, becomes "distracted" by C.'s bewildering claims (MT 433). Generic hybridity and dramatic form thus intertwine to divide the text from within. Instead of a theoretical argument expressing an undivided authorial intention, we are confronted with a riven texture of diverse speakers, genres, and voices competing for representational authority.

Implicit in this model is another form of hybridity. If there is a conventional habitat for fencing bears and dancing puppets, it is the marketplace and other venues of popular entertainment. As Christopher Wild has shown, in the very year Kleist wrote his essay, the Prussian police targeted puppet theaters in Berlin on the grounds that they attracted people of low class and corrupted public morality, an attitude that is reflected, within the essay, in the narrator's dismissive statement that puppet theaters are for the enjoyment of "the rabble [*der Pöbel*]" (MT 426). As we shall see, Kleist's essay yanks these lowly objects out of their received contexts and places them at the intersection of two highbrow philosophical discussions of the time: the aesthetic discourse on grace, and the philosophical-historical rewriting of Genesis. In doing so, he not only undercuts contemporary distinctions between "high" and "low" culture[19] but also stirs up the received ontological order. A puppet transformed

---

18. Paul de Man, "Aesthetic Formalization: Kleist's 'Über das Marionetten-theater,'" in *The Rhetoric of Romanticism* (New York: Columbia University Press, 1986), 268.

19. See Christopher J. Wild, *Theater der Keuschheit, Keuschheit des Theaters: Zu einer Geschichte der (Anti-)Theatralität von Gryphius bis Kleist* (Freiburg: Rombach, 2003), 16; and Alexander Weigel, "König, Polizist, Kasperle . . . und Kleist. Auch ein Kapitel deutscher Theatergeschichte, nach bisher unbekannten

into a vehicle of grace and redemption is insurrectionary—it has abandoned its assigned place within the order of beings, and within the order of speech. I will say more about this impropriety of speech, but for the moment it suffices to point out that Kleist's use of hybridity extends to the level of concepts, discourses, and genres. In displacing words from their traditional contexts, Kleist's essay confounds the established networks of sense and context and forges new conceptual hybrids.

With these last comments, we have moved to the essay's famous title story, the discussion of marionettes. Asked by the narrator about his interest in the puppet theater, C. puts forth two provocative claims: (a) that dancing marionettes are capable of achieving a level of aesthetic elegance—of grace—that is unavailable to human beings; and (b) that this mechanically generated grace can restore the innocence man lost through his desire for knowledge, thus providing humanity with a backdoor return to paradise. It is hardly surprising that the somewhat conservative narrator is taken aback by C.'s curious invocation of grace and redemption. In suggesting that only a mechanical puppet can fulfill the aspirations of aesthetic, religious, and philosophical-historical thought, C. launches a full-scale attack on the anthropocentric underpinnings of these discourses, on the very idea of "the human." C's wager thus brings to the fore an aspect of hybridity that is more veiled within the bear anecdote: its violent implications for *human* life.

The medium of this violence is, of course, the puppet. C. spares no rhetorical effort to highlight the marionette's mechanical and artificial nature, detailing its form and operation in the language of classical physics and mathematics (*Schwerpunkt, Pendel, Linie, Kurve, Logarithmen, Asymptote*, etc.). There are, however, two sides to the dancing puppet. On the one hand there is the puppet itself, a wooden contraption composed of interlocking parts, which is subject to natural causality and laws of gravity. On the other hand there is the puppeteer—Kleist calls him the "machinist" (MT 426)—who orchestrates (*regieren*) the puppet's movements through his own

---

Akten," in *Impulse. Aufsätze, Quellen, Berichte zur deutschen Klassik und Romantik, Folge 4* (Berlin: Aufbau-Verlag, 1982), 253–77.

hand movements, thus producing its dance. C's overall rhetorical strategy is to downplay the latter in favor of the former; that is, to subordinate rational will to mechanical law. To this end, he provides three slightly different descriptions. The first description is framed in the language of classical physics and highlights the puppet's lack of internal motivation: "Every movement, he said, had a high center of gravity; it sufficed if this, inside the figure, were controlled; the limbs, which were nothing but pendula, followed without further interference, mechanically, of their own accord [*Jede Bewegung, sagte er, hätte einen Schwerpunct; es wäre genug, diesen, in dem Innern der Figur, zu regieren; die Glieder, welche nichts als Pendel wären, folgten, ohne irgend ein Zuthun, auf eine mechanische Weise von selbst*]" (MT 426). Asked by the narrator whether "the machinist who orchestrates the marionettes must be a dancer himself or at least have some notion of what constitutes beauty [*der Machinist, der diese Puppen regierte, selbst ein Tänzer sein, oder wenigstens einen Begriff vom Schönen haben müsse*]" (MT 427), C. offers an enigmatic second description that is couched first in metaphysical and then in mathematical language. The line traced by the puppet's moving center of gravity, C. claims, is identical with "*the way of the dancer's soul [der Weg der Seele des Tänzers]*" (MT 427; Kleist's emphasis); to perfect this line and produce the most graceful movement, the machinist has to "place himself in the gravitational center of the marionette, which is to say, *dance*" (MT 427). However, this apparent appeal to empathy and identification is immediately recast in terms that emphasize its purely formal and impersonal character: when properly aligned, the fingers of the puppeteer and the motion of the puppets relate "quite like that of numbers to their logarithms or the asymptotes to the hyperbola [*etwa wie Zahlen zu ihren Logarithmen oder die Asymptote zur Hyperbel*]" (MT 427). And C. goes even further, adding a third description that altogether removes the puppeteer from the arrangement. C. continues "that the last fraction of spirit, of which he had been speaking, could itself be taken out of the marionettes; that their dancing could be shifted wholly into the realm of mechanical forces and produced by turning a handle, as I had supposed [*daß auch dieser letzte Bruch von Geist, von dem er gesprochen, aus den Marionetten entfernt werden,*

daß ihr Tanz gänzlich ins Reich mechanischer Kräfte hinüberspielt,
und vermittelst einer Kurbel, so wie ich es mir gedacht, hervorge-
bracht werden könne]" (MT 427).

The crank expresses C.'s ideal of a completely mechanized movement. In removing the puppeteer from the puppet's dance, C. suggests, the crank-driven mechanism generates a motion that is pure
grace because it is purely physical, existing wholly in the realm of
mechanical cause. But is a puppet that is moved by a crank truly
freed from the nonmechanical? As in the anecdote of the fencing
bear, we should take C.'s pronouncements with a grain of salt. What
is supposed to make the crank-driven dance so radical is the removal
of the last "fraction of spirit." However, recall my claim that the
fencing bear is not a mere animal but part of an apparatus that includes its training as well as its trainer. The same logic applies to the
marionette. Just as the bear's fencing is manipulated by the invisible
agency of the trainer, so the puppet's dance, even in its crank-driven
form, is orchestrated by the invisible agency of the puppeteer. In
both cases, the *spirit*, while remote, is far from absent—intention
and volition remain the primary source of movement, albeit one that
operates at a distance, displaced from the physical locus of action. It
is this *dislocation of agency from motion*—this split between a mechanical medium and an organizing but invisible rational will—that
structures the apparatus of the dancing puppet and finds its ideal
articulation in the crank. The crank, this product of rational invention and human design, is meant to perfect the split between instrument and purpose by removing the last traces of consciousness-
inflected *movement* (the puppeteer's finger movement) from the
arrangement. In short, what interferes with true grace is not the
"spirit" as such, but its materialization in, and as, the human body.
Despite C.'s rhetorical efforts to persuade us otherwise, the dancing
marionette is not a mere machine but a *Gestell*: a hybrid conglomerate of rationality and mechanics, intention and contraption.

What makes the human body resistant to aesthetic perfection, C.
suggests in a rather funny passage, is its irrepressible expressiveness—
that is, its sensitivity to the dynamics of the soul to which it is organically bound. Human movement is forever broken by an inner
discord that interferes with true grace.

"Watch P.," he went on, "when she is playing Daphne and, pursued by Apollo, turns to look at him: her soul is at the bottom of her spine [. . .] And watch young F. when, as Paris, he faces the three goddesses and hands Venus the apple: his soul (it is painful to see) is actually in his elbow" [*Sehen sie nur die P . . . an, fuhr er fort, wenn sie die Daphne spielt, und sich, verfolgt vom Apoll, nach ihm umsieht; die Seele sitzt ihr in den Wirbeln des Kreuzes . . . Sehen Sie den jungen F . . . an, wenn er, als Paris, unter den drei Göttinnen steht, und der Venus den Apfel überreicht: die Seele sitzt ihm gar (es ist ein Schrecken, es zu sehen) im Ellenbogen*]. (MT 429)

For C., the soul is not a substance but the fulcrum of intention: it is consciousness, conceived as the attendance of mind to the motions and attitudes of the body. The problem is that the mobility of the mind is not always in alignment with the mobility of the body. Physical and intellectual centers of gravity can diverge, as happens with F., whose focus on the elbow—the pivot of concern as his arm holds up the apple—distracts from the gestural totality of the action. This gap between mind and motion is further heightened by desire, which adds yet another layer of concern: the self's concern for the concern of the other, resulting in the urge to imagine one's body and movement as seen from outside. (Both the example of F. and the later anecdote about the *Dornauszieher* depict scenes of erotic seduction.) C.'s account of human discord helps us gain a clearer sense of the crank's aesthetic significance. Unlike the fingers of the puppeteer, which, as part of the human body, are vulnerable to the potentially distorting effects of consciousness and desire, the crank would appear to neatly separate mind from matter, movement from agency. Made by and for humans, yet generating a purely mechanical motion, the crank is a cultural tool that seems to enable cultural activity to transcend its human origins.

As I mentioned earlier, C. places his comments on man's dividedness in a biblical context, claiming that man's loss of aesthetic grace coincides with his expulsion from paradise. With consciousness cast as original sin, the puppet's mechanical grace assumes redemptive significance: it promises man's recovery of innocence, his return to paradise, and "the last chapter in the history of the world" (MT 433). C.'s reference to Genesis evokes an influential Enlightenment discourse.[20] In the second half of the eighteenth century, a number of German Enlightenment thinkers (Reimarus, Lessing, Herder, Kant, Schiller, Fichte) set out to refashion the somber biblical story of man's fall from grace into a more optimistic anthropological and historical parable. Man's lapsarian yielding to lust and curiosity is both bad and good news: bad, because it testifies to his lack of instinctual guidance and his susceptibility to preternatural desire and cognitive errors; and ultimately good, because this instinctual weakness opens up space for reflection, learning, and human freedom. Kant, in his *Conjectures on the Beginning of Human History*, clearly articulates the philosophical-historical implications of this new anthropology. History and culture, Kant suggests, both begin with and depend on humans going astray. Because transgression—our deviation from both God and instinct—is the very condition for human history and humanity's moral and political progress, what may look like original sin—our first misstep—is really the inaugural step in humanity's path to emancipation. Our fall from grace is really a happy fall: *felix culpa*. Kleist's essay taps into this discourse in ways that radically subvert it. For one thing, in equating the loss of innocence with the loss of *physical* grace, he aestheticizes the story of the Fall, avoiding its dominant moral-political interpretation. For another, his solution to the anthropological split—mechanical grace—dismantles the very entity the anthropological rewriting of Genesis was meant to throw into relief: the human.

The Enlightenment theory of human instinctual weakness acknowledged the split within humans only to turn it into an engine of humanity's moral-political progress. Man's lack is his luck, in that it enables him to set (moral) ends for himself and become truly human. Kleist breaks with this narrative of human self-perfection. Not only is the object of perfection no longer man but a particular

---

20. See Odo Marquard, "Felix Culpa? Bemerkungen zu einem Applikations-schicksal von Genesis 3," in *Text und Appplikation*, ed. Manfred Fuhrmann (Munich: Wilhelm Fink, 1981), 53–71, and Wilhelm Schmidt-Biggemann, "Geschichte der Erbsünde in der Aufklärung: Philosophiegeschichtliche Mutmaßungen," in *Theodizee und Tatsachen—Das philosophische Profil der deutschen Aufklärung* (Frankfurt: Suhrkamp Taschenbuch Wissenschaft, 1988), 88–116.

cultural activity (dancing, for instance); the perfection of this activity requires the dismantling of the human. Marionettes "heal" the anthropological split by artificializing it. The puppet, in Kleist, functions as the mechanical prosthesis of the mind; it is a technological supplement, an external and inorganic material support that perfects human movement through its mechanization.

To see how radical this conception of human hybridity is, consider the other contemporary humanist discourse Kleist targets: the aesthetic discourse on grace. Where Kant seeks to reunite humanity on the level of moral-political institutions, Schiller's *On Grace and Dignity*, the canonical Classicist treatise on the subject, flaunts the role of art in healing man's divided nature. Grace is embodied wholeness, the representation, in a single human being, of the harmonious integration of mind, body, and desire. Like Kleist, Schiller links grace to motion: grace is a *"moveable* [bewegliche] beauty."[21] But not all bodies are capable of grace. For a body to be considered graceful, its movement must be caused not only from within—which is true of animals and plants as defined by Kant, on whom Schiller heavily depends—but also by an *immaterial* force: "Wherever there is grace, then, the soul is the moving principle" (GD 127; AW 256). Grace, in other words, is bound up with freedom and morality: it is the bodily expression of true humanity, "a beauty not granted by nature, but brought forth by the subject itself" (GD 127; AW 256). What recommends the beauty of graceful motion over ordinary moral manifestations, Schiller argues, is its bodily character. Although grace is the product of man's work on his self, *a personal and moral achievement*, it nonetheless *appears* to be entirely artless. This is so because in the graceful person morality has shed its intel-

---

21. Schiller, "Über Anmuth und Würde," in *Schillers Werke. Nationalausgabe*, vol. 20, ed. Julius Petersen and Gerhard Fricke (Weimar: H. Böhlaus Nachfolger, 1962), 252. References to the English translation of this essay are to Friedrich Schiller, "On Grace and Dignity," in *Schiller's "On Grace and Dignity" in Its Cultural Context: Essays and a New Translation*, ed. Jane V. Curran and Christophe Fricker (Rochester, NY: Camden House, 2005), 125. Hereafter, extracts from Schiller's essay will be indicated by GD and page number, followed by AW and page number to indicate the reference to the pagination of Schiller's "Über Anmuth und Würde" in *Schillers Werke*.

lectual character and become a moral disposition; that is, an embodied affect. Hence the aesthetic surplus of grace over ordinary moral acts: the sensible sign of an inward harmony, graceful motion affords a redemptive vision of human life in which body and soul, freedom and the flesh, are effortlessly united.

Little of this vision survives in Kleist. While Schiller's graceful bodies are moved from within, Kleist extols a medium that lacks any interiority. Puppets need no organs, nor do they contain the principle of motion within themselves, as Kant had argued about organisms. Kleist's "natural organization of points of gravity [*naturgemäße Anordnung der Schwerpunkte*]" (MT 429) refers to a purely mechanical conception of nature, one in which movements are caused by external forces working on, rather than emanating from, bodies. "A physical point of gravity of members that are 'dead, pure pendulas,'" Petra Gehring writes, "is the exact opposite of an organ."[22] Accordingly, the illusion of naturalness, so crucial to Schiller's (and Kant's) idea of beauty, is absent from Kleist. On the one hand, puppets are unabashedly artificial. Made of wood, displayed on a makeshift stage, and moved by strings attached to distinct physical parts, the marionette is an artifact, a man-made contraption, a mechanical assemblage. On the other hand, the puppet's graceful movement—its beautiful dance—is the product of overt technological manipulation, the result of a rational will that produces the illusion of animation. Instead of approximating art to natural organisms, then, Kleist pushes art in the opposite direction, parading it as an inorganic machine. And once this machine runs, it disassembles "the human" that Schiller had so carefully sought to unite. Under the pressure of aesthetic perfection, the body's organic integrity breaks. This threat to the natural body, already implicit in C.'s praise of the mechanical puppet, becomes fully obvious in his comments about contemporary developments in medical technology. Mutilated Englishmen who received an artificial leg, C. claims, achieved a gracefulness of movement vastly superior to their

---

22. Petra Gehring, "Lebendigkeit oder Leben? Kleists 'Marionettentheater' und die Physiologie," in *Kleists "Über das Marionettentheater,"* ed. Michael Nerurkar (Bielefeld: Transkript Verlag, 2013), 145.

natural-legged countrymen. Cyborgs dance better: "Dance? What am I saying? [*Was sag ich, tanzen?*]" (MT 428). As for the other—spiritual—dimension of "the human," Kleist does not so much deny the soul as purge it of the vagaries of purpose and intention. Dissolved into the puppet's mechanized dance, the soul "glides, as the resultant of external fields of forces, through bodies and patterns of movement."[23]

It should be clear that this hybrid conception of human life constitutes an attack not just on eighteenth-century humanism but on deep strata of Judeo-Christian and Greek thinking. The idea of the soul as principle of motion goes back to Aristotle, and the image of the soul as animating life can be found in Plato's *Phaidos* and the Old Testament, where God breathes life into inanimate bodies. Kleist deconstructs Schiller's and Kant's humanistic rewriting of this spiritual tradition. But this deconstruction is in the service of *another* ideal. Kleist's conception is neither naturalistic nor materialistic. As with the enframing of the bear, the mechanization of human motion is in the service of a peculiar kind of aesthetic transcendence: "grace" continues to promise a state beyond human finitude. It is just that the achievement of this state entails the artificialization of the human, its extension into the nonhuman. Instead of overcoming the human split through refinement and sublation—whether by bringing body and mind in closer alignment (Schiller) or by turning their incongruity into an engine of human progress (Kant)—Kleist instrumentalizes it. "Transcending" the human means, for Kleist, literally pushing beyond the cognitive and organic limits of human life by extending human life into its inorganic, prosthetic support. And *only* such an artificially heightened life, Kleist suggests, can achieve aesthetic perfection and is worth living. Implicit in the images of the dancing puppet and the fencing bear, in other words, is a new conception of human life. Consider that grace, both in its aesthetic (*Anmut*) and biblical sense (*Gnade*), is a uniquely human attribute: only human beings are in need of *Gnade* and capable of *Anmut*. In claiming that in order to achieve grace humans need to

---

23. Ibid., 155.

attach themselves to marionettes or other mechanical, nonhuman devices, Kleist transforms not only our traditional understanding of grace but also that of its bearer. What makes humans distinctly human, his essay suggests, is our openness to artificiality—our hybridity. To parody Schiller: man is wholly human only when he ceases to be a "whole" human.

Let me sum up. First, Kleist emphasizes—in fact: celebrates—the dividedness of human life. Human beings are made distinctly human through artifice, by virtue of something nonhuman or nonorganic. Human life thus comprises, but is not reducible to, organic life: what elevates humans to their proper vitality is the introduction of the nonhuman, the mechanical. Second, given the emphasis of Kleist's text on circumscribed fields of activity (dancing, fencing, etc.), it seems that grace and perfection cannot be achieved once and for all but instead require perpetual arrangement and rearrangement. For humans to recover their ideal state, in other words, they must attach themselves to countless devices and machines. C.'s praise of the artificially legged dancer is programmatic: man, for Kleist, is *prosthetic* man, an organic-mechanical assemblage. Finally, Kleist continues to think of perfection in aesthetic terms, suggesting that it is art, rather than technology, that is the prime medium—the quintessential prosthesis—capable of redeeming human life through its vital intensification. Kleist shares in what may be called the absolutization of art around 1800 but gives it a peculiar twist: art redeems human life not by providing it with a unified aesthetic form but by magnifying, and orchestrating its innate capacity for hybridization.

The Environment Strikes Back

The notion of hybridity presented thus far seems to be restricted to the obvious disjunctions of nature and culture or human and animal. But in Kleist, hybridity has a global significance, structuring the workings of language, individuals, and institutions. Consider, for such an extended notion of hybridity, the famous opening of Kleist's novella *The Marquise of O . . .*

In M . . . , an important town in upper Italy, the widowed Marquise of
O . . . , a lady of excellent reputation, and mother of several well-
brought-up children, let it be known through newspapers: that she,
without her knowledge, became pregnant; that the father of the child that
she was to bear, should declare himself; and that she, out of consideration to her family, had resolved to marry him. [*In M . . . , einer bedeutenden Stadt im oberen Italien, ließ die verwittwete Marquise von O . . . ,
eine Dame von vortrefflichem Ruf, und Mutter von mehreren wohlerzogenen Kindern, durch die Zeitungen bekannt machen: daß sie, ohne ihr
Wissen, in andre Umstände gekommen sey, daß der Vater zu dem Kinde,
das sie gebären würde, sich melden solle; und daß sie, aus Familien-
Rücksichten, entschlossen wäre, ihn zu heirathen*]. (MvO 107)

The story has barely begun in the conventionalized language of
eighteenth-century narrative before it is interrupted by another, truly
disorderly text: the Marquise's announcement is the vehicle of multiple transgressions. The first transgression occurs on the level of
genre and medium. The second half of the eighteenth century saw
a rapid rise in print culture, including the publication of journals,
broadsheets, and *Zeitungen* (news) of various kinds. Among these
publications were so-called intelligence gazettes (*Intelligenzblätter*),
which focused on regional matters and published, in addition to official proclamations (warrants, notices of crimes, bread prices,
etc.), personal announcements, including texts designed to deny ru-
mors and restore honor. It is into this imagined discursive context
that the Marquise's message irrupts. However capacious the historical gazettes' conventional range of *Zeitungen* might have been, it
clearly did not countenance anything like a victim's publication of
her rape, let alone the call to her rapist to step forth and marry her.
Improper, scandalous, offensive—the announcement violates the
communicative conventions of the medium in which it appears, thus
disrupting it from within. This is also a transgression in respect to
class. Because marriage practices concern the very reproduction of
a group, they belong to the most highly regulated social norms, especially among groups like the aristocracy, which defines itself in
terms of filiation and bloodline. The announcement breaches the
rules of the aristocratic marriage game in a number of ways: it
broadcasts an ignoble sexual occurrence, violates proper considerations of rank (whoever raped her will do as a husband), and makes

use of the new and rather common medium of the daily chronicle. Her message thus disrupts the aristocratic system at its very core—in the domain of biological-social reproduction. Which brings us to the third transgression. The late eighteenth century saw the emergence of new models of reproduction centered on the idea of motherhood. The replacement of patrilinear conceptions of biological and social reproduction by epigenetic models emphasizing the biological participation of both partners[24] idealized the link between mothers and children. But women's rising biological, pedagogical, and affective importance within the family went hand in hand with their increasing exclusion from the sphere of cultural productivity, as new notions of "genius" and "author" gendered intellectual creativity as exclusively male.[25] Against this background, the Marquise's announcement constitutes an unprecedented act of self-assertion, a truly improper arrogation of agency that upsets the existing gender regime. In usurping authorship to assume control of her maternity, she disrupts in one swoop the dominant organization of both intellectual and biological productivity. To publicize one's rape while simultaneously proposing to the rapist—it is difficult to imagine an act that fits more closely Goethe's famous definition of the novella as an "unheard-of" event (*unerhörtes Ereignis*).

This is also, I want to suggest, a hybrid act. If the Marquise's announcement is scandalous, this is not just because it says what must not be said but because it brings together what discourse has kept apart: aristocracy and newspapers, rape and the protocols of marriage, motherhood and authorship. Prior to the announcement, these instances of discourse and reality existed alongside each other by virtue of their capacity to keep their counterparts at bay: "marriage" and "marital sex" were defined in opposition to "rape"; "authorship" excluded "woman"; "aristocratic" communication shunned

24. Ludmilla Jordanova, "Interrogating the Concept of Reproduction in the Eighteenth Century," in *Conceiving the New World Order: The Global Politics of Reproduction*, ed. Faye D. Ginsburg and Rayna Rapp (Berkeley: University of California Press, 1995), 369–86.

25. Helmut Müller-Sievers, *Self-Generation: Biology, Philosophy, and Literature Around 1800*, Writing Science (Redwood Hills, CA: Stanford University Press, 1997).

the "medium of reportage"; and so on. The scare quotes are meant to emphasize that we are not dealing with empirical facts but with orders of speech and behavior—that is, with *systems* that use their own operations to distinguish themselves from what they are *not*. The announcement reverses this labor of systemic differentiation. Short-circuiting distinct semantics, it blurs the established boundaries both within discourse and between words and things, collapsing, in the space of two sentences, rape into marriage, pregnancy into authorship, and aristocratic decorum into journalistic news. The announcement, in short, is not just about rape, pregnancy, and reproduction; it is itself an instrument of hybridization, of the emergence of new and unheard-of cultural and linguistic entities.

And these new entities are literally fertile; linguistic hybridity breeds *biological* offspring. Strange as this claim might sound, note that the announcement sets into motion a chain of events that culminates in the marriage between the Marquise and the Count and the birth of many more children: "A series of young Russians now followed the first [*Eine ganze Reihe von jungen Russen folgt ejetzt noch dem ersten*]" (MvO 147). What began as a traumatic interruption of the status quo results in the revitalization of the aristocratic order: recast as marital intercourse, the rape becomes an agent of restitution, a catalyst for the rejuvenation of two noble families. In fact, the text highlights the rape's generative force through its sharp contrast between beginning and end. Prior to the Count's assault, the widowed Marquise had "returned with her two children to her father's house, in the fortress. Here, occupying herself with art and literature, with the education of her children and the care of her parents, she had spent the following years in the greatest solitude [*in der größten Eingezogenheit*]: until the— war suddenly filled the surrounding country with troops of nearly all the powers, Russians among them" (MvO 107). Peace, associated with sterility and self-enclosure, will not do. The attack and subsequent rape disrupt the Marquise's retreat from the world and reinsert her into the chain of biological and social reproduction. For life to become productive again, its protective barriers—the walls of the fortress, the routines of family life, the integrity of the body—must be breached.

Let me connect all of this back to my earlier discussion of organisms and self-organization. Models of self-organization, I claimed, emphasize both the homogeneity of living systems and their capacity to turn the environment into a resource for their own reproduction. The two axes are intertwined; the function of the system is to convert the potentially destructive (external) environment into building blocks for the system's (internal) homeostatic balance. Events in Kleist's story follow precisely the opposite logic. As with the announcement, the military attack and subsequent rape depict the violent intrusion of the environment into an established organization. In each case, the outside disrupts the organization's internal balance, causing it to perish or undergo fundamental transformations. The rape—the invasion and impregnation of the Marquise's body—expresses this dynamic most clearly; but it only crystallizes and, literally, embodies a logic that structures the narrative as a whole. Kleist's novella unfolds as a series of environmental catastrophes.

- *Pregnancy vs. family.* After the attack, everything seems to have "returned to the old order of things" (MvO 112). But this reconstitution of the familial order is soon disturbed by the very reality on whose absence it was built. As we saw, the Marquise's decision to live with her parents rested on her self-understanding as a sexually inactive widow and mother; her pregnancy, undermining this vision, triggers a dynamic whereby the status quo is undone by its constitutive exterior. The Marquise's reproductive body, consigned to the environment of the "old order of things," invades the latter and destroys it from within.
- *Body vs. consciousness.* Because the Marquise was unconscious during the rape, her pregnancy confounds and traumatizes her. The biological agency of the female body overwhelms consciousness and its cultural resources, causing them to unravel and split open. On the one hand, the more irrefutable the Marquise's pregnancy, the more fervently she resists acknowledging its violent cause, creating an internal conflict that pits her against herself and codes all her words

and actions as hysterical. On the other hand, her continued insistence, in the face of her pregnancy, on having been sexually inactive, challenges the bedrock of all cultural explanation—causality—and threatens to "overthrow the order of the world [*Umwälzung der Weltordnung*]" (MvO 126).

• *Patriarchy vs. religious miracle.* After being expelled by her father, the Marquise withdraws with her children to a country home. There she begins to conceive of her pregnancy as a religious miracle, and to entertain fantasies of her child's divine origin. Her mother eventually joins in these transcendent narratives, and the two, empowered by a sense of divine innocence and injustice, return home and overthrow the father's authority. Aristocratic patriarchy crumbles under the impact of a religiously inspired female revolt, culminating in an erotically charged reunion between father and daughter that fuses incest and the cult of Mary into a monstrous collage.

Rape, pregnancy, religious fantasy, announcement, female revolt—Kleist's novella unfolds through a series of events that upend the ordinary power dynamic between system and environment. And yet, as we saw, this chain of upheavals ends up reconstituting the dominant order. The rape triggers a process of revitalization, embodied in the "series of young Russians" emanating from the marital union between the Count and the Marquise but extending beyond the biological. Under the pressure of female action, aristocratic masculinity undergoes a process of affective modernization: the rapist becomes a loving husband, the tyrannical father a sentimental one. Yet this transformation, while reviving the aristocratic family, also serves to contain the anarchic vitality that threatened it. Channeled into the institution of marriage, the reproductive vitality of the female body loses its disruptiveness and becomes a vehicle of patrilinear continuity (note that the union between the Marquise and the Count produces "young *Russians*"). What began as a traumatic breakdown of the gallant aristocratic code—the Count's rape of the unconscious Marquise—ends up reviving the patriarchal aristocratic order.

This last statement needs further refinement. As we saw, it is not just the rape but its figuration within the announcement that generates the renewal of the old order. This is clearly evidenced by the plot structure: initiating the reunion of mother and daughter as well as the subsequent legal communications between the Count and the Marquise's parents, the announcement, rather than the rape, constitutes the story's narrative pivot, the medium and turning point through with interruption is transformed into continuity. Given the announcement's scandalous character, we might generalize the logic at work here in the following way: the renewal of the social system is triggered by the radical upheaval of established semantic and conceptual relations. The announcement, in other words, functions as a linguistic catalyst that precipitates broader social changes. It is the capacity of language to disrupt itself—to attack its own regularizing codes and thus destroy, via language, the world we know through language—that is, for Kleist, the major source of newness and vitality in the world.

Such self-disruption is necessary, it seems, because language, like all other systems, tends toward its own devitalization. The processes of iteration that ground meaning and reference can also normalize language to the point of dissipating it. But when language loses its expressive and assertoric force and becomes a graveyard of ready-made distinctions, speech runs on autopilot, and words, as well as the world these words are supposed to open up, grow dull and lifeless. To save life from its petrification in routine and habit, Kleist's novella suggests, the normative tendencies of language must be disrupted. This is the function of the Marquise's scandalous announcement; but it is also the function of Kleist's own text, as the novella's opening suggests, and it is worth referencing again:

In M . . . , an important town in upper Italy, the widowed Marquise of O . . . , a lady of excellent reputation, and mother of several well-brought-up children, let it be known through newspapers: that she, without her knowledge, became pregnant; that the father of the child that she was to bear, should declare himself; and that she, out of consideration to her family, had resolved to marry him. [*In M . . . , einer bedeutenden Stadt im oberen Italien, ließ die verwittwete Marquise von O . . . , eine Dame von vortrefflichem Ruf, und Mutter von mehreren wohlerzogenen Kindern, durch die Zeitungen bekannt machen: daß sie, ohne ihr Wissen, in andre Umstände gekommen sey, daß der Vater zu dem Kinde, das sie gebären würde, sich melden solle; und daß sie, aus Familien-Rücksichten, entschlossen wäre, ihn zu heirathen]. (MvO 107)*

The words preceding the colon evoke the conventions of eighteenth-century realist narrative; the words following it constitute an emphatically singular—and unmistakably Kleistian—speech act. Taken together, and pivoting on punctuation that signifies nothing but the momentary shift in signification, the two parts of Kleist's opening sentence frame the novella as *a disruption of narrative, and more generally sociolinguistic, conventions.* What follows, then, is not just another fictional evocation of reality but the novella's attempt to undo, through its idiosyncratic realignment of language and practice, the ordinary relations between fiction and reality, words and world. And it is the novella's irregular language, its own aesthetically orchestrated generation of linguistic hybrids, that revitalizes the existing cultural and natural orders. After all, does the serial generation of children at the end of the story—*the whole series of young Russians* springing forth from the Marquise's womb—not have a tinge of the mechanical about it?

Heteropoietics

My readings so far suggest that Kleist's hybrid organisms are defined by *heteropoietic* rather than autopoietic operations. As we saw, autopoietic models, such as Kant's account of the organism, emphasize an entity's capacity to treat its environment as a resource to reproduce itself. For this to be possible, the organism must regulate its relationship to the environment (a) by creating physical boundaries that reduce its contact with the outside, and (b) by organizing its internal operations into a tightly knit network. To live, on this model, is to convert a chaotic outside into a structured inside, heterogeneity into homogeneity. Kleist's texts attack this model of the living by dramatizing the vital importance of boundary violations. Whether a bear is submitted to fencing drills, the Marquise to rape, or existing gender, class, and genre conventions to a scandalous announcement, Kleist's stories celebrate the violation of boundaries and the creation of something new. Moreover, the hybrid beings that emerge from these heteropoietic operations are characterized by a heightened level of vitality and power: the fencing bear outfences humans; the marital union between rapist and victim generates more offspring than the Marquise's first harmonious marriage; the announcement revives an insulated and outmoded aristocratic order; and so on.

I want to extrapolate what I take to be Kleist's implicit critique of the self-organizing model of life from these episodes. The autopoietic organization of life is problematic, Kleist's texts suggest, because it overprotects the living entity from the vitality of interaction with its environment. Recall the two fundamental characteristics of autopoiesis: (1) the living being's interaction with the environment occurs only at the periphery, and (2) these interactions are filtered through the system's own operations, such that whatever gets into the system does so only by virtue of being converted into an operable and useful form *for* the system. For Kleist, forms of life that submit to these mechanisms become *too* remote from and insensitive to their environment, deadening themselves in the very process of staying alive. As the system's operations, shielded from the unruly forces of the environment, increasingly stabilize around an *inner* norm, the system petrifies into routine and loses its edge. For life to regain its intensity and become worth living again, its existing forms must be smashed and the stuff of life—bodies, words, institutions—newly reassembled.[26]

Just as the theory of autopoiesis has been extended beyond the realm of biology, so the mechanisms of hybridity and heteropoiesis in Kleist are fully general in the sense that they apply to every discernible entity within the text's organization of the world: bodies, families, social groups, legal and political orders, patterns of interaction, etc. In fact, heteropoiesis extends not only to the text's

---

26. See also my "Breaking Skulls: Kleist, Hegel and the Force of Assertion," in *Heinrich von Kleist and Modernity*, ed. Bernd Fischer and Tim Mehigan (Rochester, NY: Camden House, 2011), 243–57.

depiction *of* the world but also to the way the text organizes itself
in relation *to* the world, a world that comprises, but is not limited
to, other texts as well as actual readers. It is this hetero-*poietic* dimension of heteropoiesis, already touched on at the end of the last
section, that I now want to elaborate by way of conclusion. I will
restrict my observations to a few passages from Kleist's short reflection on a painting by Caspar David Friedrich.

Kleist's reflection on a painting by Caspar David Friedrich ("Diverse Feelings before Friedrich's Seascape" [1810]) is itself a product of boundary violations. The text by Kleist draws heavily, if se-
lectively, on a longer essay submitted by Clemens Brentano and
Achim von Arnim to the *Berliner Abendblätter*, a newspaper of
which Kleist was the editor at the time. As Silke-Maria Weineck observes, "Kleist remorselessly butchers the piece. He eliminates the
dialogue altogether, heavily edits the introductory paragraph, adds
observations and judgments alien to its tone . . . and prints the result above the signature 'cb.'"[27] In other words, Kleist does what we
have been observing him do throughout this chapter: destroy the
integrity of existing forms in order to assemble new, hybrid ones.
Like the bear and the Marquise's body, Brentano and Arnim's essay
is subjected to the intensifying violence of heteropoietic operations.
"Kleist," Weineck writes, "turns a sophisticated feuilleton into one
of the most-quoted pieces of modern art criticism of all time."[28]
There is broad agreement that the fame of Kleist's re-vision hinges
on a single line, a single, indelible image. Following the first three
long sentences, which Kleist takes almost *verbatim* from Brentano
and Arnim, he adds: "Nothing can be sadder or more uncomfortable
than this position in the world: the sole spark of life within the wide
realm of death, the lonely midpoint within the lonely circle. The picture, with its two or three enigmatic objects, lies there like the
apocalypse, as if it had Young's Night Thoughts, and since, in its
uniformity and shorelessness, it has nothing as its foreground but

---

27. Silke-Maria Weineck, "Thoughts before a Line by Kleist," *Germanic Review* 85, no. 1 (2010): 63.
28. Ibid., 66.

the frame, *it is, while one gazes at it, as if one's eyelids have been cut away*" (EF 362; FF 66).

As if one'e eyelids have been cut away: the line condenses the logic of Kleistian heteropoiesis into a single terrifying image. The act of seeing offers a paradigm for the normal interaction between organism and environment. A complex system, the eye "collects light from the surrounding environment, regulates its intensity through a diaphragm, [and] focuses it through an adjustable assembly of lenses to form an image."[29] Converted into electrical signals, the information captured through the eye is then transmitted, via complex neural pathways, to the brain where it is decoded and interpreted. The images we see, in other words, are the products of "interactive processes determined solely by the organism's own organization";[30] seeing is an autopoietic organic process. (It is perhaps no accident that Humbert Maturana, who introduced the theory of autopoiesis into biology, drew for its elaboration on his earlier empirical research on the neurophysiology of visual perception in frogs.[31]) But for this intricate process to unfold, the eye must have physical boundaries that protect it from the outside and regulate its interaction with the environment. In cutting off the eyelids, Kleist removes this protective filter, thus destroying the basis of organic vision. Instead of the eye modulating and transforming the environment, Kleist paints a scene in which the environment transforms the eye, subjecting it to what lies before it without limit, to an unimpeded flood of stimuli.

The effect of this arrangement would be excruciating pain. Patients suffering from a mysterious case of oversensitivity to light, a recent medical article suggests, experience their condition as a physical attack on the eye: "Imagine a knife in your eye. Forever," one

---

29. Laurence A. Cole, Peter R. Kramer, *Human Physiology, Biochemistry and Basic Medicine* (Amsterdam: Elsevier, 2016), 101.

30. N. Katherine Hayles, *How We Became Post-Human: Virtual Bodies in Cybernetics, Literature, and Informatics* (Chicago: University of Chicago Press, 1999), 136.

31. J. Y. Lettvin, H. R. Maturana, W. S. McCulloch, W. H. Pitts, "What the Frog's Eye Tells the Frog's Brain," *Proceedings of the Ire* 47, no. 11 (1959): 1940–51.

patient writes, while others speak of "barbed wires" or "razor blades,"[32] unwittingly conjuring up the opening shot of Buñuel's *Un Chien Andalou*, one of the most horrific and famous scenes in film history. More than a century before Buñuel, Kleist envisions such an attack on the eye. A creature that is unable to close its eyes suffers the environment as a force that literally burns itself into its nervous system, producing a sensation of pain that, in its raw and unmediated intensity, not only collapses the distinction between sight and its object but also destroys the sense of self that depends on and develops out of this distinction. To see without eyelids is to be thrown back to an impossible form of perceptual encounter, to a vision that occludes and predates the organism's differentiation from its environment.

And yet this impossible vision is also a transcendent one. In removing the boundary that circumscribes the visual field, Kleist evokes a specific kind of infinite vision. It is here, in its dissatisfaction with ordinary perception, that Kleist's sadistic attack on the eye reveals its broader cultural significance. Leaving aside the essay's obvious evocation and critique of the discourse of Romantic longing,[33] the attempt to transcend the limits of natural vision was key, as we saw, to both Kant and Goethe's reflections on mind and nature. In Goethe's case, the problem arose in the context of his botanical studies. The question was how to reconcile the temporal limitation of ordinary vision—the fact that the eye only sees what is physically present—with the need to observe the growth of

---

32.   Bryn Nelson, "In the Blink of an Eye," *Mosaic*, September 7, 2015, https://mosaicscience.com/story/severe-eye-pain/.

33.   Briefly, whereas Romantic "longing" rests on the fantasy of an unrestricted freedom of the imagination that projects its own boundlessness onto nature, Kleist, following Arnim and Brentano, emphasizes the constitutive role of negation and conflict that sustains this projection. Longing, the text insists, is structured by "an appeal, which the heart makes, and, to put it this way, an abruption [*Abbruch*], which nature inflicts on one" (EFS 362; FF 65). Note that Kleist's text explicitly connects the illusion of infinite longing to the utopia of a "life" freed from limitations, a utopia that evidently has no place in Kleist's hybrid conception of life. For a good discussion of Kleist's critique of "longing," see Christian Begeman, "Brentano und Kleist vor Friedrichs *Mönch am Meer*. Aspekte eines Umbruchs in der Geschichte der Wahrnehmung," *DVJS* 64 (1990): 89–145.

plants over time. Goethe's solution to the problem involved the development of an extended mode of seeing, a continuous and synoptic vision in which conceptual thought and sensual perception presumably merge into what Goethe calls "the *mind's* eye." Kant, while skeptical of attempts to close the gap between concept and percept, nonetheless recognized the need to make moral ideas palpable. The complex visual experience of the sublime was designed to combine both realms without collapsing them. Faced with the sight of a terrifying or overwhelming object—for instance, shipwrecks or mountains—the subject's initial feeling of impotence gives way to his rapturous recognition of his inviolability as a moral creature. But for the frightening object to induce, even indirectly, such "ecstatic [moral] pleasure [*begeisternde Wohlgefallen*]" (KU §28, 5: 262), the subject must remain at a physical remove from it— he must be safe. Kleist collapses this protective distance, thus exposing the organic underside on which Goethe's and Kant's ideas of transcendence are built. For the pleasures of higher vision— whether moral (Kant) or epistemic (Goethe)—depend on the smooth functioning of natural vision; there is no mind's eye without a physical eye, no (indirect) presentation of moral ideas without actual seeing. Kleist's sadistic image returns vision to its bodily rudiments in sensation and nerve impulses, thus reversing this upward movement from lower to higher faculty built into the humanist idea of transcendence. It is as if Kleist were saying: you want infinite vision—well, here it is! We have thus returned to the radical opposition between cultivation and enframing: where Kant and, especially, Goethe think of the perfection of vision in terms of the pleasurable expansion of man's natural capacities, Kleist conceives of it as a painful cut into the biological organism. There is no higher life without the sacrifice of natural form.

In fact, (en)framing plays an explicit role in Kleist's text. Note that Kleist, following Arnim and Brentano, moves the frame *into* the picture—the "picture . . . has nothing at its foreground but the frame"—thus highlighting the role of negation at the core of the observational act. Frames are ordinarily not part of paintings but mark them out—frame them—*as* paintings, that is, as images to be looked at. In moving the frame into the foreground, Kleist blurs the distinction between medium and image on which acts of seeing rest. As the art historian Hans Belting reminds us, "no visible images reach us unmediated. Their visibility rests on their particular mediality, which controls the perception of them and creates the viewer's attention."[34] Yet while images obtain visibility only through their media, we can, in our acts of looking, pay attention only to one *or* the other, the canvas or the image. This impossibility of simultaneously seeing image and medium rests on another impossibility constitutive of the act of seeing: the impossibility of seeing the eye that sees. It is this impossibility that Kleist's text brings to the fore. The frame-as-foreground marks, within the image, that which cannot be seen—the observer who is outside of yet produces the image that she sees. This is the paradox of self-reflexivity that Arnim and Brentano had already highlighted in their text. But whereas in Arnim and Brentano the presentation of this paradox is followed by a turn toward ironic metacommentary (in the form of several pages of banal conversations about Friedrich's painting by philistine gallery visitors), Kleist drives the paradox of observation into the body of the observer. Rather than observing himself, thereby confirming his status as the origin or ground of his visual field, the lidless viewer suffers the impossibility of self-observation as a painful "abruption [*Abbruch*], which nature inflicts on one" (EFS 362; FF 65). A meager eight words, Kleist's image of the lidless observer installs a neurological blind spot at the heart of the production of image- and meaning-making. Just as the symbolic power of a painting depends on the meaninglessness of the frame that makes it visible *as* a painting, so the meaning we ascribe to our perceptions rests on presymbolic bodily processes. Belting has suggested that the dialectic of medium and image, absence and presence that shapes all artistic representation rests on the analogy with our bodies, which "serve as a living medium that makes us perceive, project, or remember images."[35] Kleist mobilizes this analogy to show that all symbols and representations—including the "indirect representation" of

---

34. Hans Belting, "Image, Medium, Body: A New Approch to Iconology," *Critical Inquiry* 31 (Winter 2005): 304.

35. Ibid., 306.

our infinite moral capacities that Kant derived from the failure of natural perception in the sublime—rest on negation, hybridity, and the violent immixture of body and meaning.

There is another feature of Kleist's essay that underscores his violently antinaturalist stance. Given Kant's and Goethe's interest in bridging the gap between nature and mind, it is hardly accidental that their reflections on higher vision center on objects taken from the natural world: plants for Goethe, mountains and storms for Kant. Kleist, by contrast, focuses on a mode of seeing induced by *art*. Kleist takes Caspar David Friedrich's famous painting *Monk by the Sea*, which foregrounds the act of seeing—the painting depicts a tiny and forlorn figure standing on a dune, gazing out onto a vast expanse of ocean and sky—as an occasion to reflect on the dehumanizing power of art. It is art and art alone, according to Kleist, that is capable of disrupting the naturalness of vision. Friedrich's painting accomplishes this by drawing the viewer into its own desolate sightscape. In blurring the contours separating the vast monochromatic expanses of ocean and sky, Friedrich produces a visual field deprived of discrete objects, a world of no-thing-ness that, due to its lack of internal distinction, engulfs the viewer, imposing on him a total vision without interruption—*as if one's eyelids have been cut away.*

What Kleist imagines apropos of Friedrich's painting, in other words, is the aesthetic production of a *hybrid* vision. *Monk by the Sea*, he insists, neither pleases the senses nor appeals to the viewer's mind; rather, it *grafts* its artificial images onto his natural vision, which collapses under the demand to see what cannot be seen—the emptiness of the infinite. Like the fencing bear or the Marquise, then, Kleist's viewer is drawn into the violent machinery of hybridization and vital intensification. But there is one important difference. In most of the earlier scenarios, the production of the hybrid is subordinated to a larger goal; hybridity produces a biopolitical surplus, enhancing the vitality of society and the body politic—the fencing bear is a lethal combatant, the "series of young Russians" revitalizes an effete aristocracy. "Diverse Feelings," by contrast, seems to be about the aesthetic production of "pure" hybridity. In fact, infinite vision is not only a purely aesthetic construct; it is ultimately impossible. No matter how much the painting aspires to denaturalize vision, art's power to break the limits of the organic remain uncertain and hypothetical, suspended in the conditional mode: as if . . .

How to read this "failure"? Here is one way to think about the impossible demand of pure hybridity. Earlier I mentioned that hybridity is traditionally thought of as the creation, or figuration, of a third kind. Cross a horse and a donkey and you get a mule. But once the mule is created, it has, at least in principle, stopped being a singularly queer entity and instead becomes its own genus. The breaking of boundaries, in other words, risks producing merely another "normal" creature, another generic kind of being that, like all forms of life, will articulate its own conventions and norms. The end of the *Marquise of O . . .* , with its production of a *"series* of young Russians,"* hints at this intersection of hybridity with reproductive stability, but we can also picture, say, the founding of an academy for the training of fencing bears. (After all, even Nietzsche—and the Nazis inspired by him—dreamt of breeding [*züchten*] a new race of super-men.) In short, the logics of vital intensification and of hybridization collide at their limits. If one really wants to do away with the boundary between system and environment, then the breaking of boundaries must not produce a new boundary, and the *operations* of hybridization not result in a new hybrid *organism*. Conceived along these lines, the failure of hybrid vision might be indicative of an irreconcilable tension, within Kleist's writing, between the demands of bioaesthetics and the demands of biopolitics. While Kleistian biopolitics, in order to achieve actual political force, must aim at the social reproduction of its new model of human life, Kleistian bioaesthetics, in order to reach its goal of vital intensification, must resist the temptation to produce a new *kind* of writing. From the point of view of Kleistian aesthetics, there must never be a series of young Kleistians.

4

LIFE AS WILL (NIETZSCHE)

For all its tendency to close the gap between nature and culture, the Idealist conception of "life" has always upheld a distinction between biological processes on the one hand and the domain of value and evaluation on the other. Where the connection between "value" and "life" was explicitly discussed, as in Kant and Hegel, it was in terms of human beings imposing value *on* life, as a means to an end that lay outside the biological and in the intellectual or moral realm. As Kant declares apodictically in the *Critique of the Power of Judgment*, it is reason alone that gives value to the existence of the world (KU §87). Nietzsche's writings mark a radical break with this thinking. With Nietzsche, life becomes not only the *highest* value, but is itself understood *in terms of valuation*. "Isn't living evaluating, preferring, being unfair, being limited, wanting to be different?" (KSA 5:22; JGB §9). "Valuations [*Werthschätzungen*] lie in all functions of the organic being." (KSA 11:26 [72]) "'Alive': that means already esteeming:—In all willing is esteeming—and will is there in the organic" (KSA 11:25 [433]).

The notion of "will" at work here clearly has little to do with reason and volition. If the traditional idea of the will as conscious volition served to shore up the distinction between human freedom and natural determination, intellect and body, Nietzsche drives the will and its evaluative processes into the depths of the body, thus redefining both. To will is to affirm—hence to value—one's existence, an affirmation that is already operative on the most basic level of organic life. Every living being, down to the smallest protoplasm, is driven by and endowed with the power to assert itself, to will its own being. On the most fundamental level, we can think of this assertion of power as the capacity to impose boundaries against an impinging environment. In distinguishing what is allowed access and what is not, the living entity engages in a basic act of regulation and evaluation, of "yes" and "no," affirmation or negation. In fact, Nietzsche even goes so far as to call this basic evaluative act an "interpretation": "The will to power interprets: the formation of an organ is a matter of interpretation; it defines limits, determines degrees, variations of power. Mere variations of power could not feel themselves to be such: there must be present something that wills to grow, that interprets the value of whatever else wants to grow. . . . (The organic process constantly presupposes interpretations)" (WP 643). Willing, interpreting, evaluating—as words traditionally used to define intellectual acts are applied to the physiological realm, the distinctions between moral-cognitive and organic processes break down. Accordingly, Nietzsche declares that "the self-spiritual [das Ich-Geistige] is already given with the cell," (KSA 11:26 [36]) and that "down to and into the cell there are, in this sense, no other movements than these 'moral' ones" (KSA 9:6 [297]).

Gregory Moore has argued that Nietzsche's will to power is essentially a Bildungstrieb and "virtually indistinguishable from the widespread crypto-idealism of contemporary German biology."[1] Moore shows that Nietzsche was familiar with a strand of mid-

1. Gregory Moore, Nietzsche, Biology and Metaphor (Cambridge: Cambridge University Press, 2006), 55; for a similar assessment, see Henry Staten, "A

nineteenth-century biological theories that recuperated the older idea of the *Bildungstrieb* to develop an account of organic development that stressed, against Darwin's emphasis on natural selection, the organism's *intrinsic* power to generate new forms. In positing that there is, at the heart of the living, an intrinsic tendency (*nisus*) toward an increase of power, Nietzsche, according to Moore, "reintroduces a teleological aspect to evolution," thus simply reiterating "the many errors and misunderstandings perpetrated by his contemporaries."[2] But Nietzsche's engagement with contemporary biology is more complicated. As we shall see, not only does he retain aspects of Darwin's theory of selection; his radicalization of the notion of the *Bildungstrieb* breaks with the latter's theoretical raison d'etre and its emphasis on the unity of (organic) form. To begin with, Nietzsche's will to power exists only in the plural, as a "multiplicity of forces" (KSA 10:24 [14]; WP 641) that operate throughout the body, within each of its elements. For Nietzsche, an organism is an assemblage of smaller organisms, which in turn are composed of yet smaller elements, each of which exerts its own power to exist.

> What every smallest part of a living organism wants is an increase of power [*ein plus von Macht*] (KSA 13:14 [174]; WP 702).
> If the quality of a cell is constituted chemically in such a way, assimilation exceeds decomposition, i.e., overcompensation of the consumed, growth occurs: then this important quality constitutes the *domination* over the other q[ualities].
> We know no organisms, no cell, which did not have this force in a stadium of its life: without it life could not *expand*. (KSA 10:7 [95])

Life, both within and between individual organisms, is thus conceived as a battlefield of countless wills and drives. One implication of this conception is the opening up of the mind to the body and the unconscious. As what I normally call "my will" is reconceived as "a kind of resultant of the struggle within me of various drives, impulses, and desires,"[3] each of which is itself a kind of "will," the mind loses its autonomy vis-à-vis the body. At the same time, the body itself is fundamentally reconceived. Where Blumenbach's *Bildungstrieb* emphasizes the dynamic *unity* of the organism, Nietzsche's pluralization of drives highlights the agonistic heterogeneity of the living. The result is an essentially *biopolitical*[4] conception of the organism.

> The absolute momentariness [*Augenblicklichkeit*] of the will to power dominates [*regirt*]; in the human being (and already in the cell) this ordering [*Feststellung*] is a process which given the growth of all participants constantly shifts—a conflict [*Kampf*], provided that one understands this word so broadly and deeply as to conceive even of the relation between dominator and dominated [*Herrschenden zum Beherrschten*] as a struggle [*ein Ringen*], and of the relation of the obedient to the dominator as a resisting [*Widerstreben*]. (KSA 11:40 [55])

Nietzsche is adamant that this struggle not be conceived in terms of self-preservation or its utilitarian moral version, the pursuit of happiness. "Human beings do no strive for happiness, only the English do" (KSA 6:61; GD §12). And more precisely, if less humorous: "Physiologists should think twice before putting down the self-preservation-drive as the cardinal drive of an organic being. A living thing [*etwas Lebendiges*] wills above all to *discharge* its strength—life itself is will to power—: self-preservation is only one of the indirect and most frequent *results*" (KSA 5:27; JGB I.13). Unlike the drive of self-preservation, which emphasizes the organism's identity over time, Nietzsche's talk of the "absolute momentariness of the will to power" highlights its instability, its organization through the interaction of competing forces into a short-lived, evanescent unity that "given the growth of all participants incessantly shifts." Recalling my discussion of Blumenbach's *Bildungstrieb* in

---

3. Raymond Geuss, "Nietzsche and Geneaology," in *Morality, Culture, and History: Essays on German Philosophy* (Cambridge: Cambridge University Press, 1999), 12.

4. Biopolitical in the sense that the political is understood as concerned not with the polis but with the administration of power.

the introduction, we might say that Nietzsche defines the living in terms of a constitutive *excess of force over form*, where what is established as form, self, or unity is immediately undone either by a countervalent force or by the internal drive to expand and alter the territory of the "self."

The first—external—dimension of the struggle of wills is clearly illustrated in Nietzsche's agonistic depiction of nutritional processes. For Nietzsche, eating is an example of life's innate drive to incorporate others and extend its power: "Let us take the simplest case, that of primitive nourishing: the protoplasm stretches its pseudopods out, in search of something that opposes it—not out of hunger, but will to power" (KSA 13:14[174]; WP702). And: "Appropriation and incorporation is above all a willing to overwhelm, a forming, shaping and reshaping until finally the overwhelmed has gone completely over into the power of the attacker and has increased it" (KSA 12:9[151]; WP656). But life's drive to grow by overcoming is also directed inward. More precisely: overwhelming others is only the outward manifestation of the organism's more fundamental drive of *self-overcoming*. To live is not simply to grow and become more, as the traditional notion of the formative drive would have it, but to become *other*. It is to constantly change form, break whatever mold or unity life has assumed at a particular moment. This attempt to conceive of form as pure actualization or becoming has two important implications, which will become clearer in the following chapters. First, it means that formation is now seen to imply *deformation*; there is no form without *Entformung* (Benn), no gestalt without *Entstaltung* (Benjamin), no growth without alteration and decay. Second, form and unity, rather than being cherished as the expression of a successful maturational process, come to be associated with the adoption of artificial masks. Whether this mask be understood negatively, in terms of a reifying or deadening role, or positively, as the playful and ironic performance of (non) identity, for modernists writing in Nietzsche's wake, the humanist conception of form as *Bildung* becomes aesthetically obsolete and politically suspect.

Cultural Values

Much of recent scholarship on Nietzsche has explored his engagement with the sciences of his time in order to develop a "naturalized" account of his philosophy. On these interpretations, Nietzsche drew on the writings of Darwin, Spencer, Roux, and others to dismantle metaphysical explanations and provide a naturalized account of morality, culture, reason, and value.[5] As we saw, there is much in Nietzsche's writings that supports such a view. Not only does Nietzsche describe the will in terms of a movement of a quantity of energy or force,[6] he says that "'spirit' itself is, after all, nothing but a kind of metabolism" (KSA 6:282) and peppers his writings with physiological metaphors. In short, Nietzsche's entire philosophy constitutes an attack on the mind-body dualism that rules much of the philosophical tradition. The question is, therefore, not whether Nietzsche draws on contemporary biology but how and why he appropriates it. Put differently, one says little in declaring that Nietzsche "naturalizes" morality or the mind unless one also shows how "the natural" itself is transformed in his work. Nietzsche's use of digestive metaphors gives us an inkling of what his new image of the natural amounts to. In describing nutritional processes as acts of appropriation, evaluation, and overwhelming, Nietzsche depicts the body—and by extension life itself—as a site of incessant *creation and evaluation*. Every act of living is creative in the sense that it transforms both the living entity and its environment, brings about something that has not been there before. At every moment, the living affirms its power to exist, recreates its own existence through an act of assertion that is simultaneously constructive and destructive. Thus when Nietzsche says we should understand intellect, consciousness, and morality "along the guiding thread of the body [*am Leitfaden des Leibes*],"[7] he does not

---

5. Besides the work by Moore, see especially Richardson, *Nietzsche's New Darwinism* (Oxford: Oxford University Press, 2004).

6. For instance: "A quantum of force is just such a quantum of drive, will, action, in fact it is nothing but this driving, willing and acting" (KSA 5:279; GM 26).

7. KSA 11:26 [374]; KSA 11:27 [27]; KSA 11:36 [35].

simply mean that all intellectual processes are ultimately physiological but that the body, *viewed from a particular perspective,* gives us the best model of the antagonisms and dynamic processes that also dominate "higher" forms of life. Nietzsche's physiological metaphors open up the body in order to make us see the "creative drive" (KSA 11:36[31]; WP 619) that already affirms itself at the most basic level of the living. What motivates Nietzsche's philosophy, down to its hyperbolic rhetoric, is an existential and aesthetic urge: to harness the creative vitality that is trapped in our bodies.

This urge derives its fundamental orientation not from Nietzsche's scientific readings but from his broader engagement with contemporary culture and society. Long before he read Darwin, Spencer, or Roux, Nietzsche seized on the notion of "life" to combat what he considered the greatest danger of his time: the threat of *creative extinction.* In his first major publication, *The Birth of Tragedy* (1872), Nietzsche returns to Greek tragedy to attack the rationalism of the Enlightenment, whose exclusive pursuit of theoretical knowledge, he claims, has cut us off from the energetic and irrational core of inner and outer reality, resulting in the flattening of psychic and cultural life. To make "life possible and worth living" (KSA 1:27–28; GT §1), nothing short of a large-scale renewal of tragic culture is needed: "for only as an *aesthetic phenomenon* is existence and the world eternally justified" (KSA 1:47; GT §5). This critical vitalism becomes even more pronounced in Nietzsche's subsequent work. Whether he examines the "Use and Abuse of History for Life" (1874) or traces the effect of Christian morality and modern science[8] on nineteenth-century Europe, the elevation of life as the standard and measure of everything underpins a critique of cultural practices that are seen to stifle intellectual and somatic creativity. This concern with creative extinction culminates in Nietzsche's depiction of the "last man," who is characterized, tellingly, not by a lack of energy but by workaholism[9] and the restless pursuit

---

8. See Nietzsche's claim that modern science is an instance of the "ascetic ideal": KSA 5:395–411; GM III:23–27 and KSA 3:574–75; FW §344.

9. KSA 5:382; GM III:18.

of happiness.[10] What threatens vitality more than anything else, for Nietzsche, is *compliance* with the environment, a view that clearly flies in the face of nineteenth-century evolutionary biology. Nietzsche's use of contemporary theories of "life" is itself an instance of the will-to-power—that is, it is an act of creative and violent appropriation.

But elevating "life" to the highest value poses a theoretical problem. If all activities are expressions of the will-to-power by which life affirms itself, how is it even possible for life to become depleted and lose vitality, as Nietzsche claims has happened in contemporary Europe? How can life turn against itself, develop forms that diminish its creative energies?[11] For Nietzsche to answer these questions, he must complicate his account of the nexus between life and valuation and introduce, if silently and without ever explicitly acknowledging it, a *distinction* between natural and cultural values.[12] *Natural values* are built into the organic by a process of natural selection. They are embodied in the organism's makeup, which enables it to carry out its specific functions, and in this sense, affirm its own wills or drives. *Cultural values* are closer to our ordinary notion of "value," though not identical with it. They are expressed in our beliefs and aspirations, but also, more deeply and unconsciously, in our habits, diets, desires, dispositions, and ways of feeling, perceiving, and acting. The difference between these two kinds of value is thus not framed in terms of an opposition between body and mind. *Cultural values*, too, are deeply embedded in our bodies; they have become, through a process that Nietzsche calls "breeding [*züchten*]," *second* nature. The crucial difference is that cultural values carry *symbolic* meanings and are the product of *social* mechanisms of selection; that is, they are selected by groups of people both in order to affirm themselves against a hostile environment and to make sense of their experience. Like natural values, all cultural val-

---

10.   KSA 5:163–64; JGB §228.

11.   To this we might add another question: "If no act of will can be seen as a diminution of life, what does it mean to condemn any given volition—any positing of value—by any subject whatsoever?" James I. Porter, "Nietzsche's Highest Value (Affirmation of Life) and Its Limits," *Nietzsche-Studien* 44, no. 1 (2015): 67.

12.   Here I draw on Richardson, *Nietzsche's New Darwinism*, 67–94.

ues are therefore expressions of a will-to-power, forms in which life's drive to dominate and grow affirms itself. And yet, natural and cultural values can come into conflict with one another. In fact, to give an account of how such conflicts come about is precisely the task of Nietzsche's genealogical method. Genealogy, for Nietzsche, is the reconstruction of the mechanisms by which the will-to-power that is embedded in a specific set of cultural values has given rise to a form of life that stifles our, and primarily Nietzsche's own, creative vitality. Hence the unabashed perspectivism of Nietzsche's writing, in which he pits his own idiosyncratic existence—his thoughts, illnesses, tastes, and sensibilities—against the entire history of Western truth and morality.

And there is another layer to the distinction between natural and cultural values. Even the most sophisticated naturalizing readings, such as that of John Richardson, on whose distinction between natural and cultural value I partly draw, fail to pay sufficient attention to an important *non*naturalizing strand within Nietzsche's thought. Nietzsche leaves no doubt that human life is susceptible to a unique kind of vulnerability: the *threat of pointlessness*. In *The Birth of Tragedy*, Nietzsche argues that Greek tragedy emerges in response to a fundamental pessimistic crisis, which he sees encapsulated in the answer given by Silenus, the companion of Dionysus, when asked what the best thing for human beings is: "The best thing of all is entirely unreachable for you: not to have been born, not to *be*, to be *nothing*. But the next best thing for you is—soon to die" (KSA 1:35; GT §3). In view of this metaphysical truth, as David Wellbery comments, "human existence can find itself bereft of the will to go on. Nietzsche speaks in this connection of the value of existence coming under threat of denial. A structural feature of human life (of the ontology of human existence) is that it can turn against itself in this way."[13] This possibility of pointlessness also informs Nietzsche's interpretation of Christian morality. Like Greek tragedy, though more problematically, Christian morality provides

---

13.   David Wellbery, "Nietzsche on Tragedy," in *Oxford Encyclopedia of Aesthetics*, 2nd ed., ed. Michael Kelly (Oxford: Oxford University Press), accessed April 10, 2019, www.oxfordreference.com.

a solution to the danger of a paralyzing pessimism that slaves under Roman rule must have felt: "What actually arouses indignation over suffering is not the suffering itself, but the senselessness of suffering: but neither for the Christian, who saw in suffering a whole, hidden machinery of salvation, nor for naïve man in ancient times, who saw all suffering in relation to spectators or to instigators of suffering, was there any such *senseless* suffering" (KSA 5:304; GM II:7). Hence Nietzsche's defense, in his 1886 preface to *The Birth of Tragedy*, of Greek pessimism against Enlightenment optimism (KSA 1:12; BT 4). Pessimism and nihilism are not aberrations of the mind; they are built into the very structure of human existence: "*That* the ascetic ideal has meant so much to man reveals a basic fact of human will, its *horror vacui: it needs an aim—*, and it prefers to will *nothingness* rather than *not* will" (KSA 5:339; GM III:1).

Let us combine this strand of Nietzsche's thought with his insistence on the multiplicity of wills. All complex organisms contain countless competing forces and wills. For the organism to become *one*, it must therefore recruit the multiplicity of forces and vitalities within it to its own perspective, impose its governing will onto them. In the case of natural organisms, this higher-level governing will is the product of a complex history of natural selection, and is built into the body and its drives. Thus, simply by virtue of existing, the organism affirms its will and pursues its distinctive aims.[14] The problem with *human* existence is that it lacks an intrinsic governing aim. More precisely, while human life also "needs an aim," the object of this aim—*what* the will wills—is organically underdetermined. This has two implications. On the one hand, it means that human beings must actively determine the direction and intentionality of mere life. The form and directedness of human life necessarily assumes an *aesthetic* dimension. On the other hand, it means that the will is highly susceptible to outside forces, and in particular to the forms of life that individuals inhabit. In fact, Nietzsche believes that the weaker the individual and his will, the stronger his tendency to adopt the aims and values—the will—of society. This

---

14. This is why Nietzsche says that the body, not consciousness, is the most admirable historical invention.

is problematic not only because genealogy shows that cultural values and the collective forms of life in which they are embedded are the products of mechanisms of social selection that benefit groups rather than individuals; these forms of life, precisely because they were selected to fit the needs of the weak, also tend to *overprotect* human life against its inescapable vulnerability, surrounding it with security mechanisms that sap its vitality and make it "sick."

Genealogy, Morality, and Nihilism

Let me briefly flesh out these comments, using as my example Nietzsche's genealogy of Christian morality. As I suggested, the task of Nietzsche's genealogical method is to show how life turns against itself, and more precisely, how the will-to-power embodied in cultural values and collective forms of life comes into conflict with the will-to-power embedded in our bodies. Phrasing the task of genealogy this way makes it immediately clear that the simplistic reading of Nietzsche's genealogy as a straightforward story of decline from master to slave morality won't do. Not only do human beings become more interesting in the course of this history; slave morality is itself, to some extent, an expression of life's creativity. The first creative act of Christianity occurs with Jesus himself, who breaks away from the customs and belief systems of his time and instantiates a new form of life, which consists of the unconditional forgiveness of enemies, abstention from use of force, and the moral condemnation of others, etc.[15] The second creative act occurs with Jesus's apostles, and in particular with Paul, who imposes his own will on Jesus's form of life, submitting it to a violent interpretation that "annuls original Christianity" (KSA 13:11 [282]) and lays the foundation for the institutionalization of Christian faith. Moreover, since "Paul's successful attempt to take over the Christian form of life by reinterpreting it is only the first of a series of such episodes,"[16]

---

15. See Geuss, "Nietzsche and Genealogy," 9. The relevant passages in Nietzsche are A §§33, 35, 39, and KSA 13:11 [239], [243], [257], [280], [294], [378].

16. Geuss, "Nietzsche and Genealogy," 11.

the entire history of Christianity is shaped by creative acts of interpretation and appropriation. In fact, even early Christian asceticism
is a creative response to a real problem in that it "had the positive
value of seducing inherently weak and despairing creatures who
would otherwise have been tempted to do away with themselves
into continuing to live, by giving their suffering . . . an imaginary
meaning."[17] The problem with Christianity is that it uses this creativity to invent practices, values, and institutions that attack the
source of human creativity—the vitality of the body. In Nietzsche's
view, whereas Jesus himself embodied love and had no conception
of sin, guilt, punishment, or even a transcendent "beyond" (KSA
6:205–6; A §33), Paul transforms Jesus's exemplary life into a moral
catalogue and guilt-ridden asceticism that rids human life of its
buoyancy.

The first problem with Pauline Christianity, according to Nietzsche, is its universalism. Even though it emerges in response to the
needs and experiences of a specific social group (slaves in Roman
society), Christian morality claims to be unconditionally true and
apply to all human beings, regardless of rank, history, or individual
makeup. From a Nietzschean point of view, universalist forms of
valuation are wrong, in fact "immoral" (KSA 5:156; JGB §221),
because they negate life's "necessary perspectivism, by virtue of
which every force-center—and not only the human—construes from
itself outwards all the rest of the world, i.e., measures, touches,
shapes according to its force" (KSA 13:14 [186]; WP 636 [1888]).
In shaping their lives according to universal values, individuals actively undermine the perspectival forces of their body, suppressing
the multiple vitalities within them. Second, this tendency is exacer-
bated by the fact that Christian values benefit the masses, which are
weak and feeble. Christian morality not only arose out of the needs
of the "herd"; it also succeeded historically (was "selected") because
it satisfied ("fit") the modest forces, talents, and aspirations of the
masses. But what is good for the masses is not good for the higher
and stronger individual. Finally, driven by the resentment of the
weak against the strong, Christianity frames the source of all

---

17. Ibid., 18.

strength—the vitality of the body—as evil. Christian ideas of "sin," "salvation," "eternal life," "pity," "chastity," etc., and the ascetic practices in which they are embodied, valorize the suppression of bodily drives as the highest value. Born from suffering, Christian asceticism turns suffering into a form of life.

This last comment requires elaboration. As is often the case with Nietzsche, his polemicism obscures some of his more fundamental insights. When Nietzsche writes in the third essay of the *Genealogy of Morals* that "read from a distant planet, the majuscule script of our earthly existence would perhaps seduce the reader to the conclusion that the earth was the ascetic planet *par excellence*" (KSA 5:362; GM III:11), he articulates, beneath the explicit critique of *Christian* asceticism, an important insight into the role of ascetic practices in human life. With a view to the late Foucault, we might say that Nietzsche identifies under the rubric of ascetic practice a mode of power that derives from the fact that human beings can, and indeed must, relate to themselves the power of working on themselves. As Peter Sloterdijk has suggested,[18] Nietzsche's truly important break from the Idealist tradition is that he conceives of self-relation not primarily in cognitive terms, as self-reflexivity, but as a practice that involves things such as diet, physical activity, the choice of climate and air, and physical habits. With this expansion of self-relation into the bodily realm, Nietzsche undermines the intellectualist definition of the human being and reframes the relation between humans and animals. "Read from a distant planet," the decisive difference is not that humans think whereas animals do not but that humans, in relating to themselves, work on and transform their *vital* form. The human being is the animal that incessantly shapes itself. "The ascetic ideal is a device for the preservation of life [*ein Kunstgriff in der Erhaltung des Lebens*]" (KSA 5:366)—a *Kunstgriff*, or cultural technology, that is made necessary by the particular vulnerability and malleability of human life: "For man is more ill, uncertain, changeable [*wechselnder*] and unstable [*unfestgestellter*] than any other animal, without a doubt" (KSA 5:367;

---

18. Peter Sloterdijk, *Du mußt dein Leben ändern* (Frankfurt am Main: Suhrkamp, 2011), 52–69.

GM III:13). Once again, we do well to read Nietzsche's talk of illness and sickness against his own more polemical uses. The "illness"
Nietzsche identifies here is more fundamental than European decadence; it is nothing other than the *existential* vulnerability of
human life, its lack of an intrinsic governing aim, which, as one of
its possibilities, carries within it the danger of the will turning against
itself and denying existence.

One implication of Nietzsche's emphasis on the instability of
human life is that it undercuts any straightforward biological reading of his work. If the human being is the animal that incessantly
shapes itself, there is no essence or biological destiny that human
life, qua human, must realize. This opens up a genuinely ethical dimension of Nietzsche's work, one that links him closely to thinkers
like Cavell and the late Foucault. But the focus on human malleability also points toward a deeper vision of the processes of socialization. For Nietzsche, cultural values are not simply intellectual
commitments; they are bodily investments, "bred" into the human
being, inculcated in the particularities of the body itself. Nietzsche's
most vivid description of these mechanisms occurs in the second essay of his *Genealogy of Morals*, whose programmatic opening lines
announce the fundamental orientation of his argument: "To breed
an animal with the prerogative to *promise*—is that not precisely the
paradoxical task which nature has set herself with regard to humankind? Is it not the real problem *of* humankind?" (KSA 5:291; GM
II:1). Despite the essay's emphasis on punishment and torture, it is
important to see that "breeding" is not simply a matter of deter-
rence and prohibition. "Breeding" is what *makes* us human beings.
It is because of "the labor performed by man upon himself during
the greater part of the existence of the human race" (KSA 5:293;
GM II:2) that man has become an "interesting animal" and developed some "depth" (KSA 5:266; GM I:6). Nietzsche's genealogy depicts intellectual capacities as the historical product of cultural
technologies and practices, rather than the other way around. In
fact, on Nietzsche's account, even the most cherished of these
capacities—self-determination—is *bred* into the human. Hence the
pivotal role of promising, which requires a form of self-relation—a
relation to one's own drives and commitments—that undercuts the

division between body and mind. On the one hand, the capacity for promising is the result of basic cultural technologies that work on and against the body. Since to promise is to remember one's promise, and since remembering runs counter to our natural tendency to forget, promise-making rests on cultivating remembering as a force that overcomes the instinct of forgetting. This is achieved, according to Nietzsche, through mechanisms of punishment that link forgetting to pain, thus searing the value of remembering into the nervous system (KSA 5:292–302; GM II:1–6). On the other hand, making promises is crucial to becoming a "sovereign individual" (KSA 5:293; GM II:2). In learning to promise, human beings acquire "self-mastery" (KSA 5:294; GM II:2), the foundation of autonomy. "What is freedom? That one has the will to assume responsibility for oneself" (KSA 6:139). Whether or not the "freedom" and "sovereignty" at stake here are problematic or a signature feature of the *overman* Nietzsche heralds in his *Thus Spoke Zarathustra*,[19] it is clear that Nietzsche leaves no space for a transcendent and noumenal realm. Everything that makes us human beings, down to our capacity for self-determination, has been shaped by the "labor performed by man upon himself." Human life is the product of *second* nature.

Nietzsche's account of promising gives us a measure of the depth of this second nature. For Nietzsche, our desires, drives, aspirations, tastes, and modes of feeling and acting are all "bred" into us through mechanisms that originate in, and primarily serve the needs of, society at large. This is not a straightforward or mechanical process, in part because the body on which breeding works is not a blank slate but contains its own countervailing drives and forces, and in part because "society" itself is made up of a multiplicity of forces

---

19. While most scholars assume that the "soevereignty" Nietzsche mentions in GM II:2 is an ideal for which we should strive, Lawrence J. Hatab and, above all, Christa Davis Acampara argue that the "sovereign individual" is a problematic category for Nietzsche and is linked to the type of subjectivity created in the context of slave morality. See Lawrence J. Hatab, *A Nietzschean Defense of Democracy: An Experiment in Postmodern Politics* (Chicago, IL: Open Court, 1999), 37–38; and Christa Davis Acampara, "On Sovereignty and Overhumanity," *International Studies in Philosophy* 36, no. 3 (2004): 127–45.

aimed at competing goals and values, an agonistic constitution that reverberates within the individual subjectivities of that society. Moreover, despite Nietzsche's penchant for metaphors of struggle, the mechanisms of breeding are not exclusively agonistic. For society to instill its values in individuals, it must *recruit* their innate drives and forces to its own perspective, bend their powers to its own purposes. This is possible because cultural values appeal to the most fundamental vulnerability of human existence: its lack of an innate governing will. Collective values free human beings from the burden of actively determining the direction of their will. "All moralities seek to implant habits, that is: to suspend the question of 'why' for many actions so that they are done instinctively" (KSA 9:4 [67]). But to "suspend the question of 'why'" by dissolving it through habitual practice carries a high price. In protecting themselves against the anxiety and burden of having to give form to their will, individuals diminish their intrinsic powers and deplete their lives. The above quote continues: "In the long run, this brings with it a strong *curtailment of reason* [*Beeinträchtigung der Vernunft*]. Moreover, 'acting from habit' is acting from comfort, in view of the next impulse, also a fear of the unusual, of what others do, a *curtailment of the individual*. To breed a race with strong instincts— that is what morality wants" (KSA 9:4 [67]). Morality gives meaning to life—but it does so at the price of diminishing life's powers and creative vitality.

This is true for all moral systems. All moralities—in fact, all collective forms of life—generate dense webs of practices, scripts, codes, customs, laws, and habits that entangle human life and regulate its vitality. But Nietzsche believes this regulation has become particularly fine-grained in nineteenth-century European society, whose unholy mix of capitalist ethos, scientific rationality, historicism, Christian ascetic morality, and egalitarianism—not to mention the rise of new mass media and the expansion of the state's legal, welfare, and educational apparatus—has enabled it to infiltrate the daily life of human beings to an historically unprecedented degree. The work of a number of twentieth-century historians, many of whom were inspired by Nietzsche, could be adduced here to flesh out this thesis: Max Weber's analysis of the influence of Christian asceticism on the capitalist work ethic; Foucault's study of disciplinary apparatuses; Daston and Gallison's discussion of the moral economy underpinning nineteenth-century scientific ideals of objectivity and factual truth; and the writings of literary historians concerned with modern literature's increasing interest in the quotidian, in the everyday life of average actors.[20] All of these writers follow Nietzsche in emphasizing the embodied nature of cultural values and tracking processes of socialization in the work that subjects do on *themselves*. For the technologies of "breeding" to fully penetrate the human being, they must enlist the individual's capacity to work on himself. If *The Genealogy of Morals* concludes with an essay on asceticism, this is because ascetic practices constitute the royal road through which Christian morality has used the creativity of human life to attack its source—the vivacity of the body.

Nietzsche believes that this process has reached a moment of crisis that is also a potential turning point. Christian asceticism and its suppression of bodily drives has not only depleted human vitality;[21] it has also undermined the very values on which it rests. As Nietzsche puts it, transforming a recent neologism into a world-historical category,[22] contemporary Europe has entered a phase of thoroughgoing *nihilism*. Nihilism constitutes a threat to what Nietzsche considers the most basic feature of life: its ability to value anything at all. As we saw, the possibility of this threat is embedded in the very structure of human existence; that is, the absence of an intrinsic governing aim, which becomes particularly problematic under conditions of extreme suffering such as slavery. Christian morality emerged in response to just such a circumstance in the midst of Roman imperialism, giving meaning and direction to people on the brink of despair. Christianity "prevented man from despising

---

20. Weber, *Protestant Ethic and the Spirit of Capitalism*; Foucault's work between *Birth of the Clinic* and *History of Sexuality*; Lorraine Daston and Peter Galison, *Objectivity* (New York: Zone, 2010), esp. 27–42 and 191–252; Lorraine Daston, "The Moral Economy of Science," *Osiris* 10 (1995): 2–24; Moretti, *The Way of the World*; Fleming *Exemplarity and Mediocrity*.

21. The contemporary fixation on happiness and self-preservation are, for Nietzsche, symptoms of this depletion.

22. Malcolm Bull, *Anti-Nietzsche* (London: Verso, 2011), 55.

himself as man, from taking sides against life; from despairing of knowledge; it was a means of preservation. In sum: morality was the great antidote [*Gegenmittel*] against practical and theoretical nihilism" (KSA 12:5 [71]; WP 10). But this antidote proved to be a poison. On the one hand, by positing a true world in opposition to the one we inhabit, Christian ascetic practices hollowed out the values and forces intrinsic to somatic life. On the other hand, in cultivating truthfulness and introspection, Christian asceticism ended up legitimating the critique of its own, otherworldly values: "But among the forces cultivated by morality was truthfulness: this eventually turned against morality, discovered its teleology, its partial perspective" (KSA 12:5 [71]; WP 10). According to Nietzsche, Christian truthfulness culminates in modern science (KSA 3:574–77; FW §344), whose will-to-truth—the belief that truth is more important than anything else—ends up exposing the *untruth* of Christian beliefs in a transcendent world, thus destroying the ideological foundation of ascetic practices. Nihilism is thus the end of a genealogical arc that began with the slave revolt in morality. Born as an antidote to the threat of pointlessness, Christian asceticism culminates in an all-consuming pessimism: "What does nihilism mean? That the *highest values devaluate themselves*. The aim is lacking: 'Why?' finds no answer" (KSA 12:5 [71]; WP 9).

Revaluing Life

As Malcom Bull emphasized,[23] unlike virtually all other contemporary authors who use this term, Nietzsche embraces "nihilism" as both necessary and salutary. The progressive undermining of all values opens up the space for the new and epochal realization that there is only one irreducible value—*the act of valuation itself*. Since values are "merely a symptom of strength on the part of the value-positers" (KSA 12:9 [35]), the decay of substantive values, if properly understood, reveals the irreducible kernel within all values, *the capacity to posit value*, which Nietzsche, as we have seen,

---

23. Ibid., esp. 44–46, 55–78.

equates with life itself: "When we speak of values we do so under the inspiration and from the perspective of life [*unter der Optik des Lebens*]: life itself evaluates through us *when* we establish values" (KSA 6:86; GD 5.5). Nihilism must therefore be completed, not avoided. Instead of mourning the loss of transcendent values, Nietzsche seeks to accelerate the history of nihilism. The task is to destroy the last remnants of our attachment to slave morality and to reevaluate all values "from the perspective of life"—from the perspective, that is, of life's immanent power to grow and assert its own value.

The first step in this project is the genealogical method itself, which analyzes the historical process that has led us to conceive of ourselves and the world the way we do. The goal of this analysis is not, as in Hegel, to justify our life by revealing its implicit rationality but to problematize the web of reasons, norms, beliefs, assumptions, and commitments that shape our everyday life and give it, and us, the appearance of coherence and stability. Problematization is not critique in the traditional Enlightenment sense of the term. It does not aim to show that our norms are contradictory or insufficiently rational; it attacks them because they are *dangerous* to our lives, stifle our vitality. Moreover, since these norms are not simply intellectual commitments but are embedded in our tastes, habits, routine assumptions, and unconscious bodily investments, the real destructiveness of traditional life and morality is that it has made us unaware of the forces that have shaped us and that we *exert on ourselves*. Genealogy counters this process by tracing our beliefs and commitments back to the violence that gave rise to them. In depicting our identities as the product of a highly contested historical process, genealogy shows that the apparent coherence and stability of our lives masks a struggle of competing wills-to-power, a struggle that is still being waged within and around us. From the standpoint of Nietzschean genealogy, norms and reasons are the symbolic death masks of *vital acts of valuation*.

Moreover, genealogy not only frames history in terms of the will to power; it is itself an expression of this will. The goal of a genealogical description is to unmask history as a series of violent encodings. Since these encodings have also shaped language, a full genealogical critique must go beyond the level of content and extend into the form of genealogical representation. Hence the crucial importance of style and voice in Nietzsche. If Nietzsche's writing is always unmistakably *his*, this is because it is propelled by the agonistic drive to overpower the social forces sedimented in the received idioms and protocols of language. Hyperbole and poetic excess are not accidental to Nietzsche's philosophy but intrinsic to the task of retrieving value and vitality from the scaffolding of language and culture. In short, Nietzsche's tendency to push the limits of linguistic expression is an assertion of *his* will-to-power. It announces, with each turn of phrase, that the authority of his writing rests not on shared norms or impersonal standards but on its *own* expressive force. Wittgenstein, fighting the philosophical belief in the logical underpinnings of language, suggested that the meaning of our words depends on nothing more than the regularities of our speaking, acting, and perceiving—that is, on our shared form of life. Nietzsche's writing attacks both logic and ordinary practice. Instead of endorsing what *we* do and say, his hyperbolic rhetoric pushes language to its outer boundary, pitting the singularity of his speech against the received forms and values of linguistic expression.

While Nietzsche's linguistic will-to-power is perhaps most visible in his hyperbolic rhetoric, it also shapes his, often risky, metaphors. Metaphors compress incongruent regions of language and expression. In connecting semantic fields that are ordinarily kept apart, metaphors reorganize, and potentially expand or disturb, the regimented territories of knowledge and culture. This is clearly the function of some of Nietzsche's most vivid and characteristic metaphors, which undermine one of the fundamental underpinnings of European culture: the distinction between body and mind, between biological process and moral value. I will confine myself to two examples. The first concerns Nietzsche's use of the term "breeding" (*züchten, Zucht*),[24] which seems to corroborate the biological reading of his philosophy eventually appropriated by National Social-

---

24. For a detailed analysis of Nietzsche's use of these terms, see Gerd Schank, *"Rasse" und "Züchtung" bei Nietzsche* (Berlin: Walter de Gruyter, 2000), who

ism. In fact, the second half of the nineteenth century witnesses a significant shift in the semantics of *Züchtung*.[25] If *Züchtung* up to this point carried an educational and ethical meaning (*Züchtung* as *Zucht* and discipline) when associated with humans, and a biological meaning when applied to plants and animals (similar to the current usage of "breeding"), the two meanings began to converge under the influence of Darwinism and the writings of Francis Galton, giving rise to the new biopolitical conception of "breeding" as the strategic intervention into the gene pool of human populations. In the works of racial hygienists such as Alfred Ploetz, *Züchtung* comes to designate medical measures aimed at improving the genetic quality of the *Volk*, such as the eradication (*Ausmerzen*) of weak or deformed infants.[26] However, Nietzsche's use of "breeding" follows a different path. Whereas the eugenicists abandon the older ethic-educational sense and define *Züchtung* in strictly biological terms (as intervention into organic matter), Nietzsche combines the two semantic strands in such a way as to reframe our understanding of morality. From the perspective of Nietzsche's genealogy, biological engineering and ethical education are two sides of a single process. Morality itself is in part determined through corporeal intervention; moreover, this process is constitutive of human life, and thus more fundamental than the political incursions into organic life identified by theorists of the biopolitical.

Nietzsche's tendency to blur the distinction between bodily and cognitive and evaluative processes is perhaps most obvious in his persistent employment of the trope of digestion, as Silke-Maria Weineck in particular has shown.[27] "Digestion is more venerable" than Kant's starry skies (KSA 13:7 [62]) Nietzsche writes provocatively,

---

argues, perhaps a bit too strongly, that Nietzsche always keeps a critical distance to the language of evolutionary biology and eugenicism.

25.   On the complex history of ideas of breeding and the history of the term *Züchtung*, see Gehring, *Was ist Biomacht*, 154–83, esp. 160–69.

26.   Alfred J. Ploetz, *Die Tüchtigkeit unserer Rasse und der Schutz der Schwachen* (Berlin: S. Fischer, 1895), 144–45. Ploetz quotes Nietzsche for the motto for his book, and also quotes him approvingly in the introduction of his work.

27.   Silke-Maria Weineck, "Digesting the Nineteenth Century: Nietzsche and the Stomach," *Romanticism* 12, no. 1 (2006): 35–43.

echoing his claim that the unity of the body is a more amazing evolutionary achievement than the emergence of human consciousness. As we have already seen, the goal of such metaphors is not to
reduce intellectual to somatic processes but to transform our received understanding of body and mind and their relationship. In
fact, in Nietzsche's varied uses of the term, "digestion" becomes a
cipher for a vast field of activities and processes involving chewing,
defecating, vomiting, spitting, constipation, assimilation, retention,
destruction, chemical transformation, health, sickness, and taste, as
well as countless body parts with "all the considerable tropic po-
tentials these body parts offer."[28] And as these bodily processes
come into view, our understanding of cognition and culture is transformed. Creative individuals and cultures, Nietzsche makes clear,
need to pay attention to what and how much they are taking into
their body; they need to learn when to throw up or otherwise ex-
crete cognitive "stuff" that weighs them down or makes them tired
and unproductive. Earlier we observed that Nietzsche described nutritive capacities not in terms of survival and sustenance but as an
expression of the organism's basic directedness, its will-to-power.
In extending digestion into the realm of mental and cultural life,
Nietzsche accords to the latter analogous operations of appropriation, assimilation, differentiation, and evaluation. From this perspective, the problem with modern man is precisely the lack of dietary
discrimination and the tendency to ingest too much: "The nutrition
of modern man—he knows how to digest much, yes, almost everything—that is his sort of ambition: he would be of a higher order,
however, if he were not capable of exactly that; homo pamphagus
is not the most refined species" (KSA 3:152; MR §171). Nietzsche's
"finer species"—his overman—is clearly very different from the
blond beast, who is unlikely to be a discriminating eater. Being
healthy, for Nietzsche, means being able to discriminate appropriately, that is, in view of *one's own* taste and constitution, abilities
and history—and this is equally true with respect to culinary and
intellectual diets. The point of Nietzsche's digestive metaphors is not
to assimilate thinking to physiological processes but to make us

28. Ibid., 37.

aware of the common current of vitality that runs through both, and to the will-to-power that already asserts itself deep in our bowels.

The goal of Nietzsche's revaluation of values is not the articulation of new norms but the total unleashing of our corporeal and intellectual vitality. For thinking to recover its intensity, the mind must open itself to the creative resources of the body. Thinking must become sensorial—become *aesthesis*—to an extent no philosopher before Nietzsche had dared to formulate. In *Beyond Good and Evil* Nietzsche complains that the Germans are unable to listen *with a third ear* (KSA 5:189; JGB §246), a notion that would have a significant career in psychoanalysis.[29] While Nietzsche's explicit concern in this passage is the ability to hear the rhythmic and acoustic dimension of language, the phrase may perhaps articulate the fundamental aesthetic, ethical, and existential demand of Nietzsche's thinking. To listen with the third ear, I suggest, is to become receptive of the totality of life, to hear the demands of vitality in every cell, and, more specifically, to summon and recruit into one's own will the countless wills that vibrate within us.

---

29. While Freud never uses the phrase, the idea of an unconscious mode of listening is crucial to his conceptualization of the analyst's attitude toward the analysand's speech. Freud recommends that the analyst, when listening to the analysand, restrain from conscious "reflection" in favor of a "state of evenly suspended attention" ("Recommendations to Physicians Practicing Psycho-analysis" (1912), in *The Standard Edition of the Complete Works by Sigmund Freud*, trans. and ed. James Strachey (London: Hograth Press, 1953) [SE], 12:111) that allows the analyst to "catch the drift of the patient's unconscious with his own unconscious" ("Two Encyclopedia Articles" (1923), in SE, 18:239). This heightened and unconscious receptivity of the analyst has been discussed by every generation of analysts since Freud. Theodor Reik, one of Freud's first students in Vienna, used Nietzsche's metaphor of the "third ear" as the title of his book about the work of psychoanalytic listening and thinking: *Listening with the Third Ear: The Inner Experience of a Psychoanalyst* (Garden City, NY: Garden City Books, 1948). Wilfred Bion, Melanie Klein's most famous student, uses the term "reverie" to describe the analyst's unconscious attitude (Bion, *Learning from Experience* [Northvale, NJ: Jason Aronson INC, 1962]); and Christopher Bollas, one of the most influential contemporary psychoanalysts, writes that the "third ear," which he also calls the analyst's "inner, intuitional ear," "listens to the latent comments concealed in the manifest text": *Cracking Up: The Work of Unconscious Experience* (London: Routledge, 1995), 171.

After Nietzsche

No philosopher before or after had as pervasive an influence on his time as Nietzsche.[30] It is the untimeliness of Nietzsche's thought—his relentless critique of modern culture at the very moment this culture seemed to reach its zenith—that accounts for its explosive impact. Wilhelminian Germany offered the perfect setting for this eruption. Predominantly rural at the beginning of the century, Germany's massive social and economic transformations during the second half of the nineteenth century, and especially after its unification in 1871, had infused the country with a feverish sense of importance and historical mission. Nietzsche's writings articulate the split-off sense of depletion, depression, and disorientation that lurked beneath Germany's—and by extension, Europe's—manic belief in progress. Nietzsche shows that the frantic pace of socioeconomic change masks a fundamental exhaustion of ideological form that neither older idealist nor newer materialist models are able to enliven. Hence the complexity of Nietzsche's engagement with the discourse of "life": on the one hand, his relentless attack on both humanist models of organic growth and contemporary theories of evolution; on the other, an increasing focus on the question of the form of human life to come. What shape must human life and thought assume?

It is this question of the "new man," crystallized in Nietzsche's metaphor of contemporary man as a "bridge" to the *Übermensch*, that informs countless aesthetic, cultural, social, and political projects after 1900. It influences artistic movements such as symbolism, expressionism, and futurism; drives the *Lebensreformbewegung* and its obsession with health, bodily purification, and the return to nature (vegetarianism, nudism, homeopathy, etc.); inspires youth movements such as the *Wandervögel*; and underlies the development of a broad range of biomedical and biopolitical measures aimed at reshaping the social body. What connects all these move-

---

30. For Nietzsche's impact on German culture, see, in particular, Steven E. Aschheim, *The Nietzsche Legacy in Germany 1890–1990* (Berkeley: University of California Press, 1992).

ments and distinguishes them from older Christian projects of spiritual rebirth is their resolutely nonintellectualist conception of human self-formation that Nietzsche's writing opened up. With Nietzsche, as we saw, the human being becomes the animal that shapes itself down to the elements of its biological processes. Human life becomes a matter of style, not because everything is art but because life's form, whether cultural or biological, is fundamentally underdetermined and thus the product of cultural practices and technologies. The impact of Nietzsche's emphasis on the artificiality of the human life-form can be seen most vividly and synoptically in two strands of writings after 1900: one explicitly political and focusing on the power of the will to shape the social body; the other aesthetic, embracing the "disgregation of the will" (KSA 6:27) and the fragmentation of the human life-form. The goal is to grasp these seemingly opposed developments as related expressions of a new moment in the discourse of life.

The aesthetic path can be approached most clearly through a passage in Nietzsche's *The Case of Wagner*:

> For the moment I am only going to look at the question of style. - What is the hallmark of all *literary* decadence? The fact that life does not reside in the totality any longer. The word becomes sovereign and jumps out of the sentence, the sentence reaches out and blots out the meaning of the page, the page comes to life at the expense of the whole - the whole is not whole any more. But this is the image of every decadent style: there is always an anarchy of the atom, disgregation of the will, "freedom of the individual," morally speaking—or, expanded into a political theory, "equal rights for all." Life, equal vitality, the vibration and exuberance of life pushed back into the smallest structures, all the rest impoverished of life. Paralysis everywhere, exhaustion, numbness or hostility and chaos: both becoming increasingly obvious the higher you climb in the forms of organization. The whole does not live at all any more: it is cobbled together, calculated, synthetic, an artifact. (KSA 6:27; CW 245, translation modified)

"Life does not reside in the totality any longer [*nicht mehr im Ganzen wohnt*]." What Nietzsche calls decadence, Gottfried Benn, as we will see in the next chapter, will reframe as *Entformung* (disformation)—the dissolution of wholes into their disordered elements (the very undoing of Kantian synthesis). For Nietzsche, as for Benn, this is at once a stylistic and an ontological event. The fragmentation of formal unity corresponds to, and in fact is caused by, the "disgregation" of the will, a term Nietzsche imports from nineteenth-century thermodynamics which expresses the degree to which the molecules of a body are separated from each other. Applied to Nietzsche's dynamics of the will-to-power, decadence is thus understood as the "symptom of a loss of the organising force" of the will,[31] which is no longer able to subdue the countless microforces of body and mind and bend them to its own aims and interests. As the will's synthesizing force diminishes, "life" migrates from the larger organized whole to its constitutive parts: the word jumps out of the phrase, the individual becomes sovereign, and the hypersensitive organ absorbs all psychic and libidinal energies. Decadence is the dispersal of life.

Despite the critical tone of the above passage, Nietzsche's attitude to this transformation is not simply negative. "Decadence is a word that . . . is not meant to reject but to designate."[32] Precisely because it affects the internal structure of the will, decadence cannot be willed away but must be acknowledged and transformed from within. There is no path back to the old organicist models of life. First, because once the will loses its organizing power the character of the "whole" is irreveversibly transformed: forms of life and expression that in the past may have seemed quasi-natural now appear "cobbled together, calculated, synthetic, an artifact." Viewed from the present period of decadence, *all* organized wholes—from narratives and communites to bodies and personalities—are heterogeneous assemblages, contingent and precarious products of the struggle of countless centers of will, countless micropowers within and between them. Second, this instability points to a structural feature of the will, which is, as we saw, always in excess of itself, hence constantly undoing whatever form it has established. The task

---

31. Letter to Carl Fuchs, August 26, 1888; KGA 3:3, 177; cited in Moritz Baßler, *Deutsche Erzählprosa 1850–1950: Eine Geschichte literarischer Verfahren* (Berlin: Erich Schmidt, 2015), 157 (footnote 308).

32. Letter to Carl Fuchs, April 1886; KGA 3:5, 401; cited in Baßler, *Deusche Erzählprosa*, 157 (footnote 307).

therefore is not to avoid the disgregation of the will but to free its creative potential. Decadence no longer signifies for Nietzsche the "final phase of an organic system but an alternative to such large systemic and quasi-natural organizations."[33] It carries a utopian potential.

Nietzsche's notion of decadence registers the breakdown of the earlier organicist model of life, which now becomes visible in its constructedness, as an historically contingent, and increasingly inadequate and outdated, cultural style. The retrospective recognition of the artificiality of organic form—of its status as artifact rather than biological fact—undercuts any nostalgic longing for wholeness and opens up the possibility to think of fragmentation as a potentially creative refashioning of life. This dialectic of decomposition and utopia enframes central strands of modernist literature. Echos of Nietzsche's account of the disgregation of the will can be found, for instance, in Rilke's poem "The Panther" (1902), which projects Nietzsche's metaphor of European man as a "caged animal" onto a big cat—a panther—held captive in a Parisian zoo in the Jardin des Plantes. Divorced from its natural surroundings, the panther's gaze loses its innate power to grasp the world, which consequently disintegrates into repetitive visual fragments on the one hand,[34] and an anaesthetized (*betäubt*) will on the other.[35] "The Panther" is the first of Rilke's so-called *Dinggedichte* (thing poems), whose diction and physical imagery, in W. H. Auden's words, seek to "think the human in terms of the non-human, of what [Rilke] calls Things."[36] This posthuman poetics is spelled out in greater detail in Rilke's novel *The Notebooks of Malte Laurids Brigge* (1910), which is overtly structured around the Nietzschean dialectic of destruction

---

33. Baßler, *Deutsche Erzählprosa*, 157.

34. "*Sein Blick ist vom Vorübergehn der Stäbe / so müd geworden, daß er nichts mehr hält. / Ihm ist, als ob es tausend Stäube gäbe / und hinter tausend Stäben keine Welt.*" Rainer Maria Rilke, *Die Gedichte* (Frankfurt am Main: Insel, 2006), 447.

35. Ibid., 447. "*Der weiche Gang geschmeidig starker Schritte, / der sich im allerkleinsten Kreise dreht, / ist wie ein Tanz von Kraft um eine Mitte, / in der betäubt ein großer Wille steht.*"

36. W. H. Auden, "Rilke in English," The New Republic, September 6, 1939, https://newrepublic.com/article/102274/rilke-in-english.

and utopia, fragmentation and invention. On the one hand, the novel abounds in descriptions of death and decay, images of fragmented bodies, and fantasies of splitting and psychic breakdown; on the other, Malte, a poet and impoverished aristocrat, believes himself to be on the brink of a radically new kind of vision and language that would transcend all established distinctions between bodies and things, self and object, the animate and the inanimate. As in Nietzsche, the decay of larger wholes is framed as the beginning of a new form of living and speaking.

Nowhere is Nietzsche's analysis of decadence more clearly on display than in Hofmannsthal's famous *Letter of Lord Chandos* (1902). Chandos's paralysis is characterized by a breakdown of the capacity to think and preceive organized wholes. "Everything came to pieces, the pieces broke into more pieces, and nothing could be encompassed by one idea."[37] An educated aristocrat and author of learned books, Chandos finds himself increasingly unable to "think or speak coherently" and to utter opinions "ordinarily offered with the sureness of a sleepwalker" (AL 121; EB 465). At the same time, and closely matching Nietzsche's decription of the displacement of meaning and vitality from whole to parts, Chandos is riveted by mundane objects in which he senses a "swelling tide of higher life [*einer überschwellenden Flut höheren Lebens*]": "A watering can, a harrow left in the field, a dog in the sun, a shabby churchyard, a cripple, a small farmhouse—any of these can become the vessel of my revelation" (AL 123; EB 467). As Malcom Bull has argued, drawing on Heidegger's distinction between (human) *Welt* and (animal) *Umwelten*, Chandos has lost the capacity to apprehend something *as* something.[38] Unmediated by categorical understanding or "the simpflifying gaze of habit," Chandos's perceptions assail him like external forces, with the result that the objects of the

---

37. Hugo von Hofmannsthal, *The Lord Chandos Letter and Other Writings*, ed. John Banville (New York: New York Review of Books, 2005), 122 (hereafter cited as AL and page number). Also, Hugo von Hofmannsthal, *Gesammelte Werke. Band 7. Erzählungen. Erfundene Gespräche und Briefe. Reisen* (Frankfurt am Main: Fischer, 2009), 466 (hereafter cited as EB and page number).

38. Bull, *Anti-Nietzsche*, 105–13. My reading of Hofmannsthal's text owes much to Bull's interpretation.

world appear "terrifyingly close" (AL 122; EB 466). This is what Heidegger, in *The Fundamental Concepts of Metaphysics*, describes as the animal's *captivation* (*Benommenheit*, which also means numbness). Captivation, Bull quotes from Heidegger, "signifies 'having every apprehending of something as something withheld,' with the direct consequence that 'in having this withheld from it, the animal is precisely taken by things.'"[39] However, as Bull points out, whereas Heidegger discusses animal captivation solely as a deficiency relative to human intentionality, Hofmannsthal discerns in Chandos's breakdown a revelatory opening. The loss of the "as-structure" enables Chandos to experience a rapturous kinship with animals and objects formerly discarded as irrelevant or repulsive. Fragmentation thus serves both a critical and utopian function: while pointing to a new way of being and understanding, it also retroactively highlights the artificial character of the earlier, seemingly natural and organic, forms of life and meaning. It shows that the "as-structure" of the world is itself a willful anthropocentric illusion, or as Musil says, a product of the *"perspectivische Verkürzung des Verstandes."*

This dual function of fragmentation continued to shape expressionist and avant-garde literature. The modernist will to disgregation takes the form of an active destruction of the nineteenth-century repertoire of social practices, language games, and aesthetic conventions. What comes under attack are the symbolic codes that sutured the particulars of both bourgeois life and its realist representation into seemingly organic and natural wholes. Accordingly, the modernist fragmentation of stylistic devices that enabled realist texts to create coherent fictional worlds (recognizable plot structures, established hermeneutic codes, stable narrators, etc.[40]) is mirrored, on the level of content and psychological structure, by an increasing emphasis on borderline themes or characters (madness, human-animal hybrids, etc.) that dramatize the breakdown of the

---

39. Ibid., 108.

40. See Baßler, *Deutsche Erzählprosa*, 158. As Hofmannsthal wrote in 1893: "Minimal is the pleasure in action, the interplay of inner and outer forces of life, the Wilhem-Meister-like learning-of-life, and the Shakespearian course-of-the-world." Cited in Baßler, 158.

"symplifying gaze of habit." Nietzsche's dual definition of decadence as an ontological and stylistic event thus remains operative long after the fin de siècle. Fragmentation of style and disgregation of the will mark the two trajectories through which modernism and the avant-garde attack the idea, first articulated in Kant's reflection on the relation between art and biological organisms, of human culture as a *second nature.*

The second, explicitly political trajectory opened up by Nietzsche's emphasis on the plasticity of (human) life follows the seemingly opposed strategy of shaping the social body through the imposition of political will. Consider the following quote from Nietzsche's diaries from the 1880s:

> Create a party of life, strong enough for *great politics*; *great politics* makes physiology the queen of all other questions—it wants to *breed* mankind as a whole; it measures the order of race, peoples, individuals, according to their future, according to the guarantee of life that their future contains—it puts an end without pity to all that is degenerate and parasitic (KSA 13:25 [1]).

Written between December 1888 and January 1889, the note forms part of a set of sustained reflections in which Nietzsche entertains the geopolitical vision of a unified continental Europe led by a transnational and transracial European caste.[41] Like the "party of life" that will support it, the new caste of leaders transcends petty national politics and pursues a "great politics" trained on the real question of "what type of man should be bred, should be willed as having greater value, as being more deserving of life, as being more certain of a future."[42] It is not difficult to see the impact of these passages on right-wing thinkers, who were quick to suppress Nietzsche's antinationalism at the expense of his vehemently antidemocratic and seemingly racist rhetoric. But the importance of Nietzsche's "great politics" of life goes beyond its fascist and anti-Semitic reception. The idea that it is the function of politics and the state to

---

41. See Hugo Drochon, *Nietzsche's Great Politics* (Princeton, NJ: Princeton University Press, 2016), esp. 160–70.
42. Ibid., 165.

"breed" a new kind of humanity marks a decisive step in the development of biopolitics, and, with it, a new conception of "life." Whereas Kant and Goethe still upheld a distinction between first and second nature, Nietzsche's expansion of the will into the organic realm blurs any clear distinction between biological and cultural processes. This conceptual shift is echoed, on the level of empirical politics, by an increasing intervention into the somatic substance of the population, which around 1900 gives rise to an explosion of social welfare programs aimed at the self-intensification of life and the creation of a "new human."[43] At the heart of these programs is a new imbrication of "value" and "life." As Petra Gehring has shown, the concept of life opens itself toward the social world in a way that cannot be reduced to the slogan of a "biologization of the social." Rather, "life" is no longer conceived in strictly biological terms but as an activity that realizes itself through actions and decisions. Life comes to signify the plasticity of the social: a space that is *intrinsically* geared toward evaluation and affirmation. Questions of life and questions of power thus blend into one another: "Reflection about life does not take the form of (natural-scientific) explanation but of the articulation of (political) maxims of action."[44] Nor is this pragmatic understanding of life restricted to a particular ideological position. Echoes of Nietzsche's call for the reshaping of man can be heard in Max Weber's famous inaugural lecture in 1895 and the work of the leading left-liberal reformer Friedrich Naumann,[45] but also in the eugenic writings of Wilhelm Schallmayer, who coined the phrase "biological politics" in 1905.[46] In fact, the blurring of

---

43. Petra Gehring, "Naturalisierung und Biomacht. Das Leben verschaltet Natur und Kultur," *Zeitschrift für Kulturphilosophie* 2011, no. 1 (2011): 118–32. On the rise of biopolitics around 1900, see also Dickinson, "Biopolitics, Fascism, Democracy."

44. Petra Gehring, "Wert, Wirklichkeit, Macht. Lebenswissenschaft um 1900," *Allgemeine Zeitschrift für Philosophie* 34, no. 1 (2009): 117–35, 133.

45. On Weber, see Drochon, *Nietzsche's Great Politics*, 164 (footnote 24). Naumann wrote in 1902: "The most important factor in the shaping of culture [*Kulturgestaltung*] is the quantity and quality of the human material itself." Cited in Dickinson, "Biopolitics, Fascism, Democracy," 29.

46. On Nietzsche's influence on eugenic thinkers such as Schallmayer and Ploetz, see Moore, *Nietzsche, Biology, and Metaphor*, 5–6 and 136.

the culture-nature distinction is reflected in the rise of new disciplines that cut across the established distinction between the humanities and natural sciences: sociology, economics, and public health, among others. Irreducible to either biology or culture, the reality at issue in these disciplines rests on the conception of life as power and evaluation that Nietzsche articulated. As Gehring writes, "The 'life' of the life sciences around 1900 is neither naturalist nor vitalist, nor does it privilege biology. Gone also are any teleologies of vital forces associated with *Naturphilosophie*. Rather, the new discourse of life postulates evaluative decisiveness, a turn toward the "real" understood as action, as well as a polemical economy of power."[47]

Philosophy does not transform history directly, but it does, from time to time, open up conceptual horizons that make new cultural and political logics possible. It would be foolish to claim that modernism and fascism, the dominant cultural and political movements of the early twentieth century, are the *products* of Nietzsche's philosophy. But the peculiar intensity and radicalism these movements assume in Germany has everything to do with Nietzsche's attempt to rethink the form of life. Modernism and fascism, aesthetic fragmentation and totalitarian imposition, are distinct yet connected responses to Nietzsche's insistence on the artificiality of the human life-form.

---

47. Gehring, "Wert, Wirklichkeit, Macht," 132.

PART III

DEFORMATION

5

BRAINS (BENN)

Zersprengtes Ich—o aufgetrunkene Schwäre—
Verwehte Fieber—süß zerborstene Wehr—:
Verströme, o verströme Du—gebäre
Blutbäuchig das Entformte her.

[Exploded I—oh, drunken-up pustule—
Blown away fever—sweetly burst weir—:
Emit, oh emit You—give birth
Bloody-bellied to the disformed.]

—"COCAIN," 1917

Blood, belly, the disformed (*das Entformte*)—the writings of the young Gottfried Benn are replete with images of anatomical dismemberment and biological decay. Benn's first collection of poems (1912) is set in a morgue and features diaphragms, esophagi, thoracic cavities, livers, kidneys, molars, skulls, pimples, testicles, and cancerous wombs. His subsequent poetry cycle, published in 1917, is called *Flesh*. His first collection of stories, published in 1916, bears the title *Brains*. Wherever we look, in prose and poetry, title and text, the body is dissected, torn apart, disjointed. Benn, a trained doctor who worked as a pathologist in a Berlin hospital before opening a practice treating venereal and dermatological diseases, writes literature as a pathology report.

But the "disformed" also carries utopian promises. The *zersprengtes* (fragmented, exploded) "I," itself bereft of any discernible unity, calls into linguistic being a "you" tasked with bringing forth an as yet unheard-of entity, a creature beyond form. The prefix *ent* has an active and elevating rather than a privative force: formlessness is imagined as the generation of a new reality liberated from received forms. Poetic speech, so conceived, is emphatically transformative, effecting an ontological shift from a world of forms to a world "beyond" form. This shift, however, leaves destruction in its wake; the birth of the disformed breaks the vessel of its delivery. Will the bloody-bellied mother survive her child, or does the birth of the disformed spell the end of all bounded forms of life, or even biological life as such? And what about meaning? Does a disformed word still carry meaning, or will its creation entail the dissolution not just of received sense but of sense as such? Finally, how are we to think the shape of this new entity? Given the invocation of the disformed in a poem that is clearly not formless, what is the relation between articulation and disarticulation, violence and *poesis*?

On the one hand, the discourse of pathology; on the other, the utopia of a new language. Science and avant-garde, dismemberment and absolute writing meet in Benn's early texts in unique and intricate ways. Yet what is unclear is the exact nature of their link. Why is poetic speech figured as anatomical dissection? And what happens to a world reduced to "words and the brain," as Benn put it in an early scenic arrangement?[1] To begin to answer these questions, it may help to notice that the phrase *words and the brain* expresses less an antithesis than a collocation. Words as such, whether spoken or written, are fundamentally material in nature, just as the brain, separated from the body, is a mere parcel of organic matter. Yet a world of mere words and brains is one without meaning, sense, unity, or coherence, and thus is no world at all. In the traditional Kantian view, what connects words and brains to one another and to language and thought is of course the mind, the dynamic faculty of cognition. Benn's early writings, I suggest, record the vanishing of this unifying agency by exposing its remainder, the detached material expressions of mind—brains, its material substrate, and words, its material effects.

The logic at work here is diametrically opposed to Kant's project in the third *Critique*, the founding text not only of modern aesthetics but also of the biological notion of the organism. As we saw in chapter 1, Kant argues that human beings can comprehend nature only if they conceive it in terms derived from their own experience as moral agents. It is the notion of purposiveness—a type of causality, Kant claims, that we infer from intentional human action—that allows us to understand the complexity of nature and discern within it the plurality of unified organisms. The Kantian idea of purposiveness serves two related functions: to envision natural bodies as dynamically integrated and "intelligent" wholes, that is, as organisms, and thus to bring nature and mind, biological and moral life, into closer proximity. Benn attacks both of these aspects. Not only does he depict, to invert Gilles Deleuze, organs without

---

1. "*Ich habe den ganzen Kosmos mit meinem Schädel zerkaut! Ich habe gedacht, bis mir der Speichel floß. Ich war logisch bis zum Koterbrechen. Und als sich der Nebel verzogen hatte, was war dann alles? Worte und das Gehirn* [I've chewed the whole cosmos to pieces inside my head. I've sat and thought till I slavered at the mouth. I've been so out and out logical I nearly vomited shit. And once the mists had cleared, what was left? Words and the brain]." Benn, "Ithaka," in *Sämtliche Werke*, ed. Gerhard Schuster and Holger Hof (Stuttgart: Klett-Cotta, 1989), 7.1:12; Benn, "Ithaka," in Ernst Schürer, *German Expressionist Plays: Gottfried Benn, Georg Kaiser, Ernst Toller and Others* (New York: Continuum, 1997), 17.

bodies—livers, brains, and limbs torn from their natural home in the body, deprived of any function—but he also reduces mind and meaning to their discrete material correlates, to "brains" and "words." The result of this twofold repudiation of purposiveness is at once a rejection of any notion of organic form and a new vision of life: "After all, one need not always say: to live is to think and produce a unity; one might also say for once: to live is to be able to discharge pus [*eitern*], for dead things do not fester [*eitert*] any longer."[2] This is life conceived as the power not of coming to be, as in Kant or Goethe, but of coming not to be. More than any writer of his generation, Benn reads the disintegration of language and thought in the corruption proper to nature, thus literally pathologizing meaning.[3] Where Ludwig Wittgenstein, drawing on biological terminology, appropriates the concept of an organized *Lebensform* (form of life) to capture the dynamic coherence of linguistic communities, Benn uses medical discourse to figure the dissolution of shared meaning. Whether understood biologically (as natural organism) or culturally (as collective practice), his writings target the very core of the notion of a *form of life*: the idea that life generates and is embodied in coherent forms.

Nowhere is this dismemberment of body and meaning and its relation to poetic practice more evident than in Benn's so-called Rönne novellas: *Brains* (*Gehirne*, 1914), *Conquest* (*Die Eroberung*, 1915), *The Journey* (*Die Reise*, 1915), *Birthday* (*Der Geburtstag*, 1916), and *The Island* (*Die Insel*, 1916).[4] Written during Benn's

---

2. Benn, "Unter der Großhirnrinde," in *Künstlerische Prosa*, ed. Holger Hof (Stuttgart: Klett-Cotta, 2006), 10.

3. For a comparable conjunction of avant-garde writing with organic imagery, one would need to look at the work of Antonin Artaud from the 1930s and 1940s. Not only were Artaud's pertinent texts written twenty years after Benn's, they also lack references to medical terminology and scientific discourse. Benn is unique in figuring bodily dismemberment as the result of scientific knowledge.

4. There is general agreement in the critical literature that despite their traditional classification as novellas, Benn's texts do not fit the critique of this genre as it was developed in the nineteenth century. While not entirely wrong, this claim rests on a restricted understanding of the novella genre. Elsewhere I have suggested a reconceptualization of the genre that emphasizes its relation to crisis, trauma, and the breakdown of received models of interpretation. Conceived along these lines, Benn's Rönne texts might be understood as radicalizing the tradition to a

tenure as a military physician in Brussels, the five loosely connected texts "narrate" episodes in the life of Werff Rönne, a trained pathologist interested in psychiatry and brain physiology, who in the opening story takes up a position in a sanatorium, where he is expected to temporarily replace the chief physician, who is on vacation. Yet as soon as Rönne arrives, he begins to suffer a deep professional and existential crisis. Alienated from his surroundings and unable to work, Rönne oscillates between despair and ecstasy, paralysis and intensely poetic flights of association. Science and literature—biological matter and free-form improvisation—are thus intricately interwoven: *Brains* records and enacts the disintegration of subjectivity in a medical discourse that gives way to an experimental prose freed from the constraints of reference and meaning.

In what follows I suggest that Benn's fictional conjunction of subjective crisis, scientific discourse, and avant-garde writing complicates contemporary scholarly reflections on the politics of life in modernity. Recall the distinction, emphasized by Canguilhem, between "*le vivant*" (living matter) and "*le vécu*" (lived experience).[5] Much of the modern discourse of life is built on the disciplinary disaggregation of these two dimensions of vitality, with the life sciences taking as their subject matter the former ("*le vivant*"), leaving the latter ("*le vécu*") to literature and the humanities. *Brains*, by contrast, interweaves the experiential and material meaning of the notion of "life." Through its protagonist Rönne, a physician captive to the scientific reduction of mind to brain, Benn's novella cycle asks what happens to subjective life when it seeks to understand *itself* in terms of living matter. Benn's critique of the idea of "life itself" unfolds in two steps: while the opening novella, "Brains," depicts Rönne's psychological breakdown—the unforming of the self—as the result of his immersion in the life sciences of his day, the following stories systematically undo conventional modes of writing and experiencing. To the violence of the scientific-political *Entformung*

---

point where its operative distinctions (between norm and deviation, frame and embedded narrative, crisis and normalcy, etc.) break down. See Gailus, "Form and Chance: The German Novella," in *The Novel, Volume 2: Forms and Themes*, ed. Franco Moretti (Princeton, NJ: Princeton University Press, 2006), 739–76.

5. Canguilhem, *Études d'histoire*, 335.

of qualified life, Benn opposes the aesthetic *Entformung* of received social forms of life.

Rönne's Breakdown

Following Foucault's archaeology of the modern clinic, much has been written about the medical gaze—the detached vision of the doctor that dissects the patient's body into an array of signs so as to better penetrate its depth.[6] Helmut Lethen, for instance, has shown how the avant-garde after World War I modeled its cult of coldness on the figure of the doctor.[7] For writers like Bertolt Brecht, Ernst Jünger, and Benn, approaching the world like a doctor meant keeping it at an observational distance, scanning it for signs of danger while assuming a pose of steely indifference toward it. But the eye is not the only organ doctors rely on. Doctors also learn to grasp the world through their hands, using and shaping them as instruments of knowledge. And then there are the surgeons, the pianists of medical practice, whose hands transform esoteric scientific knowledge into breathtaking feats of physical modification and restoral. The surgeon's hand is astonishingly nimble and sensitive; relaxed and determined, it reigns over the body not by suppressing its particularities but by adapting itself to its intricate folds and textures. Benn's protagonist Rönne is also a man of hands,

> turning the handle, fixing the lamps, starting the motors, focusing light on this or that with the help of a mirror; he took comfort in seeing science broken down into a series of hand movements [*Handgriffe*], some calling for the brute strength of a blacksmith, others the delicacy of a watchmaker.
>
> Then he took his hands, passed them over the X-ray tube, adjusted the gap through which light fell on to a back, inserted a funnel into an

---

6. Michel Foucault, *The Birth of the Clinic: An Archaeology of Medical Perception* (New York: Vintage, 1975).

7. Helmut Lethen, *Cool Conduct: The Culture of Distance in Weimar Germany* (Berkeley: University of California Press, 2002); Helmut Lethen, *Der Sound der Väter: Gottfried Benn und seine Zeit* (Berlin: Rowohlt, 2006), 56–61.

ear, took cotton-wool, placed it in the ear-duct, and was at once absorbed in the consequences of this operation on the owner of the ear.[8]

Rönne's professional identity is concentrated in his hands. Medicine, for him, is not a body of theoretical knowledge but a practice, a way to do things with one's hands. As such, it can be broken down into a series of movements that form part of a unified sequence of actions, a physically enacted narrative. While Rönne's confidence as a doctor rests on his utter familiarity with each move in this narrative, the pleasure he derives from his hands also feeds on the technological apparatus he manipulates. That apparatus is not a mere instrument of his will; rather, machine and hand—technical appliance and bodily skill—belong to a broader constellation that unifies its parts. Rönne's sense of professional identity is a function of his total immersion in the medical *Gestell*, and the feeling of power he derives from this is predicated on the fragmentation of its object, the living human being, into a congeries of organs, their unity a matter of mere possession by an abstract "owner of the ear."[9]

Benn's novella cycle traces the progress of this fragmentation. *Brains* opens at a moment when the depersonalizing logic of the medical *Gestell* has already affected its purported author, the almighty doctor:

> Rönne, a young doctor who in the past had done many dissections, was traveling through southern Germany on his way north. He had done nothing for some months now; for two years he had held a position in an institute of pathology—that is to say, approximately two thousand corpses had passed through his unthinking hands, and for some reason this had left him strangely and inexplicably exhausted [*es waren ungefähr zweitausend Leichen ohne Besinnen durch seine Hände gegangen,*

---

8. Benn, "Gehirne," in *Gesammelte Werke*, 2:19–20 (hereafter cited as GW).

9. The notion of *Gestell* is of course borrowed from Martin Heidegger, "The Question Concerning Technology," in *The Question Concerning Technology and Other Essays*, trans. William Lovitt (New York: Harper & Row, 1977), 3–35. On the connection between Heidegger's *Gestell* and Foucault's *dispositif*, see Giorgio Agamben, "What Is an Apparatus?," in *What Is an Apparatus? and Other Essays*, trans. David Kishik and Stefan Pedatella (Redwood Hills, CA: Stanford University Press, 2009), 1–24.

*und das hatte ihn in einer merkwürdigen und ungeklärten Weise er-
schöpft].* (GW 2:19)

That two thousand corpses have passed through Rönne's hands
without thought or reflection (*"ohne Besinnen"*) does not mean that
his surgical hands are opposed to concept and thought; it suggests,
on the contrary, that the elaborate medical knowledge informing
pathological dissection has so completely shaped his body as to
leave no role for consciousness. Rönne's hands are truly an "organ
of the mind," to quote the title of a recent collection of essays on
the cultural agency of hands.[10] It is against this background that
the text's description of Rönne's gestures assumes its full significance. For it is Rönne's hands, not just his mind, that go mad:

> Often when he got back to his room from one of these rounds he would
> twist his hands this way and that and look at them. And once a nurse
> observed him smelling them or rather going over them as though testing
> their air, and she watched him putting his lightly cupped hands together,
> little finger to little finger, then pressing them open and shut, as though
> squeezing open the halves of a large, soft fruit or bending something in
> two. She told the other nurses but no one knew what it might mean. Till
> the day when an animal of larger than usual size was being slaughtered
> in the hospital. Rönne came along, apparently by chance, just as the head
> was being split open, took the contents in both hands and forced the two
> halves apart. In a flash the nurse realized that this was the gesture she
> had witnessed in the corridor. But she could see no connection between
> this and anything else and soon forgot about it. (GW 2:21–22)

At this point Rönne, having left his position at a pathological institute, is substituting for the clinic's director at a sanatorium. Removed
from both morgue and corpse, Rönne's misplaced gestures testify
to his intense temporal and spatial dislocation. Rönne is haunted
by the routines that shaped him; he is a ghost of his professional
self. Like all action, conducting an autopsy binds together different
systems: the body, medical observation and knowledge, institutional
routines and hierarchies, and others. To "conduct an autopsy," you

---

10. Zdravko Radman, *The Hand, an Organ of the Mind* (Cambridge, MA:
MIT Press, 2013).

need not just proper hand gestures but also a corpse, a knife, a specific environment, a set of procedures, and so on. The trouble with Rönne is that his bodily movements are dissociated from the context in which they could amount to a practice. Rönne makes surgical movements, but he does not engage in the act of autopsying.

Rönne's gestures bring into focus two interrelated points. First, they highlight the complexity of social practices and the forms of life that demarcate them. To engage in the form of life of a surgeon is not only to transform one's body, down to the nerves of each finger, into an organ of scientific knowledge; it also requires immersion in the countless protocols of the medical system. Forms of life comprise a potentially infinite number of smaller forms and in this sense are open-ended rather than "organically" closed. Second, Rönne's gestures illuminate the link between body, self, and society. They show that because personal identity is lived and embodied, inculcated into the somatic structure of the subject, psychological disintegration can be experienced as corporeal fragmentation. Hence the sociopolitical implications of the term *Entformung*. Although Rönne's hands are not physically separated from his body, they are disarticulated, cut off from the collective forms of life that infused them with meaning.

This is not a merely cognitive or physical problem. Rönne is still capable of making the appropriate bodily movements, just as he abstractly knows what is involved in "conducting an autopsy." In the language of contemporary cognitive theory, Rönne still remembers the *scripts* that structure and organize the ensemble of movements that constitute "conducting an autopsy." What is unraveling, instead, is his interior connection to these scripts, his capacity to *inhabit* the form of life of a doctor. Rönne can no longer operate because the *reasons* for operating—the ideas and purposes that unify the practice of a doctor—are disappearing. *Brains* figures this loss of reason in terms of the dissolution of a synthesizing mind.

> And once I too had a pair of eyes, always running backward with their gaze [*Und ich hatte auch einmal zwei Augen, die liefen rückwärts mit ihren Blicken*]; yes, indeed; I existed, without questions and composed. Where have I come to? Where am I? A gentle fluttering, a breeze blowing past.

> Something is weakening me from above. There is nothing solid behind my eyes. Space surges off into infinity; once surely it flowed together at one spot. Rotten is the cortex that carried me. (GW 2:21)

Kant argued that the unity of experience, hence, of our world, is a product of the mind's active synthesis. In Michael Hampe's useful formulation, "World is world for a subject, and this subject constitutes the world through the ordering of experience and its own unity. If the unity of subjectivity and the coherence of the ordering rules of pure reason and judgment were to break up, according to Kant's conception, the lawful unity of the world would also disappear."[11] This is precisely what happens in Benn's novella cycle, which depicts Rönne's dissolution of world in terms of his inability to collect his thoughts and sensations.[12] This symbolic collapse is particularly pronounced with respect to the two categories that, according to Kant, provide the fundamental coordinates of worldly experience: time and space. Space, formerly centered on the experiencing subject (*"einst floß er [der Raum] doch auf eine Stelle"*), begins to split off and expand infinitely, drowning Rönne in a world without bounded shapes: "He was no longer facing any object; he had lost all power over space, he said once [*er sei keinem Ding mehr gegenüber; er habe keine Macht mehr über den Raum, äußerte er einmal*]" (GW 2:23). As for time, *Brains* tellingly begins with Rönne's exhortation to himself to stem the increasing pull of forgetfulness by writing: "I must buy a notebook and a pencil; I must take down everything I can from now on so that things don't flash past out of sight. So many years to my life, and it's all sunk without a trace.

---

11. Michael Hampe, *Eine kleine Geschichte des Naturgesetzbegriffs* (Frankfurt am Main: Suhrkamp, 2007), 78.

12. In his reading of Benn's novellas, Andreas Huyssen has pointed out that the word *Rinde* used here can mean both the bark of the tree and the cerebral cortex, the latter being, according to contemporary science, the seat of rational thought. Rönne thus may be said to naturalize and localize his depersonalization. See Andreas Huyssen, *Miniature Metropolis: Literature in an Age of Photography and Film* (Cambridge, MA: Harvard University Press, 2015), 100. I would add that Rönne's neurological self-conception points to his inability to grasp the larger sociosymbolic and psychological reasons for his breakdown. Rönne is losing not only his mind but also the very language of the mind that would allow him to describe what is happening to him.

When I was starting out, did things stay with me? I can't remember" (GW 2:19). Kant claimed that the unity of experience, and thus the presence of a world, depends on the subject's apperceptive unity—its continuous ascription of its mental states to itself.[13] Herein lies Rönne's malady: his drifting impressions suggest the breakdown of apperception and, as a consequence, the bedlam of a self and world without unity, a confusion of inner and outer experience. What remains of (Kantian) reason, at most, is a vague memory of its essential tie to the "I." "One just needs to connect everything that one sees to something else, align it with earlier experiences and place it under general aspects—that is the function of reason, as I remember it" (*Die Eroberung*, GW 2:28). We are now in a better position to make sense of the novella's title and the opening reference to the disorienting effect of autopsies on Rönne. What Rönne registers when he claims that he has "nothing solid behind [the] eyes"—or that he once had but no longer has two eyes "running backward with their gaze"—is the loss of reason, the agent of synthesis, unity, and sense. The autopsies trigger this feeling of loss because they confront the subject with his own absence, an absence that is, somewhat paradoxically, embodied in the self's corporeal remnant. Convinced of the revelatory power of the new life sciences, Rönne approaches autopsies as a gateway to the mysteries of life and mind. Yet what he finds in anatomical dissection is not life but death, not mind and thought but an extended and deracinated piece of organic matter: "Look, I held them in these hands of mine, a hundred, maybe even a thousand of them; some soft, some hard, all very runny [*sehr zerfließlich*]" (*Gehirne*, GW 2:23). In short, the brain functions as the materialization of an absence, the mind depleted of reason. Benn's novella cycle is about the consequences of reducing the mind to the brain, a reductionism at the core of scientific discourse around 1900.

The immediate result of this sort of materialism can be seen in the dissociation of Rönne's thought and the consequent fragmentation of his experience: all the unities of character, action, and linguistic and social systems that immerse the subject in a communally

---

13. Kant, *Critique of Pure Reason*, B 131–32.

shared life have lost their hold on Rönne. Cognitive scientists speak of these unifying forms in terms of schemata—scripts, frames, and descriptions that "characterize the cultural and generic information we use to make sense of what is going on in situations and to construct relevance and coherence in discourse."[14] Given our observations about gestures, we might add that these schemata and scripts do more than channel the surfeit of words and perception into typical and familiar forms; they also integrate the countless microforms of daily life into larger patterns, linking diverse systems (linguistic, bodily, institutional, etc.) in such a way as to turn otherwise disjointed utterances, objects, and movements into meaningful and publicly recognizable phenomena. Moreover, Rönne's breakdown shows that these public patterns—and the coherence of daily life they ground—are held in place by acts of affective investment. Unable to attach to and inhabit them from within, Rönne relates to the scripts and frames of everyday life at best from the third-person perspective of an ironic—and, most often, disgusted—observer. And it is not just the first-person perspective that has become unavailable. "Rönne lived by himself, dedicated to his development and working hard. His studies concerned the creation of a new syntax. The worldview, which the work of the past century had created, had to be completed. To eliminate the you-character of the grammatical seemed honestly important to him, since the address had become mythical" (*Die Insel*, GW 2:56). Defined by communally recognized activity, forms of life are anchored in the daily to-and-fro of conversational and bodily engagement in which people continually evaluate one another. Anthropologists like Webb Keane have emphasized how such evaluation is driven by the constant work of projecting a sense of self and responding to the sense of self projected by others.[15] Rönne's abandonment of the second-person pronoun signifies a full-scale retreat from this dialectic of recognition and, as such, amounts to a refusal of the most basic form of relational-

---

14. Elissa Asp and Jessica de Villiers, *When Language Breaks Down* (Cambridge: Cambridge University Press, 2010), 87.

15. Webb Keane, *Ethical Life: Its Social and Natural Histories* (Princeton, NJ: Princeton University Pres, 2016), 110–22.

ity. There are obvious advantages to such a refusal, for to immerse oneself in a publicly shared human world is to expose oneself to the possibility that others will refuse to acknowledge one's self-expression. Yet the avoidance of vulnerability to others comes at a heavy price. To abandon the second-person pronoun because "the address ha[s] become mythical" is to make myself unknowable, for who could acknowledge and confirm my existence if not another person?[16]

I will return to the refusal of empathy and the corresponding dream of an impersonal language, which are constant themes in German discourses of life between the wars. At the moment it suffices to note that Rönne frames his retreat from the world of others in historical terms, as a deliberate and programmatic response to a broader transformation of thought and knowledge. The goal is to develop a "new syntax" that is radically divorced from the scripts and schemata underpinning everyday life and speech. Before we can explore this new language in detail, however, we must get a clearer sense of the "work of the last century" (*Die Insel*, GW 2:56) that presumably has hollowed out the language of intersubjectivity and mythologized the second-person pronoun. Doing so allows us to situate Rönne's breakdown in a broader historical context and helps us grasp more clearly the link between medical discourse and avant-garde experimentation.

Science

"I hail from the scientific century," Benn writes in the epilogue to his first collection of literary writings in 1921.[17] The young Benn encounters the century of science as a student at the Militärärztliche Akademie in Berlin, also known as the Pépenière. The Pépenière was one of the leading medical institutions of the time: its library

---

16. The self's dependence on the acknowledgment by the other and the temptation to make oneself unknowable are at the core of Stanley Cavell's work. See *Claim of Reason*, part 4.

17. Benn, "Epilog," GW 2:252.

held 67,700 volumes, 115 microscopes were available for training purposes, and 1,554 square meters of lab space were dedicated to the practical teaching of chemistry, physics, pathology, roentgenology, and bacteriology.[18] Emil Fischer, winner of the 1902 Nobel Prize in Chemistry, and Rudolf Virchow, the founder of modern pathology, taught there; scientific luminaries like Hermann von Helmholtz and Ernst von Leyden received their education at the Akademie. Benn learns the epistemic practices and virtues of nineteenth-century empiricism: inductive and statistical thinking, precise observation, and methods of experimentation. Beyond factual knowledge, he soaks up an entire habitus, as he remembers fondly many years later: "For one more time there came together in those years the whole sum of the inductive period, its methods, values, jargon. . . . Coldness of thought, sobriety, ultimate precision of concepts, readiness to provide evidence for every judgment . . . and above all the deep skepticism that creates style."[19]

The methods of thinking and observing Benn absorbs at the Pépenière are trained on the great new object of nineteenth-century science: "life" understood as living matter and biological process rather than as lived experience or biographical unity. As an attentive Nietzsche reader, and at a time when the notion of life has assumed broader cultural and political significance, Benn knows that the rise of the life sciences is part of a broader shift in the evaluation of reality.[20] For society to invest so heavily in the scientific study of biological life, the very materiality of life must have become a supreme value. Far from being the simple result of impartial observation, then, the emergence of the new object implies a radical reappraisal of the real and is thus a historical and political event. "For a long time I have begun to wonder," Benn writes in a late essay, "how strange it is that this concept of life has become

---

18. See Werner Rübe, *Provoziertes Leben. Gottfried Benn* (Stuttgart: Klett-Cotta, 1993), 93 and Lethen, *Der Sound der Väter*, 61–62. On Benn's medical background, see the rich and detailed work by Marcus Hahn, *Gottfried Benn und das Wissen der Moderne* (Göttingen: Wallstein, 2011).

19. Benn, "Lebensweg eines Intellektuellen," GW 2:312.

20. For the cultural and political valence of the discourse of life around 1900, see Gehring, "Wert, Wirklichkeit, Macht."

the highest concept of our state of conscience and consciousness. . . . Only for us, within a certain geographic zone, has it become the fundamental ordering concept that stops everybody in their tracks, the abyss into which everything precipitates despite all other decay of values, around which it gathers and falls silent in awe."[21]

Nowhere is this gravitational force more palpable than at the point where life turns in on itself. What would it mean to look through the microscope and capture, in a scientifically precise way, the thinking and observing subject? Between 1905 and 1911 Benn studies the "three sciences" that explore the life of the brain[22]— brain physiology, psychiatry, and experimental psychology—and publishes papers that pay tribute to the "new era of scientific researchers" that "made *tabula rasa* by sweeping clean the temple" of metaphysical speculation.[23] Despite the revolutionary language, Benn does not lose sight of the larger philosophical and metaphysical issues. It is the "psychophysical question"—the traditional mind-body problem—that interests him more than anything else.[24]

The nineteenth-century project of "rewriting the soul" sought to raze the metaphysical temple by framing the mind on the model of the body.[25] As Johann Friedrich Herbart wrote in 1824, "Just as [physiology] construes the body out of fibers, so [psychology] the mind out of chains of ideas."[26] Forty years later Gustav Theodor Fechner provided the conceptual infrastructure for Herbart's analogy. Under the new designation "psychophysics," Fechner articulated

21. Benn, "Soll die Dichtung das Leben bessern?," GW 3:594.

22. Benn, "Unter der Großhirnrinde," in *Künstlerische Prosa*, 9.

23. Benn, "Zur Geschichte der Naturwissenschaften," GW 3:21. See also Benn's comments on Flechsig und Fritsch: "*Es interessierte am Gehirn gar nicht mehr der Sitz und das Ergehen der Seele; es war viel wichtiger, daß beim Stich in den vierten Ventrikel Zucker im Harn auftrat und daß bei einer enthirnten Taube bestimmte psychische Funktionen ausfielen und andere bestehen blieben* [What was interesting about the brain was no longer the seat or action of the soul; it was much more important that with the puncture of the fourth ventricle sugar appeared in the urine and that a debrained pigeon lacked certain psychic functions while others remained]" (GW 3:21).

24. Benn, "Beitrag zur Geschichte der Psychiatrie," GW 3:15.

25. Ian Hacking, *Rewriting the Soul: Multiple Personality and the Sciences of Memory* (Princeton, NJ: Princeton University Press, 1995).

26. Quoted in Hahn, *Gottfried Benn und das Wissen*, 156.

the theoretical paradigm that allowed psychology to become, in the minds of its practitioners, an exact science. Differences notwithstanding, the new students of the mind agreed on one fundamental point: "the necessity to carry out psychology according to the scientific method and in every respect link up to the natural sciences, above all to nerve and brain physiology."[27] Accordingly, most psychological research programs around 1900 were based on three premises:[28] every mental act, in fact consciousness as a whole, can be broken down into isolatable atomic elements; the connection among these elements is determined by laws of mechanical causality, expressible in mathematical terms (teleological explanations in terms of purposes were excluded); and these laws—hence the mind in its totality—can be grasped only from an external, third-person perspective.

These principles still undergird the cutting-edge research program that Benn encounters during his studies at Berlin: the psychology of association. As Marcus Hahn and Ursula Kirchdörfer-Boßmann have shown, the central figure in this context is one of Benn's teachers at the Pépenière, the psychologist and psychiatrist Theodor Ziehen.[29] Ziehen claims to offer empirical solutions to fundamental problems of modern philosophy that have persisted since René Descartes. This concerns not only mind-body dualism but also concepts such as "I" and "world," which according to Ziehen have "no reality and not even any sense outside their existence as representations." "Neither a subject nor a plurality of subjects is given; all that is given is a chain of sensations and representations."[30]

---

27. Richard Müller-Freienfels, *Die Hauptrichtungen der gegenwärtigen Psychologie* (Leipzig: Quelle und Meyer, 1929), 9.

28. I say "most" because in the late nineteenth century a more holistic strand of psychology emerged in opposition to the prevailing mechanical positivism. See Harrington, *Reenchanted Science*.

29. On Ziehen, see Hahn, *Gottfried Benn und das Wissen*, 151–67; and Ursula Kirchdörfer-Boßmann, "'Eine Pranke in den Nacken der Erkenntnis': Zur Beziehung von Dichtung und Naturwissenschaft im Frühwerk Gottfried Benns" (St. Ingbert: Röhring, 2003), 54–59.

30. Theodor Ziehen, *Psychophysiologische Erkenntnistheorie* (Jena: Fischer, 1898), 4–5, 37.

Hahn's claim that Ziehen's conception of thinking is fundamentally idealistic is only half correct. Ziehen's theory is a conglomerate of two seemingly opposed philosophical positions. Ziehen embraces a psychic monism: "Everything that is or is given, is either sensation or representation. Initially, sensations are given, which leave behind remembered images [*Erinnerungsbilder*] or representations. . . . Not given to us are the objects that we sense."[31] The reliance on Kant's epistemological limitation to the world of appearances is obvious. But unlike Kant, whose transcendental idealism rests on a complex web of a priori categories and intellectual acts of syntheses, Ziehen bases the entire world of appearances, hence everything that counts for him as reality, on the mechanisms of association, which follow two and only two principles: "similarity" and "contiguity or simultaneity."[32] Speech and thought, the laws of logic, the order of aesthetic objects or political institutions—all are products of associative connections, whose principles of construction (similarity, contiguity) are as unproblematically given as the material of sensation or representation that they connect.

That is the idealistic side of Ziehen's theory. The other side entails a materialist reductionism that reduces the play of symbols to the asymbolic play of nerve cells. To be sure, Ziehen claims "to have never undergone a materialist phase," and his interpreters, including Hahn, tend to follow him in this self-description.[33] Yet Ziehen's refusal to clarify the relation between association and brain function does not prevent him from repeatedly avowing their identity. As the title of Ziehen's most famous textbook unmistakably announces, Ziehen's theory is a *physiologische Psychologie*; that is, the sensations and representations that make up our associative world have their precise correlates in "physiological excitations of the cortex."[34] That these physiological excitations are accessible to

---

31. Ibid., 2.

32. Theodor Ziehen, *Leitfaden der physiologischen Psychologie* (Jena: Fischer, 1906), 146.

33. Quoted in Hahn, *Gottfried Benn und das Wissen*, 160.

34. Ibid., 160. See also the following: "*Dem Denken eines allgemeinen sinnlichen Begriffs entspricht also in noch viel größerem Grade als dem Denken eines spezielleren sinnlichen Begriffs ein fast über die ganze Großhirnrinde ausgebreiteter*

us only in the form of representations, and are thus not directly given but only logically inferred, does not undermine Ziehen's main claim: every association, thought, or word has its physiological correlate in the movement and excitation of nerve cells.

In short, Ziehen is an epistemological idealist and a metaphysical materialist. From either perspective, the premises of nineteenth-century psychology—ideational atomism, causal determination, impersonal description—remain intact. And it is here, in this methodological and conceptual positivism, that the broader (bio) political dimension of Ziehen's work can be found. Ziehen's neuropositivism is part of the larger positivist attempt of nineteenth-century psychiatry to fix and *feststellen* (Heidegger) subjective life by reducing it to its material substrate, whether understood as an organic brain or, in Ziehen's more refined version, as identifiable and mechanically connected items of association. At stake is the "scientific penetration and psychotechnological availability" of the mind for purposes of its economic and political control,[35] a process that, as Foucault's work on the nineteenth-century takeoff of the human sciences has shown, is a crucial dimension of the biopolitical regime. *Brains* unmasks the violence of this operation by enacting, in narrative form, psychiatry's reduction of experience to bare life. Two aspects of this deconstruction can be distinguished. First, through its narrative avatar Rönne, *Brains* shows that the scientific picture of the mind, if taken up and internalized by the subject, leads to the disintegration of the human life it claims to capture. It is because Rönne seeks to live and embody, rather than merely think, the psychiatry of his time that he experiences its conceptual violence as an *Entformung* of mind and body. Second, in pushing association to the point of psychic and semantic incoherence, the novellas illustrate that thinking is held in place not by intrapsychic laws or pro-

---

physiologischer Prozeß [The thinking of a general sensuous concept corresponds to a physiological process spread over almost the entire cerebral cortex to a much greater degree than does the thinking of a more specialized sensuous concept]," Ziehen, *Leitfaden*, 146.

35. Friedrich Balke, "Heidegger und Ernst Jünger. Kontroversen über den Nihilismus," in *Heidegger-Handbuch. Leben—Werk—Wirkung*, ed. Dieter Thomä (Stuttgart: Metzler, 2003), 371.

cesses, as Ziehen and contemporary psychiatry believed, but by public practices and norms—in other words, by *communal forms of life*.

We have already begun to look at the issue of embodiment. *Brains* transplants the theoretical discourse of the materiality of thought into the infinitely more complex materiality of a lived life. Instead of engaging contemporary psychology at the level of propositional content, Rönne interiorizes its tenets in body and soul. The transfer from third to first person—from the impartial description of mechanical processes to the internal vantage point from which these processes are experienced—undoes the self whose psychic life the description is meant to grasp. The reason for this has to do with the neuropsychiatric emphasis on mechanical causality. Eager to embrace the "scientific method and in every respect link up to the natural sciences,"[36] nineteenth-century psychology adopts a causal determinism that does away with questions of purpose, intention, and normative commitments, and thus has difficulty thinking about self-awareness, reflexivity, or the capacity of the subject to direct itself toward its feelings, thoughts, or surroundings. In general, the scientists of the mind or brain do not suffer the consequences of their own reductionism, because they treat the mind on the level of *theoria*, as an observable object that, in Heideggerian terminology, is *vorhanden* (present at hand) rather than *zuhanden* (ready to hand).[37] By contrast, Benn's narrative projects the medical discourse onto the axis of performance and praxis—that is, into the productive life of a speaking and thinking subject. Rönne enacts the scientific picture of the mind, applying it to *himself*—with the result that he loses the capacity to think *why* he is doing what he is doing. Hence the increasing incoherence of his actions and thoughts, as exemplified in his decontextualized surgical movements. Rönne's breakdown, in other words, stems from his identification with the stance of the scientific observer who treats thinking as the effect of

---

36. Müller-Freienfels, *Hauptrichtungen der gegenwärtigen Psychologie*, 9.

37. This is also why Ziehen can write *about* association in a style that is entirely unaffected *by* association. For the distinction between *vorhanden* and *zuhanden*, see Heidegger, *Being and Time*, parts 12 through 16.

"physiological excitations of the cortex," lived life as living matter.[38] Thus in his most apathetic moments, Rönne becomes a nonperson in the strict sense that, in observing his thoughts and feelings as if from without, as objectively *vorhanden* rather than lived, he no longer recognizes his experiences as *his*. This is why Benn's opening story culminates in Rönne's projecting the identification of his self onto the organic matter of brains. *Brains* narrates the reduction of human to bare life.

If Benn's opening story dramatizes the materialist reduction of mind to brain, the following novellas take aim at the idealist core of Ziehen's theory, his associative model of thought. Ziehen's theory continues to rely on key epistemological premises of nerve and brain physiology. Ziehen believes that the causal relations and associations among representations are sufficient to explain the coherence of both psychic life and meaning-making. The mind, for him, is essentially a natural physical system that, like all other such systems, follows identifiable causal laws. Benn's prose homes in on the core of this claim, the connection between association and concept formation. Ziehen recognizes that for word associations to produce meaningful thought, the metonymic slide of basic representations must be anchored in a vertical axis of condensation. He thus holds that general representations—concepts—are made out of basic representations that, according to mechanical laws of contiguity and similarity, crystallize into complex associative clusters, into

---

38. Hahn, *Gottfried Benn und das Wissen*, 160. This materialist dimension of Rönne's breakdown is most obvious in *Brains*. See, for instance, Rönne's reflections toward the end of this novella: "*Sie lebten in Gesetzen, die nicht von uns seien und ihr Schicksal sei uns so fremd wie das eines Flusses, auf dem wir fahren. Und dann ganz erloschen, den Blick schon in einer Nacht: um zwölf chemische Elemente handele es sich, die zusammengetreten wären nicht auf sein Geheiß, und die sich trennen würden, ohne ihn zu fragen* [They [brains] were ruled by laws not made by man, their fate was as foreign to us as that of a river on which we happen to be sailing. And then he gave way completely, his eyes already in darkness: it was a question of twelve chemical substances which had combined without awaiting his command and which would separate again without consulting him]" (*Gehirne*, GW 2:22). Hahn's claim that the Rönne novellas are exclusively shaped by Ziehen's idealist theory of association overlooks the importance of this materialist reductionism.

Allgemeinvorstellungen.[39] Since the condensation via similarity is only partial, Ziehen also describes complex concepts as "reductive representations" (*Reduktionsvorstellungen*).[40] Whether "rose," "god," "self," or "scientific theory," "they are simply the most frequent and for many associations the most obvious reductive representations."[41]

As Hahn was the first to show, Rönne's problem consists in his *inability* to generate, through the modality of association, these "most obvious reductive representations."[42] Rönne conducts himself in strict accordance with Ziehen's associative model, as attempting to derive ideas from sensations, meaningful associative complexes from stimuli. "To apprehend, he advised himself, to order and confirm what could be ignored, that was what was needed. To construct from the influx of things, the rustling of sounds, the flooding of lights, the quiet level that he signified [*die stille Ebene herzustellen, die er bedeutete*]" (*Die Reise*, GW 2:36). Yet these experiments invariably founder, and their underlying program—the observation of the emergence of meaning—disintegrates. In fact, Rönne's inability to synthesize isolates him from his surroundings and places him in sharp contrast to the comfortable generalizations of others, be they patients who good-heartedly reduce him to a "helper" or "good doctor" (*Gehirne*, GW 2:20), passersby who think of him as a "forgetful sir" (*Die Eroberung*, GW 2:27), or colleagues talking during lunch about avocados and "the dangers of tropical fruit [*das Gefahrvolle der Tropenfrucht*]" (*Die Reise*, GW 2:35).[43]

Building on Hahn's work, Andreas Huyssen has argued that Benn's stories employ Ziehen's theory of association in ways that satirize its positivist core.[44] I want to push this line of argument and suggest that Benn's parody unmasks the biopolitics of scientific reductionism. The slapstick discussion of Rönne's colleagues about

---

39. Ziehen, *Leitfaden*, 146.
40. Ziehen, *Physiologische Erkenntnistheorie*, 91.
41. Ibid., 91.
42. Hahn, *Gottfried Benn und das Wissen*, 172.
43. The formulation is the narrator's, or perhaps Rönne's, referring to his colleagues' absurd discussion about an avocado.
44. Huyssen, *Miniature Metropolis*, 94–95.

avocados and "the dangers of tropical fruit" ridicules not just bourgeois thought but also the presumed scientism of Ziehen's theory. In linking associations to the formation of clichés[45] and to stereotypical images of military or sexual conquest (*Die Eroberung*, GW 2:25–33; *Der Geburtstag*, GW 2:41–51), *Brains* points to the conventional character of both Ziehen's "typical" concepts and his theory of concepts. Where Ziehen thinks that concepts form according to mechanical laws that operate in the privacy of minds, Benn's caricature shows them to be publicly available scripts or schemata that codify thinking according to *social* norms. Rönne's identification as a "good doctor" by his patients, for instance, draws on and captures not only an array of perceptual clues but also a complex set of institutional realities, professional conventions, and social hierarchies. Ziehen's internalist approach to conceptualization—his exclusive focus on intrapsychic processes—cannot account for the normative dimension of this or other "typical" concepts, because it cannot take the dependence of meaning on intersubjectivity and public practices into consideration. Like the man in Wittgenstein's critique of private language who bangs on his chest to underscore that only he can feel his pain, Ziehen can only hit his own head to explain the source from which words and meanings derive their force.[46]

There is an institutional and political dimension to this reductionism. From the perspective of the novellas, contemporary psychology fails to grasp not only the complexity of the mind it observes but also the complexity of its own observations. Like the

---

45. Besides the conversation about avocados in *The Journey*, see various passages in *Conquest* (*Die Eroberung*, GW 2:27, 29) and, perhaps most obviously, the following reflection from *The Island* (*Die Insel*, GW 2:57): "*Immer blaut etwas bald herab, zum Beispiel der Kalbsbraten, den doch jeder kennt. Jäh tritt er an einem Stammtisch auf, und es ranken sich um ihn die Individualitäten. . . . Es wird branden der Streit und das Erschlaffen, der Angriff und die Versöhnung um den Kalbsbraten, den Entfesseler des Psychischen*" (Something is always coming down, for instance the roast veal, which everybody knows. Suddenly it appears at a *Stammtisch*, and the individualities creep around it. . . . The quarrel will surge and there will be the slackening, the attack and the conciliatory gesture around the roast veal, the unleasher of psychic activity).

46. Wittgenstein, PI §253.

words and thoughts the psychologist seeks to account for, the scientific observation of the mind is embedded in a complex set of practices, is part of a form of life—the life of the social system of science. Ziehen cannot but ignore this institutional dimension because his solipsistic model of meaning rests on the fantasy of an isolated extramundane observer, what Thomas Nagel has called "the view from nowhere."[47] But the view from nowhere comes from somewhere; it is the product of a particular technology of knowledge. As Lorraine Daston and Peter Galison have shown, the idea of "objectivity" gained scientific currency only in the second half of the nineteenth century—precisely when psychology established itself as an "exact" science. Unlike the naturalist "truth-to-nature" paradigm that preceded it, objectivity was defined in stark opposition to its shadowy other—subjectivity. "To be objective," Daston and Galison write, "is to aspire to knowledge that bears no trace of the knower—knowledge unmarked by prejudice or skill, fantasy or judgment, wishing or striving. Objectivity is blind sight, seeing without interference, interpretation, or intelligence."[48] Yet this idea of context-free observation was itself shaped by an array of historically specific objects, practices, institutions, and values: mechanical machines for image making, peer-reviewed journals that enforced norms of seeing and reasoning, the rise of the research institute with its disciplinary divisions and institutional hierarchies, and so forth. In short, "objectivity" is the result of a *systemic* operation—a form of observation that originates not in an extramundane subject but within the normative practices of a scientific system that in turn stands in dynamic exchange with the norms and practices of other social systems, such as the political and the economic.[49]

It is this broader political and economic dimension of science, only hinted at in the novellas, that Benn's later essays openly attack. The scientific reduction of reality to "the schema of cause and effect, the continuous thread of chemico-physical conditions" serves specific purposes; it is a "utility positivism [*Nützlichkeitspositivismus*]"

---

47. Nagel, *View from Nowhere*.
48. Daston and Galison, *Objectivity*, 17.
49. Ibid., 203.

that frames nature in view of its exploitation.[50] What makes this operation so pernicious, according to Benn, is that it hides its will-to-power under the guise of neutrality. The reduction of "life" to the status of a scientific fact veils the unequal treatment of actual living beings that it enables. Benn gives a concrete example of this logic in a 1928 review of a novel by Victor Margueritte dealing with abortion.[51] Allegedly an expression of the inviolability of life, Paragraph 218—the German law prohibiting abortion—in fact entails a value judgment about what *kinds* of life matter to the state. Paragraph 218 is a murderous machine that kills in the name of "life." On the one hand, the law draws on two ideologies that fetishize the idea of "life as such": the theologically inflected notion of the sanctity of life and the scientific notion of life as living matter.

> The state calls on its sciences when it legitimates this law. Theology and philology come to their help . . . as does biology. By nature and tendency normatively indifferent, rejecting any philosophy other than its own empirical one, which is no philosophy, as well as any theory of value, biology all of a sudden discovers its own idol: life itself, the protoplasm as such, the organic quantity for its own sake and *en masse*, *katexochen* and at all costs. (GW 3:74)

On the other hand, this reduction of life to a "bare life" shared by all heightens existing social inequalities. The presumably impartial notion of biological life underwrites concrete acts of political violence against marginalized members of society. About forty-four thousand women, most of them poor, Benn notes, die annually because of a policy that privileges the biological life of the fetus over the biographical life of the mother, living matter over lived experience:

---

50. Benn, "Bezugssysteme," GW 3:389; Benn, "Irrationalismus und moderne Medizin," GW 3:171.

51. The novel appeared in French as *Ton corps est à toi* in 1922 and in German as *Dein Körper gehört dir* in 1926. On Margueritte's novel and the theme of abortion in literature and legal discourse during the 1920s, see Kerstin Barndt, *Sentiment und Sachlichkeit. Der Roman der Neuen Frau in der Weimarer Republik* (Cologne: Böhlau, 2003), 70–86. For Benn's review, "Dein Körper gehört dir," see GW 3:71–75.

Poor circles provide the dead, workers and servants who run to abortionists who for 10 marks work with dirty syringes, or with soapy water pushed into the abdominal cavity, women who try out everything on themselves from petroleum to chalk, from hour-long tickling of the breasts to multiple daily intercourse to explode the uterus. 44,000 victims of living life, sacrificed to the germinating, unborn life: 44,000 victims of a law whose meaning is supposed to be the preservation of life. (GW 3:74)

Benn's short essay points to weaknesses in today's master theories of biopolitics. In contrast to Agamben, who focuses on law and sovereignty, Benn reminds us that the modern notion of bare life is bound up with the rise of the life sciences; and in contrast to Foucault, who brackets questions of value and inequality, Benn's text shows that the biopolitical regulation of populations rests on a moral economy that imparts *unequal* value to different groups and individuals: "to make live," Benn shows, is always also to "reject into death."[52] Abortion illustrates that the conceptual reduction of life to a purely biological phenomenon—the shift from lived life to living matter—is an act of violence. Spi, the protagonist of Margueritte's novel, is also the victim of late nineteenth-century science:

Her body was not hers, whom did it serve, certain wider views and institutions, certain influential organizations with currency, which she [Spi] does not even see: biology with its quantification lies [*Quantitätschwindel*]; sociology with its class forgeries [*Klassenfälschungen*]; historiography with its inconclusiveness; eugenics with its feuilleton; medicine with its biopsychosis [*Biopsychose*]. (GW 3:73)

For all their differences, Benn's book review and his Rönne novellas address themselves to the same question: What are the existential consequences of the scientific reduction of life to living matter? While the book review focuses on the politics of this process, the novellas explore its psychological dimension. In both cases, Benn's texts highlight the *violence* of scientific reductionism: the death of thousands of poor women in one case and the traumatic breakdown of self and world in the other. Far from a mere piece of organic

---

52. Foucault, *Histoire de la sexualité*, 180.

matter, the brain emerges from Benn's novella cycle as the corporeal remnant of mind depleted of reason, and of human existence deprived of meaning.

Writing

But this is only half the story, for Rönne's crisis opens up another side of Benn's project—the creation of a new form of writing. Benn's texts respond to the violence of the scientific-political *Entformung* of qualified life to living matter with a violent literary technique centered on the *Entformung* of received cultural forms of life. Creative destruction fundamentally changes what it negates, which loses its status as a binding form and instead becomes mere material, mere content, to be worked on and disfigured. It is in this broader context of an avant-garde aesthetics of destruction that we must situate Benn's emphasis on bodily dismemberment and psychological dissociation.[53] Rönne's crisis has a precise function. It provides a diegetic frame through which the text launches its poetic attack on dominant models of living matter and lived experience: the Kantian notion of the organism and the scientific conception of "bare life"; the idea of consciousness as the source of unified experience; the language of purpose, intention, and agency; but also more historically specific scripts and frames that structure early twentieth-century everyday life and align individual consciousness with public communication and the operations of institutions.

Given the intertwinement of the institution of art with these broader cognitive, linguistic, and social models, it is not surprising

---

53. On Benn's prose in the context of the avant-garde, see Peter-Uwe Hohendahl, "The Loss of Reality: Gottfried Benn's Early Prose," in *Modernity and Text*, ed. Andreas Huyssen and David Bathrick (New York: Columbia University Press, 1989), 81–94; and Baßler, *Deutsche Erzählprosa*, esp. 220–26, 232–40. Although he slightly exaggerates the continuity of Benn's early prose with Benn's own later self-interpretation in terms of "absolute prose," Baßler offers the most astute and fine-grained analysis of Benn's poetic techniques and of the German avant-garde more generally.

that the violence of Benn's texts is also directed against the conventions of literary realism. His experimental prose attacks the core of realist narrative—the illusion of a coherent and easily recognizable fictional world—from multiple angles. Especially in novellas such as *Birthday* and *The Journey*, plot and narrative structures disintegrate, often making it impossible to locate the events in time and space; rapid oscillations in voice and perspective undermine the reader's ability to clearly differentiate between narrator, implied author, and protagonist; the distinction between external and internal reality, the depiction of things and states of mind, is increasingly blurred; and, on the level of syntax and grammar, Benn's associative style explodes even basic elements of linguistic coherence, giving rise to a text that is opaque and at times unintelligible.

The notion of script, usefully employed by Moritz Baßler in his analysis of realist and modernist writing styles, can help us flesh out this latter point.[54] The power of realist narrative rests on the legibility of its fictional worlds, which in turn depends on the familiarity of the codes that structure the realist narrative. When Thomas Mann writes in *Buddenbrooks*, "*Drinnen im Eßsaale herrschte Aufbruch* (Inside, in the dining room, things were breaking up)," most readers will easily grasp this sentence and imagine the world it evokes because they are familiar with the architecture of bourgeois homes and the conventions of festive family dinners. To understand a text is to decode its implicit frames and scripts in a way that locates the narrated events in a broader story world, an interpretative act that is easier the more closely the implied cognitive models of the fictional world of the text resemble those structuring the reader's lifeworld. Rönne's breakdown—his dissociation from the frames and scripts of ordinary life—disrupts this smooth interplay between fiction and reader. Thus the more dislocated Rönne becomes—the more extreme his departure from ordinary scripts—the denser the experimental and poetic structure of the text. And in due course, the collapse of the embodied self releases the *entformte*

---

54. See Baßler, *Deutsche Erzählprosa*.

counterspeech of avant-garde writing. Just such a release occurs at the end of *Brains*:

> The doctor was recalled. . . . But Rönne said: Look, I held them [brains] in these hands of mine. . . . What is it about brains? I always wanted to soar up out of the ravine like a bird; now I live outside in the crystal. Please now, let me through, I am taking flight once more—I have been so weary—I am borne aloft by wings—with my sword of blue anemones—in a midday cataract of light—in ruins of the south—crumbling cloudbanks—dustings of the front—rovings of the temple. (GW 2:23)

What begins as a recognizable speech act in an identifiable setting turns, via Rönne's meditation on brains, into a still-intelligible metaphor, only to end in associative reveries that border on the incomprehensible. Through its dislodged protagonist, the text breaks away from its diegetic world, as if moving through a door into another space. Yet the subsequent novellas don't lose themselves in this other—hallucinatory—space. Instead, "each of these texts . . . will begin anew with an epic situation that is relatively comprehensible to the reader . . . only to then problematize this 'realistic' setting. Throughout, Rönne is under the observation of the narrator and, as a doctor, is also capable of competently observing himself."[55] Benn's prose, that is, stages a highly self-reflexive, continuous movement between frame and hallucination, bound and unbound text, ordinary script and its disarticulation. And it is through this repeated citation and contravention of codes, not through the renunciation of form as such, that the forms and institutions of life will give way to the improvisation of free-form poetics.

The novella *Birthday* enacts most emphatically the dynamics of association. Composed of four parts, it begins with an ordinary historical and biographical event. The novella opens with "realistic" details about the protagonist: Rönne's first name is Werff, he is on the brink of his thirtieth birthday, he was born in northern Germany, and he is a doctor who treats prostitutes. But already the form in which this information is communicated casts doubt on its status as secure narrative ground. Instead of firmly identifying the subject

---

55. Baßler, *Deutsche Erzählprosa*, 221.

through the voice of an external narrator, Rönne's name and pro-fession are given in the context of a self-address, as a subjective speech act whereby Rönne *summons* his identity as a distinct and enduring subject: "What was his first name: Werff? What was his whole name: Werff Rönne. What was he? Doctor in a whorehouse" (GW 2:41). The need for this self-invocation becomes palpable when Rönne calls up his "experiences":

> What had he experienced [*erlebt*]: love, poverty and X-ray tubes; rabbit hutches and recently a black dog in an open place, occupied with a big red organ swinging to and fro between its back legs, comforting and win-ning [*gewinnend*]; children stood round about, ladies' glances sought the animal, teenagers changed their position to see the action in profile. (GW 2:41)

Love, poverty, X-ray tubes—this is a chain of incongruous phenom-ena, an asyndetic list without recognizable paradigm. Run through an uncategorizable set of categories, Rönne's experience assumes a strongly dissociative character, casting doubt on the continuity of the subject to whom these things happen. This broken list of ab-stract concepts yields to a sexually charged scene that is at once concrete and opaque. Merging grim animality with poetic indirec-tion, Benn's punctured narrative refracts and intensifies the porno-graphic gaze of the depicted spectators absorbed in what we, as readers, are invited to imagine as the dog's phallus. Yet nothing about this scene is certain, and what might count as the "experi-ence" of the passage is both inside and outside its reported content, in the sexual act and its textual (de)composition, in Rönne's head and in ours.

This blurring of identifiable referents and viewpoints is intensi-fied in the next paragraph, which abruptly shifts scale, moving from the episodic micronarrative of the dog to a synoptic view of an en-tire life:

> How had he experienced all that: he had harvested barley from the fields, on wagons, and that was great: stooks and baskets and horse harness. Then a girl's body was full of water and had to be drained and sluiced. But above everything hovered a quiet, doubting As if: as if you were really space and stars.

And now? It would be a gray insignificant day when he was buried.
(GW 2:41)

Who is the subject of this experience, and what is being experienced?
On one level, the passage presents us with a highly compressed version of Rönne's biography, reduced to its main biological events
(conception, birth, death). The text thus seems to radically literal-
ize its title (*Birthday*), suggesting a view of human life that is squarely
anchored in what Canguilhem called "living matter," as opposed to
"lived life." Yet this reduction of life to a biological phenomenon is
counteracted by its impossible focalization. Who is the "he" witnessing these events? Rönne (as the sentence before the colon would
suggest), his father ("he had harvested"), or perhaps an unlocaliz-
able voice that assumes various pronouns and perspectives? Is experience anchored in an empirical subject, or does it exist only in
the suspended mode of an imagined "as if"?

Whatever the answer to this question, it seems clear that the paragraph's hypercompressed "biography" of Rönne's life parodies
what is generally considered to be the defining feature of narrative.
If literature strives "to grasp the life that may escape the person who
lives it and to rescue it not so much from death or oblivion as from
insignificance," in Didier Fassin's words,[56] then narratives ordinarily accomplish this task by organizing the temporality of human
life, structuring the discrete elements of experience and events
into "larger interpretive wholes, working out their play of meaning and significance."[57] That larger whole—the *narrated* life—
transfigures its episodic content: a rhetorical recasting that culminates at the end of the story, which retrospectively orders and makes
sense of the events leading up to it, providing metaphorical condensation and closure to the metonymic sequence preceding it. Benn's
reduction of Rönne's life to its fundamental biological events—
conception, birth, death—mocks this model of narrative transfigu-

---

56. Fassin, "True Life, Real Lives," 40.
57. Peter Brooks, *Reading for the Plot: Design and Intention in Narrative*
(New York: Vintage, 1984), 18.

ration, which finds perhaps its clearest expression in the realist novel's attempt to wrest meaning from *everyday* life.

Yet Benn does not relinquish the idea of rescuing life from insignificance. What counts in *Brains* as a life's truth will be found not in the totality of a biographical arc but in discrete and discontinuous moments. Existence, as the story's epigraph announces, will be episodic and irregular: "Sometimes an hour, you are there; the rest is what happens. / Sometimes the two floods rise up into a dream." Hence the second meaning of "birthday," diametrically opposed to its biological literalization. The emphatic moments of existence occur when the empirical subject dissolves and the "I" *happens*—is born—in a new language:

> Now it is time, he said to himself, for me to begin. In the distance a thunderstorm is rumbling, but *I* am happening [*aber* ich *geschehe*]. The cloud is bursting into May woods, but the night is *mine*. . . . But then he wanted to summon up something image-like, but failed. He found this in turn meaningful and pregnant with future import: maybe metaphor was already an attempt at evasion, a kind of vision and a want of fidelity. (GW 2:42)

The text speaks of "happenings," not "experiences" or "actions," which suggest the existence of an underlying subject, an authorial "I" distinct from its articulations. In fact, Benn's experimental rewriting of the "I" radically transforms received models of experience. His style releases experience from its traditional aesthetic and epistemological straitjackets, granting it a discontinuity and heterogeneity that explodes both the developmental bias of realist narrative and the identitarian notion of unified experience. Indeed, *Brains* pushes the discontinuity of consciousness even beyond the level granted it in modernist techniques, such as Joycean stream of consciousness. Marrying association with poetic compression, Benn puts Ziehen's theory into aesthetic overdrive:

> Through motionless blue mist, driven inland from the nearby sea, Rönne strode out the next morning on the way to his hospital.
> There from gardens the crocus threw itself at him, the candle of early Mass in poetic speech, and especially the yellow variety, the epitome of charm to Greeks and Romans, no wonder it transported him to the

kingdom of heavenly things. In pools of crocus juices the god bathed. A wreath of blossoms kept intoxication at bay. By the Mediterranean the fields of saffron: the tripartite scar; flat pans, horsehair sieves above fires, light and open.

He drove himself further: Arabic *za-fara*, Greek *kroké*. There was a Corvinus, king of Hungary, who had known how to avoid saffron stains when eating. The dye came nearer without any trouble, the spice, the flower meadow and the Alpine valley.

Still abandoned to the satisfaction of drawing such plentiful associations, he came across a glass shield bearing the words Maita Cigarettes, illuminated by a ray of sunlight. And now by way of Maita—Malta—beaches—shining—ferry—harbor—mussel eaters—depravities—came the bright chiming of a slight splintering, and Rönne tottered in a happiness. (GW 2:42–43)

This is not just the associative release of the "I" from the constraints of regimented experiences; it is the release of the "I" from its own regimentation *as* an "I." But this splintering of the self is very different from Rönne's collapse in the first novella. Whereas in *Brains* Rönne passively suffered a breakdown, in *Birthday* he actively induces, as in a psychological self-experiment, the dissolution of his rational self. While the former results in a state of painful stasis, experienced as the self's contraction to its biological substance, the latter gives rise to an ecstatic expansion, the joyful projection of the "I" onto the infinite horizontal axis of association.

Hence the lyrical, even hymnic, character of some of these lines. But if association here undergoes a kind of poetic intensification, the rhythms and forms that result clearly differ from traditional "poetry." Not only do Rönne's flights of imagination not cohere in an overarching form or crystallize in a higher, metaphorical meaning but the various discourses and codes that run through these associations undercut any transcendent movement. Where rapture is triggered by an advertisement for cigarettes, the wings of poetic imagination are, if not clipped, at least pulled back to earth. In fact, for all the poetic release of the "I," the associating subject remains sociologically recognizable. After all, who would *know* these Greek and Arabic words, the poetic meaning of yellow crocuses in Greek and Roman literature, or the story of Corvinus and his avoidance of saffron stains, if not a subject thoroughly shaped by a late nineteenth-century humanistic education, perhaps at a Wilhelminian *Gymnasium*? What makes Benn's prose so radical is not its liberation from existing language but the fragmentation and poetic collision of its codes.

Here we glimpse what might be called the dialectics of *Entformung*. For the *Entformte* to be an active unforming rather than a static form, the reality that is to be poetically transfigured must remain at least minimally recognizable. The text, in other words, works with and on preexisting historical material, which gets cut up and newly combined—disarticulated and rearticulated—in the avant-garde laboratory of the writer. To the extent that these pieces from the historical archive remain recognizable as elements of specific discourses, practices, or institutions, their *Entformung* also entails an attack on their normative force, an attack that often generates parodic effects. Conceived along these lines, Benn's experimental style clearly resembles the Dadaist montage that artists like Kurt Schwitters developed after World War I.[58] What distinguishes Benn's prose from montage, among other things, is the centrality of association and, through it, the emphasis on the temporal discontinuity of consciousness. In fact, emphatic existence will be episodic. Barely has Rönne begun to "[totter] in a happiness" before he is recalled to reality:

> But then he entered the hospital; an unyielding stare, an uncompromising will: to link the stimuli and sensations meeting him today to the store he already had, not leaving any out, tying in each one. He imagined a secret organization [*ein geheimer Aufbau*], something of armor [*Panzerung*] and eagle's flight, a kind of Napoleonic desire, such as the conquest of a hedge behind which he was resting, Werff Rönne, thirty years old, solidified [*gefestigt*], a doctor. (*Geburtstag*, GW 2:43; *Birthday*, 341–42; changes to the translation are mine)

If *Brains* depicts the breakdown of Rönne's professional identity, this passage figures the formation of this identity as the creation of an armored subjectivity. Association here functions not in the

---

58. On Schwitters, see Patrizia McBride, "The Game of Meaning: Collage, Montage, and Parody in Kurt Schwitters' Merz," *Modernism/Modernity* 14, no. 2 (2007): 249–72.

service of escaping the scripts of everyday life, as in Rönne's previous fantasies, but in the service of spelling them out and making their normative force visible. As if preparing his medical instruments, Rönne associatively assembles the components of the person that he must become in order to join the medical institution. Werff Rönne, thirty years old, doctor—by the end of this passage, these seemingly neutral facts of biographical existence come to look like a death mask, the public face of a reified self. And, once again, the language of the passage remains historically recognizable. The demand "to link the stimuli and sensations meeting him today to the store he already had" echoes Ziehen's description of memory, while the "secret organization" of hardened subjectivity evokes the nineteenth-century image of the scientific self, which, in Daston and Galison's words, had to learn to "turn its domineering will inward—to practice self-discipline, self-restraint, self-abnegation, self-annihilation, and a multitude of other techniques of self-imposed selflessness."[59] But whereas the scientific "will to willessness" masqueraded as the *absence* of subjectivity,[60] as pure neutrality and objectivity, Benn's prose exposes its hypersubjective and gendered character. A phallic vision of conquest and impenetrability, Rönne's dream of armored subjectivity reveals the phantasmic undercurrent that sustains the scientific concept of bare life.

It is perhaps unsurprising that the flights of association Rönne conjures up to *dissolve* his scientific self remain recognizably gendered. While conducting gynecological examinations of prostitutes, Rönne abandons himself to a series of associations that culminate in a fantasy addressed to an imagined group of women:

And you [1], ladies, we know each other! Permit me to create you [2], dress you [3] up in your essences, with your [4] impressions in me, undecayed is the leading organ [*unzerfallen ist das Leitorgan*]. It will be shown how it remembers, you [5] are already emerging.

You [6] address the part you love. You [7] look into its eye, give soul and breath.—You [8] have the scars between your thighs, an Arab bey; they must have been large wounds, torn by the sinful lip of Africa.—But

59. Daston and Galison, *Objectivity*, 203.
60. Ibid., 39.

you [10] sleep with the white Egyptian rat, its eyes are rose-red; you [11] sleep on your side, with the animal on your [12] hip. Its eyes are glassy and small like red caviar eggs. In the night they [*sie*] are attacked by hunger. Across the sleeping woman climbs the animal. It climbs quietly back onto the hip, snuffling and hesitating. Often you [13] wake up when the tail snakes across your [14] upper lip, cool and slender. (GW 2:43–44)

To be sure, this is a masculine, Western fantasy of Africa merged with a dream of poetic omnipotence, insofar as Rönne's associations both create and disarticulate the women they conjure up.[61] But to see in this passage only the expression of privilege and power is to overlook how Rönne's associations also disfigure the hegemonic discourses they draw on. Arab bey, white Egyptian rat, lip of Africa— the passage evokes the vagina as a wound carved by colonialism and oppression. Who sleeps with rats if not a homeless beggar who offers her body to men in order to scrape together the money she needs for survival? Rönne's fantasy, in other words, highlights the violence that sustains both colonial and sexual relations. Moreover, the associative movement of the text runs in a direction diametrically opposed to the scientific production of bare life. Instead of reducing lived experience to living matter, the woman's body in Benn's text is shaped by the symbolic and physical violence of her surroundings. The physiognomy of the whore is not a biological fact but the expression of her life at the margins of society. Her anatomy is biographical. There is no vagina as such, only the biography of a wound.

In sum, *Brains* depicts the subject as the meeting place of countless historically specific discourses, scripts, codes, and archives of knowledge. Rönne associates the way he does because, as a humanistically and scientifically educated German male doctor at the beginning of the twentieth century, he simply knows certain things—about colonialism, the romanticism of Arabia, the female body, the life of prostitutes, the sexual act, power, and so on. Because history has unfolded in a certain manner, and he is immersed in it

---

61. On Benn's primitivism and his use of colonial imagery and discourses, see Joshua Dittrich, "Recolonizing the Mind: Gottfried Benn's Primitivism," *New German Critique* 127 (2016): 37–58.

from a specific vantage point, he has the kinds of experiences that he does. The novelty of Rönne's associations—and of Benn's prose—lies not in its material but in how this material, hence experience, is configured. Ordinarily, human life unfolds in highly regimented and territorialized modules: doctor, erotic partner, reader of historical fiction, and the like. Each of these regions of experience has its own scripts, codes, and frames, which circumscribe and anchor specific identities, between which subjects move more or less competently. Hence the earlier passage about Rönne's armored subjectivity: walking into the hospital, he is, as it were, dressed by the institution, whose scripts furnish him with the appropriate "secret structure" of identity. But there is also the secret structure of "male conversational joviality," which his colleagues, talking about "the dangers of tropical fruit," effortlessly and unconsciously inhabit, enabling them to go home and, as husbands instead of scientists, talk to their wives about their "experience" at the pub. The relevant poetic operation of Benn's prose is not to do away with these bits of historically sedimented experience but to deterritorialize them through associative fragmentation and compression that creates a written "I" (a *Bewußtseinsschrift*) without a privileged identity. Thus the creation of the disformed begins in medias res, within established discourses. There is no "view from nowhere" in Benn, nor is there an epiphanic breakthrough to a hidden layer of meaning and existence, as in Proust, early Joyce, or the avant-garde texts of Benn's contemporary Carl Einstein. Yet Rönne's "birthday" takes place. The *Entformte*: that is Rönne's associative release from the regularized structures of experience, his poetic liberation from embodied subjectivity, and the happening of an "I" that exists, in the end, only on paper.

The Infinite Specificity of Life (Musil)

Midway through the first part of Robert Musil's great unfinished novel *The Man without Qualities*, the protagonist, Ulrich, is arrested and taken in for questioning, a procedure at once bureaucratic and metaphysical:

> He felt as though he had been sucked into a machine that was dismembering him into impersonal, general components before the question of his guilt or innocence came up at all. His name, the most intellectually meaningless yet most emotionally charged words in the language for him, meant nothing here. His works, which had secured his reputation in the scientific world, a world ordinarily of such solid standing, here did not exist. His face counted only as an aggregate of officially describable features—it seemed to him that he had never before pondered the fact that his eyes were gray eyes, one of the four officially recognized kinds of eyes, one pair among millions; his hair was blond, his build tall, his face oval, and his distinguishing marks none, although he had his own opinion on that point. His own feeling was that he was tall and broad-shouldered, with a chest curving like a filled sail on the mast, and joints fastening his

muscles like small links of steel whenever he was angry or fighting or when Bonadea was clinging to him; but that he was slender, fine-boned, dark, and as soft as a jellyfish floating in the water whenever he was reading a book that moved him or felt touched by a breath of that great homeless love whose presence in the world he had never been able to understand. Thus he could, even at such a moment as this, himself appreciate this statistical demystification of his person and feel inspired by the quantitative and descriptive procedures applied to him by the police apparatus as if it were a love poem invented by Satan. The most amazing thing about it was that the police could not only dismantle a man so that nothing was left of him, they could also put him together again, recognizably and unmistakably, out of the same worthless components. All this achievement takes is that something imponderable be added, which they call "suspicion." (MoE 159; MwQ 168–69, changes to the translation are mine)

Ulrich's "statistical demystification" proceeds in two steps. First, he is analytically dismantled, divided according to an array of categories: age, height, weight, eye color, and so on. This categorical decomposition, which produces in Ulrich the feeling "that nothing remains of him," is followed by an operation of *re*composition in which the various data about his person are brought together under the empty sign of his name. The individual—"Ulrich"—thus emerges as a simple constellation of calculable properties. The outcome of this twofold operation is the institutional construction of the subject as a distinct and identifiable person. For the police, Ulrich is now visible as a man with qualities, as a case "which at one and the same time constitutes an object for a branch of knowledge and a hold for a branch of power."[1]

But the very procedure that constitutes the individual as a subject of institutional knowledge also causes his disappearance as a person. Feeling, reflection, experience—everything that pertains to Ulrich's interior perspective, to the first-person perspective of being Ulrich—is excluded from the statistical composition. A "love poem invented by Satan," the statistical demystification is a truly devilish operation that succeeds in removing the soul of the individual by canceling it through a sort of mathematical spell, resolving the in-

---

1. Michel Foucault, *Discipline and Punish: The Birth of the Prison*, trans. Alan Sheridan (New York: Vintage Books, 1995), 91.

determinate unity of the living subject into a finite catalogue of measured qualities. But what kind of being are we left with after Satan has done his work? What happens to the notion of the individual once it has been voided of its interior perspective, reduced to the inventory of its external properties?

To gauge these questions, I want to return briefly to another scene of institutionalized subjectivity discussed earlier: Wilhelm's initiation into the Tower Society in Goethe's *Wilhelm Meister's Apprenticeship*. As in Musil's novel, Goethe's protagonist is confronted with an image of himself that is fashioned by an external agency. It is the gaze of institutional authority (the police in Musil, the Tower Society in Goethe) that fixes the subject and spells out the terms of its identity. Moreover, in both cases this articulation entails a conversion of first-person experience to third-person enactment: while the interior vicissitudes of Ulrich's life are replaced by the police's statistical inventory, those of Wilhelm's life are replaced by the aesthetic and social norms of the Tower's official biographical script. Both scenes therefore suggest that human life is externally mediated, that it is a product of *institutional* articulation, of aesthetic, epistemic, and political formation. In short, Ulrich, like Wilhelm, is taken apart and put back together (*zergliedert* and *zusammengesetzt*).

And yet our two protagonists experience their reassembly very differently. While Ulrich is fascinated by the statistical procedure without identifying with its product, Wilhelm takes the Tower's narrative of his life as revealing his inner truth. Interpellation works: the institutional address captures the subject by enticing it to identify with the gaze of sovereignty, to recognize itself in, indeed passionately embrace, the picture the authorities create of it. So why does interpellation work in the one case and fail in the other? The *statistical* nature of Ulrich's demystification suggests a first answer. If language in Kakania has lost its ability to subjectivize the world, this is because the very idea of what it means to know the individual has changed. Gone is the emphasis on narrative and temporality that still structured the ideological operations of the Tower Society; in fact, gone is the idea of an *individual form* so crucial to Goethe's conception of (human) life. While the statistical machine is driven by the same goal that motivated the Tower's biographical approach, the police make use of different details and employ a different style of knowing. Instead of ordering the particulars of individual life in narrative form, as parts of a singular biographical arc, it places them in relation to a mass of data gathered from a *large number of individuals*. Within the statistical framework, Ulrich's features—his particular weight, height, eye color, and so on—are relevant not in themselves but only in relation to a group or population of individuals "characterized by a mean and a standardized dispersion."[2] What matters is not Ulrich but his location on a statistical map, not what the details of his life and being might mean to him but their measurable distance from a numerical average. Hence the complete absence of a subjective and interior perspective from the statistical picture. Whereas the Tower's narrative machine draws on and edits a structuring activity that is native to selfhood and experience—narrative organization of experience being an integral aspect of language acquisition and the human being's entry into meaning[3]—the statistical machine imposes a radical break with the first-person perspective, producing a purely quantifiable individual, a subject that is nothing but a set of coordinates in a system of numbers and classes. For the police, "Ulrich" is not a person with a unique life history, but a data point on a Gaussian curve.

I want to read these two scenes as representing two distinct phases within an overarching history—the history of the biopolitical orchestration of the subject. On the one hand, the difference between Goethe and Musil—between narrative and statistical identification—is a difference of degree rather than kind. Ulrich's reduction to numbers makes transparent the political-epistemic logic that already informs Goethe's more holistic model: it shows that the power of biopolitical forces extends from the official institutions of sovereignty to the psycho-biological institutions of individual life.

---

2. Ian Hacking, "Statistical Language, Statistical Truth and Statistical Reason: The Self-Authentification of a Style of Scientific Reasoning," in *The Social Dimensions of Science*, ed. E. McMullin (Notre Dame, IN: University of Notre Dame Press, 1992), 130–57; 148.

3. Jerome Bruner, *Acts of Meaning: Four Lectures on Mind and Culture* (Cambridge, MA: Harvard University Press, 1993), 67–98.

Whether through narrative or statistics, it is a matter of capturing life in its most profound particularity—of recording its details and subjecting them to epistemic, and thus political, regulation. But on the other hand, the technologies informing Ulrich's statistical demystification represent a radically new phase in this political-epistemic constitution of human life. First, new forms of knowing put pressure on the notion of the individual, which is increasingly conceived in relation to a reality—the reality of "population"—that can only be grasped statistically. Second, the rise of the numerical individual goes hand in hand with a crisis of ideology, and, in particular, with a weakening of narrative's power to anthropomorphize relations of power and to organize the subject's experience of itself and the world. Third, the very idea of knowing the self becomes problematic. Ulrich's statistical demystification articulates Musil's more general suspicion that to conceive of the self in epistemic terms, as an object of knowledge, is to surrender individual life to its (bio)political exploitation.

Biopolitics of Numbers

Musil's Satan speaks a distinctly modern language. Statistics emerged as a branch of mathematics in the late seventeenth century, but its broader disciplinary takeoff occurred only in the mid-nineteenth century. As Ian Hacking has shown, the rise of statistics began with "an avalanche of printed numbers at the end of the Napoleonic era."[4] State bureaucracies in Prussia began to keep numerical track of human behavior, especially wrongdoings such as crime and suicide, which turned out to be surprisingly regular from year to year. This discovery in turn gave rise to more counting and more refined models of statistical reasoning, resulting in the erosion, over the course of the nineteenth century, of the theory of determinism.[5]

---

4. Ian Hacking, *The Taming of Chance* (Cambridge: Cambridge University Press, 1990), vii.

5. Michael Hampe, *Eine kleine Geschichte des Naturgesetzbegriffs* (Frankfurt am Main: Suhrkamp, 2007), 119–24.

Whereas the deterministic model of natural law conceived of nature as a machine that operated according to a set of timeless and universally valid instructions, statistical law measured temporally and spatially circumscribed patterns of regularity among groups of individuals or events. Statistical reasoning thus reached deep into the texture of the contingent, offering a language that was descriptive of the kinds of irregularities that make up the social and natural world.

In fact, the difference between the social and the natural became blurred. Alphonse Quetelet's 1835 *Sur l'homme et le dévelopment de ses facultés, ou essai de physique sociale* condensed the two into a single phrase. *Physique sociale*—the term was not meant metaphorically.[6] Quetelet sought to show that the social world was subject to the same regularities as the natural world. As Petra Gehring put it, "The laws of the social are laws in a physical sense: natural laws of a social body made up of humans."[7] This had nothing to do with organicism or even with traditional metaphors of sovereignty: Quetelet's social body had a different shape than the one represented on the frontispiece of Hobbes's *Leviathan*. In applying the tools of statistical analysis to the social world, Quetelet helped to create a new kind of object: the "population," which is neither the "people," nor the mere sum total of individuals inhabiting a territory, but a group of individuals characterized by a mean and standardized dispersion.[8] This may sound dry and technical, but the idea of a reality that could be represented only statistically carried enormous ontological significance. John Forrester captures the ontological shift admirably:

---

6.   Lambert Adolphe Jacques Quetelet, *A Treatise on Man and the Development of his Faculties*, ed. T. Smibert, trans. R. Knox (Cambridge: Cambridge University Press, 2013; orig. 1842). On Quetelet, see Alain Desrosières, *The Politics of Large Numbers: A History of Statistical Reasoning*, trans. Camille Naish (Cambridge, MA: Harvard University Press, 2002), 67–102 and Petra Gehring, "Adolpe Quetelet: Sprache und Wirklichkeitsmacht der Bevölkerungsstatistik," in *Das bunte Gewand der Theorie: Vierzehn Begegnungen mit philosophierenden Forschern*, ed. Astrid Schwarz, Alfred Nordmann (Munich: Karl Alber, 2009), 96–113.

7.   Gehring, "Adolpe Quetelet," 99.

8.   Hacking, "Statistical Language," 148.

The pre-Darwinian Aristotelian theory of the natural world is founded, it is argued, on the category of species, arranged hierarchically in order of generality. Darwin's fundamental break with the Aristotelian tradition was to see classes or species as constituted by populations of individuals which vary along an indefinite number of axes. Whether one is to attribute this revolution in biological (and social) thought to Darwin, or to his contemporary Quetelet (the inspiration for Maxwell's probabilistic model of matter and for Buckle's account of statistical laws in history), or for that matter to Francis Galton, founder of eugenics and pioneer of statistical studies of inheritances, the claim is that it is populations of independently varying individuals that constitute the base matter of the natural and human worlds. All categories or species are artificial, imprecise and ultimately misleading attempts to portray in the outmoded Aristotelian language of predication a fundamental dynamic reality which can be represented only statistically.[9]

For Aristotle, the individual can be perceived but not known. There can only be knowledge of the universal and necessary; what is contingent is beyond the purview of theoretical reason and thus, strictly speaking, unintelligible. Statistical reasoning reversed this picture by making the seemingly unintelligible the very stuff of its calculations. Instead of denying or avoiding contingency, it measured and counted it, extracting from the erratic and fickle play of chance a new kind of law: law as numerical average and empirical norm.

It is this openness to contingency that accounts for the impact of statistics on the modern discourse of "life" and the historically specific form of power Foucault has called "biopolitics." Quetelet's phrase, *physique sociale*, captures the connection aptly insofar as the erosion of the sharp distinction between biology and politics, nature and culture, and physical and political law lies at the conceptual center of biopolitics. Biopolitical technologies of power—public health policies, fingerprinting, eugenics, and so on—no longer treat nature as an immutable substrate over and against which politics must erect its own artificial order but as a constantly changing pool of forces whose dynamic instability power must calculate and study so as to bend it to its own purposes. They conceive of nature as "life," and of the living world,

---

9. John Forrester, "If *p*, Then What?," *History of the Human Sciences* 9, no. 3 (1996): 3.

whether natural or social, as constituted by a multitude of individuals whose shape and behavior varies along an indefinite number of axes. Statistics was vital in establishing biopolitical forms of power because it provided rational access to this multitudinous reality. In replacing the old idea of human nature with a model of normal people organized around laws of dispersion, it made space for indeterminacy while simultaneously providing a tool to measure and regulate it.

However, the irregular and singular enters statistical calculation only insofar as it arranges itself into larger patterns or aggregates. In terms of politics, this means that biopolitics is *population politics*: a form of power that targets not the singular body of the individual but the more abstract "body" of a population or group, a body that is not naturally given but rather is the product of the very measurements and statistical assessments brought to bear on it.[10] The emergence of this transpersonal species body has profound consequences for the notion of the individual, who finds himself reduced to a data point on a trend line or demoted, as in Quetelet's essentially metaphysical notion of the "average man," to a contingent expression of an underlying statistical reality. As John Forrester writes: "The rise of statistical thinking put in question the notion of the individual, through the very process of refining what it might mean to have knowledge of a *number of individuals*."[11]

"Ein vom Satan erfundenes Liebesgedicht"

This returns us to Ulrich's statistical demystification, which dramatizes Forrester's point. The statistical demystification, as we saw, evokes in our hero the feeling that he has been "sucked into a ma-

---

10.   The logic at work becomes very clear with the transpersonal body of contemporary biomedical sciences: the singular body as bearer of stuff (blood, organs) or information (genetic data) that acquires economic and political value as part of a collective pool, appropriately called "banks." See also Petra Gehring, *Was ist Biomacht? Vom zweifelhaften Mehrwert des Lebens* (Frankfurt am Main: Campus, 2006).

11.   Forrester, "If *p*, Then What?," 3.

chine that was dismembering him into impersonal, general components." But this is only part of Ulrich's reaction, for his reduction to impersonal formulas both terrifies *and* elates him. Again, here is the decisive passage:

> His own feeling was that he was tall and broad-shouldered, with a chest curving like a filled sail on the mast, and joints fastening his muscles like small links of steel whenever he was angry or fighting or when Bonadea was clinging to him; but that he was slender, fine-boned, dark, and as soft as a jellyfish floating in the water whenever he was reading a book that moved him or felt touched by a breath of that great homeless love whose presence in the world he had never been able to understand. *Thus* [*Darum*] he could, even at such a moment as this, himself appreciate this statistical demystification of his person and feel inspired by the quantitative and descriptive procedures applied to him by the police apparatus as if it were a love poem invented by Satan. The most amazing thing about it was that the police could not only dismantle a man so that nothing was left of him, they could also put him together again, recognizably and unmistakably, out of the same worthless components. All this achievement takes is that something imponderable be added, which they call "suspicion."

Darum (thus)? Why the inferential expression indicating Ulrich's admiration for the statistical apparatus when it cuts through his own highly poetic perception of himself? And why then think of this statistical dissection as a *poem*, and a *love* poem to boot? And Satan? Let us unpack this dense passage step by step. *Liebes*: like lovers absorbed in every detail of the body of their beloved, the gaze of the police lingers over the contingent features of Ulrich's being, transforming the investigation into a statistical meditation on him and only him. This invocation of love invests the organizing principle behind the police procedure with erotic intensity. *Suspicion, Satan*: The "suspicion" of the police, in other words, is represented as a sadistic desire, a libidinally charged interest, which attends to and gathers the minutiae of the individual's existence in the service of political and epistemic control. Framed as a "suspect," the subject becomes the object of a political desire whose goal is to capture the animating principle—the desire—of its target. Far from being a dead mechanical device, the statistical machinery of the police is fueled by the violent drive to devour the souls of its subjects—Satan precisely. *Poem*: "The poetic function," Roman Jacobson famously writes, "projects the principle of equivalence from the axis of selection into the axis of combination."[12] Though unfamiliar with Jacobson, Ulrich would certainly have subscribed to the above formulation. His aesthetic fascination with the statistical procedure lies precisely in the force of its interior principle, in the sense that this impersonal machine, rather than letting itself be determined by the particulars of this or that individual, translates them into its own condensed self-referential language, transforming a being of flesh and feeling into a combination of terms that together refer back to the statistical whole they constitute, a combinatory matrix. From the perspective of the machine, it does not matter who gets caught in this web. The individual, every individual, is only an occasion for the activity of symbolic condensation, and it is this activity, which follows its own ethereal and ghostly logic, that Ulrich deems beautiful and poetic.

My earlier claim about the failure of interpellation in Musil thus needs to be qualified. While Ulrich does not identify with his institutionally produced self, his excitement and aesthetic appreciation point to another type of identification. Ulrich recognizes himself in the statistical procedure itself, in the impersonality of its operations, whose precision and formalized character promise a state of absolute purity, of a body and a language of unadulterated soullessness. I will say more about this fascination with the mechanical, but for the moment I take Ulrich's ambivalent reaction—part fascination with the impersonal, part fear of losing his innermost being—as signposting the novel's stance with respect to earlier attempts at writing human life. First, Ulrich's fascination with the machine highlights Musil's antihumanism. Even more than for Benn, with whom he shared a background in scientific training, Ulrich's, and thus Musil's, identification with rationality informs the novel's ironic stance toward "culture" in general, and humanistic rhetoric in particular. Under the cold gaze of mathematical calculation, the traditional languages of emotion and subjectivity dissolve into (hot) air. "If you own a slide ruler," the narrator declares early on, "and someone

---

12. Jacobson, "The Function and Structure of Language," 78.

comes along with big statements or great emotions, you say: 'Just a moment, please—let's first work out the margin for error and the most probable values.'" (MoE 37). This skepticism toward the received languages of experience extends to humanism's main rhetorical device, narrative, which is shown to have lost much of its normative force. Consider Ulrich's famous reflection on narrative and life toward the end of book 1:

> And in one of those apparently random and abstract thoughts that so often assumed importance in his life, it struck him that when one is overburdened and dreams of simplifying one's life, the basic law of this life, the law one longs for, is nothing other than that of narrative order, the simple order that enables one to say: "First this happened and then that happened. . . ." It is the simple sequence of events in which the overwhelmingly manifold nature of things is represented in a unidimensional order, as a mathematician would say, stringing all that has occurred in space and time on a single thread, which calms us, that celebrated "thread of the story," which then seems to be the thread of life itself. . . . This is the trick the novel artificially turns to account . . . and this would be hard to understand if this eternally dependable epic device . . . this tried-and-true "foreshortening of the mind's perspective," were not already part and parcel of life itself. Most people are in relation to themselves storytellers. . . . And it now came to Ulrich that he had lost this elementary, narrative mode of thought to which private life still clings, even though everything in public life has already ceased to be narrative and no longer follows a thread, but instead spreads out as an infinitely interwoven surface. (MoE 650)

This is a long way from Goethe. Where Wilhelm praises narrative selection as a means to access the truth of his life, Ulrich debunks it as an anthropomorphizing distortion, a "foreshortening of the mind's perspective [*eine perspektivische Verkürzung des Verstandes*]," that imposes illusory unity onto a scramble of experience. And while Goethe extols narrative as the aesthetic birthplace of a properly social self, Musil pans it as a retreat into anachronistic privacy. Accordingly, Musil cuts the link between individual life and biographical form that had shaped the novelistic representation of the subject from Goethe to late realism. His novel's representation of human singularity does not take the form of a narrative arc; there is no developmental story, no emplotment of life as biographical history. Irony, polyphony, essayism—Musil's novel employs all of these antinarrative forms, which are born of the suspicion that narrative has become at best anachronistic, and at worst yet another tool used for the identification and political organization of human life. Hence also Ulrich's excitement about the mathematical destruction of traditional personhood. Far from being a merely negative event, the statistical demystification is seen as a revelation, a moment of truth, in that it dissolves the false humanistic and narrative model of individuality. In identifying the subject in quantitative terms, the police procedure reveals not only the outdatedness of the old system of classification but also the emptiness of the object this system was meant to capture.

This does not mean, however, that Musil embraces the poetry of the machine. The languages of science are problematic in that they fail to give form to the nothingness that is the (in)essential core of human individual life. While the slide ruler replaces the empty rhetoric of "big statements or great emotions" with the pure language of numbers, its translation of the individual into a calculable quality omits the incalculable quality of self-conscious life. As we saw in Ulrich's statistical demystification, the mathematical destruction of humanistic essence gives rise to the objectification of subjectivity, to something that can be counted, measured, and managed. Ulrich's inability to fully identify with his statistical measurement reflects his and the novel's recognition that the objectifying languages of science, for all their salutary critical power, fail to articulate a dimension of human life that is irreducible to social identification and conceptual classification. The frenzy of identification leaves behind a remainder, an unqualifiable (*ohne Eigenschaften*) and formless (*gestaltlos*)[13] nothing that is also the site of a defiant vitality. "There was something in him that had never wanted to remain anywhere,

---

13. On Musil's notion of *Gestaltlosigkeit*, see his "Theorem der menschlichen Gestaltlosigkeit," in PSE, 1353–400. See also Klaus Amann, "Robert Musil und das 'Theorem der menschlichen Gestaltlosigkeit,'" in *Medien, Technik, Wissenschaft. Wissensübertragung bei Robert Musil und in seiner Zeit*, ed. Ulrich Johannes Beil, Michael Gamper, and Karl Wagner (Zürich: Chronos, 2011), 237–54; and, above all, Florence Vatan, *Robert Musil et la question anthropologique* (Paris: Presses Universitaires de France, 2000), 57–71.

had groped its way along the walls; it was this slowly cooling, absurd drop 'I' that refused to give up its fire, its tiny glowing core [*dieser langsam erkaltende, lächerliche Tropfen Ich, der sein Feuer, den winzigen Glutkern nicht abgeben wollte*]" (MoE 153).

The utopian task of Musil's novel will be to find a new language for this "*winzigen Glutkern*," and thus a new form of life that enables the self to creatively reengage both itself and the objects of the world. Unlike in the traditional bildungsroman, Musil seeks the intensity of self in the liminality of the single moment, in transience rather than linearity. Individual life, or to use Musil's favorite term, the *soul*, is unqualifiable (*eigenschaftslos*), a mystic energy that both drives attempts at its (bio)political organization and is irreducible to it. The title of Musil's novel, then, carries a double meaning: to be a man without qualities is not only the symptom of a crisis of individuality brought about by the proliferation of attempts to qualify the human; being *eigenschaftslos* is also an achievement and utopian goal, the name for a new ethics and aesthetics of human life.

How (Not) to Begin a Novel

The road to the mystical language of *Eigenschaftslosigkeit* is a long one, and it passes through the novel's exploration of the mechanisms of averaging that have petrified human life. In fact, the opening chapter of the novel already highlights the consequences of normalization for the novel's own form. The novel begins by not beginning, and it fails to take off because the element that would be needed for such a beginning—a singular constellation, an infraction, an event worth telling about—dissolves under the pressures of the regularizing frames and languages enlisted to express it. Narrative presupposes, to use D. A. Miller's term, *narratability*. In *Narrative and Its Discontents*, Miller defines the narratable as "the instances of disequilibrium, suspense, and general insufficiency from which a given narrative appears to arise."[14] The opening chapter invokes

---

14. D. A. Miller, *Narrative and its Discontents: Problems of Closure in the Traditional Novel* (Princeton, NJ: Princeton University Press, 1981), ix.

the paradigm of the narratable event—an accident—only to narrate
its evaporation into institutional routine and statistical law:

> The victim was lifted onto a stretcher and both together were then slid
> into the ambulance. Men in a sort of uniform were attending to him,
> and the inside of the vehicle, or what one could see of it, looked as clean
> and tidy as a hospital ward. People dispersed almost as if justified in feel-
> ing that they had just witnessed something entirely lawful and orderly.
>
> "According to American statistics," the gentleman said, "one hundred
> ninety thousand people are killed there every year by cars and four hun-
> dred fifty thousand are injured." (MoE 11; MwQ 5)[15]

Narrative unfolds in the dialectic between familiarity and surprise,
law and deviation. Rooted in the ordinary, narrative explores moments of rupture and disequilibrium to make the familiar strange
again, while simultaneously domesticating unexpectedness, giving
it "a sheen of ordinariness."[16] No genre has exploited this dialectic
more thoroughly than the realist novel, which "revives the everyday with [a] sense of possibility,"[17] finding surprise and deviation
in the midst of ordinary life. But when a traffic accident comes to
be interpreted almost instantaneously as a "lawful and orderly
event," the dialectic of familiarity comes to a standstill, and narrative and traditional realism lose their symbolic power to word the
world. Musil makes this crisis of representation the explicit subject
matter of the novel's opening chapter. Instead of fictionalizing a possible reality, the opening chapter, appropriately entitled "From
Which, Remarkably Enough, Nothing Develops [*Woraus be-*

---

15. Note that the image of modern urban life that emerges from these sentences is diametrically opposed to the discourses on shock and trauma from the
works of Simmel, Freud, Benjamin, and others. From the observational perspective
of the novel, the problem with reality is not that it is too real but that it is not real
enough. To be more exact, reality has morphed into a formless world of communicative differences that no longer make a difference.

16. Jerome Bruner, *Making Stories: Law, Literature, Life* (Cambridge, MA:
Harvard University Press, 2003), 90. "The narrative gift," writes Jerome Bruner,
"seems to be our natural way of using language for characterizing those deviations
from the expected state of things that characterize living in a human culture" (85).

17. Franco Moretti, *The Bourgeois: Between Literature and History* (London: Verso, 2013), 75.

merkenswerter Weise nichts hervorgeht]," fictionalizes the disappearance of possibilities under descriptions. Here are the famous opening lines of the novel:

> A barometric low hung over the Atlantic. It moved eastward toward a high-pressure area over Russia without as yet showing any inclination to bypass this high in a northerly direction. The isotherms and isotheres were functioning as they should. The air temperature was appropriate relative to the annual mean temperature and to the aperiodic monthly fluctuations of the temperature. . . . In a word that characterizes the facts fairly accurately, even if it is a bit old-fashioned: It was a fine day in August 1913. (MoE 9; MwQ 3)

Isotherme, aperiodic variations, fine August day—this is, among other things, an ironic commentary on the literary conventions of nineteenth-century novels, the realistic pretenses of which are unmasked, together with the old-fashioned expression of "fine August day," as just that: a linguistic, and somewhat outdated, convention. Note how these lines both cite and undermine narrative conventions. Traditional novel openings articulate the world in which the story will take place, thus creating a backdrop of normalcy against which the singularity of character and story can emerge as surprise and deviation, as narratable events worth telling about. Musil's doubling of the opening frame—scientific weather report, realistic novel—undermines this narrative convention by making the activity of framing itself visible. Instead of observing events within a world, we are made to observe the linguistic mechanisms that produce that world and the events within it.

Again, as with the nonstory of the traffic accident, the text draws attention to the power of these linguistic frames to *absorb* contingency. Since Goethe and Howard at least, weather patterns have been a test case for the thinking of aesthetic and natural form.[18]

---

18. Joseph Vogl, "Wolkenbotschaft," in *Wolken*, ed. Lorenz Engell, Bernhard Siegert, and Joseph Vogl (Weimar: Verlag der Bauhaus-Universität, 2005), 69–79; Christian Begemann, "Wolken. Sprache. Goethe, Howard, die Wissenschaft und die Poesie," in *Die Gabe des Gedichts. Goethes Lyrik im Wechel der Töne*, ed. Gerhard Neumann and David Wellbery (Freiburg: Rombach, 2008), 225–34.

The opening lines of Musil's novel frame the weather as a thermo-dynamic system, thus highlighting the status of singularity—of eventfulness—at the heart of probabilistic knowledge.[19] Changes in weather were precisely the kind of phenomena that classical physics, with its emphasis on reversibility and causality, was unable to account for. The decisive innovation occurred with the statistical interpretation of the second law of thermodynamics in 1872, which posits "that natural processes are in principle irreversible and unrepeatable."[20] Statistical thermodynamics thus provided a conceptual framework to model contingent phenomena such as weather changes. It made it possible, in other words, to describe events and calculate surprises.

In citing the meteorological description, the novel turns the calculation of the event into the event itself. Placed at a referential remove, meteorology becomes visible as a system of representation that draws reality into its own operational code. The result is a kind of meteorological mantra, a scientific incantation that ostensibly tames contingency by enfolding it in a network of reassuring terms: isotherms, isotheres, aperiodic variation, and so on. Yet this incantation is problematic, as is highlighted by an ironic detail that Christian Kassung noted: the weather report refers to statistical averages typical of winter days, rather than to the "*schöner Augusttag des Jahres 1913*" of the novel's setting.[21] A simple mistake? Perhaps, but given Musil's scientific knowledge and the prominent position of the quote, it seems likely that more is at stake. The "mistake" draws attention to the allure of language as such, to the beauty of the hermetic surface, as opposed to the irregularity of what lies beneath. The point, in other words, is not that thermodynamic language is wrongly applied but that its pull toward formalization and interior coherence is so powerful as to seduce us into believing whatever it asserts. Specialized scientific language has become a kind of automatic writing, an autonomous system of notation that threat-

19. Christian Kassung, *EntropieGeschichten. Robert Musils "Der Mann ohne Eigenschaften" im Diskurs der modernen Physik* (Munich: Fink, 2001), 267–98.

20. Carl Friedrich von Weizsäcker, *Die Geschichte der Natur. Zwölf Vorlesungen*, 10.

21. Kassung, *EntropieGeschichten*, 285.

ens to overshadow the singularity of the world it claims to illuminate. "*Woraus bemerkenswerter Weise nichts hervorgeht.*"

Moreover, the formalized languages of science have become not
just autonomous but in fact incommensurable with the anthropocentric style of nineteenth-century narrative. The conjoining of scientific concepts with everyday speech throws into relief the gap that
separates them from each other *and* from the world they claim to
capture. Placed alongside the specialized language of science, the
style of nineteenth-century realism, this unique experiment in join-
ing descriptive detail with human experience, loses its expressive
power and appears hackneyed and outdated—an arsenal of conventions and commonplaces. But how, then, to regain the expressiveness of language, its power to word the infinite richness of inner
and outer life? What form must literary language take to give voice
to the singularity of events and human experience? Musil's opening chapter does not yet answer these questions, but the novel's
ironic (non)beginning marks out the problematic historical terrain—
Western Europe on the brink of World War I—within which the
literary recovery of reality must take place. And in that sense, the
novel does, after all, begin.

Averages

In figuring this state of affairs in thermodynamic and probabilistic
language, Musil associates the proliferation of differences with the
scientific discourse on entropy. Boltzmann's probabilistic expansion
of thermodynamics helped secure the second law of thermodynamics, which states that isolated systems irreversibly evolve toward
greater equilibrium and increased entropy. With time, then, the chaotic movement of particles will "*fluctuate* around the attractor
state,"[22] and "the most probable state available to a system is the
one in which the multitude of events taking place simultaneously

---

22.   Ilya Prigogine and Isabelle Stengers, *Order out of Chaos: Man's New Dia-*
logue with Nature (Toronto: Bantam Books, 1984), 124.

in the system *compensates for one another statistically.*"[23] A multitude of events that compensate for one another statistically; a reality that fluctuates around the average: Musil extends these mechanisms to the world of culture and morality.

> Look at it this way, Gerda. Suppose the moral sphere works exactly like the physical as described by the kinetic theory of gases; everything whirling around at random, each element doing what it will, but as soon as you work out rationally what is least likely to result from all this, that's precisely the result you get! Such correspondences, strange as they are, do exist. So suppose we also assume that there is a certain number of ideas circulating in our day, resulting in some average value that keeps shifting, very slowly and automatically—it's what we call progress, or the historical situation. What matters most about this, however, is that our personal, individual share in all this makes no difference; whether we individually move to the right or the left, whether we think and act on a high or low level, in an unpredictable or a calculated fashion, a new or an old style, does not affect this average case, which is all that God and the world care about. (MoE 491; MwQ 535; changes to the translation are mine)

The average value forms independently of the individual and his actions. "But little by little it enwraps him, and penetrates into his very brain."[24]

> "A young man with an active mind," Ulrich reflected ... "is constantly sending out ideas in every direction. But only those that find a resonance in his environment will be reflected back to him and consolidate, while all the other dispatches are scattered in space and lost!".... Ulrich thought that what he had just thought was not entirely without significance. For if, in the course of time, commonplace and impersonal ideas are automatically reinforced while unusual ideas fade away, so that almost everyone, with a mechanical certainty, is bound to become increasingly mediocre, this explains why, despite the thousandfold possibilities available to him, the average human being is in fact average. (MoE 116–17; MwQ 121)

---

23. Prigogine and Stengers, *Order out of Chaos*, 124.

24. Franco Moretti, *Modern Epic: The World-System from Goethe to García Márquez* (London: Verso, 1996), 70. Moretti situates Musil's discourse on average in the context of the development of the modern epic's encyclopedic aspirations to give symbolic form to the proliferation of discourse and knowledge in modernity.

From the weather report, to statistics on traffic accidents, to the averaging of human individuality: we have returned to Quetelet's theory of the average man, but with an important twist. Musil's novel extends the dynamics of normalization into the domain of morality, and thus into a region that lies beyond the ordinary application of statistical measurement, whose social use was closely tied to explicit governmental policy.[25] Put schematically, whereas Quetelet is concerned with the political regulation of populations, Musil is interested in cultural dynamics that bear on the ethics and aesthetics of self-formation.

To gauge the full scale of modernity's regulation of human life, then, we must go beyond Quetelet's "realism of macrosocial objects"[26] and engage another—aesthetic—kind of realism. Musil's reflections on the dialectic of self-fashioning and social averaging bear on the core symbolic problem of the nineteenth-century realist novel: its attempt to reconcile the new values of self-determination and individual freedom with society's demand for regularity and order. The realist novel "solves" this problem by representing the unfolding of individual life in terms of the discovery, enjoyment, and eventual stabilization of this life's *possibilities*. In doing so, the novel projects and indeed extends the regulatory thrust of population politics into the microscopic domain of self-care. Goethe's *Wilhelm Meister*, the paradigm of the realist bildungsroman, gave us an inkling of the genre's symbolic politics. If for Goethe the regulation of possibilities is still tied to a discernible authority, three-quarters of a century later, in George Eliot's *Middlemarch*, the averaging of life—its oscillation around a socially accepted range of possibilities— seems to occur entirely on its own.[27] Lydgate, the young doctor who arrives in Middlemarch filled with "professional enthusiasm" and eager to "shape [his own] deeds and alter the world a little bit,"

---

25. Desrosières, *The Politics of Large Numbers*, 147–209. Desrosières also points out that the connection between statistics and governmental policy was embodied in the person of Quetelet, who organized the census and built up a statistical bureau (74).

26. Desrosières, *The Politics of Large Numbers*, 68.

27. On the increasing power of the average in realist literature, see Moretti, *The Bourgeois*, 76–79.

becomes within the course of a few years what he dreaded most, an ordinary man "shapen after the average and fit to be packed by the gross."[28] Before he knows it, and without any extraordinary event having occurred, Lydgate's creativity has atrophied and his "earlier self walked like a ghost in its old home and made the furniture ghastly."[29] "Nothing in the world is more subtle than the process of their gradual change! In the beginning they inhaled it unknowingly; you and I must have sent some of our breath toward infecting them, when we uttered our conforming falsities or drew our silly conclusions: or perhaps it came with the vibration of a woman's glance."[30]

Musil's Ulrich is heir to Eliot's Lydgate. Both authors locate the threat of psychic and moral deadness in a maze of minuscule and ordinary events. "Conforming falsities, silly conclusions, a woman's glance" (Eliot); "commonplace and impersonal ideas" (Musil): these are the things that cool down Lydgate's youthful "ardour" and derail Musil's "young man with an active mind." Eliot and Musil throw into relief a type of impersonal force that operates alongside the more official mechanisms of biopolitical regulation. It is a force without author or discernible source, a power that works, not by regulating behavior or disciplining bodies, but by hollowing out the media of articulation—words, ideas, perceptions—through which the self gains access to itself and constitutes itself as a subject. Commonplace and impersonal ideas throttle human life by blunting its creativity, its capacity to feel, think, and say what is not yet the case. And in a world in which the scope of human potentiality is circumscribed by clichés, individual freedom and social norms reinforce each other, since "it will always be the same possibilities, in sum or on average, that go on repeating themselves" (MoE 17; MwQ 12).

---

28. George Eliot, *Middlemarch*, ed. Bert G. Hornback (New York: Norton, 2000), 93.
29. Ibid.
30. Ibid.

Specialization, Dilettantism, Stupidity

The rise of the cliché is part of a dialectic process whose other pole is the increase in scientific specialization, whose formalized language we have already encountered in the novel's opening and in Ulrich's statistical demystification. The differentiation of knowledge is fueled by a fundamental trope of scientific rationality—the drawing of distinctions.[31] Driven by the demand for precision, scientific knowledge is ceaseless since every concept or distinction it generates is the starting point for yet another, further act of differentiation and discrimination. Scientific thinking thus proceeds through a series of conceptual cuts, where every cut demarcates a form that in turn becomes the object of another distinguishing cut, giving rise to a dynamic process that moves toward ever smaller and finer distinctions. Once set into motion, the relentlessly particularizing work of the precisionist turns into "dust" [*Staub*] all that is solid, dissolving every identity (MoE 254). Reality thus comes to appear as a "dreadful blend of acuity in matters of detail and indifference toward the whole [*ungeheuerliche Mischung von Schärfe im Einzelnen und Gleichgültigkeit im Ganzen*]" (MoE 40; MwQ 36)—that is, as a profusion of facts that lies beyond the grasp of any individual.[32] This endless differentiation of knowledge highlights one of the central concerns of Musil's thinking, which we might call the infinite specificity of the singular.

> "Have you ever seen a dog?" [Ulrich] asked. "You only think you have. What you see is only something you feel more or less justified in regarding a dog. It isn't a dog in every respect, and always has some personal quality no other dog has. . . . Has a tile ever fallen off the roof in precise

---

31. For a more detailed account of this dynamic, see my "Ein Theater des Infinitesimalen: Musil und die Grenzen der Genauigkeit," in *Dilettantismus als Wissenschaft*, ed. Safia Azzouni and Uwe Wirth (Berlin: Kulturverlag Kadmos, 2010), 65–83.

32. Note that Musil's account differs from the Foucaultian model in that it grants greater autonomy to the dynamic of scientific innovation, suggesting that it is the self-differentiation of the social system of science that puts pressure on the political system, rather than the other way around.

accord with the law of falling bodies? Never. Even in the lab, things never behave just as they should. They diverge from the ideal course in all possible directions, while we keep up a fiction that this is to be blamed on our faulty execution of the experiment, and that somewhere midway a perfect result is obtainable." (MoE 572; MwQ 624)

Neither natural law nor experiment can close the "margins for error [*Fehlergrenzen*]" (MoE 37) that separate them from their ideal of absolute precision. Absolute precision is an impossibility: a fiction. Yet it is precisely this fiction that sustains and feeds scientific activity. It is *because* scientific precision keeps falling short of its own ideal that it generates ever finer distinctions, thus driving the machinery of specialization.

The above quote highlights a major reason for Ulrich's ultimate dissatisfaction with science: the commitment to generality and law prevents science from fully grasping the infinite particularity of the world of experience. Ulrich's (and Musil's) point seems to be that scientific thinking is driven by competing goals—precision and generality—and that the drive to precision must be disentangled from its intertwinement with law and regularity. Musil's critique here is not only epistemological but political. As we have seen in Ulrich's statistical demystification, the scientific interplay of precision and generality provides the ideal *dispositif* for a biopolitical machinery that seeks to convert the indeterminate unity of the living subject into a finite catalogue of measured qualities. If science, in the police interrogation, works so perfectly in the service of power, this is because both frame the singular in terms of a sovereign will to know and control that threatens to cancel out its specificity. Like the dog that is only seen *as* a dog, the infinite specificity of Ulrich's experience—his "soul"—is on the brink of disappearing under the pressure of descriptive annihilation.

From this perspective, Ulrich's statistical demystification represents only the most blatant example of a drama of descriptive annihilation that permeates the modern world of fin de siécle Vienna. Satan is everywhere, speaking in many tongues. Just as the police subdivides Ulrich into a distinct set of categories, so every institution in the novel segments the world according to its own selective code. In every domain of society, reality is reconstituted according to abstract categories and general types. This network of functional practices is what Musil calls "the world of qualities without man": a system of systems that, through the assignment of specific functions and roles, describes, differentiates, locates, and identifies individuals and objects in countless institutional and discursive grids. In fact, the reach of these grids is not limited to institutions in the narrow sense but extends into all aspects of social and personal life. Every act of self-representation, be it in the public sphere of communicative expression or in the most private of thoughts, passes the subject through a categorical machinery of symbols that operates in the service of the same infinitesimal taxonomy of types as the police bureaucracy. In such a fully homogenized society, even Ulrich's thinking cannot escape the force of normalization, and is experienced as nothing more than the meeting place of ready-made distinctions: "But the man without qualities was now thinking. One may draw the conclusion from this that it was, at least in part, not a personal affair. But then what is it? World in, and world out; aspects of world falling into place inside a head [*Der Mann ohne Eigenschaften dachte aber nun einmal nach. Man ziehe den Schluß daraus, daß dies wenigstens zum Teil keine persönliche Angelegenheit war. Was ist es dann? Aus-und eingehende Welt; Seiten der Welt, die sich in einem Kopf zusammenbilden*]" (MoE 112; MwQ 116).

We are now in a position to return to the problem of the commonplace, for the commonplace is both a reaction against and a force contributing to the drama of descriptive annihilation. On the one hand, the commonplace is a defensive reaction against the differentiation of knowledge. As such it has become a cultural movement, a dilettante search for transcendence that has spread in rebellion against the language of specialists. "The period of turning away from specialists had already begun" (MoE 111), and under the new reign of the "unfocused type of person" (MoE 269), the critique of scientific rationality and the search for soul have become a topic of universal chatter. Thus, on the other hand, precisely by plunging the quest for a new language and life into the medium of vague and empty formulas, the commonplace intensifies the inexpressiveness of the self it sought to remedy. Musil's treatment of the commonplace and his analysis of the differentiation of knowledge and languages are intimately intertwined. Numbers and clichés, statistical and communicative averaging, precision and vagueness, are two poles of a single process that give rise to a world of qualities without man.

Throughout his career, Musil repeatedly returned to the problem of the commonplace, dedicating to it, as late as 1937, a long lecture entitled "On Stupidity." Stupidity is not so much a cognitive problem as the symptom of an imbalance between feeling and thinking. "To Musil," writes J. M. Coetzee, "the most stubborn and retrogressive feature of German culture . . . was its tendency to compartmentalize intellect from feeling, to favor an unreflective stupidity of the emotions."[33] Musil saw this split "among the scientists with whom he worked: men of intellect living coarse emotional lives."[34] But he was even more worried about a type of stupidity that masqueraded as culture. Especially in its elevated guise, as a "disease of Bildung [*Bildungskrankheit*]" (PSE 1287),[35] stupidity is a "mysterious malady of the time [*geheimnisvolle Zeitkrankheit*]" (MoE 56) that undermines the search for a proper ethical and political life at its very basis, in the self's reflective relation to itself. It is therefore the "most lethal illness; a dangerous disease of the mind that endangers life itself" (PSE 1288).

Stupid communication is diametrically opposed to the meticulous semantics of scientific speech. Whereas the proliferation of scientific communication rests on the extensional force of its concepts, dilettantish communication derives its power from its ability to connote everything (intension) without saying anything specific (extension).

---

33. J. M. Coetzee, *Stranger Shores: Literary Essays* (New York: Penguin, 2002), 93–94.

34. Coetzee, *Stranger Shores*, 93–94.

35. Robert Musil, "Über die Dummheit," in PSE, 1270–93; Robert Musil, "On Stupidity," in PS. On Musil's notion of stupidity, see also Avital Ronell, *Stupidity* (Champaign: University of Illinois Press, 2003), 61–94; Inka Mülder-Bach, *Robert Musil, Der Mann Ohne Eigenschaften. Ein Versuch über den Roman* (Munich: Carl Hanser Verlag, 2013), 135–42; and Florence Vatan, "Flaubert, Musil und der Reiz der Dummheit," in *Robert Musil–Ironie, Satire, falsche Gefühle*, ed. Kevin Mulligan and Armin Westerhoff (Paderborn: Mentis, 2009), 149–71.

Stupid communication replaces "a specific action with a voluminous one [*ein gezieltes Handeln durch ein Voluminöses*]" (PSE 1283), extension with intension. Its defining features are therefore not fixity and rigidity but flexibility and fluidity. "There is absolutely no significant idea stupidity would not know how to apply; stupidity is mobile in every direction and can dress up in all the clothes of truth" (PSE 1288). Hence the expansive force of stupid communication.[36] It is "precisely their [clichés'] lack of precision and factuality that enables them to suppress, when they are used, whole realms of words that are more accurate, more relevant, and more correct" (PSE 1282). Where nothing precise is being stated, everybody may at any time add to what has been said.

Musil's description of stupidity as an imbalance between intellect and feeling places it in an illustrious tradition. Stupid communication is not only opposed to the semantics of specialized discourse; it also represents a perversion of what Kant had identified as the political promise of aesthetic communication. The open-endedness of aesthetic conversation, in which speakers, articulating their pleasurable feelings about the beautiful in a universal voice that *calls for* the agreement of others without being able to *demand* consent, provided a model for a properly democratic mode of conversation, and thus of a community built on, rather than excluding, the diverse sensibilities and voices of its citizens. Art and aesthetic communication offer a medium that connects self and society, converting the subject's seemingly private sensibilities and pleasure, occasioned by the reciprocal enlivening of its mental faculties, into a force that animates communal and political life. Stupidity inverts the democratizing direction of aesthetic communication. Instead of animating the faculties, the clichés of stupidity petrify both thinking and sensibility; and instead of extending the scope and depth of judgment, they give rise to aimless chatter. And yet, stupid communication can pervert aesthetic communication

---

36. This accounts for Musil's tendency to connect the dyanmics of stupidity with mass panics. On Musil's representation of the masses, see Stefan Jonsson, *Crowds and Democracy: The Idea and Image of the Masses from Revolution to Fascism* (New York: Columbia University Press, 2013), 166–74.

precisely because it draws on and mimics it. This is not only because stupid communication, like its aesthetic counterpart, admits, and in fact appeals to, everybody but also because it voices its idiocies under the cover of what Kant had identified as the core of aesthetic judgment: conceptual indeterminacy. It is the emptiness of elevated stupid speech (the absence of an *object* of cognition) that creates its unverifiable and suggestive aura. Hence Musil's description of stupidity as a *Bildungskrankheit* and its association with the *Bildungsbürgertum*, the nineteenth-century heir to the Idealist program of aesthetic education. Stupidity, for Musil, is not a psychological phenomenon but a symptom of the decay and bankruptcy of high culture.[37]

Nowhere is the bankruptcy of culture and its intersection with scientific and political developments more apparent than in the novel's central dilettantish action: the so-called Parallel Campaign, the goal of which is to unify the many nations, peoples, and parties of Kakanian society in a celebration of the seventieth anniversary of Emperor Franz Joseph's rule.

Against the relentless production of specialized knowledge, the "great patriotic campaign [*große vaterländische Aktion*]," composed of leaders from science, culture, politics, industry, and the military, initiates the search for a "sublime symbol" [*erhabenen Symbol*] which shall express, as a "splendorous life affirmation of Austria [*glanzvolle Lebenskundgebung Österreichs*]," the Empire's innermost being (MoE 88). The longing for synthesis and unity beyond fragmentation aims at a transcendental meaning, at a deep mythical signified beneath the proliferation of dialects, scientific facts, and ethnic pluralism of the Habsburg Empire. Yet the very attempt at synopsis sets into motion a machinery whose manic productions—an avalanche of reports, recommendations, applications, and committees—merely intensifies the feeling of fragmentation by extending its dynamic beyond the differentiation of knowledge into

---

37. See PSE 1284, where Musil connects the rise of stupidity to the destruction of the culture of German Idealism *by the bourgeois friends of that culture.* Rather than facing up to this process and seeking to articulate new modes of expression and thought, the *Bildungsbürgertum* harks back to the old phrases, which in their mouths become pseudoeducated clichés and inanities.

the domain of cultural identity. If the scientific language of precision disintegrates its objects into "dust," the empty rhetoric of unity deprives words of their meaning and so hollows out their socially binding force.

This dialectic of knowledge and dilettantism is captured beautifully in the most comedic chapter of Musil's novel, in which General Stumm von Bordwehr, a member of the Parallel Campaign, visits the state library in Vienna. Frustrated with the Campaign's interminable production of meetings and competing proposals, Stumm decides to attack the repository of all knowledge—the library—to locate the organizing idea that lies beneath the maze of heterogeneous values and interests that make up early twentieth-century Austrian society. As a military man, Stumm expects the world of culture and knowledge to be organized along the same principle of hierarchical differentiation that structures the army: the supreme idea, Stumm imagines, must be a kind of conceptual commander in chief; it must be the "highest ranking among all ideas [*ranghöchste unter allen Ideen*] (MoE 371)." Stumm's hopes are dashed when the main librarian takes him to the catalogue room, where it begins to dawn on him that the production of knowledge generates a nonsynthesizable complexity that exceeds the grasp of any individual. "'General,' [the librarian] said, 'if you want to know how I know about every book here, I can tell you: because I never read one of them. . . . Anyone who lets himself go and starts reading a book is lost as a librarian. . . . He will never be able to survey all of them'" (MoE 462). Stumm thus learns, as David Wellbery puts it, that "knowledge or science [*Wissenschaft*] might be a subsystem of society . . . but it is not for that fact an *organization*" in the hierarchical sense that Stumm is accustomed to from the military. There is no sovereign in the world of knowledge.[38]

Stumm's and the Campaign's efforts to capture the essence of empire end up revealing the very absence of the substance of meaning they aim to celebrate. Generating countless proposals and endless

---

38. David Wellbery, "The General Enters the Library: A Note on Disciplines and Complexity," in "The Fate of Disciplines," ed. James Chandler and Arnold I. Davidson, special issue, *Critical Inquiry* 35, no. 4 (Summer 2009): 984.

discussions, the encyclopedic stupidity of the Campaign, a kind of Bouvard and Pecuchet writ large, unfolds the literal truth of the claim the narrator makes earlier in the book that "the Emperor and King of Kakania was a legendary old gentleman" (MoE 83), the meaning of which now becomes clear: the image of a patriarchal Sovereign is an archaic fable that has lost credibility and currency. The Campaign thus reveals a fundamental problem of Kakanian society: the discrepancy between Kakania's received symbolism of power and its production of epistemic, economic, and linguistic distinctions. Kakania is a society that is no longer capable of representing itself to itself; it is a world of symbolic differences that no longer make a difference. Framed in these terms, Stumm's encounter with the card catalogue can be read as a parable about the dialectic of symbolization and the real in Musil's novel. The episode makes visible the symbolic hole at the center of Kakanian society; but it also shows that this hole—this unrepresentable real—is itself the product of new forms of knowing and ordering, a fissure carved out by the very languages designed to fill it. Hence the urgency and despair that permeates life in Kakania. Kakania is a society whose manic production of languages, rituals, and ideas is driven by an inexorable and ultimately violent feeling of hollowness. "Somehow or other," Stumm muses in front of the card catalogue, "order turns into a desire for homicide [*Irgendwie geht Ordnung in das Bedürfnis nach Totschlag über*]" (MoE 465).

This allows us to specify the lethal danger stupidity, in its elevated form, poses to society. In its ceaseless attempts to plug the symbolic hole at the heart of society, stupidity's grandiose pronouncements delay its acknowledgment and block its proper analysis. In the figure of Ulrich's great opponent, Paul Arnheim, an industrial magnate who writes famous quasi-philosophical books and quotes obscure literary texts, this danger finds its most eloquent embodiment. Not that Arnheim is stupid in the ordinary sense of the term; besides being a brilliant steward of his own economic empire, he speaks five languages and has an impressive breadth of knowledge in the areas of philosophy, literature, music, science, politics, and sports. But that is precisely the point. Combining, in his person, the most diverse strands of German-speaking culture—

"What all Others are separately, Arnheim is in one Person [*Was alle getrennt sind, ist Arnheim in einer Person*]" (MoE 188)—Arnheim's speeches hold out the promise of fullness, a release from the unbearable feeling of hollowness that afflicts Kakanian culture. "In Arnheim's discourse," David Wellbery writes, "items drawn from incommensurable disciplinary vocabularies are interwoven in a metadiscourse that uses its terms in a systematically nonserious way. This is not in order to deceive or mislead but rather to create an unverifiable—infinitely suggestive—aura."[39]

But stupidity does not always proceed through recourse to an already established semantic. It can also work through a sort of evacuating mimicry. Toward the end of the first book, Ulrich hears his cousin Diotima, the queen of official culture, echo his own mystic language:

> "When I speak of the emerging from the shadows, I mean from the unreality, from that flickering concealment in which we sometimes sense the presence of the unusual. It is spread out like a net that torments us because it will neither hold us nor let us go. Don't you think that there have been times when it was otherwise? When the inner life was a stronger presence, when there were individuals who walked in the light or, as people used to say, walked in holiness, and miracles could happen in reality because they *are* an ever-present form of another reality, and nothing else!"
>
> Diotima surprised herself by the firmness with which it seemed possible to say this sort of thing, without any special elation, as though she were walking on solid ground. Ulrich felt secretly infuriated, but actually he was deeply shocked. Has it come to this, he thought, that this giant hen can talk the way I do? (MoE 566; MwQ 618, Musil's emphasis)

Diotima's speech, which blocks every movement of thought by mimicking its communicative side, helps us understand why stupidity, according to Musil, is the "most lethal illness; a dangerous disease of the mind that endangers life itself" (PSE 1288). Between Diotima's and Ulrich's talk, there is a consonance of words but not of meaning. Diotima speaks Ulrich's language, but she does not inhabit it the way Ulrich does. Ulrich speaks in order to trigger new verbal,

---

39. Wellbery, "The General Enters the Library," 986.

emotional, and intellectual processes; his metaphors are instruments of self-orientation, forms of indirection and incitement designed to restore to words their lost subjective resonance. In Diotima's speech Ulrich's search for his voice returns to him as a meaningless verbal shell that exists independently of him. He hears the echo of his own voice, but deprived of the impulse that enlivens this voice and makes it expressive of his life. Ulrich consequently experiences Diotima's words as a denuding force that strips him of all affective and cognitive life. What Ulrich experiences through Diotima's speech, we might say, is the loss of his own loss, which thus becomes absolute, making him a homeless ghost in a cabinet devoid of objects:

> But one could also say that his solitude—a condition that was present within him as well as around him, binding both his worlds—it could be said, and he felt it himself, that this solitude was growing greater or denser all the time. It flowed through the walls, flooded the city, then, without actually expanding, inundated the world. "What world?" he thought. "There is none!" (MoE 664; MwQ 724)

Skepticism

Musil's account of the "unreflective stupidity of emotions" highlights the indissoluble bond that links words, intellect, and feelings. It should therefore not come as a surprise that the political and communicative crisis the novel traces is also a libidinal one. This is nowhere more visible than in the figure of the psychotic sex murderer Moosbrugger, who may be thought of as Kakania's penumbral double. If the mania of communication in Kakania is built on the repression of desire, Moosbrugger's psychotic episodes, characterized by obscene hallucinatory provocations, represent the return of repressed desire in reality.

> This was clearly madness, and just as clearly it was no more than a distorted connection of our own elements of being. Cracked and obscure it was; but it somehow occurred to Ulrich that if mankind could dream as a whole, that dream would be Moosbrugger. (MoE 76)

A sovereign of the Kakanian unconscious, Moosbrugger is the living symbol that the Parallel Campaign has been looking for. But whereas the Campaign sought a supreme Idea that would synthesize the totality of Kakania's culture, Moosbrugger's fascination for his countrymen rests on his externality to this culture, on his *transgression* of all established language games. Moreover, in his psychotic episodes, Moosbrugger attacks not only all consensually established forms of meaning but the apparatus of reflection itself, the distance separating the subject of reflection from its object. In such moments, referential and more general symbolic relations collapse under the unsublimated force of drive energy, which destroys the function of the ego and triggers in Moosbrugger a vertiginous instinctual demand for absolute unity. Hence his mad use of language: Moosbrugger inhabits the world of words and names, but as a stranger sealed off from the mysteries of their symbolic employment.

> When he was feeling on top of things Moosbrugger paid no attention at all to his voices and visions but spent his time in thinking. He called it thinking because he had always been impressed with the word. He thought better than other people because he thought both inside and outside.... Now Moosbrugger had let his head drop and was looking down at the wood between his fingers. "A squirrel in these parts is called a tree kitten," it occurred to him, "but just let somebody try to talk about a tree cat with a straight face! Everyone would prick up their ears as if a real shot had gone off among the farting sound of blanks on maneuvers. In Hesse, on the other hand, it's called a tree fox. Any man who's traveled around knows such things." But oh, how curious the psychiatrists got when they showed him a picture of a squirrel and he said: "That's a fox, I guess, or it could be a hare, or maybe a cat or something." They'd always shoot a question right back at him then: "How much is fourteen plus fourteen?" and he would say in his deliberate way, "Oh, about twenty-eight to forty." This "about" gave them trouble, which made Moosbrugger grin. It was really so simple. He knew perfectly well that you get twenty-eight when you go on from fourteen to another fourteen; but who says you have to stop there? (MoE 240; MwQ 258–59, changes to the translation are mine)

Why stop at twenty-eight? In his *Philosophical Investigations*, Musil's compatriot Ludwig Wittgenstein used the example of adding numbers to inquire into the foundations of meaning and subjectivity.

Why do we add numbers—and by extension, employ words, make
gestures, eat, etc.—the way we do? What makes us believe that the
right answer to the question "what is nine plus six" is "fifteen"
rather than, say, "one hundred and thirty-nine"? Are there rules
that determine our performances in adding and if so, what kinds
of rules are they? Wittgenstein shows that the idea of transcendent
rules controlling or determining our cultural practices is misguided
since rules require application, and no metarule exists that unambiguously regulates such application. Thus, no matter how often
a rule has been applied in the past, this does not determine how we
will apply it in the future: "this was our paradox: no course of action could be determined by a rule, because every course of action
can be made out to accord with the rule" (PI §201). But given the
unavailability of logical rules, how do we account for the fact that
we ordinarily know how to add numbers? According to one interpretation, made famous by Saul Kripke, Wittgenstein argues that
our practices are "grounded" in nothing other than the status quo:
they are mere conventions, socially sanctioned ways of doings
things, deviations from which are discarded as unacceptable or
even deemed unintelligible or abnormal. To be intelligible, to
make sense, the individual must submit to the communal standards
of evaluation. Stanley Cavell has taken issue with this conventionalist reading, arguing that it fails to gauge the full force of Wittgenstein's antifoundationalism.[40] According to Cavell, Kripke's appeal
to convention overly substantializes our human life with words. Instead of explaining our shared uses of language in terms of communal conventions, Cavell's Wittgenstein helps us realize that such
a thing as a community exists only through our agreement in (not
on) language, an agreement that in turn depends on "our sharing
routes of interest and feeling, senses of humor and of significance
and of fulfillment, of what is outrageous, of what is similar to what
else, what a rebuke, what forgiveness, of when an utterance is an

---

40.   Stanley Cavell, "The Argument of the Ordinary: Scenes of Instruction in
Wittgenstein and in Kripke," in *Conditions Handsome and Unhandsome: The
Constitution of Emersonian Perfectionism* (Chicago: University of Chicago Press,
1990), 64–100.

assertion, when an appeal, when an explanation—all the whirl of organism Wittgenstein calls 'forms of life.'"[41]

Moosbrugger's madness is characterized by his inability to share "routes of interest and feeling" with others. His bizarre utterances— "why stop at twenty-eight?"—place him outside the world of common sense, but in so doing also reveal the boundaries of this and every sense, the fragility of the human life with words. Why indeed stop at twenty-eight if no transcendent truth or absolute authority commands us to do so? Insofar as he articulates and lives these questions, Moosbrugger is the symptom of Kakanian society, the embodiment of a doubt about cultural foundations that afflicts each of its citizens. One way for them to respond to Moosbrugger would be to acknowledge him as one of their own, to recognize in his distorted life a possibility that belongs to their own lives. It would be, in other words, to recognize in the psychotic sex murderer the terrifying lack of foundation that characterize the human form of life. But this is clearly not their reaction. Instead of acknowledging Moosbrugger's and their own humanness, they treat him as both more and less human: as monstrous freak and transcendent redeemer. In transgressing the rules of ordinary sense, Moosbrugger holds out the promise of another kind of language and existence, a life beyond all established forms of life. He captivates Kakanian society, in other words, because he embodies the dream of an absolute Real that every Kakanian dreams. To inhabit this Real is to be freed from the anxiety about foundations that afflicts and drives life in Kakania. But on the Wittgensteinian picture, a certain measure of this anxiety is unavoidable in that any reflection on our forms of life will eventually push up against an element of inexplicability and unreason, a mystery we cannot solve. "Explanations come to an end somewhere" (PI §1). And: "If I have exhausted the explanations, I have reached bedrock and my spade is turned. Then I am inclined to say: 'This is simply what I do'" (PI §217). In Kakania, however, to "simply do" won't do any longer. Anxiety over the lack of foundation has become unbearable, and Moosbrugger's psychotic

---

41. Stanley Cavell, *Must We Mean What We Say?* (Cambridge: Cambridge University Press, 1969), 52.

intensity, characterized by utter certainty, augurs a release from doubt and a complete attachment to one's words and actions.

How questionable a solution this is can be gauged not only by the fact that Moosbrugger's intense investment in words comes at the price of depriving them of their meaning; the dream of full speech is also accompanied by vengeance on the *objects* of libidinal attachment. Moosbrugger's psychosis is intrinsically bound up with his violence against women, onto whom he projects the doubts he is unable to bear within himself. More precisely, what Moosbrugger attacks in women is the mystery of his own vitality, whose incomprehensible swerve terrifies him:

> Moosbrugger asserted that he could not possibly be a sex murderer, because these females had inspired only feelings of aversion in him. This is not implausible. . . . There is in the attitude toward the living, moving, silently rolling or flitting a secret aversion to the fellow creature that enjoys its own existence [*Da ist im Verhalten zum Lebendigen, Bewegten, stumm vor sich hin Rollenden oder Huschenden eine geheime Abneigung gegen das sich seiner selbst freuende Mitgeschöpf berührt*]. And then what could one do when she started screaming? One could only come to one's senses, or else, if one simply couldn't do that, press her face to the ground and stuff earth into her mouth. (MoE 71)

Moosbrugger's flight from vitality, which carries him into the wilderness of unreason, finds its sophisticated mirror image in Ulrich's intellectualism. Like Moosbrugger's madness, Ulrich's rationality is, at least in part, a defense against his own vitality. Ulrich's excitement during his police interrogation already gave us an inkling into the dynamic at play here. His fascination with the impersonality of the statistical procedure reveals his profound identification with rationality. Ulrich's ironic stance toward his surroundings is born of an overproximity to the mechanisms of conceptual reduction, which he has applied to himself. Ulrich is the purest embodiment of the scientific rationalism of his age, a modern Oedipus who rejects tradition and insists on the mastery of reason and intellect. And, like Oedipus, Ulrich's mastery is built on repression and violence. This is perhaps most visible in the hyperphallic masculinity of Urich's relations with women. For the Ulrich of book 1, women are neither intellectual companions nor objects of tenderness or desire but composite creatures, split between a cultural surface that is utterly conventionalized and an organic depth whose soulless automaticity is utterly meaningless. Be it the "provocatively lifeless" Leona—a cabaret singer devoted to romantic music and voracious eating—in whom "the dream of being [was] only loosely draped over its matter" (MoE 25) or his cousin Diotima, under whose "soulful expression [*seelenvolle Ausdruck*]" Ulrich divines the "instinctive vegetative processes at work every day beneath the cover of the body [*instinktive, vegetative Arbeit, die täglich unter der Decke des Leibes vor sich geht*]" (MoE 103–4), women are, for Ulrich, archaic and subhuman enigmas, ciphers of an unacknowledged part of his self that invoke in him the fear, as he recognizes in a moment of clarity with Diotima, that they want "to devour him [*ihn zu verschlingen*]" (MoE 95). In short, Ulrich's aggressive masculinity and intellectualism constitute a defense against an unapproachable femininity that stands at the center of his desire.

The effect of this phallic intellectualism is the theatricalization of self and world, the feeling, persistent in Ulrich's stance toward his surroundings, that the world has become unreal and dead.

> Thus was the dream of being only loosely draped over its matter.
> But Leona knew that such elegant entertainment entitled the host to something more than a guest who was merely there to be gaped at, even when he asked for nothing more; so she rose to her feet as soon as she was able and serenely broke into full-throated song. Her friend regarded such an evening as a ripped-out page, alive with all sorts of suggestions and ideas but mummified, like everything torn from its context, full of the tyranny of that eternally fixed stance that accounts for the uncanny fascination of tableaux vivants, as though life had suddenly been given a sleeping pill and was now standing there stiff, full of inner meaning, sharply outlined, and yet, in sum, making absolutely no sense at all. (MoE 25; MwQ 20, changes to the translation are mine)

In a 1925 review of a book by friend and film critic Béla Balázs, Musil suggested that silent film's photographic transformation of reality provided a gateway into the "other state." Film transfigures the world by animating the inanimate, conjuring up a reality in which things, rather than being means to an end, become expressive of the self, symbolic faces of the life of the soul. "One could in fact call this symbolic face of things the mysticism of film, or at least its romanticism, if it played more than an episodic role in the shadowy realm of living photography" (PSE 1143; PS 198).[42] Leona's becoming-image represents the distorted flip side of the mysticism of "*lebende Photographie*." Instead of reconnecting the self with reality, the world-turned-image unhinges the self even further, sealing it in a state of absolute inexpressiveness. Rather than bringing the world back to life, the photographic image conjures up the threat of the world's irrevocable petrification.

Stanley Cavell captured the logic of derealization at stake here in a book devoted to the "ontology of film." "Photography," Cavell writes, "maintains the presentness of the world by accepting our absence from it. The reality in a photograph is present to me while I am not present to it: and a world I know, and see, but to which I am nevertheless not present . . . is a world past."[43] Cavell's reflections on film are part of his lifelong exploration of modern skepticism, understood as a doubt, "intensifying in the West since the Reformation,"[44] in the mind's capacity to "know with certainty of the existence of the external world and of myself and others in it."[45] According to Cavell, modern arts record the catastrophic consequences of this loss of conviction in reality while seeking to reconnect the self with the world through a route that, at least since Romanticism, passes through the subject, thereby acknowledging that the recovery of the world must proceed through the recovery of the self's presence to itself.

Ulrich embodies this skeptical attitude perhaps more than any other modern literary hero. His "vacation from life," his wish "to do away with reality" (MoE 289) because it blocks access to "that

---

42. Robert Musil, "Ansätze zu neuer Ästhetik. Bemerkungen über eine Dramaturgie des Films," in PSE; "Toward a New Aesthetic: Observations on a Dramaturgy of Film" in PS.

43. Stanley Cavell, *The World Viewed: Reflections on the Ontology of Film* (Cambridge, MA: Harvard University Press, 1979), 23.

44. Ibid., 21.

45. Stanley Cavell, *Disowning Knowledge in Seven Plays of Shakespeare* (Cambridge: Cambridge University Press, 2003), 3.

which truly moves us" (MoE 289), and his experiments with possibility and the "other state," express both the skeptical unhinging
of the world from consciousness and the desire to go beyond skepticism and recover the lost conviction in reality through the transformation of his self. But Ulrich's relation to women also highlights
the role of gender and desire in skepticism. Leona's deadness is his
own: it is the product of his refusal to grant her existence as a living human being. Nor is this attitude limited to her. Ulrich persis-
tently reduces the female body to an unthinking organic machine—
referring to Leona's voracious eating, Bonadea's nymphomania,
Diotima's vegetative processes—denying women interiority and depriving them expressiveness. Turning each woman's body into a
purely biological reality, as if nothing more about her existence can
be known with certainty, least of all the presence of feeling and
thoughts, Ulrich retreats from the difficult task of acknowledging
the other. Ulrich's stance is continuous with the novel's overall skeptical attitude, as articulated, for instance, in the narrator's previously quoted hilarious pronouncement about the virtues of mathematical precision. To be sure, given the Parallel Campaign's tireless
production of nonsense, the call for precision is both understandable and salutary. But as the image of the slide ruler, "sensed as a
hard white line over one's heart," indicates, the confrontation of
mathematical formulas with great emotions is overdetermined,
carrying an element of violence against human embodiment as such.
As Stanley Cavell has argued, the skeptic uses epistemological doubt
to deny the other's humanity:

> To withhold, or hedge, our concepts of psychological states from a given
> creature, on the ground that our criteria cannot reach the inner life of
> the creature, is specifically to withhold the source of my idea that living
> beings are things that feel; it is to withhold myself, to reject my response
> to anything as a living being; to blank so much as my idea of anything
> as *having a body*. To describe *this* condition as one in which I do not
> know (am not certain) of the existence of other minds, is empty. There
> is nothing there, of the right kind, to be known.[46]

---

46. Stanley Cavell, *The Claim of Reason: Wittgenstein, Skepticism, Morality,
and Tragedy* (Oxford: Oxford University Press, 1979), 83–84.

Ulrich's relationship to women reveals this violent underside of the skeptical stance. In withholding attribution of an inner life, Ulrich refuses to acknowledge the existence of the other's soul, thus rejecting the claim for recognition the other makes on him. Yet insofar as this failure of acknowledgment is also a denial of responsiveness, a refusal to respond to the other's call, Ulrich's coldness toward women masks a coldness toward *himself*, an aggressive desire to make himself inexpressible, unknowable by the other. Failing to give himself expression before the other, Ulrich in fact denies his own embodiment, his own peculiarly human vitality, thus becoming dead to himself.

Ulrich's attitude is reminiscent of Benn's medical gaze and belongs to the broader, antibourgeois "cult of coldness" that shaped the thinking of countless critics of the Weimar Republic on the left and the right. What sets Musil apart from these writers is that, rather than merely flaunting coldness and antihumanism as properly postbourgeois stances, his novel explores their broader social, political, and psychological contexts, thus submitting them to critical analysis. It is not just that Ulrich's hyperphallic attitude highlights the extent to which the "cult of coldness" perpetuates the patriarchal underpinnings of bourgeois culture that this attitude claims to attack. The cult of coldness and its denial of interiority its also shown to be both a critical response to a broader biopolitical reification of human life *and* an act of despair that turns the process of descriptive annihilation against the subject, thus intensifying it. Book 1 of Musil's novel pushes the problem of skepticism to its extreme point. Ulrich's skeptical stance toward reality is not limited to the conventionalized forms of social life but extends into the deepest regions of his own emotional and libidinal life. His disappointment with reality engulfs his self, threatening to destroy the very affective core—"this slowly cooling, absurd drop 'I' that refused to give up its fire, its tiny glowing core [*dieser langsam erkaltende, lächerliche Tropfen Ich, der sein Feuer, den winzigen Glutkern nicht abgeben wollte*]" (MoE 153; MwQ 162)—that fuels his critique of the status quo. This threat of psychic deadness, first palpable in the freezing of time with Leona, increases throughout book 1. And it is precisely at the height of this development, at the moment when the theatricalization of self and world seems to have become absolute, that Musil opens the door into the "other state" that is the subject of the second part of the novel:

> Ulrich suddenly realized that it was he, who had been standing at the window the whole time, who was being taken for the Count. All the eyes down there seemed focused on his face, and sticks were being brandished at him. A few steps beyond, where the street curved from view as though it were slipping into the wings, the performers were already beginning to take off the greasepaint, as it were; there was no point in looking fierce for no one in particular, so they naturally let their faces relax, and some even began to joke and laugh as if they were on a picnic. Ulrich noticed this and laughed too, but the newcomers took him for the Count laughing and their rage rose to a fearsome pitch, which only made Ulrich laugh all the more and without restraint.
>
> But all at once he broke off in disgust. With his eyes still moving from the threatening open-mouthed faces to the high-spirited ones farther back, and his mind refusing to absorb any more of this spectacle, he was undergoing a strange transformation. I can't go on with this life, and I can't keep on rebelling against it any longer, either, was what he felt, while keenly aware of the room behind him with perpendicular lines of draperies and bell ropes, like another, smaller stage, with him standing up front on the apron, in the opening between the curtains, facing the drama running its course on the greater stage outside. The two stages had their own way of fusing into one without regard for the fact that he was standing between them. Then his sense of the room behind him contracted and turned inside out, passing through him or flowing past him as if turned to water, making for a strange spatial inversion, Ulrich thought. . . . It was an experience beyond his understanding; he was chiefly aware of the glassiness, emptiness, tranquility of the state in which he found himself. Is it really possible, he wondered, to leave one's own space for some hidden other space? He felt as though chance had led him through a secret door. (MoE 631–32; MwQ 688–89)

The Dead Father

The above scene already highlights the form in which book 2 seeks to overcome the problem of skepticism. The recovery of self and world unfolds under the logic of a threefold inversion—of space, sexuality, and language—designed to open up new modes of being and speaking: an inversion of space, inspired by contemporary

Gestalt theory, designed to undermine the strict distinction between inner and outer, mind and world;[47] an inversion of sexuality, aimed at weakening phallic aggression in favor of bisexual complementarity; and an inversion of language privileging analogical relations between words over reference and propositional content. The opening chapters of book 2 articulate the crucial role of sexual inversion. Ulrich must undergo a therapy of desire, figured in its initial stage as the recovery of an archaic, pre-oedipal phase of narcissism. The medium of this narcissistic relation is Ulrich's "forgotten" (MoE 671) sister Agathe, who only makes her first appearance now, roughly seven hundred pages into the text. Separated by their father after their mother's death and sent to different boarding schools, Ulrich and Agathe had barely seen each other "since their childhood, where however they had loved each other very much" (MoE 673). The first step on the "Journey to the New Millenium," the title of book 2, harks back to this period of early love, to a phase of primary narcissism predating the paternal separation of self and other, man and woman. The self-reflective structure of narcissism, dramatized in the siblings' first encounter while dressed in identical Pierrot costumes, signals the irruption of a new perspective of the self on itself.

> But when he entered the room where his sister was waiting, he was amazed at his costume, for by some mysterious directive of chance he found his appearance echoed in that of a tall, blond Pierrot in a pattern of delicate gray and rust stripes and lozenges, who at first glance looked quite like himself.
> "I had no idea we were twins!" Agathe said, her face lighting up with a smile. (MoE 676; MwQ 734)

Dressed in identical Pierrot costumes, Ulrich and Agathe appear as virtual doubles. If this is a picture of narcissism and similarity, it is, however, a similarity with difference, a narcissism of complemen-

---

47. On the spatial logic in Musil's writings, see Oliver Simons, *Raumgeschichten: Topograophien der Moderne in Philosophie, Wissenschaft und Literatur* (Munich: Wilhelm Fink, 2007), 279–338 (331–38 in MoE). On Musil's engagement with Gestalt psychology, see Vatan, *Robert Musil et la question anthropologique.*

tarity rather than repetition. Crucial to this model is the difference, against a background of similarity, separating Ulrich and Agathe, a corporeal and sexual difference Ulrich is repeatedly drawn to. The negotiation of distance and proximity is characteristic of the analogic relationship Ulrich and Agathe seek to establish: a relationship not of identicals but of constructive equivalents. That the analogy functions in book 2 as a sexual as well as a semantic model is already indicated in the doubling of the siblings as Pierrots. For while a single Pierrot, a joker figure from the commedia dell'arte, may be thought of as a symbolic wild card, a zero symbol capable of referring to everything because it designates nothing, the *double* Pierrot of the siblings redirects the verticality of reference into the horizontality of analogy, indicating a semantics not of reference but of revelatory association.[48]

But let us stick to the sexual aspect of analogy. The new self-reflective and "narcissistic" perspective of the self on itself reverses what I earlier described as the inversion of reason in Ulrich's hyperphallic masculine stance. If the latter is characterized by the self's over-identification with rationality, a turning of the operation of conceptual cutting against the self, narcissism recovers the self as "a thing of care and commitment."[49] It thus recuperates an original attraction, a love that precedes the organization of desire along the socially enforced paths of strict sexual difference. Violently separated by their father at an early age, the siblings restage after his death a mode of relating and desiring that precedes the rule of the father, consciously exploring a primordial phase that is "much older than the distinction of the sexes, which later complemented their spiritual dresses out of it [*viel älter als der Unterschied der Geschlechter, die sich daraus später ihre seelische Kleidung ergänzt haben*]" (MoE 689).

This is why the "Journey to the New Millenium" begins with the explicit demolition of the law of the father. The reunification of

---

48. On the figure of Pierrot, see also Stefan Jonsson, *Subject Without Nation: Robert Musil and the History of Modern Identity* (Durham, NC: Duke University Press, 2001), 175–81.

49. Stanley Cavell, *A Pitch of Philosophy: Autobiographical Exercises* (Cambridge, MA: Harvard University Press, 1996), 142.

brother and sister takes place against the background of the death, not just of Ulrich's and Agathe's father, but of paternity. The first six chapters of book 2 dramatize a rite of passage, transition, through a series of ritualized transgressions, from the reign of the father to the reign of siblinghood. Crucially, these transgressions take the form of messages authored by the siblings and addressed to their dead father. The reign of analogy is founded on the violation of paternal language, thus aiming at the destruction of what Lacan has called "the symbolic order." This decay of the symbolic is already announced in a message authored by Ulrich's father himself, albeit in a way that throws doubts upon the very notion of authorship and authority. Walking through the city of his childhood, Ulrich makes the following reflections:

> In his pocket he carried his father's eccentric telegram, which he knew by heart: "This is to inform you that I am deceased" was the old gentleman's message for him—or was it to him?—as indicated by the signature at the end: "Your father." His excellency, the Privy Councillor, never went in for levity at serious moments. The weird information of the message was consequently infernally logical, since he was himself notifying his son when, in expectation of his end, he wrote or dictated word for word the message that was to be dispatched the instant he had drawn his last breath; the facts could really not be more correctly stated, and yet this act by which the present tried to dominate a future it could not live to see emitted from the grave an uncanny whiff of an angrily decayed will! (MoE 672; MwQ 730)

Ulrich's father's message is indeed uncanny, though perhaps not only in the way he intends it. On the surface, the message attests to the father's will to extend his authority beyond his physical existence and to outlive his death. But this heroic act, intended to arrest the demise of the traditional order through a sheer act of will, falls in upon itself, and in doing so reveals the very opposite of what it intended. The father is drawn into the decadence of the symbolic, and the message he leaves, rather than upholding the status quo, initiates its end.

On one level, the father's testament is paradigmatic of symbolic speech as such. Generally speaking, the symbolic depends upon the directedness of communication, on the fact that a message originates from an addressor and points toward an addressee. The mark of this origin is, of course, the signature. The signature marks the thisness, the utter specificity, of a message, thus endowing it with authenticity and individuality. This mark of particularity implies an invocation of authority that necessarily exceeds the individuality of the addressor and the specificity of the message. Put simply, a signature signals that I am entitled to speak because I *own* my words, because I am the sovereign of my utterance. Yet this sovereignty is of course a borrowed one. The words I use are never entirely mine, and the authority I claim is never more than the invocation or appropriation of the authority of him in whose name I speak, be this a specific institution that has invested me with a symbolic mandate, the notion of truth or God to which I appeal, or, finally and in the last instance, the totality of the symbolic order that is the guarantor of the meaning I claim. As a communicative act whose authority is upheld, beyond the physical existence of its author, by the legal-political order as a whole, the father's will thus perfectly embodies the promissory and transpersonal character of the symbolic order.

What makes the father's message disorienting, however, is that it draws the promissory temporality of symbolic speech into the *content* of the message itself. Ulrich's difficulty in pinpointing the origin of the message hits its paradoxical core. In stating, in the present tense, that he who is signing this message no longer exists, the father subverts his own signature, thus enacting, against his intention, his removal from the world of communication. What follows, then, is the final cancellation of the symbolic father through the transgressions of his descendants. The first transgression consists in violating the father's request that his imperial medals remain attached to his corpse as long as possible. For the father, the medals are a symbol of a "universalist" theory of state according to which "man receives his extra-personal purpose, mercy, and justice, only from the creative community of the state; by himself man is nothing, which is why the Emperor represents a spiritual symbol" (MoE 695). The siblings replace the original medals with duplicates immediately, rather than just prior to the closing of the casket as stipulated by the father, thus violating not only the father's will but also the system of royal sovereignty the medals were meant to sustain. Yet this violation of the institutional letter is not enough, and is thus followed by a second, explicitly *sexual* transgression aimed at the father's body:

> But Agathe had already bent down, slid from her leg a wide silk garter that she wore to relieve the pull on her girdle, lifted the pall, and slipped it into her father's pocket. And Ulrich? He could hardly believe his eyes . . . the barbaric notion of sending the frosty dead man on his way with a garter still warm from his daughter's thigh tightened his throat and muddled his brain. (MoE 707; MwQ 768)

Agathe's symbolic rape of her father wrenches sexuality from its association with patrilineal procreation, thus separating it from the domain of kinship and generation. Her act, then, is meant to seal the end of the old order and signal the dawn of a new one: "[Ulrich] almost leapt forward to stop her, just because it was so completely out of order. But he caught in his sister's eyes a flash of the dewy fresh innocence of early morning that is still untainted by any of the drab routines of the day, and it held him back" (MoE 707; MwQ 768).

A New Millenial?

What follows is the siblings' "journey to the margin of possibility [*Reise an den Rand des Möglichen*]"—that is to say, to the margin of what I have been calling a form of life. Musil referred to this liminal space as "the other state" and famously associated it with mystical experience.[50] Through Ulrich and Agathe, book 2 of *The Man*

---

50. On Musil's use of mystical language, see in particular the work by Niklaus Largier, who argues that Musil transposes "the eschatological goal of a union with the divine" associated with early medieval mysticism into an art of living, a *Lebenskunst*, "that has its ground in an art of perception shaped by the use of mystical tropes" (51). Largier traces the genealogy of this projection of mystical tropes into a new epistemological space, the realm of (aesthetic) experience and self-fashioning, which begins ironically with Luther's disjunction of the secular and the spiritual. Niklaus Largier, "Mysticism, Modernity and the Invention of Aesthetic Experi-

without Qualities explores modes of thinking, feeling, and perceiving that are characterized by "that miraculous feeling of the lifting of all bounds, the boundlessness of the outer and inner that love and mysticism have in common [*dieses wunderbare Gefühl der Entgrenzung und Grenzenlosigkeit des Äußeren und Inneren, das der Liebe und der Mystik gemeinsam ist*]" (MoE 765; MwQ 830). The broader implications of this seemingly apolitical turn toward love and mysticism are best approached by way of Musil's previously mentioned essay "Toward a New Aesthetics," which contains his most programmatic description of the "other state." Here as elsewhere, Musil draws a stark opposition between ordinary and liminal experience, between a normal and an "other" condition. Ordinary experience is sustained by a "ratioed" attitude, anchored in the reassuring regularity of the ego and its institutions, calculative reasoning, practical and scientific judgment, and an aggressive focus on self-preservation and self-interest. Rooted in archaic strata of an "aboriginal mistrust and struggle for existence [*urverwurzelten Mißtrauens und Daseinskampfes*]" (PSE 1143; PS 199), the ratioed attitude drives capitalism's reduction of qualities to monetized quantity and underlies traditional morality, whose very form "as rule, norm, command, threat, law, or the quantifying and weighting of good as well as evil, reveals the shaping influence of the metric, calculating, mistrusting, annihilating will of the spirit" (PSE 1143; PS 199). Diametrically opposed to the aggressiveness of the ratioed attitude stands the heightened receptiveness of the "other condition," in which the "rigid formulas of ordinary experience" (PSE 1152, PS 206) dissolve, giving rise to the feeling of a "secret rising and ebbing of our being with that of things and other people" (PSE 1144; PS 199). Musil associates this fluidity with madness and unreason on the one hand and mystical experience on the other. But at the heart of his essay lies the claim that art's calculated "disturbance" of reality provides a unique access to this other condition. In

---

ence," *Representations* 105, no. 1 (Winter 2009): 37–60. See also his "'A Sense of Possibility': Robert Musil, Meister Eckhart, and the 'Culture of Film,'" in *Religion: Beyond a Concept*, ed. Hent de Vries (New York: Fordham University Press, 2008), 739–49.

"exploding the normal totality of experience" (PSE 1145; PS 200) through mechanisms of abstraction, condensation, and displacement, art articulates the physiognomy of another world, a "symbolic face" (PSE 1142; PS 198) of things, thus provoking new modes of thinking, feeling, and perceiving.

To get a clearer sense of what is at stake here, it will help to reframe Musil's strict opposition between ordinary and liminal experience in terms of the infinitesimal topography of a *form of life*. According to this model, the closer we move to the center of a form of life, the more routinized and formulaic actions and expressions become. This center is the domain of highly conventionalized scripts and supposedly fixed rules, where what happens next seems already to be predetermined, traced out in advance. As Wittgenstein suggests in the *Philosophical Investigations*, life at the center is sustained by an ultimately transcendental vision of rules: "'All the steps are really already taken' means: I no longer have any choice. The rule, once stamped with a particular meaning, traces the lines along which it is to be followed through the whole of space" (PI §219). Although Wittgenstein's attack on the idea of fixed rules is aimed primarily at issues in the philosophy of logic and mathematics, it is not difficult to see the broader existential and even political implications of his critique. In a world in which all rails are "invisibly laid to infinity" (PI §218), individual and collective life loses its creativity and vibrancy, and with it, meaning and the very *sense* of possibilities. To revive this *Möglichkeitssinn*, Musil and Wittgenstein take us to the boundaries of established forms of life, that is, to situations in which it is not yet clear, as Wittgenstein puts it, "how to go on." At this perimeter, where action and communication are no longer tied to established routines and protocols of culture and history, the image of the world undergoes a deep transformation: what appeared as firm reality made up of "objective relations" (PSE 1153; PS 207) and compact actualities now gives way to the experience of a fluid and open field of possibilities. Musil describes this "journey to the margin of possibility" in terms of the progressive dissolution of both the conceptual framework underpinning ordinary modes of thinking and perceiving and the sense of self anchoring these modes. In its most extreme form, the journey to the margin catapults the subject beyond the boundaries of communal forms of life and into madness, as happens to Moosbrugger. But even in less extreme cases, the absence of regulative habits and rules immobilizes thought, and is accompanied by an ecstatic surge of unbound affect that threatens to overwhelm the subject and push it toward an unsustainable, and ultimately unbearable, experience of formlessness.

This is precisely where art enters Musil's theory of the *other condition*. Aesthetic form allows for the reflectively controlled and experimental engagement with the ecstatic intensity of the other condition. This is so because the language of art in general, and of literature in particular, never completely loses its connection to the world of concepts and thinking, which provide an intelligible framework—a "scaffolding [*Gerüst*]" as Musil puts it—for guiding the extrarational dynamics of aesthetic experience. In other words, rather than simply identifying aesthetic experience with the *other condition*, Musil conceives of literature as setting into motion an oscillation between concept and affect, structure and force, ordinary experience and the *other condition*. A back-and-forth "journey to the margin of possibility," poetic figuration (metaphor, analogy, rhythmic patterning, etc.) stretches thinking and perception to the limits of sense only to return, time and again, to some measure of intersubjective meaning and consensually validated reality. The goal of this movement is to upset the routinization of everyday perceptions and judgment and to induce forms of experience that, from the point of view of the center of the communal form of life, appear as anomalous, nonsensical, or even mad. On the one hand, these experiences point back to archaic, preverbal phases of psychic development, to a period of life when inside and outside were not yet separate, and when language was mere voice, sensory experience (sound, rhythm, tone) without signification and symbolic value. Literary language reaches into and revives these strata of archaic mentation, what psychoanalysis calls "primary processes," which are normally covered over by the more developed "secondary processes" dominant in the ratioed attitude. On the other hand, through its conceptual scaffolding, literature brings these two processes into systematic contact with each other, thus creating a space in which "meaning, perceived sensuous form, and emotional excitement" mix and stimulate one another (PSE 1150; PS 204). It is this intermingling of concept, percept, and affect that enables literature to weaken the hold of regulative formulae at the center of a form of life and open up new modes of thinking, perceiving, and feeling.

For Musil, the task of literature is thus at once epistemological, ethical, and political. It is epistemological because the new modes of thinking and perceiving opened up by art "serve not only the production of specific sensual and emotional experience but also the constitution of a specific knowledge of the world and the self."[51] Seeing the world in terms of open possibilities rather than fixed facts changes our sense not only of the world but also of what it means to lead a human life. Epistemology is thus intimately connected with questions of ethics and aesthetics. Like Wittgenstein, Musil conceives of writing in experimental terms, as a playful exploration of incongruous modes of being in the world. Where Wittgenstein invents surreal language games and bizarre tribes to probe the bounds of our forms of life, Musil takes his reader into the mind of a mad man (Moosbrugger) and to the mystical edge of speech and expression (Ulrich and Agathe). In both cases, writing is employed not discursively but to involve readers in an experiment in which their "natural attitude is subverted and their inner dynamics realigned so that they come to see things in a new way."[52] The goal of this experimental aesthetics is to transform cognition and affect. For Musil, as for Wittgenstein, writing is a spiritual exercise, a work of the self on itself.

This ethical work also carries political implications, for the transcendental conception of rules as "rails invisibly laid to infinity" is an illusion that distorts individual and collective life. There is no big Other—no impersonal rule, law, or authority—that fully determines how to go on and absolves us from the democratic task of

---

51. Largier, "Mysticism, Modernity and the Invention of Aesthetic Practice," 51.

52. Joel Whitebook, "Against Interiority: Foucault's Struggle with Psychoanalysis," in *The Cambridge Companion to Foucault*, ed. Gary Gutting (Cambridge: Cambridge University Press, 2005), 324–25.

determining the scope of our agreements. To be sure, as long as we stay close to the center of a communal form of life, our lives *seem* to be governed by rules that leave little space for contingency. But this sense of strict determination is a fiction, and even the ordinary is not quite as rigid as it appears:

> We may take as a point of departure the average, ordinary condition that is regarded as orderly, whose most important characteristics include the fact that we acquire experiences. I have already said that between the experience that one has and the concepts with whose help one has it there exists a peculiarly labile relationship; each new experience escapes the formula of previous experiences, and is at the same time formed in their image. This is valid for ethics as it is for physics or psychology. What we call our spiritual and intellectual being finds itself continuously in this process of expansion and contraction. (PSE 1151–52; PS 206)

As we have seen, a vague sense of the fundamental indeterminacy of rules and roles, of a *lack* of firm foundation, permeates Kakanian society and drives its manic search for scientific precision, cultural identity, and universal political symbols. The problem is that the languages of precision and the sublime equally and systematically disavow the lack of foundation that drives them, thereby heightening the division between concept and feeling, surrendering individual and collective life to the inexpressiveness of rigid, formulaic, and, ultimately, empty speech. In this situation, literature's controlled journey to the margin of established forms of life is meant not only to reconnect feeling and concept within the individual but also to free thinking from the hegemony of fixed and transcendent laws. In reviving the process of expansion and contraction that operates at the heart of individual *and* public life, art shakes up our reified understanding of reality and the centrality of indeterminacy and possibility.

> He suspects that the given order of things is not as solid as it pretends to be; no thing, no self, no form, no principle, is safe, everything is undergoing an invisible but ceaseless transformation, the unsettled holds more of the future than the settled, and the present is nothing but a hypothesis that has not yet been surmounted. (MoE 250; MwQ 269)

This, at least, is the idea behind the aesthetic use of the "other condition" as outlined in the 1925 essay. The above quote is from book 1, in which the goal of expanding the field of possibilities is predominantly associated with a new style of writing and thinking that Musil captures under the title of "essayism." But by 1930, when Musil began to work on book 2, the stakes have been raised and the *other condition* is framed in the context of Ulrich and Agathe's attempt to create, not just an expansion of possibilities, but a new millennial—a new form of life—that radically breaks with the political and symbolic regulations of the Kakanian epoch. After Agathe's symbolic rape of her father, the question haunting all insurrection (How to go on? What shape to give the new order?) imposes itself on the siblings. Moreover, given the explicitly sexual form of Agathe's rebellion and the obvious attraction between Ulrich and Agathe, the Wittgensteinian question as to how to go on is now extended into a domain of life that Wittgenstein, at least in his work, strenuously avoided: the domain of erotic desire.

The topography of the "other condition" as located at the perimeter of an established form of life is given novelistic form in the setting of one of the crucial chapters of book 2, entitled *Atemzüge eines Sommertags*, which finds Ulrich and Agathe, absorbed in each other's presence, sitting in the garden of their father's home, separated from the outside world by lush vegetation and a semitransparent fence through which they intermittently observe the activities of passerby. The fence marks the boundary between two sides: the side of ordinary life, in which people stop to tie their shoelaces (MoE 1316; MwQ 1390) and go about their business, and the side of yearning and contemplation, of open possibilities that need to be taken up and given an as-yet undetermined form. Recalling Wittgenstein's example of counting, we might say that the siblings, having dislodged the paternal law, find themselves in a situation in which the ordinary practices of counting have been suspended and the question of how to go on poses itself in a newly exhilarating but anxiety-provoking manner. In fact, and following the Wittgensteinian analogy, once the sovereignty of the rule has been overturned, it is not even clear that the next step ought to take place within the domain of counting and numbers rather than, say, that of drawing, singing, or dance. This amounts not merely to an intellectual question but an existential impasse; at issue here is what form to give to one's life, and to all life comprises: thought, feeling, perception, action, and, above all for Musil, desire.

> And finally the unavoidable discovery dawned on him, although he had so far avoided it, that all these strange, individual temptations of the emotions and emotional experiences, which intermingled and hovered within him like the shadows cast by the foliage of a restless tree when the sun is high, could be encompassed and understood at a single glance if he regarded his love for his sister as their origin. For evidently this emotion and this alone was the hero of his breaking down, of his blocked path, and of all the ambiguous adventures and detours associated with this. Even the psychology of the emotions, which he was pursuing on his own in his diaries, now seemed to him merely an attempt to conceal the love between him and his sister in a quixotic edifice of ideas. Did he, then, desire her? He was really astonished that he was confessing this to himself for the first time, and he now clearly saw the possibilities between which he had to make up his mind. Either he really had to believe that he was making ready for an adventure such as had never existed before, an adventure that he needed only to urge on and set out on with no second thoughts. . . . Or he had to yield to his emotion, even should this feeling be unnatural, in the natural way, or forbid himself to; and was all he was accomplishing through his irresolution to become inventive in subterfuges? When he asked himself this second, rather contemptible question, he did not fail to ask the third it entailed: What was there to prevent him from doing what he wanted? A biological superstition, a moral one? In short, the judgment of others? (MoE 1312–13; MwQ 1387–88)

Ulrich's desire for his sister, which is at once sexual, moral, and existential—a desire to beget a different form of being—involves a seemingly irresolvable predicament. On the one hand, *not* acting on their desire would seem to amount to a concession to the world of convention, morality, and law that the siblings are determined to leave behind. This would mean yielding to the "judgment of others" and remaining caught in the old psycho-political forms of life. On the other hand, acting on this desire and breaking with all established laws would seem to reinscribe the *Geschwisterliebe* into the logic of transgression which remains tied, if negatively, to the system of prohibitions it seeks to transcend. Would incest, even sibling incest, not keep them bound to the kinship structures their symbolic rape of their father was meant to sever? What holds Ulrich back, in other words, is the difficulty of disentangling desire from its biopolitical determination. And yet Ulrich knows that whatever form the next step will take, it must salvage the vitality of the erotic, for what pulls Ulrich to Agathe is not simply the wish to have and possess her. Rather, Agathe is for Ulrich the fulcrum of a world that receives illumination through her. The text frames Ulrich's desire for Agathe—and, through it, desire as such—as an originating power, as the creative force that drives the human search for other possibilities of living and being from its very inception. Conceived along these lines, Ulrich's desire for Agathe is nothing other than, to requote an earlier passage, that "something in him that had never wanted to remain anywhere, had groped its way along the walls; . . . this slowly cooling, absurd drop 'I' that refused to give up its fire, its tiny glowing core," the loss of which would amount to the death of meaning and possibility. The conversations of the siblings in book 2 are driven by the urgent sense that the time has come for this *Feuer* to be released into the world, to be converted into a new language, a new form, that transcends the biopolitical discourse of law and transgression. But what language will allow them to *go on* and open up a new form of life?

Musil seems never to have found a clear answer to this question, but one of the major options the text explores in response to it is the conversion of erotic desire into a quasi-mystical form of "love." We get an inkling of the structure of this idealizing conversion, which hinges on the suspension of the will's drive to seize its object, in the following passage:

> He could not keep from admitting to himself that separated out from the stream, such emotion could also wash around the love for a dead person, whose countenance belongs with a more profound defenselessness than any living one to the glances which it cannot drive off . . . but when he cautiously directed his glance at Agathe and allowed it to drink from the sight of her, there still dominated in his feelings, in spite of their miserable sublimity, an uncanny absence of will, a marked displacement or being carried away into the vicinity of sleep, of death, of the image, of the immobile, the imprisoned, the powerless. Ideas drained away, every

energetic drive dissipated, the unutterable paralyzed every limb, the world slipped away remote and unheeding, and the unstable armistice on the borderline between the enhanced and the diminished was barely to be borne any longer. But precisely with the entrance of this enormous draining away of power something different began, for their bodies seemed to be losing something of their boundaries, of which they no longer had any need. "It's like the frenzy of the bee swarm that's trying to surround the queen!" Ulrich thought silently. (MoE 1312; MwQ 1386–87)

As erotic desire is drained of its aggressivity, it gives rise to a different kind of energy that dissolves the dichotomy of desiring (subject and self) and desired (object). This is love as the *other condition*. While the distinction between self and other is not entirely erased in this state, it brings about a blurring of boundaries on the one hand and a rush of symbolic creativity on the other. Ulrich's comparison of this state to a swarm of bees encircling the queen goes beyond the received imagery of romantic love or mystical states, and in this sense does break new symbolic ground. And yet, there are reasons to question the scope of this accomplishment. It is not just that it is unclear how to move on from this new state and expression; perhaps more problematically, the love Ulrich invokes seems to be more a defense against desire than its successful sublimation. As Ulrich himself admits, there is something "necrophilic" (MoE 1312) about this new state, "an uncanny absence of the will, a noticeable removal from or descent into the region of sleep, of death, of the image, of immobility, arrest, impotence" (MoE 1312). "He could not fail to admit that such a feeling, removed from its currents, could also wash around the love of a dead person, whose face, deeply defenseless in a way no living face was, belonged to the gaze it was unable to shake off" (MoE 1312). Ulrich's reflections here and elsewhere suggest that the feeling of "limitless love" experienced in the other condition is purchased at the price of the death of any real, hence mortal, object of love. In other words, Ulrich's "love" may be an idealizing defense not only against the aggressiveness of desire but also, and perhaps more fundamentally, against the fragility of human love itself, which is inherently threatened by loss. Conceived along these lines, Ulrich (and Musil?) can be seen to belong to what Henry Staten has described as a "tradition of thanatoerotophobic metaphysics that has always attempted to keep the lid on mourning by keeping libidinal expenditure in check whenever a mortal being is the object."[53] While cautioning "that no object that may be lost is to be loved in an unreserved fashion,"[54] this Platonic-Stoic-Christian tradition has also generated a counter-model of transcendent love whose Greco-Christian name is *agape*.[55] And is Agathe not also *agape*, that "highest form of love"? To pose this question is also to highlight a fundamental gender asymmetry that links Musil's novel to the "tradition of thanatoerotophobic metaphysics." For just as the latter is authored by male writers for whom "the paradigm of the libidinal snare set by mortal beings . . . has been the erotic lure of a woman,"[56] for Musil all reflections about love-beyond-desire come from Ulrich, who is clearly troubled by his erotic attraction to his sister. So have our siblings, and Ulrich in particular, really succeeded in breaking free from patriarchy?

There are strong reasons to believe that the siblings' attempt to found a new form of life fails. In fact, Musil himself seems to have envisioned this failure. Musil's unpublished material suggest that he planned for the various narrative strands of his novel to converge in war, as indeed the opening paragraph of the entire book, which begins the fictional action exactly one year prior to the outbreak of World War I, indicated.[57] But there is another, more external reason for the failure of the siblings' experiment, one that may also point to Musil's own failure, if this is what it is, to find a conclusion to his novel. For the simple fact is that while Musil tried to figure out the contours of the siblings' journey "into the new mil-

53. Henry Staten, *Eros in Mourning: Homer to Lacan* (Baltimore: Johns Hopkins University Press, 1995), 16.

54. Ibid., 10.

55. On the relation between eros and agape, see, besides Staten's work, Anders Nygren, *Agape and Eros*, trans. Philip S. Watson (London: SPCK, 1953).

56. Staten, *Eros and Mourning*, 16.

57. "*Fundamental idea*: War. All lines lead to the war" (MoE 1851; MwQ 1747, Musil's emphasis). See also the comments on MoE 1876, which directly link the failure of sibling love to the war: "Ulrich-Agathe is really an attempt at anarchy in love. Which ends negatively even there. That's the deeper link between the love story and the war. (Also its connection to the Moosbrugger problem.)"

lennial," plans for another, very different, *tausendjähriges Reich* had been announced.[58] National Socialism not only drove Musil into exile and banned his books; it also made him suspect that in view of the Nazi's mass mobilization of "the unreflective stupidity of the emotions,"[59] his own aesthetic attempt to reconnect feeling and thinking had become hopelessly individualistic and outdated.[60] While Musil and his protagonists experimented with the *other condition*, the world outside the siblings' garden was sucked into the vortex of a totalitarian experiment aimed at the unification of all forms of life. Musil died of a cerebral hemorrhage on April 15, 1942. At the time of his death, he was working on a new draft of the chapter of "Breaths of a Summer Day."

---

58. The first part of book 2 was published in 1932. One year later, on September 1, 1933, Hitler declared that the Third Reich would last "a thousand years." See Wolfgang Wippermann, "Drittes Reich," in *Enzyklopädie des Nationalsozialismus*, ed. Wolfgang Benz, Hermann Graml, and Hermann Weiß (Stuttgart: Klett-Cotta, 1998), 479.

59. Coetzee, *Stranger Shores*, 94.

60. "C. [Hitler]. You must believe either in the future of N[ational] S[ocialism] or the downfall of [Germany]. At any rate, in a break in the tradition in which I know I am embedded. How is it possible still to work when one is in this position?"

The effect one has even on individuals functions only via totalities. . . . My homegrown theory—about transcending the conditions and questions of the time through mental leaps leading to indirect influence on people whoc are practically involved in creative work or on later spirits—is rendered invalid by this idea" (D, 389).

EPILOGUE

"Life as Formation," "The Conflict of Forms," "Deformation"—the preceding pages have sought to identify three pivotal moments in the German discourse on the relation between form and life from the late eighteenth to the mid-twentieth century. Each of my chapters has focused on a specific text or body of texts, seeking to extract from it in as much detail as possible the logic of life it articulates. Rather than retracing the historical arc of my argument, I want to conclude with an overview of the positions and claims I stake out. While (for reasons articulated in the preface) these will not amount to a *definition* of life, I hope that they will both provide a useful map for the book as a whole and throw into sharper relief its broader theoretical implications.

1. German vitalism conceives of life as a process of self-constitution.

When Kant, in the second part of the *Critique of the Power of Judgement*, argued that in order for us to grasp an organism we must assume not only "*first*, that its parts . . . are possible only through their relation to the whole," but also "*second*, that its parts be combined into a whole by being reciprocally the cause and effect of their form" (KU §65, 5:373; CPJ 244–45), he introduced a conception of organic life that became foundational for subsequent German vitalist thought. According to this conception, living things are governed by processes that both constitute their form and conform to it—they are, in this sense, self-constituting.

This model ascribes to the living a particular kind of normativity that is distinct from that of prescriptive norms or statistical averages. The form and organization of living beings express an immanent self-governance, a dynamic order that is less imposed upon than determined by the living being itself. Following Georges Canguilhem,[1] we can speak of a vital norm—a norm that is actualized in the process of living and that has no other guarantee than the factuality of this process.

2. The notion of life replaces the earlier model of nature-culture.

The idea of life as a self-constituting process helped to overcome the stark dualism of body and mind, as of nature and culture, that had dominated Western thought since Descartes, and that Kant himself had broadly upheld prior to the third *Critique*. Instead of opposing the determinism of nature to the autonomy of human reason, as he had done in his moral theory, Kant's conception of the organism as a complex unity governed both by material and teleological laws highlighted the continuity between natural and rational processes. It was this new hylomorphism that inspired Hegel to

---

1. Canguilhem, *A Vital Rationalist*, esp. 351–57.

(re)introduce the idiom of a "first" and "second" nature[2] and that informed Wittgenstein's famous claim in the *Philosophical Investigations* that "Giving orders, asking questions, telling stories, having a chat, are as much a part of our natural history as walking, eating, drinking, playing" (PI §25).

Kant himself offered two basic models to conceive of the continuity between nature and culture: (1) that of the organism, suggesting a structural homology between natural self-organization and moral self-determination; and (2) that of aesthetic judgment, in which body and mind are singularly attuned. Insofar as aesthetic judgment rests on the feeling of an accord between the cognitive faculties, the third *Critique* describes embodiment as a condition for, rather than an obstacle to, thinking. Whether conceived analogically or in terms of an internal connection, Kant's work marked a break with Cartesian dualism and helped initiate a turn toward a broadly conceived Spinozist vitalism that would shape German culture for the next one hundred fifty years.[3]

3. Life's immanent normativity is built around a dialectic of force and form.

Starting with Blumenbach's notion of the *Bildungstrieb*, German vitalism conceives of form as formation, as a dynamic process rather than a static, determinate structure. On the one hand, living beings display some kind of unity and form; on the other hand, this unity is subject to continuous transformation and change. The vitalist concept of life is thus built around a dialectic of change and continuity, of force and form.[4] Living beings are the manifestations of an intrinsic force that "not only generates forms but supercedes and transgresses them in the course of development."[5]

---

2. On Hegel's conception of first and second nature, see Khurana, *Das Leben der Freiheit.*

3. On Spinoza's influence on German culture around 1800, see the essays in *Spinoza and German Idealism*, ed. Eckart Förster (Cambridge: Cambridge University Press, 2015).

4. For an excellent articulation of this dialectic, see Khurana, "Force and Form."

5. Ibid., 22.

Canguilhem's work on the normative creativity of the living provides a useful articulation and extension of this dialectic. Canguilhem conceives of the health and pathology of living beings as a dynamic interchange between a living being's conservative tendency to preserve its own state and its creative capacity to adapt to its internal and external circumstances, generating new norms of living.[6] Authentic normativity—health—consists in the living being's capacity to respond to systemic and environmental fluctuations by deviating from its established norm and producing new ones; this alternation in rule between perpetuation and transformation defines the organic dialectic between force and form.

4. Speaking is a form of life.

Although the modern conception of "life" as an organizing force internal to living beings emerged first in biological thought, German thinkers quickly extended this organic notion of life from the biological realm to processes and structures of the social, political, and psychological worlds. This extension finds its most powerful articulation in Wittgenstein's appropriation of the notion of *Lebensform*. Contrary to its contemporary conservative usage, Wittgenstein employs the term to highlight the open-ended character of meaning and its dependence on a natural life that is essentially metamorphic. Speaking is a form of life because, like all life, it constantly creates and transgresses its own norms.

Wittgenstein's account of linguistic practices draws on two features of the earlier discourse of life: (1) the idea of immanent normativity, and (2) the dialectic of force and form. (1) According to Wittgenstein, the normativity of linguistic practices does not rest on abstract rules that precede these practices but is created by the activity of speaking itself. As in Canguilhem's notion of vital norms, the norms governing speech are actualized in and through the process of speaking, and thus have no other guarantee than the factuality of this process. There is no external meaning-authority—no

---

6. Canguilhem, *The Normal and the Pathological*, esp. 181–231.

logical rule or political power—that grounds meaning and determines the proper use of signs. Instead, it is the repeated use of signs
itself that produces the norms and forms of usage. (2) Wittgenstein
compares the rule-bound character of linguistic practice to games
in order to emphasize its irreducible diversity and malleability. Language is made up of countless "language-games" which, while constraining the range of acceptable moves in specific contexts, remain
open to innovation and contestation.[7] Like Canguilhem, he thus
conceives of normativity in terms of a dynamic interplay between
a conservative tendency toward repetition and a creative force of
deviation.

Moreover, the dialectic of force and form is not limited to speech,
narrowly understood, but shapes all human activity. The use of language is constitutively interwoven with nonlinguistic activities,[8]
and it is the interplay of these larger patterns of behavior that "determines our judgments, our concepts, and our reactions" (RPP
§629). Meaning thus rests on a tacit agreement in action—on a
shared "form of life"—that provides the prereflective background
of all normative practices. What is more, this background is itself in
perpetual flux. The patterns of activity that make up a community's
form of life are *essentially* heterogeneous and fluctuating, a "complicated filigree" (RPP §624) and "hurly-burly" (RPP §629) that cannot
be systematized: "The background is the bustle of life" (RPP §625).

5. A "mutual absorption of the natural and the social."[9]

Wittgenstein's notion of *Lebensform*, then, is not intended to explain or ground meaning or invest the linguistic community with
uncontestable normative sovereignty. There is no sovereign power

---

7.   On the role of contestability in Wittgenstein's conception of language and
normativity, see José Medina, "Wittgenstein as a Rebel: Dissidence and Contestation in Discursive Practices," *International Journal of Philosophical Studies* 18,
no. 1 (2010): 1–29.

8.   "The word *language-game* is used here to emphasize the fact that the
speaking of language is part of an activity, or of a form of life" (PI §23).

9.   Stanley Cavell, "Declining Decline," in *The Cavell-Reader*, ed. Stephen
Mulhall (Malden, MA: Blackwell, 1996), 330.

over practice, no indivisible source of normativity, whether individual or collective.[10] Instead, the phrase draws attention to the "mutual absorption of the natural and the social" that characterizes human life. At the most basic level, human life is shaped by "extremely general facts of nature" (PI §142)—gravity, mortality, the need for food and air, and so on—that sustain our practices and silently inform our concepts. Language and meaning unfold against a background of natural regularities that are taken for granted. Moreover, these general facts include what Wittgenstein calls the "common behavior of mankind," (PI §206), which comprises a set of primitive language games and instinctual responses found across all human societies, the product of evolutionary history. This is the dimension of *Lebensform* that informs Wittgenstein's understanding of linguistic life as "a part of our *natural* history" (PI §25; my emphasis).

The idea of a "common behavior of mankind" highlights what Cavell has called the vertical sense of the notion of *Lebensform*,[11] which points to the evolutionary roots of human language. Talking is not added to our biological existence but is natural to us, part of *our* natural history.[12] This vertical sense of "form of life," which emphasizes features shared by all humans, must be distinguished from the horizontal and ethnological sense of the term, which refers to sociocultural differences between particular cultures. The practice of "giving orders" or "asking questions" is common to all human life, but the specific form these activities take will differ according to geographical and historical contexts. While analytically distinct, these two aspects of *Lebensform* are always dynamically interwoven. There is no universal language-game of "commanding" that is prior to or distinct from its particular historical actualization.

---

10. See Medina, "Wittgenstein as a Rebel," 12.

11. Cavell, "Declining Decline," 328.

12. In his last writings, Wittgenstein pushes this line of thought even further, suggesting that our basic language-games evolve out of primitive, prelinguistic behavioral patterns that can already be found in nonhuman animals—a radically anti-intellectualist conception of language that breaks with the dualism underpinning the ancient definition of humans as rational animals: "Language did not emerge from some kind of ratiocination (*Raisonnement*)" (OC 475).

All there is is what people do and say—actual human practice—which is shaped both by human commonalities and sociocultural difference, our natural and social histories.

6. Forms exert a distinct kind of force.

Whether understood vertically or horizontally, Wittgenstein's appropriation of the notion of *Lebensform* highlights the ineluctable historicity of human life. Cultures are not only internally heterogeneous, composed of countless practices and language games; these games are themselves subject to constant change and innovation: "new types of language, new language-games . . . come into existence, and others become obsolete and get forgotten" (PI §23).

This historicity is at the core of Wittgenstein's conception of normativity. Normativity is not dictated by transcendent rules or laws, but established through precedent. For something to become part of a meaningful practice, it must repeat, conforming to, but necessarily without ever duplicating, those preceding acts or moves that realize and instantiate the relevant practice. What regulates and defines a sequence of acts is not a rule or law but the succession itself of structurally equivalent acts, the *patterns* of connectedness—conventions, customs, etc.—that distinguish practices from one another and orient future extensions of those practices.

Wittgenstein's historical conception of cultural regulation has two important implications. On the one hand, it highlights the variability of our normative practices. Because practices exist only insofar as they are repeatedly articulated through concrete individual actions, their form is intrinsically subject to change. Past instantiations of practice—collectively its tradition—never fully determine the future course of events, whose shape hinges on the present moment of actualization. But on the other hand, the weight of past actions is precisely what constrains the range of possible moves in the present. For an utterance or action to be recognizable as part of a practice, it must be seen as participating in, and thus resembling in the relevant aspects, a preexisting pattern of activity. Our earlier discussion of the dialectic of force and form will thus not suffice. Forms are not simply opposed to force but themselves exert a distinct kind of force—the force of regularity. Forms are regulative, constraining expressions by virtue of their historical continuity. When Wittgenstein writes, "What has to be accepted, the given, is, so one could say, forms of life" (PPF §345; PI, Part II, 192), he is referring to this basic normativity, which is already at work in our most ordinary practices and language-games and which has no other source than the regularity of what we do and say.

7. Human life is open to the threat of unintelligibility.

The regularity of our actions provides the prereflective background that must be in place for anything to become intelligible at all. As Wittgenstein puts it, what enables language to function, and thus must be "given," is "agreement not in opinion, but rather in forms of life" (PI §241). Hence the particular kind of threat associated with the authority or force of such normativity. Since meaning rests on agreement in action, on regular patterns of activity, every action that deviates too much from these patterns risks becoming *unintelligible*. This may not be critical in the case of mispronunciations or simple mistakes, but unintelligibility poses an obvious existential threat to a life that is essentially social. Our sanity depends on our "good enough" conformity to the routines of language and practice on the one hand, and on their tolerance of variation and improvisation on the other.

Crucially, what counts as "good enough"—hence, as intelligible and sane—can never be determined in advance. Precisely because the norms guiding social practices do not have the status of abstract rules but are created through these practices, there is no metarule to determine whether a certain action is intelligible or unintelligible, normal or abnormal, innovative or erratic. This opens the boundaries of ethical life and political contestation. Instead of recourse to transcendent, invariable rules, ethical, political, and aesthetic evaluation depends upon recognition and decision—that is, normative judgment—for which individuals and communities must bear responsibility.

As suggested in chapter 6, it is helpful to visualize the normativity of practices and forms of life in terms of an infinitesimal topography. The closer we move to the center of a practice or form of life, the more routine and repetitive actions become. This center is the domain of highly conventionalized scripts and tightly coupled actions, where what happens next seems to be decided in advance. As we move outward, away from more entrenched forms and formulae, the identity of action and meaning is more loosely defined, making room for innovation, improvisation, and the projection of new possibilities. But this freedom of expression comes at a price. To the extent that an action, in deviating from formulaic repetition, gains vibrancy and expressiveness, it also risks becoming unintelligible and indecipherable (think of metaphors). If the action is taken up, it will have been successful and intelligible, expanding the range of expression, or perhaps even creating a new, contiguous practice. But if it remains unintelligible, or is deemed too eccentric, it will be excluded from the domain of normality and its author will have to contend with having violated the normative force of social form.

8. Vital and social norms.

We are now in a better position to compare the normativity of organic and social forms of life. Living beings and social practices are both forms of *life* in that both constitute, reproduce, and modify their characteristic forms. Social and natural forms are thus intrinsically dynamic, built around a dialectic of change and continuity, force and form. As in Canguilhem's notion of vital norms, the norms guiding social practices are built into these practices, actualized in and through their temporal unfolding.

Moreover, natural and social forms are *mutually determinative*. To use a term first developed in the psychology of visual experience, human life unfolds through the interplay of social and biological *affordances*.[13] On the one hand, language acquisition, ethical be-

---

13. The term was coined by the psychologist James J. Gibson; see his "The Theory of Affordances," in *Perceiving, Acting, and Knowing: Toward an Ecological Psychology*, ed. R. Shaw and J. Bransford (Hillsdale, NJ: Lawrence Erlbaum, 1977), 67–82. For an excellent articulation of the notion of "affordance" and its importance for an understanding of social and ethical behavior, see Keane, *Ethical Life*, esp. 27–32 and 39–73. The following two paragraphs draw heavily on Keane's brilliant work.

havior, and social coordination depend on certain basic capacities and propensities—openness to others, intention-seeking, basic empathy—that "get their initial impulse from the child him- or herself" and thus "are not, in the first instance, things that the child is taught by other people."[14] These specifically human affordances are the product of our natural, organic history. But on the other hand, these natural potentialities depend for their development and expression on relevant social affordances. The child's innate capacities will be shaped by interactions with his or her familial and social environment, that is, by cultural resources, including that of language. And like language, these interactions will "bear the mark of specific social histories,"[15] hence of forms of social life.

Finally, human life's dependence on symbolic articulation also *differentiates* it from other forms of life in a number of important respects. First, human life is characterized by an enormous variety of language games and practices: basic language games—claiming, asking questions, promising, commanding, telling stories, joking, insinuating, and so on—are interwoven with other games and practices, giving rise to complex discourses and patterns of activity that open up and regulate new ways of being human. Second, human symbolic life is not only open-ended and indeterminate but also heterogeneous and divided. The more elaborate social forms become, the more closely they follow their own hermetic logic, dividing human life from within. Each of us is traversed by multiple ways of being human—artistic, moral, political, erotic, legal, and so on— that are in potential conflict with one another. Unlike organic life, human life is subject to competing normative pressures. Third, these competing regulative systems also permeate society at large, driving its internal dynamic. Organized into complex subsystems— institutions, groups, professions, classes, and so on—each social form imposes itself on its adjacent forms, which in turn impose themselves on it, opening up a space for distinctly *political* forms of disagreement and contestation.

---

14. Keane, *Ethical Life*, 71.
15. Ibid., 30.

9. A short critique of recent political ontologies.

As the preceding observations indicate, my understanding of the place of politics in human life differs from recent ontological theories of "the political" that conceive of the latter as coextensive with social being in its entirety. As opposed to Agamben, I insist that human life is not a mere political artifact. Politics is not reducible to the production of "bare" life, nor is life as such, whether human or nonhuman, ever "bare" in the sense of being formless. While Agamben is correct in observing that Nazi politics seeks to rob human life of its form, this project does not reveal the essence of either politics or life. Life produces vital and social forms, including, in its most sinister manifestation, political forms that systematically seek to extinguish life's intrinsic creativity. The camps expose the destructive potential of the human *Lebensform*; not more, but also not less.

Ontological theories of the political such as Agamben's distinguish sharply between politics as an empirical social subsystem and "the political," which is meant to refer to the groundlessness of society whose historical shape is said to be the result of conflict and antagonism, hence essentially political. In the words of Oliver Marchart, who analyzed this paradigm most lucidly, "*all* things social"[16] are grounded "through instances of conflict, power, subordination, oppression."[17] While I also insist that human symbolic life lacks a transcendent foundation, I take issue with the claim that therefore "*all* things social" are the result of antagonism and power. The problem consists in the argumentative leap from normative groundlessness to conflict and power, which in turn rests on the faulty equation of symbolic difference with political antagonism. The practice of "cooking" or "playing games," or of "asking a question" and "telling a story," though all internally differentiated and distinguished from other practices and games, are not therefore necessarily founded through antagonism and power. All forms are differentiating, but not all differences are antagonistic. Moreover, as

---

16. Oliver Marchart, *Thinking Antagonism. Political Ontology after Laclau* (Edinburgh: Edinburgh University Press, 2018), 88.
17. Ibid., 12.

we saw, disagreements or antagonisms between social actors or groups presuppose a background of shared practices and agreements that opens up the horizon of intelligibility—the space of meaning—within which something as complex as "actors" or recognizable "conflicts" can emerge. The idea of a thoroughgoing antagonistic *Lebensform*—of social being as inherently rivalrous, and thus *essentially* political—is incoherent.

A similar criticism can be levelled at Eric Santner's Lacanian account of human symbolic life. While Santner and I share an emphasis on the ineluctably normative dimension of human existence, Santner, following the ontological trend in political philosophy, grounds the social in the political, claiming that all meaning and sociality are ultimately held in place by the authority invested in the political sovereign. Against this political grounding of normativity, I insist that the basic coherence of social life rests on the prepolitical force embedded in the regularities of speech, habits, and practices. Hence when Santner, following Jonathan Lear, defines the "ontological vulnerability" of human life in terms of its exposure to historical contingency, he misidentifies the basis of this vulnerability. Any form of human life can succumb to incoherence, thus existential crisis, not only when its cultural way of life breaks down or disappears; even the slightest departure from cultural regularity carries with it the threat of unintelligibility. There is no escape from the normative force of social forms.

10. The place of politics in human life.

What, then, is the place of politics in human life? My attempt at answering this question is framed by two postulates. First, politics is a subset of social relations. Not all social relations and practices are political, even though all can, under certain circumstances, become a matter of distinctly political forms of contestation. Second, politics owes its essential place in human life to the latter's normative indeterminacy. There is politics because the constraints governing social life are produced, maintained, and reformed through social activity itself and thus lack any transcendent—rational or divine—grounding. Put together, these two claims allow us to rephrase our opening question in ways that relate it to the broader concerns of this book: What is the place of the political in the *self-constitution* of human life?

As we saw, at its most basic level, forms govern through their regularity and historical continuity. While at any point any such regularity can be explicitly formulated and/or contested, contestation is possible, and intelligible *as* contestation, only against a background of practices and forms of life whose normative authority is taken for granted and silently accepted. Political disagreement and conflict always presuppose a more basic agreement, which is "not agreement in opinions but in form of life" (PI §80).

This is not to say that political contestation leaves social life untouched. In fact, the political might be defined as that region of communal life in which actors publicly debate and contest the conditions of participation in their shared forms of life. Such contestation concerns, in the first place, *who* is entitled to have a say in this debate, that is, who is granted the authority to make political claims and thus allowed to participate in the processes of collective self-constitution. In framing access to self-constitution in terms of authority, rights, and laws, politics introduces into human life a type of force that differs not only from the mere imposition of physical power, which already occurs among all animals, human or otherwise, but also from the regulative force of social norms. More often than not, contest over the overall shape of human life, of the sort that I am calling *political*, deploys resources of power that originate in "socially located and conditioned abilities to do things" to others.[18] The domain of the political begins where (a) the authority of social forms is backed by institutional sources of power and (b) a conflict emerges between the freedom of social participation and the force of institutional authority.

This last formulation allows us to see "how politics can be a pervasive potential of every social relation without identifying every

---

18. Raymond Geuss, *History and Illusion in Politics* (Cambridge: Cambridge University Press, 2001), 28.

social relation with politics."[19] Social practices and relations *become* politicized when citizens challenge the constraints these practices inevitably impose upon human life. The possibility, indeed necessity, of such challenges derives from the normative indeterminacy of human life. The political is a (and, since the advent of modernity, *the*) fundamental way through which societies manage this constitutive indeterminacy and the vulnerability it imparts to individual and collective existence. Politics, so understood, refers to the ensemble of symbolic forms and institutional mechanisms whereby a *Lebensform* regulates its groundlessness, giving form and direction to the "whirl of organism"[20] that is the insubstantial source of its normativity.

11. From politics to biopolitics.

While all politics is to some extent concerned with the regulation and organization of human life, not all politics is therefore biopolitical in the strong sense of the term. As I have argued throughout this book, biopolitics emerges in the late eighteenth century in the context of, and in response to, a newly dynamic understanding of life in general, and human life in particular. There is biopolitics because life is conceived to be intrinsically powerful, endowed with the force to create its own forms. Against this vision of life, which was first articulated in biology, literature, and philosophy, biopolitics emerges as a set of technologies and institutions aimed at organizing, regulating, and exploiting the newly discovered vitality of life for economic and political purposes.

Thus, while all politics attempts to manage the "hurly-burly" of social life, biopolitics represents an historically distinct and more pragmatically radical approach to this task, one that targets life in all of its modalities and expressions. I suggest we restrict the term to refer to political mechanisms that repress the insubstantiality of the social by defining society in naturalist terms, as an empirical

---

19.   Mark Warren, "What Is Political?," *Journal of Theoretical Politics* 11, no. 2 (1999): 207–31.

20.   Cavell, "The Availability of Wittgenstein's Later Philosophy," 52.

object. For analytical purposes, two types of biopolitical naturalization can be distinguished. What I call "epistemological" biopolitics refers to the set of practices, analyzed in great detail by Foucault, that seek to control the contingency of social life by framing it in terms of statistical regularities, as a "population" of independently varying individuals. This type of biopolitics does not so much deny the dynamic nature of collective life as translate it into a set of data and algorithms (probabilities, laws of dispersion, etc.), which then serve as the basis for interventions and regulatory controls. The fundamental move here is to quantify human life, whether individual or collective, to reduce it to a calculable system of forces and thus to convert it into a resource for economic and political manipulation.

If epistemological biopolitics seeks to *regulate* human vitality, "metaphysical" biopolitics, which finds its most deadening manifestation in Nazi-politics, *mortifies* life by reducing it to a pseudobiological substance, to "blood." The racially defined *Volkskörper* collapses the older distinction between mystical and natural body. "Blood" here refers to a substance that is at once sublime, connecting the true members of the *Volkskörper*, and natural, that is, (supposedly) verifiable through genealogies and the methods and instruments of the empirical sciences. Unlike epistemological biopolitics, which flourishes in liberal and capitalist societies, metaphysical biopolitics is essentially totalitarian, seeking to impose a single political form on every configuration of social and natural life, and indeed on the "bustle of life" itself. As such, the appeal to "blood" constitutes the most extreme political deflection of, and defense against, the groundlessness of normativity Wittgenstein captured in his notion of *Lebensform.*

12. Beyond biopolitics.

However, let me end on a less tragic note. Not only is it unnecessary to accept biopolitics as the ultimate vision of twenty-first-century life, it is necessary that we not do so. Life, as I hope I have shown, is irrepressibly creative, and thus resistant to the totalizing project of biopolitics. Whatever a new and expanded politics of life looks like, it will need to be based on a recognition of its subversive drive. While life is always already formed, it is at the same time driven by the power to create and disrupt the forms and norms that govern it. To treat life as a mere resource or material is itself an expression of political violence. This view has consequences for the relationship we bear both to the natural world and to our own bodies within it. That the human *Lebenform* is shaped by the mutual absorption of the natural and the social means, among other things, that human life is essentially embodied. We never stop being natural creatures, endowed with a body that has its own forms of vitality, its own idioms of expression and creativity, which never fully coincide with the forms of ethical and political life. This tension points to the open-endedness of life in general, and human life in particular. Neither individuals nor cultures are self-contained and internally consistent unities but are instead shaped by a multiplicity of diverse ways of acting and judging. While the temptation to transcend internal conflict through recourse to force or rational or divine law is seductive, to yield to it is to relinquish life itself. Conflict is essential to human life, both the expression and the condition of its creativity. This means, finally, that there cannot be such a thing as a comprehensive politics of life. Life's creativity expresses itself in countless different yet interconnected forms: political and biological, legal and erotic, ethical and perceptual. It is the art of life itself that protects it from becoming entirely political.

INDEX

acknowledgment: and aspect seeing, 61–63; Cavell on, 273n16; failure of, 60–61, 65, 182, 273, 324, 329, 334; and form of life, 54, 62; of relation to other, 59–63; self's dependence on, 273; of shared vulnerability with animals, 56–57, 60–63

Adorno, Theodor, 14

aesthesis: Kant's recalibration of, 82–83; thinking as, 249

aesthetic experience: and aesthetic life, 64, 154; and attunement (*Überein-stimmung*), 95–98; autonomy of, 119; autopoietic character of, 192; communal character of, 59, 105; and desire, 126, 150; extraconceptual dimension of, 78–85; feeling of freedom in, 11–14, 154; and *Lebensgefühl*, 79–84, 104; and the life of cognition, 83–85, 104–14;

and mimesis, 152–53; and the nature of human symbolic life, xiii–xv, 80; and ontological vulnerability, 153; and organic life, 78; and the other condition (Musil), 343; and purposiveness, 36, 98; and second nature, 120–21. See also *Wilhelm Meister's Apprenticeship* (Goethe)

aesthetic judgment: and aspect seeing, 59; and the attunement of the mind, 95–98; and beauty, 87; indetermi-nacy of concept in, 97, 322; and *Lebensgefühl*, 79–84; and *sensus communis*, 99, 108–12; subjective universality of, 99, 108–12

aesthetics: anti-Cartesian orientation of modern, 59; and art of living, 45; in Baumgarten, 81, 81n4; as bioaesthetics, 140; critique of organicist conception in Kleist,

CPSIA information can be obtained
at www.ICGtesting.com
Printed in the USA
LVHW050745230322
714108LV00006B/264